Evangelicalism

Evangelicalism

An Americanized Christianity

Richard Kyle

Transaction Publishers
New Brunswick (U.S.A.) and London (U.K.)

Library of Congress Catalog Number: 2006040444
ISBN: 0-7658-0324-0
Printed in the United States of America

Library of Congress Cataloging-in-Publication Data

Kyle, Richard G.
    Evangelicalism : an Americanized Christianity / Richard G. Kyle.
        p. cm.
    Includes bibliographical references (p.   ) and index.
    ISBN 0-7658-0324-0 (alk. paper)
        1. Evangelicalism. I. Title.

BR1640.K95   2006
270.8'2—dc22   2006040444

In Memory of My Son, Bryan R. Kyle

Contents

Introduction

This volume surveys the relationship of two strong forces—evangelicalism and American popular culture. Currently, evangelicalism may be the most Americanized and dynamic brand of religion in the United States. While its roots can be found in Europe, if evangelicalism were a garment its label would read: "Made In America." But this is not a new development. While it has reached new heights in the last twenty-five years, evangelicalism and American popular culture have interacted extensively since the colonial era.

And the relationship has been complex and paradoxical. It has run in both directions. In its attempt to create a Christian American, evangelicals have powerfully shaped the nation's public values. The influence, however, has run more in the other direction. The popular culture has had a tremendous impact on evangelicalism—so much so that many conservative Protestants regard evangelical and American values as one and the same. Evangelicals also have had a hate-love relationship with American culture. While many view America's political and economic systems as divinely inspired, they have hated what they regard as the nation's departure from these perceived biblical principles.

This book is more about popular evangelicalism than its serious varieties. I do not wish to tar all evangelicals with the same brush. Evangelicals have achieved much in recent years—rising from being ridiculed fundamentalists to a respected element in American society. Politically, two evangelicals have occupied the White House and many others have been in the president's cabinet or elected to Congress. Conservative Protestants are well organized and represent a powerful political voice. Evangelicals are also a growing and significant aspect of the American economy. They often vote with their pocketbooks. Of the best selling books, a number cater to the interests of the evangelical subculture. Intellectually, many evangelicals have shed the "ignorant fundamentalist" and "Bible thumping" images. They have some outstanding academic institutions, some very respectable scholars, and have produced many serious publications. And of great importance, evangelicalism is the most dynamic and growth-oriented segment of American religion.

Having said all of this, the evangelical subculture is driven by its popular elements. The popularizers have carried the day—not the scholars or the serious thinkers. Why? Evangelicals are deeply populist and pragmatic and the popularizers connect with their interests and aspirations. They scratch where it itches. They deal with immediate issues not theory. With the decline of doctrine and tradition in religion, evangelicals are left with experiences, feelings, and celebrities. And these popular personalities have become the last word in religion, politics, money matters, history, music, the rearing of children, health issues, science, and more. The televangelists, megachurch preachers, pop psychologists, and popular authors have indeed powerfully shaped the evangelical mindset. Unfortunately, many of these celebrities are unqualified to give such advice.

Authors are often prompted by personal issues to write a book. To this I must plead guilty, but I hope that my personal motives have not clouded my interpretation of evangelical history. Hopefully, this study can be regarded as a fair and friendly criticism of the evangelical subculture but also an affirmation of its achievements. Two of my motives connect with observable evangelical and denominational trends and one relates more to national issues. A person's religious background also shapes his/her view of evangelical history. My theological training has been at Baptist and Presbyterian divinity schools. For over thirty years, however, my membership has been in a Mennonite Brethren church—a denomination with its roots in the Anabaptist tradition that can be considered as both theologically conservative and evangelical.

Several years ago, I returned from Kiev where I had been teaching as a Fulbright scholar. In Kiev, I had attended an Anglican church and here enjoyed some of the best expository preaching that I had ever heard. (Those English preachers just pack their sermons with substance and include few anecdotes). The services were also worshipful. Anticipating some of the same when I came home, I visited a number of Mennonite Brethren churches. To my surprise, things had changed. I encountered a series of sermons based on the Jabez Prayer, many personal illustrations, big screens displaying hymns and Bible verses, and Praise and Worship teams.

In the next few years, I visited more Mennonite Brethren churches and witnessed much of the same. At times, announcements came in the form of a dialogue, skits introduced the sermons, and large screens flashed the hymns and Scripture verses. In worship, Praise and Worship teams had replaced the choirs, singing in four-part harmony was gone, guitars had pushed out the organs, and drums boomed so loud that the singing often could not be heard. A number of churches had centered their services around the best-selling book, *The Purpose Driven Life.* When we come to the sermons, they were often light and on relevant subjects. Expository preaching was a thing of the past. Some pastors began with their ideas and found verses to support what they wanted to say. Moreover, in some of the churches the pastor was operating more as a CEO than as a pastor of the flock. Rather than working in close connection with the congregation, he was attempting to control it.

This is not to say that all of the above is bad. It is to illustrate trends within evangelical churches. The pace of adapting to contemporary developments has indeed progressed much faster in many other evangelical churches than it has in the small Mennonite Brethren denomination. This illustration also points out the tension that has divided evangelical churches between the traditionalists and the advocates of a contemporary church service more in tune with American culture.

Another motivation for penning this work relates to the denominational framework from which evangelicalism has been interpreted. Most studies regarding evangelicalism have been written by evangelical scholars, largely from the perspective of their own denominational tradition. Most common are books from Reformed scholars. But there are several studies representing the Wesleyan-Arminian, Anglican, dispensational, Pentecostal, and Baptist traditions.

But few Anabaptist-Mennonite scholars have written about evangelicalism. Why? In part, some Mennonites do not like to call themselves evangelicals. They are embarrassed by the excesses of popular evangelicalism. *Evangelicalism and Anabaptism* (1979), edited by C. Norman Kraus, attempts to place a distance between the Anabaptist and evangelical traditions, pointing out the differences between the two. In general, Mennonites are ambivalent about their relationship with American evangelicalism. Despite having many differences from popular evangelicalism, Mennonites do uphold the major elements common to the evangelical heritage. Given a broad view of evangelicalism, this study thus regards the Anabaptist-Mennonite tradition as a form of evangelicalism and attempts to examine evangelical history from a perspective that considers the Anabaptist-Mennonite and free church vantage points.

Some national trends have also prompted me to write this book. At one time, economic questions divided America. Currently, cultural issues are driving the disagreements. The great watershed separating Americans pertains to their faith. On one side of the divide we have the more secular people, whether they be mainline Protestants or liberal Catholics. On the other are the evangelical Protestants, conservative Catholics, and others who attend church on a regular basis. A person's voting preference can often be predicted by how often he/she attends church.

While evangelicals are only one component of this conservative coalition, they are its driving force. It must be noted, however, that all evangelicals are not Republicans or supporters of the Religious Right. However, if the elections of 2000 and 2004 are any indication of where most evangelicals stand, they lineup solidly in the Republican camp. In these elections about 80 percent of those calling themselves evangelicals voted for George W. Bush.

As I write this introduction, two incidents serve to illustrate the intensity of the linkage between conservative Protestants and the Religious Right. Should Terry Schiavo's feeding tubes be removed thus ending her life? With the evangelical vote in mind, Republicans jumped on the band- wagon. Majority Leader and evangelical Tom DeLay indicated that God had given them Terry Schiavo for an issue. Congress then passed a law for one person and President Bush returned from Crawford, Texas, in the wee hours of the morning to sign the legislation. A more local issue concerned East Waynesville Baptist Church in North Carolina. Nine members were ousted during a church gathering because they refused to support President Bush.

This survey of evangelicalism makes no claim to comprehensiveness. Instead, I have focused on one aspect of evangelical history—its interaction with American culture. The relationship of evangelicalism with American culture has been considerable, complex, and paradoxical. This study attempts to balance the past with current interests and follows a pattern. One chapter introduces the major issues. Four chapters then look at evangelical activities from the eighteenth century to 1960. Three chapters note the major developments after 1960. An epilogue summarizes the major issues.

Chapter 1, "The Evangelical Paradox," introduces the general theme of the volume. It also establishes a working definition for evangelicalism, looks at the impact of the separation of church and state on American religion, and surveys the major characteristics of American culture and how they have helped to shape the evangelical faith. The next chapter, "Evangelicalism in the Driver's Seat," begins our journey through American history and focuses on the early national period. It tackles the question of just how Christian America has been. It points out that Christianity, republicanism, and democracy share many values, but they also have diverse sources. The chapter then moves on to some specific developments prior to the Civil War when evangelicalism had its greatest impact on American society.

Chapter 3, "Cracks in the Evangelical Empire," looks at evangelicalism from the Civil War to early in the twentieth century. During this time, evangelicalism remained strong but cracks in its dominance began to appear. Rather than shape the nation, American culture substantially influenced the evangelicals. New intellectual challenges threatened the evangelical worldview. They embraced capitalism and bought wholeheartedly into the values of the industrial age. To be sure some groups such as the holiness churches dissented.

Chapter 4, "From Mainline to Sideline: Evangelicalism in Retreat," surveys the period from the early twentieth century to the 1940s. The evangelical cultural dominance was now gone. Evangelicals were defeated in the struggles concerning control of several denominations and the teaching of evolution in the public schools. They were down and retreated from American society as never before or since. But they were not out. Now known as the fundamentalists, they rebuilt their institutions and several recent evangelical movements —dispensationism and Pentecostalism—gained strength and influence.

Chapter 5, "Reaction and Renewal," looks at evangelicalism in the 1940s and 1950s. Prompted by the return of prosperity and the fear of communism, along with the revival of religion in general, evangelicalism staged a comeback. It was now in the process of establishing an identity separate from fundamentalism and Billy Graham emerged to lead the evangelical resurgence. The next three chapters take a topical approach to evangelical developments in the late twentieth and early twenty-first centuries.

Chapter 6, "God is a Conservative," focuses on the ever important marriage between evangelicalism and conservative political and economic ideas. It looks at the rise of the Religious Right, the uncritical embrace of consumerism and the market economy, and the feminist threat. But this chapter also points out that there exists an evangelical left. The next chapter, "Selling Jesus: The Megachurches and Televangelism," focuses on the tremendous impact of these two religious expressions. Following the old market principle of giving the consumer what he or she wants, evangelicals have changed how they are doing church. They are catering to contemporary cultural trends.

Chapter 8, "If You Can't Beat 'em Join 'em, examines how popular evangelism has swallowed the latest cultural fads "hook, line, and sinker." The exception would be what they regard as immoral practices. Otherwise there is little difference between the evangelical subculture and mainstream culture. In fact, evangelicals have created their own counterfeit culture, which contains most elements of American society. More specifically, this chapter looks at issues such as publishing, movies, television, music, and the Word-Faith and Possibility Thinking movements. The "Epilogue" ties things together. It puts the spotlight on the book's major themes—the Americanization of evangelicalism and its paradoxical relationship with the surrounding culture.

No one writes a book alone. In the time that this book has been in gestation, I have accumulated debts to several individuals and institutions. I hope that my memory is not short in this regard and that I do not inadvertently omit any thanks that are due. Appreciation must go to Adam Wathen, Rosella Epp, and the library staff of Tabor College for arranging the acquisition of many books and articles through interlibrary loan. Without these sources my work would not have been possible. Thanks must go to Jonah Kliewer for reading the chapter concerning evangelicals and music. Materials drawn from chapter 7 have appeared in an article published in the journal *Direction*. Appreciation must be expressed to Dale Johnson of Erskine Seminary and members of the Tabor College faculty for some ideas that have found their way into this study.

Debts have also been incurred in the production of this book. I thank Ellie Rempel and Melanie Wehrman for taking my various drafts and putting them in a publishable condition and for researching materials on the Internet. Appreciation must be offered to Deborah Penner for her timely comments regarding matters of writing style. Thanks must go to Tabor College and Howard Keim for my 2003 sabbatical, the time when this book was begun. Academic publishing entails its own problems. Therefore, much appreciation must go to the staff of Transaction Publishers of Rutgers University for publishing this volume.

Finally, my gratitude goes to some who were involved only indirectly with the writing and publishing process. In particular, I am grateful to my wife Joyce, and two sons, Bryan and Brent, for sharing me with this project. My oldest son, Bryan, passed away from leukemia while this book was in the works. Thus, I have dedicated it to his memory.

Richard Kyle
Hillsboro, Kansas

1

The Evangelical Paradox

"We cannot view the church as an island isolated from the rest of society. It cannot be isolated. As the culture changes, the church changes"—says Leith Anderson, an advocate of the church growth movement.[1] Most forms of religion have a close relationship with the surrounding culture. At times they influence culture and on other occasions they are shaped by the civilization in which they reside. This may be particularly true with American culture, especially its popular version. Few religious groups (and secular entities for that matter) have successfully resisted its powerful tug. Immigrant Catholicism became Americanized; mainline Protestantism accommodated itself to the modern world; Reform Judaism is at home in American society; and even some Eastern religions have had to make adjustments in order to market their faith.

In *Christ and Culture,* theologian H. Richard Niebuhr noted the ways in which Christ could transform culture. In the United States the opposite has happened—"culture has transformed Christ, as well as all other religions found within these shores. In every aspect of religious life, American faith has met American culture—and the culture has triumphed," notes Alan Wolfe.[2] Still, all religious bodies have not caved in. Eastern Orthodoxy has remained more traditional and some Old Order Mennonite groups have dug in their heels.

This book is about evangelicalism's paradoxical relationship with American culture. While noting conservative Protestantism's resistance to aspects of the modern world, the focus will be on evangelicalism's romance with popular culture. For the most part, evangelicalism has been thoroughly acculturated—perhaps more than any other religious body in America. Evangelicals have not created a Christian America. Rather, they have developed an Americanized Christianity and they cannot tell the difference between the two. In the other direction, two trends are observable. Acculturation is a two-way street. Evangelicals have also influenced American culture, especially its religious component. Viewing the growth of evangelical churches, other religious bodies have adopted some of its methods and characteristics. But in other ways evangelicalism has been a counterculture movement. It has resisted certain national moral trends and its fundamentalist branch has often retreated from society. (This opposition to national sins, however, is often more talk than walk. As will be noted later, evangelical moral practices frequently parallel those of the general population.)

The first tendency—the acculturation of evangelicalism—has dominated and has been a key to evangelicalism's numerical success. Rather than develop a viable subculture, evangelicals have created a counterfeit culture— that is, they have baptized and sanctified secular culture. For a religious group to be successful, it must be culturally relevant. For any religious body, however, there is only a fine line between being relevant to its surrounding culture and being absorbed by the culture. American evangelicalism has stepped over this line.

Granted that evangelicalism is tremendously diverse—nearly defying definition—generalizations are extremely difficult. Still, an attempt will be made to survey evangelicalism's relationship with American culture since the eighteenth century. For much of its history, evangelicalism has accommodated popular culture. This trend has accelerated in the late twentieth century, but it is certainly not new. The popular character of evangelicalism was evident even in colonial America. Because this accommodation has increased in recent years, special emphasis will be placed on the late twentieth century and movements that have been most adaptable to contemporary American culture.

Martin Marty and James Hunter also note the evangelical paradox. They contend that "evangelicalism has remained a cognitive minority but has emerged as a sociocultural majority." Evangelicalism still embraces its core beliefs and values. But at the same time, it has adapted itself to the secular world. In so doing, evangelicalism has become a middle-class movement, which dominates America's culture. Because evangelicals have become culturally mainstream, their social acceptance has greatly increased. All of this has come about because of the tremendous pressure on evangelicalism to accommodate itself to American culture—something it has done very well.[3]

To a large extent, the evangelical paradox is unavoidable. On one hand, evangelicals are a traditional people. They embrace traditional values and the historic faith. Thus, evangelicalism can be called "the old-time religion." On the other hand, they take very seriously the great commission—that is, to bring the good news to other people. They believe in reaching out and in church growth. Like the rest of American society, evangelicals are quantitatively, not qualitatively oriented. The disestablishment of religion in America has created a free market for religion. To succeed in a free market, a religion (or anything else for that matter) must appeal to the people. And this often entails incorporating the latest cultural fads into worship and other aspects of religious life. As a result, evangelicals are at once a very traditional but culturally accommodating people.

Church-State Separation

It would be difficult to exaggerate the impact of religious disestablishment upon American religion, especially its evangelical version. On one hand, the First Amendment has created an exciting, diverse, and vibrant religious climate—"one unmatched in any Western culture…"notes Randall Balmer. The government's laissez-faire attitude toward religion has made it a market economy with no government support or restrictions. Perhaps more than any other religious type, the evangelicals have capitalized on this dynamic and innovative religious climate. They have emphasized the experiential aspect of religion and used the most creative methods to promote their faith. In doing so, their numbers have grown dramatically.[4]

On the other hand, this free exercise of religious freedom has come at a price. It has prompted American religion—especially evangelicalism—to become "unabashedly populist." Evangelicals have championed the spiritual superiority of the common person against the elite or learned clergy. In doing so, they have reduced serious religious thinking to its lowest common denominator. Evangelicalism's obsession with numbers since the mid- twentieth century has caused the movement to pander unashamedly to the popular tastes of American culture. Serious worship has "degenerated into showmanship," often with a circus atmosphere. Evangelicals view America as God's chosen nation and feel that they (and the nation, too) have a corner on divine truth and righteousness. They have sanctified large segments of American culture, especially its consumerism and middle-class values. Worse yet, evangelicals have a tendency to gravitate toward charismatic personalities who embody the traits they desire—populist, sensational, nonconformist, and independent. American evangelicals have indeed embraced the cult of personality. They do not gather around doctrines or church organizations but tend to follow a charismatic leader.[5]

Paradoxically, in the late twentieth and early twenty-first centuries many evangelicals—especially those identified with the Religious Right—have little desire to maintain the separation of church and state. They contend that the "wall of separation between church and state" cannot be found in the First Amendment. Rather, the Supreme Court drew this language from Jefferson's 1802 Danbury letter and has since interpreted the Constitution in such a way. And even if the separation of church and state is legitimate, this interpretation should not entail the separation of religion from culture and the demand that religion should be removed from all aspects of public life. To employ a phrase coined by Richard John Neuhaus, a "naked public square" is not required by the First Amendment.[6]

Throughout the nineteenth century, religious disestablishment greatly benefited the evangelicals. It enabled them to expand numerically and to establish a cultural consensus around their values. But the twentieth century has not been as kind to evangelical values. A combination of social, intellectual, and demographic assaults destroyed their cultural dominance. As a result, many evangelicals now desire to restore their cultural hegemony by means of legislation. They want the government to legalize prayer in the classroom, provide public support for private education, and ban abortion and same sex marriages. And in pressuring the government to enact such provisions, they are undermining church-state separation.[7]

The Flow of Culture

The acculturation of Christianity flows in several directions. The more mainstream liberal denominations have tended to accommodate their faith to the elite culture, that is, science, psychology, sociology and more. Conversely, evangelicals have adjusted their faith to the popular culture, including its highly personal, experiential, intellectually shallow, and growth-oriented tendencies. But the result has often been the same. The elite culture is frequently hostile to Christianity and thus promotes a more secular society. Conversely, evangelicalism has Christianized secular society, often with the same results. Society is superficially Christian but with a secular core.

The influence, however, can run the other way. From the White House to the halls of Congress, politicians know that evangelicals are a powerful voice with which they must reckon. In the elections of 2000 and 2004, about 35 to 40 percent of George W. Bush's votes came from conservative Protestants. Consequently, few Republicans can ignore their agenda and expect to remain in office. Even other religious bodies have noted evangelicalism's numerical success and to some extent emulated it. The characteristics of the evangelical style—"its strongly personalist and therapeutic tendencies, its market savvy approaches to expanding the flock, and even a certain theological fuzziness—have permeated other faith traditions in America, including Roman Catholicism and Judaism."[8]

If numerical growth is the standard, evangelicalism has been enormously successful since the mid-twentieth century. During the same time, mainline Protestantism has experienced a significant decline. Some estimates suggest that up to one-half of the Protestants in America may be regarded as evangelicals. What has caused this situation? In his 1972 book, *Why Conservative Churches are Growing,* Dean Kelley set forth an idea that dominated for years. He argued that people are seeking the meaning to life. In maintaining both their faith and lifestyle standards, conservative churches have exhibited "traits of strictness": absolute beliefs, moral and social nonconformity, and a missionary zeal.[9]

This study will argue that such an idea is only part of the answer. Yes, evangelicals have generally maintained their belief system and resisted a number of contemporary moral trends. But at the same time they have bought heavily into the popular culture—so much so that in many respects the evangelical subculture is really secular culture sprayed over lightly with a coating of Christianity.

Several scholars note the acculturation of American evangelicalism. "The Christian faith is unrivaled among the world religions for its genius in innovation and adaptation. And no branch of the Christian faith has demonstrated this genius more often and more successfully than the evangelical movement," argues Os Guinness. Or as he puts it differently elsewhere, "Fundamentalism...prided itself on being world-denying by definition. Today...it has become world-affirming in a worldlier and more compromising way than...liberalism."[10] For this and other reasons, Mark Noll includes the words *flexible* and *adaptable* in his list of evangelical characteristics. Indeed, evangelicals have been "pervasively shaped by their particular cultures."[11]

Thanks to television and other innovations in the last thirty years or so, popular culture has become a more dominant force than ever before—so much so that success in many areas of life depends on how one relates to popular trends. Because of the free religious market in America and evangelicalism's emphasis on winning converts, it has fallen prey to the winds of popular culture more than has either mainline Protestantism or Catholicism.

In some evangelical churches, this accommodation to popular culture has reached ridiculous proportions. One large Texas church has stated its plan— namely, "to create a worship service...that is fast-paced, light on doctrine, and very heavy on music and drama." They were not concerned with be being "holier-than-thou" but rather with being "trendier-than-thou." Another church advertises, "Church Like You've Never Seen It Before! Outstanding music...no choirs or pipe organs here. Our music is crisp, contemporary, professional, and yes, even hot! World Class Drama...presents a dramatic performance specifically designed to enhance...messages...tailored for people in the 90s." Several years ago in another Texas church service, the pastor honored an individual and his wife for bringing six friends to church. Wearing Troy Aikman's jersey, the pastor tossed a football signed by the Dallas star quarterback to Michel Wood and his spouse, who were sitting in the pews and also dressed in football duds. This was their reward.[12]

Some churches have designed most of their activities to capture the interest of people who want to be entertained. In one large charismatic church, the pastor interjects dramatic acts into his sermons. Eye-popping antics include using live camels, ascending to the skylights via invisible wires, and chain sawing down potted trees. Some other evangelical services feature body-builders breaking boards, skydivers dropping in during sermons, and prayer warriors dressed in combat fatigues doing battle with the forces of darkness. In many conservative Protestant settings, Martin Marty sees too much "Christian bodybuilding and beautyqueening," rock music "with a Jesus gloss on it," and entrepreneurs "hawking a complete line of Christian celebrity cosmetics and panty-hose." So he observes that few modern religious groups have become more worldly than the fundamentalists.[13]

Both in the World and of the World

The issue is not so simple as evangelicalism drowning in contemporary culture. With many evangelicals, the Christian faith is synonymous with the "American way of life." They are two sides of the same coin. Still, the problem is more complex than this. Evangelicalism has had a paradoxical relationship with American culture—at times it has acted as a counterculture while on other occasions it has become thoroughly secular. In doing so, evangelicalism has simply reflected the paradox of American society, which is "both remarkably religious and secular."[14] Observers from Alexis de Tocqueville in the 1830s to modern pollsters have agreed on this issue.

Patrick Allitt notes four of these paradoxes. While industrialization and urbanization have caused religion to decline in Europe, in America it has become vigorous. Post-World War II America is a "highly religious and highly secular place." Second, while Jesus spoke out against wealth, American Christians are very materialistic and at times ostentatiously display their wealth. Next, in their rhetoric and values American Christians are quite traditional, but in their methods of ministry they are "innovative and technologically sophisticated." Lastly, while America is the most technologically advanced and wealthiest nation, it has large segments of Christians who believe society to be in disrepair and long for the return of Christ to correct this hopeless situation.[15]

At various times and places, evangelicals have evidenced a hate/love relationship with American culture. This connection began with the Puritans. While revivalism largely dismantled Puritan beliefs, American evangelicalism is usually seen as rooted in Puritanism and its focus on Scripture, biblical preaching, and experiential approach to salvation. The Puritans were the most educated and articulate of the early immigrants to North America and as a result they helped shape early American society more than any other religious movement. And this immense influence continued into the twentieth century. The Puritan vision of a new nation in a covenant with God helped give America a sense of mission—that is, a chosen nation, the new Israel, and a beacon to the world, which resulted in the "manifest destiny" of the nineteenth century. Through the years, Puritanism has also helped to shape how Americans view politics, morals, work, welfare, education, and the Sabbath.[16]

For much of the nineteenth century, especially the first sixty years, evangelicalism was the dominant cultural influence. To separate evangelicalism from nineteenth-century American culture would be as difficult as unscrambling a mixed omelet, argues William McLoughlin. "The story of American Evangelicalism is the story of America itself in the years 1800 to 1900.... To understand it is to understand the whole temper of American life in the nineteenth century." In respect to southern culture, Donald Matthews makes a similar statement. Evangelicalism was "the single most influential strain of religious activity in the South during the formative years before 1860."[17]

In the mind of most people, to be a Protestant and perhaps even a good American was to be an evangelical Christian. Thanks to revivalism from Finney to Moody, Americans became the most religious people in the world. Rather than conflict with the major political trends of republicanism and democracy inherited from the Revolutionary era, the evangelical faith coalesced with them. In this context, the notion of America being a Christian nation, chosen by God for a special mission, began to grow.

Not only could revivals change the hearts of individuals, they could re-make society, so it was believed. Perfectionist and postmillennial thinking drove many evangelicals to combat the various evils of the day—alcohol, slavery, prostitution, dueling, and Sabbath-breaking. Postmillennialism believed that through divine and human efforts the world could get progressively better and then Christ would return. Perfectionism insisted that as individuals could become nearly perfect, so could society. Thus, evangelical institutions became some of the leading forces for social reform. Education also felt the impact of evangelical Christianity. They built many schools and colleges, which solidified their role in shaping cultural values. The nation could not cope with the slavery problem and neither could the Protestant churches. Slavery split them into northern and southern branches and both used Scripture to justify their respective positions.[18]

After the Civil War evangelicalism continued its cultural dominance, but not without serious challenges. On one hand, it was the great age of missions, and thanks to Dwight Moody and Billy Sunday revivals continued. On the other, cracks in this evangelical hegemony began to appear. Massive immigration, industrialism, and urbanization all worked to change American culture and religion in a direction not favorable to the evangelical empire. Some new challenges also came from science, psychology, and the higher criticism of Scripture. In wake of these developments, what became known as modernism or liberalism adjusted its theology to accommodate these new intellectual trends.

But evangelicalism refused to go down this path, thanks to some evangelical scholars who defended the faith. In a different way, some new evangelical movements and theologies—dispensationalism, the holiness movement, Pentecostalism, and fundamentalism—combined to pull evangelicalism away from mainstream Protestantism and into its own subculture. Most of these movements adopted the premillennial view regarding Christ's return. This position argued that the world was getting progressively worse and that Christ would return before the millennium. So evangelicals began to abandon their efforts to redeem American society.

At the end of the nineteenth century, cultural evangelicalism still remained the dominant public ideology—that is, the definer of public values. But events would begin to change this perception. It soon became obvious that the millennium—at least in a postmillennial sense—was not dawning. Developments in the 1920s—especially the Scopes trial, which made evangelicals look intolerant, ignorant, out of touch with the world, and country bumpkins—reinforced their withdrawal from society. Many evangelicals now became known as fundamentalists and retreated to rebuild their institutions, including establishing new denominations and colleges. In doing so, rather than adopting an accommodating stance toward culture they were more like a world-rejecting sect. In the South, however, evangelicalism has remained the dominant culture throughout the twentieth century.[19]

Elsewhere, evangelicalism began to emerge from its subculture in the 1940s and 1950s, but it would not come out in full force until the 1970s. In the last thirty to forty years, several trends are visible. In respect to theology, evangelicals are generally orthodox, despite giving little serious thought to theological issues. On some moral issues—abortion, homosexual rights, same sex marriages, removal of prayer from the schools, feminism, and the teaching of evolution—they have resisted the prevailing direction of American society. And they have become politically active in support of such beliefs, working to elect politicians who will support their views. What alarmed conservative Protestants so much was the decline of evangelical Christianity as a cultural force. One hundred years or so earlier, though most Americans could not be regarded as evangelicals, evangelicalism still had much respectability as a cultural force. But throughout the twentieth century, the cultural hegemony of evangelical Christianity has deteriorated significantly. Many evangelicals, especially the Religious Right, want to restore this cultural dominance.[20]

When it comes to the popular culture, nevertheless, evangelicals may be the most acculturated religious group in America. They have, in fact, created a counterfeit culture—that is, they have baptized or sanctified many aspects of secular society. We now have Christian yellow pages, shopping malls, dating services, diets, physical fitness programs, celebrities, rock music, nightclubs, and bookstores. Moreover, evangelicals overwhelmingly embrace conservative politics and economics. Ironically, evangelicalism and mainstream Protestantism have generally gone in opposite directions in these respects. The Protestant mainstream has compromised many essentials of the historic faith but generally they have not accommodated popular culture to the extent that their evangelical cousins have. Traditionally, evangelicals have been cultural conservatives resisting the world; whereas liberals have stressed relevance in it. Today, as Guinness states, "many evangelicals are out-doing liberals as the enthusiastic religious modernizers [and] compromisers…"[21]

Not all evangelicals, however, support these political and social trends. There exists the evangelical left, which advocates social policies benefiting the poor, a less hawkish foreign policy, a more serious approach to worship, and refuses to equate the American way of life with the Christian faith.[22] Along with some confessional groups (e.g., Reformed and Lutheran bodies), these left-wing evangelicals have not traveled down the road toward cultural accommodation as extensively as have some evangelicals. The distinction of adapting to popular culture rests more with many of the independent and charismatic churches.

Who are the Evangelicals? Some Difficulties

Considering evangelicalism's extreme diversity, any definition is very difficult. Can Presbyterians, Methodists, black churches, Nazarenes, Baptists, Episcopalians, Mennonites, Pentecostals, Lutherans, fundamentalists, holiness bodies, dispensationalists, various Reformed groups, charismatics, and perhaps even Catholics all be part of the same movement? Some would say no. Donald Dayton argues that "the category evangelical has lost whatever usefulness it once had and...that we can very well do without it." Historically, the word has had three different meanings, he says. Reformational in the sixteenth century; pietist and conversionist in the eighteenth century; and fundamentalist in the twentieth century.[23] In Europe, the word *evangelical* often denotes Protestant or Lutheran.

Some groups raise particular problems. Given any common understanding of the word *evangelical*, what can be said about the vast majority of the black churches, Adventism, Anabaptist bodies, confessional groups (whether Reformed or Lutheran), or charismatic Catholics? Quite often the label *evangelical* is given to conservative or traditional Protestant bodies. But at their points of origin, one could hardly call the holiness, Adventist, or Pentecostal movements traditional.[24]

In *Deconstructing Evangelicalism*, D. G. Hart argues that evangelicalism is not an appropriate religious category. He contends that it came into existence only in the 1940s. Until the twentieth century, no clear line separated evangelicals from other Protestants. Not until the Protestant wars of the 1920s did Protestantism divide into two hostile camps, the fundamentalists and the modernists. Wanting to distance themselves from both the liberal and fundamentalists factions, a group of moderate fundamentalists adopted the name *neo-evangelicals*. In the coming years, they formed a loose coalition around a minimum of orthodox Christian doctrines and several organizations. In recent years, however, this movement has become so diverse and has failed to establish a clear institutional identity that it is better to abandon the term.[25]

While a clear evangelical category may not have existed prior to the twentieth century, most historians acknowledge an evangelical type by the eighteenth century. In such a category, they would place the revivalistic, pietistic, and non-liturgical Protestants. For example, in *Blessed Assurance*, Randall Balmer contends that North American evangelicalism derives from an eighteenth-century fusion of Puritanism and pietism. In *The Rise of Evangelicalism*, Mark Noll notes that movement's eighteenth-century roots in Britain and

America. Here he employees the term *evangelical* to denote "a set of convictions, practices, habits and oppositions that resemble what Europeans describe as pietism."[26]

The influence of Puritanism and especially pietism upon subsequent evangelicalism, particularly on ordinary believers, is difficult to calculate. The influence of Puritanism and pietism can be seen in the emphasis on personal piety and maintaining the Sabbath and prohibitions against alcohol, tobacco, and dancing. Exacting moral standards, the call for conversion, and a suspicion—if not outright rejection—of ecclesiastical structures, liturgical formulations, and theological systems can be attributed to pietism. Both Puritanism and pietism called for a warmhearted experience as a sign of conversion. And the attempt to legislate these moral standards can be attributed to Puritanism.[27]

Who are the Evangelicals? Some Common Denominators

These objections not withstanding, the term evangelical is used widely by people both inside and outside the movement. So it deserves some attempt at definition. At its most basic level, *evangelion* is the Greek word for good news, which is usually translated as "gospel" in the English Bibles. What does the gospel mean? It is the good news about Jesus Christ, his death and resurrection, and his kingdom, that is, the rule of God over humanity. On the part of people, it entails faith and repentance, and the need for a spiritual rebirth.[28] Such a definition could apply to most Christian bodies. So it would help to see how the word has been used historically.

Several metaphors have been used to describe evangelicalism. At first, Timothy Smith characterized it as a mosaic. Later he changed the metaphor to that of a kaleidoscope, which represents a changing pattern. Looking at evangelical history, Smith saw evangelism responding and adjusting to cultural, intellectual, religious, and political developments at every juncture in its development.[29] In more recent years, Robert Johnson has viewed evangelicalism as an extended family. With parents, siblings, cousins, and in-laws, family boundaries are not always well defined. So it is with evangelicalism. There is some unity but with many differences. Other scholars describe evangelicalism as a big tent, one big enough to include many diverse groups.[30]

Despite having many disconnected, even opposing parts, evangelicalism can be viewed as a whole. As George Marsden notes, "no one part [of evangelicalism] can be equated with the whole." The many subgroups have their special characteristics, but no one denomination can equate its distinctives with evangelicalism as a whole. Still, there are some common denominators running through the movement. To recognize these threads while still allowing for considerable diversity is a key to "unlocking" the puzzle of evangelicalism. So evangelicalism must be seen as movement, an ethos, and a mood that cuts across many denominational lines.[31]

What are these common denominators? When boiled down to its essentials, evangelicalism embraces certain characteristics. British historian David Bebbington notes four special marks of evangelical faith and practice: conversionism (the need to change lives, especially by the new birth); activitism (sharing the gospel); biblicicism (regarding the Bible as the ultimate authority); and crucicentricism (an emphasis on the death of Christ as the only means to salvation).[32]

Richard Quebedeaux says evangelical Christianity has exhibited three major characteristics: the "authority of Scripture in matters of faith and practice"; a personal faith in Jesus Christ as Savior and Lord; and, the necessity of actively seeking "the conversion of sinners to Christ."[33] Alister McGrath argues for six basic evangelical convictions. They are, "the supreme authority of Scripture"; the majesty of Christ as God incarnate and Lord and Savior; "the lordship of the Holy Spirit"; "the need for personal salvation"; "the priority of evangelism"; and "the importance of the Christian community."[34]

Historically, one can look at evangelicalism as either a broad or narrow movement. As a narrow movement, which this study rejects, neo-evangelicalism (as it was called) emerged from fundamentalism in the 1940s. While upholding the historic Christian faith, as did fundamentalism, evangelicalism rejected many of the cultural characteristics of fundamentalism—rigid separation from the world, militancy toward liberalism, anti-intellectualism, and a lack of social concern. In this view, evangelicalism is usually regarded as a more moderate version of fundamentalism. Whereas fundamentalism arose largely within Presbyterian and Baptist circles, evangelicalism is seen as linked primarily to these denominations plus the holiness movement. Such an approach obviously excludes many groups. So no wonder many contemporary denominations reject the label *evangelical*.[35]

A Broad Movement

Evangelicalism, therefore, should be viewed as a broad and identifiable movement stretching back to at least the revivals of the eighteenth century. Actually, its roots go back to the Protestant Reformers and their insistence on the authority of Scripture, justification by faith, and biblical preaching. They were called *evangelicals* but soon the term became equated with Protestantism in general. The term *Protestant* gradually displaced the older designation of evangelical. Next in the evangelical family tree came the Puritans, who also stressed the supreme authority of the Bible and grounded predestination in the experience of the believer.[36]

On the Continent, Protestantism had largely fallen prey to a new scholasticism, which was as lifeless as that of the Middle Ages. Correct doctrine and participation in the sacraments replaced heart commitment to Christ. Dead orthodoxy became the sum of Christianity. In the seventeenth century, German pietists led by Philipp Jacob Spener and August Hermann Franke attempted to correct this situation by insisting on a personal faith in Christ as the essence of Christianity. The excesses of pietism did inject a major dose of individualism into the Christian faith and contributed to evangelicalism's tendency to ignore the lordship of Christ over many areas of life. Still, pietism powerfully influenced future evangelicalism with its missionary impulse and insistence of personal salvation.[37]

By the eighteenth century, pietism spilled over into England, influencing the Methodist revivals. Led by George Whitefield, John and Charles Wesley, the Methodists brought great spiritual and social changes to England. Arminianism, which stressed human choice in salvation, was born in the Netherlands during the seventeenth century. John Wesley popularized this theology in England and by the nineteenth century it became dominant in America. The eighteenth-century revivals, however, were transnational. What is called the First Great Awakening in America was begun by the efforts of Theodore Frelinghuysen and Gilbert Tennent in the middle colonies. This awakening spread to New England where its leading spokesman was Jonathan Edwards. The job of connecting the revivals in England with those in America and spreading them throughout the colonies fell to George Whitefield, the greatest preacher of his day.[38]

After the 1740s, these revival fires burned low until about 1800 when they burst forth in the so-called Second Great Awakening, which operated in three primary areas: the frontier, New England, and New York. The leading figures included James McGready, Timothy Dwight, Lyman Beecher, and Charles G. Finney—one of America's greatest revivalists. These revivals differed from the First Great Awakening in several ways. Edwards and Whitefield preached the gospel with a clear-cut Calvinistic twist. On the other hand, the Second Great Awakening leaned distinctively toward theological Arminianism. Of great importance for the future of evangelicalism, these revivalists took a far more pragmatic approach to winning souls for Christ. In particular, Finney utilized contrived methods to convert sinners, namely, the "new measures," that were designed to evoke a decision for Christ. These awakenings also spawned a series of social reform movements—abolition leagues, missionary programs, temperance societies, and a host of others.[39]

Thanks to the efforts of Dwight L. Moody and Billy Sunday, the revival fires continued to burn in the late nineteenth and early twentieth centuries. These evangelists adopted and refined the revival methods begun by Finney—namely, organized rallies, business methods, fundraising, techniques for evoking decisions, and urban meetings. During these years, several new movements and their various denominations joined the evangelical family. These newcomers—the holiness movement, dispensational premillennialism, and Pentecostalism—came with some new twists and had a tremendous impact on the direction evangelicalism would take in the twentieth century.[40]

Prior to the twentieth century, evangelicalism was part of the Protestant mainstream. But the events of the late nineteenth and early twentieth centuries—namely, the fundamentalist-modernist struggle—forced the evangelicals (now called the fundamentalists) out of the mainstream. In such a position, they adopted a separationist stance and hostility towards the modern world. But many moderates within the movement disliked this new direction. So they moved down a different path. While remaining orthodox in respect to the Christian faith, they endeavored to engage the modern world in a meaningful way. In doing so and in an attempt to distance themselves from fundamentalism, they adopted the names of neo-evangelicalism or evangelicalism. During the nineteenth century, there was no need to consciously identify themselves as evangelicals. Now with the discomfort generated by both liberalism and fundamentalism, evangelicals saw the need to define their identity.[41]

At the beginning of the twentieth-first century, evangelicalism must be regarded as a big tent or large extended family. It includes many diverse elements, some in conflict with each other. But there still exists several critical issues, which forge a common bond. So rather than viewing evangelicalism as primarily emerging out of fundamentalism, it should be seen as a movement that has been shaped by three periods in modern Christianity: the Reformation, especially its expression in Puritanism; the revivals of the eighteenth and nineteenth centuries; and the twentieth-century conservative reaction to the modern world, which has been called fundamentalism.[42]

Fundamentalism and Evangelicalism—What are the Differences?

What is the relationship between evangelicalism and fundamentalism? Are they the same? Some people both inside and outside the movements confuse the two. Both are expressions of orthodox religion so it is easy for non-evangelicals to lump the two together. But neither evangelicals nor fundamentalists approve of this linkage. "Evangelicals resent being called Fundamentalists, and Fundamentalists do not usually appreciate the Evangelical designation," says Richard Quebedeaux. As a result, both often take every opportunity to distance themselves from each other, both theologically and behaviorally.[43]

Despite these efforts, the boundaries between evangelicalism and fundamentalism are not always clear. When evangelicals make efforts to distance themselves from fundamentalism, their critics often do not acknowledge or even notice the difference. In part, this is due to the human tendency to stereotype individuals and movements. Also, both evangelicals and fundamentalists share certain common beliefs. Perhaps more important is that fundamentalism has influenced the mindset of much of evangelicalism, especially the conservative side of the movement. Fundamentalism is more than a set of beliefs. It is also a tendency, a habit of mind, an ethos, and a culture—features that some evangelicals share.[44]

What then is fundamentalism? It is a movement taking shape in the late nineteenth century but organized in the early twentieth to defend orthodox Protestantism against the challenges of the modern world, especially theological liberalism, evolution, and the higher criticism of the Bible. Fundamentalism has been viewed socially (as a rural way of life); as a form of anti-intellectualism; and as growing out of a conjunction between orthodox Calvinism and millennialism.[45] The most accepted interpretation has been the one set forth by George Marsden: "Fundamentalists were evangelical Christians...who in the twentieth century militantly opposed both modernism in theology and the cultural changes that modernism endorsed."[46]

Fundamentalist historian George Dollar echoes similar words: "Historic fundamentalism is the literal exposition of all the affirmations and attitudes of the Bible and the militant exposure of all non-Biblical affirmations and attitudes." This defense of the Bible also involves a particular interpretation of Scripture—what Dollar calls the literal exposition of the Bible. And fundamentalists often equate the literal interpretation of Scripture with the Bible itself. For them, Scripture is inerrant—meaning that the Bible is not only an infallible authority in matters of faith and practice but also when it addresses scientific and historical issues.[47]

In these descriptions of fundamentalism, two concepts have emerged— militant opposition to modernity and an inerrant Bible. To these, a third must be added—separation from the world. In order to preserve purity in respect to doctrine and lifestyle, the older and more militant fundamentalists refuse to cooperate with other religious groups. "*Compromise* and *accommodation* are the most dreaded words in the Fundamentalist vocabulary," argues Nancy Ammerman. "Their insistence on separation most clearly distinguishes Fundamentalists from their closest relatives, the Evangelicals." There are, however, the so-called neo-fundamentalists who have cooperated with a variety of religious and political conservatives to combat social issues such as abortion. Still, these more moderate fundamentalists insist on separation when it comes to ecclesiastical matters.[48]

What then is the relationship of evangelicalism and fundamentalism? Both are loose coalitions, but fundamentalism is a subgroup within evangelicalism and can be seen as an extreme wing of this larger movement. All Christian fundamentalists are evangelicals but not all evangelicals are fundamentalists. Mainstream evangelicalism is not as militant or as separatist as is fundamentalism. Also, while upholding the supreme authority of Scripture, many evangelicals do not insist on the literal interpretation of an inerrant Bible. In this respect, evangelicals are more complex, believing that it is important to understand the circumstances in which Scripture was written. Regarding Christ's second coming, many fundamentalists insist on the dispensational premillennial position. Again, on this issue evangelicals hold to several interpretations. Significant differences arise regarding their respective outlooks and temperament. Fundamentalists often embrace a siege mentality and tend to be anti-intellectual. Such tendencies are less prevalent among mainstream evangelicals.[49]

A Few Categories

The great diversity within the broad evangelical movement demands that the various groups not be lumped together. Some categorization, however, helps to reduce evangelicalism's tendency toward religious anarchy. And a number of scholars have attempted to draw some order out of this chaos. On an evangelical/fundamentalist continuum, Quebedeaux has identified five subgroups. At one extreme are the "Separatist Fundamentalists," who "make up the most conservative ideological subgroup—theologically and otherwise." Examples include individuals such as Carl McIntire and Billy James Hargis and institutions like Bob Jones University and the American Council of Churches.

"Open Fundamentalism" is his next category. While almost as conservative religiously and politically, "it is less vocal and extreme about its separatist posture" and is "willing to engage in dialogue with other Orthodox schools of thought..." Dallas Theological Seminary and Moody Bible Institute fit into this group. In the middle are what Quebedeaux labels as "Establishment Evangelicalism." These evangelicals differ from both types of fundamentalists over three issues. They separate much less from apostasy. While accepting the authority of Scripture, they do not limit themselves to a literal interpretation of the Bible or dispensational hermeneutics. Examples are the National Association of Evangelicals, Wheaton College, and Fuller Theological Seminary.

The "New Evangelicals" have moved even further away from fundamentalism, embracing many liberal and neo-orthodox ideas. They place more emphasis on experience, the role of the Holy Spirit, and social concern. Quebedeaux's last group is the "charismatic renewal," which is difficult to categorize. It is a "transdenominational if not an ecumenical movement...theologically diverse but generally Orthodox and unified by a common experience—the Baptism of the Holy Spirit..."[50]

Timothy Weber sees four branches in the evangelical family tree. The classical evangelicals are "loyal primarily to the doctrines of the Protestant Reformation" and largely include the Lutheran and Reformed churches. Next are the pietistic evangelicals who "stand in the Reformation tradition" but who "seek to complete it by incorporating the experiential emphases of Puritanism and the evangelical awakenings..." He includes Methodists, Baptists, holiness groups, and Pentecostals in this branch. Third are those "shaped by the fundamentalist-modernist controversy," namely, the fundamentalist evangelicals. In this category, he lists not only the fundamentalists but their neo-evangelical offspring who came out of fundamentalism in the 1940s. Last are the progressive evangelicals, who come out of the other three branches but are more in tune with modernity. They can most often be found in the attempts to reform evangelicalism and conservative elements within the mainline Protestant churches.[51]

Sociologist James Davidson Hunter has also identified four evangelical traditions. The most prominent are the Baptists who bring revivalism and a democratic strand to evangelicalism. Next is the Holiness-Pentecostal tradition. These churches emphasize the role of the Holy Spirit in conversion, sanctification, and the gifts of the Spirit. Hunter's third stream is the Anabaptist tradition, which places the rational over the emotional, focuses on community relationships, and evidences considerable social concern. Fourth is the Reformed-Confessional wing, which also tends toward a rational view of conversion. But it differs from the Anabaptists in its adherence to Calvinistic doctrines and its emphasis on the avoidance of worldly pleasures.[52] Robert Webber also approaches evangelicalism from the vantage point of religious traditions. He lists fourteen, which I will not note.[53] But this path to evangelicalism can be useful. It best accounts for the different distinctives within evangelicalism while still allowing for some commonalties.

Culture and Character

Considering evangelicalism's close relationship with American culture, a brief look at its major characteristics would be appropriate. American culture is dynamic and in constant flux. Still, there are some threads that run the course of American history. Sometime from about 1760 to 1830, Americans and foreign observers realized that America had developed a distinct culture—one that was no longer just an appendage of European society. What was this culture like? Or, to raise Hector Crevecoeur's question, "What then is the American, this new man?" What are their aspirations? How do they think or act?

Individualism must be at the top of any list. America was a vast area, a frontier nation. This fostered many characteristics—but self-reliance, democracy, the spirit of liberty, and individualism must be numbered among them. Space helped bring about these traits. Challenged by the realities of geography, Americans had to be mobile and self-reliant. They had no one to depend on but themselves. Thus, the self-made individual became an American ideal.

This individualism and self-reliance has spilled over into politics in several ways. It can be argued that the spirit of liberty was the driving force behind the Revolutionary War. While colonial America must be regarded as pre-democratic, Americans no longer cared to be ruled by an aristocratic European power. Individualism is a key component of republicanism, political democracy, and the market economy—the pillars of the American secular gospel. Democracy came gradually, but its components are visible in the colonial and early national period. The lax British colonial rule permitted considerable local autonomy and the colonies developed a form of de facto independence.

Democracy proceeded through a series of developments—the colonial assemblies, Declaration of Independence, the Constitution, Bill of Rights, Jeffersonian republicanism, and Jacksonian democracy.

In particular, the First Amendment to the Constitution disestablished religion, guaranteeing that there would be no national church. This critical development made religion a matter of persuasion, a cultural commodity that people could accept or reject. This can be seen as the key to the dynamism of American religion. In fact, being "religious" can thus be a way of being "American." That religion became a commodity is also why it contains many superficial elements. People must buy into it or it is dead. And sometimes people do not want substance in religion.

About this time, mercantilism with its governmental control of the economy was collapsing in much of the Western world. So an incipient form of capitalism began to develop in the young nation. As religion exploded in part due to the lack of a state church, the economy also grew in leaps and bounds because the economy had few restraints. These two occurrences grow out of the dynamic individualism and free environment found in early national America.

Populism, the belief in the virtues and wisdom of the common people, came to dominate the culture of early America, and it is still a powerful force. The people who migrated to America came from European countries marked by nobility, aristocracy, and privilege. None of these could flourish in a nation conceived in liberty and equality. The Declaration of Independence said, "all men are created equal." And "where all men were equal in the sight of God, it was difficult not to admit equality in the eyes of men; and where men were equal at the ballot box, it was impolitic to encourage privilege," wrote Henry Steele Commager.

While our founding fathers were largely men of means, in general elitism was something to be frowned upon. As a result, sometime during the first fifty years of our nationhood, the common people dethroned the aristocratic elements in America. The will of the people and sensitivity to public opinion became something that any political, business, and religious leader had to consider. Popular sovereignty and equalitarianism received a boost with the election of Andrew Jackson in 1828. Public opinion could be ignored only at great peril. Such is especially true with the evangelical faith, which is driven by the will of the people and the need to win converts.

Americans are also a pragmatic people. Because of our populism and pragmatism, we are often not interested in an individual's education or background. And we certainly do not want to hear about any abstract theory. We only ask, Will it work? Can they get the job done? As a consequence, Americans are an active people, a people on the go. We often act first and ask questions afterwards. Somewhat related is our emphasis on numbers. Success is measured quantitatively, not qualitatively. We are impressed with big businesses and churches. Size is the criterion for success. From this thinking emerges evangelicalism's fascination with the large religious organizations and empires that have been built throughout American history.

To build such edifices, optimism is required. On the whole, Americans are an optimistic people. Because we believe the job can get done, we undertake some overwhelming tasks. In part, this is because we are oriented to the future. Having little tradition to build on, Americans looked forward, not to the past. We only had our empires to build. Evangelicalism has embraced this sense of empire building. Not only does it take great faith to build large churches and religious organizations, but it also requires great optimism.[54]

Notes

1. Leith Anderson, *Dying for Change* (Minneapolis: Bethany House, 1990), 43.
2. Alan Wolfe, *The Transformation of American Religion* (New York: Free Press, 2003), 2, 3 (quote). See also R. Stephen Warner, "They're Ok, We're Ok, *Books and Culture* (March/April 2004): 117; David Dark, *The Gospel According to America* (Louisville: Westminister John Knox Press, 2005); David Clark, "The Gospel According to America," *Books and Culture* (March/April 2005): 12-14, 40-42.
3. James Davidson Hunter, *American Evangelicalism: Conservative Religion and the Quandary of Modernity* (New Brunswick, NJ: Rutgers University Press, 1983), 47, 48 (quote); Martin E. Marty, *Righteous Empire* (New York: Dial Press, 1970); Martin E. Marty, *A Nation of Behavers* (Chicago: University of Chicago Press, 1976).
4. Randall Balmer, *Blessed Assurance: A History of Evangelicalism in America* (Boston: Beacon Press, 1999), 4-6, 42.
5. Ibid. 5, 6, 69.
6. Kenneth J. Collins, *The Evangelical Moment: The Promise of an American Religion* (Grand Rapids: Baker Books, 2005), 113-15 (quotes).
7. Balmer, *Blessed Assurance*, 100-102.
8. Jay Tolson, "The New Old-Time Religion," *U.S. News and World Report* (8 December 2003): 38.
9. Dean Kelley, *Why Conservative Churches Are Growing* (New York: Harper and Row, 1972), 37.
10. Os Guinness, "Sounding Out the Idols of the Church Growth," in *No God But God*, ed. Os Guinness and John Seel (Chicago: Moody Press, 1992), 154 (quote); Os Guinness, *Dining with the Devil* (Grand Rapids: Baker Books, 1993), 62.
11. Mark Noll, *American Evangelical Christianity* (Oxford: Blackwell, 2001), 14.
12. John H. Armstrong, "The Rush to Seeker Sensitive Worship," *Modern Reformation.org* http://www.modernreformation.org/mr95/janfeb/mr9501madrush.html. (12/12/02) (quote).
13. Quoted in Mark Noll, Cornelius Plantinga, Jr., and David Wells, "Evangelical Theology Today," *Theology Today* 51, 4 (1995): 497, 501 (quote on 501).
14. The paradox between America being both religious and secular is the theme of Marsden's book. See George Marsden, *Religion and American Culture* (Chicago: Harcourt Brace, 1990).
15. Patrick Allitt, *Religion in America Since 1945: A History* (New York: Columbia University Press, 2003), xi, xii (quotes). See also Jedediah Purdy, *Being America: Liberty, Commerce, and Violence in an American World* (New York: Alfred A. Knopf, 2003); Philip Jenkins, "America the Ambiguous: The Paradoxes of a Chosen Nation," *Books and Culture* (March/April 2003): 39.

16. See Sydney Ahlstrom, *A Religious History of the American People* (New Haven, CT: Yale University Press, 1972), 1079, 1090; Sydney Ahlstrom, " From Puritanism to Evangeliclism: A Critical Perspective," in *The Evangelicals*, ed. David Wells and John D. Woodbridge (Nashville: Abingdon, 1975), 269, 288; Marsden, *Religion and American Culture*, 17; Bruce Shelley, *Evangelicalism in America* (Grand Rapids: Eerdmans, 1967), 27-30.

17. William G. McLoughlin, ed., *The American Evangelicals, 1800-1900: An Anthology* (New York: Harper Torchbooks, 1968), 26 (quote); Donald G. Mathews, *Religion in the Old South* (Chicago: University of Chicago Press, 1977), xiv (quote); Leonard I. Sweet, "The Evangelical Tradition in America," in *The Evangelical Tradition in America*, ed. Leonard I. Sweet (Macon, GA: Mercer University Press, 1984), 1, 2.

18. For such general observations, see Noll, *American Evangelical Christianity;* Nathan O. Hatch, *The Democratization of American Christianity* (New Haven, CT: Yale University Press, 1989); George Marsden, ed., *Evangelicalism and Modern America* (Grand Rapids: Eerdmans, 1984); Shelley, *Evangelicalism in America*; Marsden, *Religion and American Culture*; Jon Butler, *Awash in a Sea of Faith* (Cambridge, MA: Harvard University Press, 1990); Paul E. Johnson, *A Shopkeepers' Millennium* (New York: Hill and Wang, 1978); Mark A. Noll, *America's God* (New York: Oxford University Press, 2002); Timothy L. Smith, *Revivalism and Social Reform* (Baltimore, MD: Johns Hopkins University Press, 1980).

19. For such general observations, see George Marsden, *Fundamentalism and American Culture* (New York: Oxford University Press, 1980); Noll, *American Evangelical Christianity*; Shelley, *Evangelicalism in America*; Marsden, *Religion and American Culture*; Joel A. Carpenter, *Revive Us Again* (New York: Oxford University Press); Randall Balmer, *Mine Eyes Have Seen the Glory* (New York: Oxford University Press, 1989); Douglas W. Frank, *Less Than Conquerers* (Grand Rapids: Eerdmans, 1986); Harriet Harris, *Fundamentalism and Evangelicals* (Oxford: Clarendon Press, 1998); Marty, *Righteous Empire*; D. G. Hart, *That Old-Time Religion in Modern America* (Chicago: Ivan Dee, 2002).

20. See James Davidson Hunter, *Evangelicalism: The Coming Generation* (Chicago: University of Chicago Press, 1987); Hart, *That Old-Time Religion*; Grant Wacker, "Searching for Norman Rockwell: Popular Evangelicalism in Contemporary America," in *The Evangelical Tradition in America*.

21. Guinness, *Dining with the Devil*, 55, 56 (quote). See Hart, *That Old-Time Religion*; Carol Flake, *Redemptorama: Culture, Politics, and the New Evangelicalism* (Garden City, NY: Anchor Books, 1984); Richard Quebedeaux, *The Worldly Evangelicals* (New York: Harper and Row, 1978); Shelley, *Evangelicalism in America;* Hunter, *American Evangelicalism;* Mark A. Shibley, *Resurgent Evangelicalism in the United States* (Columbia: University of South Carolina Press, 1996); Christian Smith, *American Evangelism: Embattled and Thriving* (Chicago: University of Chicago Press, 1998).

22. Robert Weber, *The Younger Evangelicals* (Grand Rapids: Baker Books, 2002); Hunter, *Evangelicalism: The Coming Generation*; Richard Quebedeaux, *The Young Evangelicals* (New York: Harper and Row, 1974); Ronald J. Sider, *Rich Christians in an Age of Hunger* (Nashville: Word, 1977); Jim Wallis, *Who Speaks for God?* (New York: Delta Books, 1996); Leslie Keylock, "Evangelical Protestants Take Over Center Field," *Publishers Weekly* (9 March 1984): 32-34.

23. Donald W. Dayton, "Some Doubts about the Usefulness of the Category Evangelical," in *The Variety of American Evangelicalism*, ed. Donald W. Dayton (Knoxville: University of Tennessee Press, 1991), 245.

24. Ibid., 246, 247.
25. D. G. Hart, *Deconstructing Evangelism* (Grand Rapids: Baker Books, 2004), 13-32. See Mark Galli, "Evangelicals: Fragmented and Thriving," *Books and Culture* (January/Februrary): 22.
26. Mark A. Noll, *The Rise of Evangelicalism* (Downers Grove, IL: InterVarsity Press, 2003), 17 (quote); Balmer, *Blessed Assurance*, 14.
27. Balmer, *Blessed Assurance*, 28-30.
28. Shelley, *Evangelicalism in America*, 14, 15; Timothy George, "If I'm an Evangelical, What Am I?" *Christianity Today* 9 (August 1999): 62.
29. Timothy L. Smith, "The Evangelical Kaleidoscope and the Call to Unity," *Christian Scholars Review* 15, 2 (1986): 125-40; Jon R. Stone, *On the Boundaries of American Evangelicalism* (New York: St. Martin's, 1997), 4-6.
30. Robert K. Johnson, "American Evangelicalism: An Extended Family," in *The Variety of American Evangelicalism*, 252-69; Cullen Murphy, "Protestantism and the Evangelicals," *The Wilson Quarterly* (autumn 1981): 105-17.
31. George M. Marsden, "Fundamentalism and American Evangelicalism," in *The Variety of American Evangelicalism*, 24, 25 (quote on 24); George Marsden, "Introduction," in *Evangelicalism and Modern America*, ed. George Marsden (Grand Rapids: Eerdmans, 1984), xiv, xv; George M. Marsden, *Understanding Fundamentalism and Evangelicalism* (Grand Rapids: Eerdmans, 1991), 1-6.
32. David Bebbington, *Evangelicalism in Modern Britain* (Grand Rapids: Baker Books, 1989), 2, 3.
33. Quebedeaux, *Young Evangelicals*, 3,4.
34. Alister McGrath, *Evangelicalism and the Future of Christianity* (Downers Grove, IL: InterVarsity Press, 1995), 55, 56.
35. For example, see John H. Gerstner, "The Theological Boundaries of Evangelicalism," in *The Evangelicals*, 21-37; C. Kraus, ed., *Evangelicalism and Anabaptism* (Scottdale, PA: Herald, Press, 1979); Hart, *Deconstructing Evangelicalism,* 22-31.
36. McGrath, *Evangelicalism and the Future of Christianity,* 20, 21, 23; Shelley, *Evangelicalism in America*, 27-30.
37. F. Ernest Stoeffler, ed., *Continental Pietism and Early American Christianity* (Grand Rapids: Eerdmans, 1976); Dale Brown, *Understanding Pietism* (Grand Rapids: Eerdmans, 1978); McGrath, *Evangelicalism and the Future of Christianity*, 25.
38. Mark A. Noll, *A History of Christianity in the United States and Canada* (Grand Rapids: Eerdmans, 1992), 103-13; Ahlstrom, *Religious History*, 265-329.
39. Bernard A. Weisberger, *They Gathered at the River* (New York: Octagon Books, 1979); William G. McLoughlin, Jr., *Modern Revivalism* (New York: Ronald Press, 1959).
40. Noll, *Christianity in the United States and Canada*, 288-309. See Weisberger, *They Gathered at the River*; McLoughlin, *Modern Revivalism*.
41. Hart, *That Old-Time Religion*, 25-114; Noll, *American Evangelical Christianity*, 18-22; Stone, *Boundaries of American Evangelicalism*, 70-118; McGrath, *Evangelicalism and the Future of Christianity*, 22, 23.
42. Noll, *American Evangelical Christianity*, 22-26; Bruce Shelley, "Evangelicalism," in *Dictionary of Christianity in America*, ed. Daniel Reid et al. (Downers Grove, IL: InterVarsity), 413; Collins, *Evangelical Moment*, 22-40.
43. Quebedeaux, *Young Evangelicals*, 19 (quote); Stone, *Boundaries of American Evangelicalism*, 29, 30.
44. Harris, *Fundamentalism and Evangelicals*, 1-11.

45. Timothy Weber, "Fundamentalism," in *Dictionary of Christianity in America*, 461, 462; Ernest Sandeen, *The Roots of Fundamentalism* (Chicago: University of Chicago Press, 1970).

46. George Marsden, *Fundamentalism and American Culture* (New York: Oxford University Press, 1980), 4.

47. George W. Dollar, *A History of Fundamentalism in America* (Greenville, SC: Bob Jones University Press, 1973), xv (quote); George Marsden, "Fundamentalism and Evangelicalism," in *The Variety of Evangelicalism*, 24, 25.

48. Nancy Tatom Ammerman, *Bible Believers: Fundamentalists in the Modern World* (New Brunswick, NJ: Rutgers University Press, 1987), 4 (quote); Harris, *Fundamentalism and Evangelicals,* 3, 4.

49. Ammerman, *Bible Believers*, 4, 5; Harris, *Fundamentalism and Evangelicals*, 3-8.

50. Quebedeaux, *Young Evangelicals*, 19-24 (quotes).

51. Timothy P. Weber, "Premillennialism and the Branches of Evangelicalism," in *The Variety of American Evangelicalism*, 12-14.

52. Hunter, *American Evangelicalism*, 7-9.

53. Robert E. Webber, *Common Roots* (Grand Rapids: Zondervan, 1978), 32.

54. This material on the American character has been drawn from several sources, especially from Henry Steele Commager, *The American Mind* (New Haven, CT: Yale University Press, 1950), 3-25 (quote on 13), and Bruce Shelley, "The American Character," Seminary Studies Series, Denver Seminary, 1963. See also John Harmon McElroy, *American Beliefs* (Chicago: Ivan R. Dee, 1999); Robert Bellah et al., *Habits of the Heart* (New York: Harper and Row, 1985); Richard Hofstadter, *Anti-Intellectualism in American Life* (New York: Vintage Books, 1963); Nathan O. Hatch, "Evangelicalism as a Democratic Movement," in *Evangelicalism and Modern America*, 71-82; Sidney E. Mead, *The Lively Experiment* (New York: Harper and Row, 1963); "America and Religion," *The Economist* (8 July 1995): 19-21.

2

Evangelicalism in the Driver's Seat

To be sure, the First Amendment disestablished religion in America. No particular religion could be recognized by law or receive special privileges from the national government. This stipulation, however, did not stop the development of a de facto evangelical establishment. From the very beginning of the colonial period, evangelical Protestantism had been a powerful cultural force in America—but by 1830 it had achieved undisputed dominance over most aspects of national life. Martin Marty, therefore, called the years from 1776 to 1877, "The Evangelical Empire." "Overall, between the years 1820 and 1860 evangelical Protestants had a greater impact on American culture than at any time before or since," says Curtis Johnson. By the time of the Civil War, the evangelical imagination had influenced nearly every aspect of American public life—politics, education, leisure activities, gender roles, reform movements, and the slavery debate. After the Civil War this evangelical cultural dominance began to weaken, but it still hung on until the end of the century.[1]

Evangelicalism's cultural importance extended well beyond its numerical strength. In the eighteenth and early nineteenth centuries, church membership was more restrictive than it is in modern times. Still, at the time of the Revolutionary War only about 4 to 7 percent of the population were members of churches. By the mid-nineteenth century, out of 30 million Americans the evangelical churches could count approximately 4 million members. If children, casual attenders, and seekers could be added to this number, perhaps 60 percent of the population came under evangelical influence.[2]

Given these numbers, how did this evangelical cultural dominance develop in the nineteenth century? What factors enabled the French observer de Tocqueville to proclaim that "there is no country in the world where the Christian religion retains a greater influence over the souls of men than in America."[3] Most obvious, the disestablishment of religion leveled the playing field, giving all denominations an equal opportunity to win adherents. This situation was well suited to evangelical groups, who aggressively sought converts, especially through the vehicle of revivalism.

Second, evangelicalism displayed both a diverse and homogeneous face. On one hand, its diversity made it possible for the movement to meet many different needs. If one denomination failed to meet an individual's needs, others certainly could. On the other hand, evangelicalism displayed a certain amount of homogeneity. Despite many sectarian differences, most evangelicals stood shoulder to shoulder on the essentials of Christian beliefs and ethics. Thus, they significantly influenced America on many cultural issues because they could present a more or less unified stance. Next, evangelicalism (and most of Protestantism for that matter) became thoroughly Americanized. It achieved an emotional and ideological identification with the expanding American society—its individualism, pragmatism, populism, democracy, free-enterprise system, and imperialism. Or as Henry May states, "in 1876 Protestantism presented a massive, almost unbroken front in its defense of the social status quo."[4]

Generalizations are always hazardous. For the most part, evangelicalism in the twenty-first century is dynamic, populist, pragmatic, highly individualistic, intellectually shallow, patriotic, and strongly supportive of "the American way of life," which many see as synonymous with conservative politics and the market economy. These trends are not new. Many were quite obvious by the mid-nineteenth century. Between the two centuries, however, there is a difference. In the nineteenth century, evangelicalism was the dominant cultural influence; its ethos had penetrated American society. For much of the twentieth century, it has been one of many influences and is currently seeking to regain its dominant role. In fact, one can argue that the salt has lost its savor, that is, except for some selective moral issues modern evangelicalism has been thoroughly acculturated. But this is a subject for the last part of this book.

A Christian America They Say!

Is America a Christian nation? Many contemporary evangelicals contend that America has Christian roots. Jerry Falwell says so. We need to "come back to the faith of our fathers, to the Bible of our fathers, and to the biblical principles that our fathers use as a premise for this nation's establishment."[5] Tim LaHaye agrees. Christians must "vote in pro-moral leaders who will return our country to the biblical base upon which it is founded." George W. Bush tells us that God is on America's side. The echo of similar themes can be heard from many pulpits. One Maine pastor said "that from Christopher Columbus to George W. Bush, God has smiled on the people who have figured large in this nation's history."[6]

In *The Light and the Glory,* Peter Marshall and David Manuel see the hand of God in nearly every event from the discovery of America to the 1960s when the United States turned its back on God. "This nation was founded by God with a special calling. The people who first came here knew that they were being led here by the Lord Jesus Christ, to found a nation where men, women, and children were to live in obedience to Him…" God had a corporate relationship with America, specifically calling the nation into a covenant relationship with him.[7] On a more sophisticated level, Francis Schaeffer also argues for America's Christian underpinnings. He does not maintain that the founding fathers were all Christians, but he does contend for a definite biblical influence on the origins of our country. Evangelicals who deny the Christian foundations of America are "playing directly into the hands of the secular humanists," says Schaeffer.[8]

The notion of a Christian America originated in the colonial period and early nineteenth century and is now ingrained in the popular evangelical mind. How did it arise? What are its ideological roots? Robert Linder and Richard Pierard deal with this subject in the context of civil religion, which they define as "the use of consensus religious sentiments, concepts and symbols by the state…for its own political purposes." This usually leads to a "blurring of religion and patriotism and of religious values with national values."[9] Civil religion is a disputed subject and while it bears close resemblance with our subject of a Christian America, the two are not synonymous.[10] Still, the origins of both civil religion and the concept of a Christian America are closely related—so much so that many evangelicals assume that America is a chosen nation with a special mission. They regard the Declaration of Independence and the Constitution as embracing biblical principles to the exclusion of secular influences.

Basic to the Christian country concept is the notion that America was a chosen nation—the New Israel, "a city on a hill." This special relationship was sealed by a covenant with God, which is implied in the quasi sacred documents of American history—namely, the Mayflower Compact, Declaration of Independence, Constitution, and Lincoln's Gettysburg Address. The notion of a sacred or chosen nation did not begin in colonial America. It has roots deep in history but most directly the Puritans brought it from England. According to Richard Hughes, William Tyndale popularized the notion of England's covenant relationship with God. Like Israel of old, God chose England for a special mission. By the time of Edward V1—and even more so during the rule of Queen Elizabeth—this idea had developed into the belief that England was God's anointed vessel, a chosen nation. The divine destiny of these "covenanted people" was to usher in the millennium. In his influential *Book of Martyrs*, John Foxe popularized these themes. During the troubled years of the first half of the seventeenth century, Parliament was to be a divine instrument enacting God's will. Oliver Cromwell's victory in the English Civil War and his rule during the Commonwealth period (1642-58) confirmed England's sense of a sacred mission.[11]

In New England, the Pilgrims gave flesh to these ideas. Modern day evangelicals who embrace the notion of a Christian America point to the

Mayflower Compact. This document drawn up by the Pilgrims envisions a just and moral society based on biblical principles. Even more than the Pilgrims, however, the Puritans established the theological-political basis for the belief in a Christian America, which was embraced by most Americans until the twentieth century. The Puritans believed that they had a covenant with God, one that demanded godly behavior and established them as a "city on a hill"— namely, that they would serve as a moral example for the nations to behold. "They had undertaken to establish a society where the will of God would be observed in every detail, a kingdom of God on earth," says Edmund Morgan. Events of the Revolutionary War era reinforced the chosen nation concept. By the end of the French and Indian War, the colonists began to blur distinctions between the kingdom of God and the new emerging nation. They, therefore, regarded America's victory over Britain as providential and the victory of liberty over tyranny.[12]

The Vision Continues

The vision of America as an elect nation continued throughout the nineteenth century. Americans gradually sacralized many documents, individuals, rites, and rituals. The Declaration of Independence, Constitution, and Gettysburg Address acquired the aura of sacred covenants. Some founding fathers—Washington, Franklin, Jefferson, and John Adams—achieved a near saintly mantle. In particular, Washington came to be seen as an American Moses: "The deliverer and political savior of the nation." Holidays such Memorial Day, the Fourth of July, and Thanksgiving merged religion and politics, often expressing a belief in America's providential history.[13]

Developing out of the chosen nation concept is the belief that America is a "redeemer nation" with a millennial mission. By the early nineteenth century there had developed a nationalistic theology, which by 1845 was called the "Manifest Destiny." Many Americans believed that God had called the United States to be "a chief means of world-wide redemption, and that as a chosen people it was assigned a new promised land," namely, a large part of the North American continent. The promises of a great land that God had given to Israel now applied to the United States, the New Israel. "As the Israelites were given the land of the pagans, so the last chosen people has been given a rich continent for its heritage," writes Ernest Tuveson. The emerging evangelical empire had two sources of unity—a common core of Christian beliefs and the growing American nationalism. Driving much of the "Lord's work" in early national America was an inflammable nationalism. Beginning with the belief that God had chosen America to be a moral example, the manifest destiny now legitimized raw force to achieve the nation's territorial objectives. "The sense of responsibility to others had given way to privilege and divine right," notes Richard Hughes.[14]

The redeemer nation concept grew out of a secularized postmillennialism. The Great Awakening of the 1740s ignited an evangelical postmillennialism that mingled human and divine efforts to usher in the golden age. But the Great Awakening failed to bring the anticipated results. To the dismay of the revivalists, a new age did not dawn. So the American believers looked for apocalyptic signs in other contemporary events—especially the French and Indian War and the Revolutionary War. Bible expositors in the 1750s and 1760s explained end-time events in both political and religious terms—a trend that would continue. The colonists politicized their view of the millennium—identifying God's prophetic plan with the British interests against the French and then with the Americans against the English. By the end of these conflicts, the Americans began to equate God's work in the world with America's national interests.[15]

Previously, the Americans believed that God's people would prepare the world for Christ's kingdom through prayer and preaching. Now they began to equate the kingdom of God with the political and moral destiny of America. Indeed, in the nineteenth century, Americans believed that God was smiling on their cause. They regarded the nation as the primary vehicle for God's activity in the world, bringing Christianity and democracy to less fortunate people. The opportunities for territorial expansion in the years after Texas revolted against Mexico combined with the general Protestant millennial theology to produce a justification for American territorial expansion in the West. In pursuit of a Christian commonwealth in America, postmillennialism sparked a number of reform efforts—abolition, temperance, Sabbath observance and more. Eventually it developed into a more secular millennialism largely devoid of religious impulses.[16]

As the nineteenth century ran its course, the concept of a redeemer nation declined. Rather than being tied to national activities, salvation now became more a matter of rescuing individual souls. But the notion of America's millennial mission did not die. Washington Gladden and Josiah Strong, who were associated with the Social Gospel movement, saw America's movement into the West as directed by God. Economic motives may have been involved in this conquest, but behind these reasons was the hand of God. Divine ordination, they believed, determined that the New World should belong to the Aryan race. In the last years of the nineteenth century, Strong attempted to rally the nation to its redeemer mission, insisting that Protestants regenerate the nation and the world in preparation for the coming of God's kingdom.[17]

A third factor driving the Christian nation belief is the evangelical consensus that arose in early nineteenth century America. Most societies have a dominant public ethic, and at this time it was an evangelical consensus. The First Great Awakening began the process of instilling evangelical values, and despite a decline during the Revolutionary era, the Second Great Awakening completed this task. While everyone did not accept evangelical theology and values, evangelical norms prevailed nationally. Remarkably, evangelical and secular standards largely converged at this time.[18]

Linder and Pierard note the basic beliefs shared by evangelical Christianity and liberal democracy. Included are a "common assent to a basic moral law, agreement...that constitutional government was necessary for the restraint of evil, the shared doctrine of the free individual, common adherence to the philosophy of progress" and accord regarding America's mission "to save the world from autocracy" and "satanic governance." Indeed, evangelicals did not have to choose between God and country. On the whole, evangelical values and their secular counterparts were acceptable to most Americans. Or, as Robert Handy puts it, "the evangelical Protestant churches and Christian civilization with its developing patterns of freedom and democracy would go on...mutually reinforcing one another."[19]

This evangelical consensus arose largely because evangelical Christian and Enlightenment values flowed together. What emerged in the years after the American Revolution as the dominant intellectual trend was a Christianized form of the Enlightenment. "By the early nineteenth century there existed in America a powerful cultural synthesis compounded from evangelical Protestantism, republicanism, and commonsense moral reasoning," says Mark Noll. Did the evangelicals influence the rationalists? Or did the Enlightenment thinking influence the evangelicals? This is a matter of debate.[20]

But it is certain that the two converged largely because they shared certain values. Evangelical Christianity insisted that true liberty came when Christ freed a person from the bondage of sin. Revivalism entailed many democratic methods of persuasions. Republicanism insisted that the exercise of political power must be sanctioned by the people. The Whig tradition as it developed in Britain and spread to America resisted tyranny. A belief in the free individual is the central tenet of liberal democracy. Freedom, individualism, moral virtue, and a well-ordered society were values shared by both the evangelical Christians and the republican founding fathers. What developed was a Christian republicanism. And this soon led to the sacralization of politics, economics, and public morals.[21]

In the nineteenth century, the evangelicals did a remarkable job of Christianizing America. But as they shaped the values of the nation, they, in turn, were less able to discern the difference between the kingdom of God and American society. The belief that America was a Christian nation thus continued strong throughout the century. According to President Woodrow Wilson in the early twentieth century, "America was born a Christian nation for the purpose of exemplifying to the nations of the world the principles of righteousness found in the Word of God."[22] But by the late twentieth century, this notion came under serious question—by both evangelicals and non-evangelicals. Despite this challenge, large segments of the evangelical community have continued to uncritically embrace Americanism and to equate it with Christianity.

Others Say No!

Are the conservative evangelicals correct in their view of America's spiritual heritage? If by a Christian nation one means a significant Christian influence, the answer is yes. America was certainly Christian in a generic sense. America indeed is a self-proclaimed Christian nation. Most people claim some connection with the Christian faith. But the same can be said about Western civilization, which has its religious and moral roots in the Judaic-Christian tradition. Until sometime in the twentieth century, the dominant public ethic in the United States gave some allegiance to the Christian tradition. The founding fathers also had a high regard for religion, believing that it was necessary for the maintenance of public virtue. People viewing America as a Christian nation regard the Declaration of Independence and Constitution as based on a Christian worldview and not a mixture of Christian and secular sources.[23]

If by a Christian nation one means that a majority of Americans were serious followers of Jesus Christ, the answer is no. Many colonialists could qualify as evangelical Christians. But by the time of the American Revolution, the nation had experienced a religious depression and church attendance was low. Among the revolutionary leaders some could be labeled as evangelicals—Patrick Henry, John Witherspoon, and Isaac Backus for example. The founding fathers, however, who had the greatest influence—Benjamin Franklin, George Washington, Thomas Jefferson, James Madison, Alexander Hamilton, and John Adams—embraced a more liberal religion, which has been called as Deism. They certainly did not embrace an orthodox Christian worldview. They did, however, regard themselves as Christians because they considered Deism to be Christian.[24]

While the Declaration of Independence and Constitution contained some traditional Christian attitudes, on the whole they rested on secular sources—especially John Locke and the Scottish Enlightenment. More specifically, the Declaration of Independence appealed to "self evident" truths or "laws of nature," and makes no mention of the Bible. Evangelicals, however, have given a meaning to this document that Jefferson never intended. And the Constitution of 1787 makes no reference to God. One would also expect a Christian society to exhibit the standards of peace, justice, and charity. Unfortunately, these virtues were often absent as illustrated by slavery, imperialism, and the nation's treatment of Native Americans, immigrants, and the poor.[25]

The terms *evangelical, Protestant, Christian America, and early America* are used quite loosely. Herein rests much of the problem. Well-meaning people often talk past each other. They are not on the same page. A general Protestant variety of Christianity played a large role in the founding of America. It provided the basis for the public morality of the day, which the founding fathers regarded as essential for the well-being of the new republic. But in their beliefs and lifestyle such people were not necessarily what people today would describe as "evangelicals" or even orthodox Christians. Unfortunately, many contemporary evangelicals anachronistically project their vision for America back upon the founding fathers. In the contemporary culture wars, they inflate the values of the founding fathers and equate them with the moral standards of conservative Protestantism.

To convey their ideas, the founding fathers often employed religious phrases and references to God—a practice quite common for that day. Contemporary evangelicals advocate a literal interpretation of their words and insist that "words are words." Such words have a plain meaning and need no special interpretation. Historical statements, however, must be interpreted in the larger historical context and general religious tenor of the time. And when such is done, such statements often have a different meaning—one that calls into question the Christian basis of the founding era.

Second, the evangelical faith did not gain importance until after 1800. From about 1815 to 1860 evangelicals became politically active, influencing the direction the nation would take. As will be noted later, evangelicalism and democracy share certain values. And both gained strength in early national America. The situation that modern-day evangelicals envision more approximates the period after 1815 than it does the era of the founding fathers.[26] Given their ahistorical mentality, most modern evangelicals do not distinguish between the founding era and early national America. In the mind of most evangelicals, these two eras are the same. Moreover, in designating either of these two historical periods as Christian, one must be selective in what one regards as Christian, emphasizing certain virtues while ignoring many shortcomings.

An early challenge to the belief in America as a Christian land came from the Puritan Roger Williams. He contended that since the coming of Christ, God has not designated any nation as his uniquely chosen people. God had chosen only one people—the Israelites. As a champion of religious liberty, Williams has significantly influenced the free-church tradition, especially the Baptists. In the early republic, other dissident movements also championed the separation of church and state. But ironically, they endowed the new republic with divine qualities as strongly as did any of the liturgical churches, which still longed for a Christian nation or a state church.[27] In modern America, the same trend is evident. Many in the free-church tradition—especially the Baptists and independent churches—staunchly support the notion that God has chosen America for a special mission. Conversely, the offspring of the state churches—Congregationalists, Presbyterians, and Anglicans—often downplay this idea.

Republicanism, Democracy, and Evangelicalism

In America democracy and evangelical Christianity have mutually and significantly influenced each other. Democratic ideals have shaped evangelical Christianity, which in turn—among other forces—has helped to forge a democratic America. Democratic and Christian values are compatible and they are so intertwined that they are often confused. But they are not the same.

The Christian belief in the existence of a fundamental law ordained by God, combined with the Enlightenment view of natural law found its way into the American democracy. Related to this concept of fundamental law are several other democratic principles—notably, a written constitution guaranteeing individual rights and limitations on the powers of government. The Christian insistence on the dignity and worth of humankind—created in the image of God—has impacted democratic thought, especially the belief in the equality of all people before the law. While the church has often been autocratic, it has functioned best when the free expression of ideas has been permitted. This practice, when combined with similar Enlightenment ideas, has resulted in the cherished American value of free speech.[28]

Democratic principles have also influenced Christianity. While Luther's notion regarding the priesthood of all believers has resulted in the importance of the individual, democratic ideals have promoted the role of the laity. An expression of democracy can be found in the separation of church and state and religious liberty. As a result, American religion depends on voluntarism. People must choose to join a church or support a religious activity. While democracy did not cause religious pluralism, religious freedom has been a major factor in this development and America's democratic institutions have allowed it to flourish.[29]

Early America was pre-democratic. How did Christianity combine with other elements to produce a republican and democratic society? To start, the Europeans who colonized America embraced a free spirit and much independence of thought. They naturally embraced individual rights and self- government. The vast geography of the North American continent, an untamed frontier, the democratic implications of Calvinism, the doctrines of the French philosophers, and strains with Britain all combined to promote a spirit of liberty and individualism.[30]

Prior to about 1830, the United States had a republican but pre-democratic form of government. The Christian faith, along with other forces, helped forge this republicanism. At this time, republicanism can be defined as the belief that the exercise of political power determines the political process. And if this power is unchecked it leads to corruption and the reduction of liberty and natural rights. In order to avoid the concentration of power, republicans thus advocated the separation of powers. Good government should not be monarchical, democratic, or aristocratic but contain elements from all three. In arriving at these conclusions, the republicans shared much with Calvinism—namely, the human capacity for evil and a view of history that saw a cosmic struggle between liberty and tyranny (or God and Satan as interpreted by the Puritans). So much did republicanism express Christian values that the early American Christians strongly supported it.[31]

The First Great Awakening furthered republican and democratic ideals, eventually influencing the American Revolution and the separation of church and state. The Great Awakening and its emphasis on an inward, heartfelt religion represents a shift in religion. From now on evangelicalism replaced Puritanism as the dominant religion in America. The messages of the revivalists—especially those of George Whitefield (1715-1770)—promoted spiritual liberty, which many came to equate with political liberty. The Awakening did not cause the Revolution but it foreshadowed many of its attitudes, especially the right of individuals from any social class to challenge established authority, whether it be political or religious.[32]

Independence from Britain and the Constitution of 1787 did not make the new nation democratic. The aristocracy expected the new Constitution to provide a governmental structure that would maintain a dominant position for people of wealth and education. While many developments in the colonial and revolutionary periods furthered the cause of democracy, full white male democracy did not come until about 1830. Democratization seemed to be blocked by the privileged classes.[33]

From about 1780 to 1830, however, the new nation witnessed earthshaking changes, which were in some ways as dramatic as the events of the revolutionary era. In respect to politics, religion, and the social structure America became democratized. The elite were dethroned and the people became sovereign. Their choices in politics, religion, and the marketplace determined the direction of American society. "America became a liberal society, individualistic, competitive, and market driven," notes Nathan Hatch.[34]

The nonrestrictive American environment permitted an explosive mixture of religion and politics that helped to Christianize and democratize American popular culture. Revivalism and politics—which were interrelated during in the eighteenth and nineteenth centuries—drove this democratization. Each asserted popular claims and challenged the authority of the elite. Both promoted charisma rather than rationalism and innovative Americanism as opposed to European tradition.[35]

Revivals advanced political democracy after 1800. The revival experience inspired people to exhort and pray publicly. Revival preachers attacked the coldness of the established churches and the authority of their preachers. Such challenges spilled over into the political arena. Common people refused to regard themselves as inferior to the aristocratic elements. Thus they pushed for the elimination of property qualifications for voting and other restrictions to democracy. As a result mass male democracy arrived about 1830. The link between religion and politics did not end here, but this is a subject for later chapters.[36]

Democracy and Popular Christianity

In the early years of the new nation, it was assumed that the educated elite would dominate in both politics and religion. As time progressed, however, these inclinations gave way to democratic impulses. Such democratic tendencies propelled the most dynamic aspects of American society—the development of political democracy, the market economy, and the Christianization of American culture. Power shifted from the elite to the people. They became sovereign in both politics and religion. And this democratization must be seen as the key to the profound Christianization that the nation experienced from the Great Awakening to about 1900. While no national state church existed, the results were about the same—the values of evangelical Christianity placed its stamp on the nation. So much was this true that Sydney Ahlstrom would call early national America the "Golden age of Democratic Evangelicalism."[37]

Religion is more important in the United States than in any other Western nation. Why? The market process has produced a dynamic economy in America. To survive a business must persuade people to buy its product. The same must be said about religion—it is democratic and populous. In religious matters the people are sovereign. Religion is not controlled by the state or the clergy but by the people. For any religion to succeed it must identify with the people, who choose to support or not support it. It cannot be aloof but must speak the language of the people—simple and direct. That Christianity became democratized from about 1780 to 1860 is the key to religious vitality in America.[38]

But in appealing to the democratic and popular instincts of the people, some problems have arisen—evangelical Christianity has become mindless and thoroughly acculturated. Or in the words of Mark Noll, "the evangelical ethos is activitistic, populist, pragmatic, and utilitarian." It is also "immediatistic and individualistic" and "allows little space for broader or deeper intellectual effort because it is dominated by the urgencies of the moment." In many ways, Alexis de Tocqueville's concerns have come true. He feared the "tyranny of the majority," which could shoot down serious ideas before they got off the ground.[39] Twenty-first-century evangelicals want a religion that works, is practical, makes them feel good, and is not intellectually challenging. Such trends are not new—they have their roots in the evangelical faith of early America.

Revivalism and Popular Christianity

What conditions promoted the democratization of American Christianity? In part it arose with the political democratization of the new nation and the rise of the market economy. The separation of church and state permitted Christian groups to compete in a free religious market. But the tool, which most evangelical bodies used as a means for growth, was revivalism. As Bruce Shelley notes, "revivalism was preaching aimed at individuals, confronting them with God's fearful judgment upon their sins…" After "sin and hell were painted in vivid tones, producing fear and dread"…the preacher then pointed the sinner to God's forgiveness.[40]

While not unique to Christianity or America, revivalism took off because it was tailor made for the new nation. Revivalism made its appeal to an individualistic society. Individualism reigned supreme in America and when combined with democracy and the freedom of conscience, the situation was ripe for revivalism. Any religion appealing to an individualistic society must make individual needs the focus of attention. This revivalism did, emphasizing that salvation is a personal matter and dependent on an individual decision. Revivalism shaped Christianity to suit America's needs and can be seen as an instrument for the Americanization of Christianity. Or as Shelley writes, "In the nineteenth century, revivalism was not a type of Christianity in America; it was Christianity in America."[41]

Revivalism personalized religion and to personalize it is to emotionalize it. The eighteenth century witnessed a major shift in the nature of Christianity. This new form of Christianity came to be known by two names: pietism on the Continent and evangelicalism in North America and Britain. Pietism or evangelicalism is often known as a "religion of the heart, rather than a religion of the head." It focused on individual redemption and appeals largely to the emotions. Pietism or evangelicalism moved away from formal, outward, and structured religion to a personal, inward, and heartfelt religion.[42]

Revivalistic preaching with its focus on emotionalism and an individual decision came to the forefront during the Great Awakening of the 1730s and 1740s and the Second Great Awakening of the early nineteenth century. These revivals produced a new type of preacher—charismatic leaders who used common language and sought practical results. To make it in America, religion had to be popular and to be popular entailed adapting to the tastes of the average person. This the revivalists did. They minimized intellectual preparation, reduced theology to its bare bones, moved away from instruction to emotional exhorting, and preached extemporaneously in lay and often crude language.[43] Narrative preaching came to the forefront. Preachers stripped their sermons of doctrine and rhetoric and adopted the uses of storytelling and humor. An indication that preaching was becoming integrated into popular culture was "the wholesale introduction of humor: jokes, sarcasm, biting ridicule, witty anecdotes, [and] clever plays on words…" writes Nathan Hatch.[44]

The most sensational example of this type of preaching prior to the Civil War came in the frontier camp meetings. People traveled for miles around to hear exciting extemporaneous preaching. While they often sought a spiritual message, they also desired to be entertained. And they were not disappointed. The itinerant evangelists put on a show. In vernacular language they railed against the religious and political elite, especially attacking Calvinist theology for its elitism. The tone of such messages "was doggedly democratic in spirit and populist in tone…" notes Randall Balmer. In their disdain for ecclesiastical hierarchies and authorities, these traveling evangelists "served as a democratic and leveling force" and embodied the individualism of Jacksonian democracy. [45]

To be sure, exceptions—notably Jonathan Edwards—to this description of the revivalists did exist. The two most prominent preachers in colonial and early national America were George Whitefield and Charles Finney (1792-1875). And in various degrees they employed these new methods of persuasion. While they did not ignore theology, their primary interest was for individuals to have an experience with God. They represented a new style of religious leadership—"direct, personal, popular, and dependent much more on the speaker's ability to draw a crowd..." than on their education or clerical credentials.[46] The enduring legacy of the revivalists was not doctrine but "a new mode of persuasion..."[47] Such a style has continued into the modern era and has exerted tremendous influence upon evangelicalism.

Whitefield, Revivalism, and Popular Culture

Breaking from the conventional pattern, Whitefield preached wherever and whenever he could gather people—any day of the week, at any hour, usually outside of the churches, and often to large crowds. With spell binding eloquence, he turned preaching into a dramatic performance and church services into entertainment. His extemporaneous and thunderous sermons focused on the new birth and had a compelling appeal to many. They evoked "tears, heightened emotions, agitated bodily movement—and above all, an intensely personal encounter with the New Birth..." Whitefield grasped the new realities of the age and knew that any religion "fit for a new consumer age, would have to be voluntary, and this meant popular and entertaining," says Harry Stout. Whitefield's method of revivalism—theatrical, passion based, non-denominational, international, experienced-centered, and self-consciously promoted through the media—outlived him."[48]

Whitefield's ministry foreshadowed another trend that has continued throughout evangelical history—he promoted revivals. Whitefield's success rested on more than his rhetorical skills. Crowds did not materialize out of nowhere to hear his preaching as one observer noted. Rather, he utilized the best marketing techniques of his day—pamphlets, newspapers, magazines, and other printed materials. Whitefield was an innovator in advertising—vigorously promoting his revivals in advance and printing up many sermons. Through creative pricing plans for his publications and tireless fund raising, he financed his ministry and more. He funded several humanitarian and evangelical interests and amassed a moderate estate. Whitefield, indeed, stood apart from his contemporaries not only as a preacher but as an innovator in promoting religion. At the beginning of the consumer age, he understood that religion was a commodity to be marketed. He knew that success in religion depended on satisfying market forces and public opinion.[49]

Whitefield contributed to another trend—the revivals challenged the religious, intellectual, and social authority of the churches. The religious establishments had been run largely by the educated classes. Whitefield and other revivalists bypassed the church, preaching a democratic message in a simple language. And their messages often had an anti-aristocracy, anti-authority, and anti-learning tone. In preaching such sermons, they often undercut the traditional, aristocratic, and hierarchical culture. Whitefield, Edwards, and other early revivalists were not democrats but they set in motion a democratic tide that would become a tidal wave in the nineteenth century.[50]

Finney, Revivalism, and Popular Religion

The Second Great Awakening was a series of revivals, which ran from about 1800 to 1830. During these awakenings a number of revivalists paraded across the American scene. While they ranged from the emotionally charged frontier revivalists to the well-educated preachers produced by Yale College, the best known was Charles Grandison Finney (1792-1875). Finney stood somewhere between the fiery frontier preachers and the educated clergy. He never encouraged excessive emotionalism, but he set the tone for future revivals—a riveting speaker who organized "controlled revivals" in urban areas. During the Second Great Awakening, the "concept of a special kind of preacher, a man with exceptional oratorical gifts...a man God had established for working up Protestant revivals, became an accepted part of the evangelical Protestant ministry," writes William McLoughlin. By the early nineteenth century, the Puritan ideal of the minister as an educated teacher gave way to the evangelical model of the pastor as a popular exhorter.[51]

More than most preachers of his day, Finney understood the connection between two rising forces—democratic culture and the competitive market. As part of the cultural market, religion had to compete with other forms of entertainment. Finney thus appreciated the importance of holding an audience. So he attempted to ascertain the nature of his audience and then preach accordingly. Standing six-foot-two with a penetrating gaze and a big voice, he was magnetic and compelling. While he ruled out theater attendance for Christians, he employed theatrical tactics from the pulpit, giving his preaching a sense of drama. Religion, indeed, had its star performers as did the theaters. His sermons were overpowering, combining emotional power with logic, denunciation with compassion. He was neither the most cultivated nor crudest of the preachers, avoiding the vulgar but speaking with great simplicity. The key to conversion he believed was forcing the audience to make a choice. As a former lawyer he thus preached for decision—as if he were arguing a case before a jury. Like Whitefield and the future revivalists, Finney scorned the use of notes and preached extemporaneously. In sum, he recognized how pervasive the influence of democracy had become on homiletics.[52]

Powerful preaching alone would not get the job done. More than that was needed for the conversion of sinners, Finney contended. Revivalists before Finney believed that conversions had to wait on God. But he insisted that God had given people the ability to repent now. Indeed, human instruments could facilitate this process. "A revival of religion is not a miracle. There is nothing in religion beyond the ordinary powers of nature," he insisted.[53]

New times and new circumstances required a novel approach to converting sinners. So he initiated a number of methods—called the "New Measures"—to complement good preaching. In doing so, he shaped the revival practices that have come down to the present. While Finney did preach in small towns, he accommodated the new urbanization trend and focused on the cities. Revivals in urban areas allowed Finney to use "protracted meetings," (nightly meetings for several weeks). The "anxious bench,"—which led to people coming to the front at the end of a service—became a standard practice for future evangelism. Finney also used popular religious music to set a tone for the revivals and expanded the role of women in services. These "new measures" aroused considerable opposition. True to the pragmatic approach of evangelicalism, Finney insisted, "The results justify my methods. Show me the fruits of your ministry, and if they so far exceed mine...I will adopt your views."[54]

In other ways, Finney's ministry complemented the democratic and populist spirit of the time. In Jacksonian America, the populist dream said that the common person—without much specialized training—could do most anything, including running the government and pursuing the professions. Though an ordained Presbyterian minister, Finney had no clerical preparation. Despite becoming a college president, he distrusted formal education, including training for ministers. The reign of Yale in the ministry came to an end. After Finney no popular evangelist until modern times would be a graduate of a first-rate university or seminary. Before pragmatism became a formal philosophy, Finney and most revivalists were pragmatists. While he did not look fondly on ignorant ministers, "he admired soul-winning results, no matter how achieved." Revivalism had succeeded where the more intellectual and coercive methods of the traditional churches had failed. Rather than by any appeal to reason, people were brought back to the churches by simple and emotional messages voiced by powerful preachers.[55]

Such developments helped dethrone the educated clergy. In the early years of the new nation, the educated elite dominated most professions. During the first thirty years of the nineteenth century, however, democratic and populist forces challenged the grip of the elite on most areas of public life—government, law, medicine, and the ministry. All were toppled from their privileged positions. State laws permitted untrained individuals to practice law and medicine. But by the twentieth century, the legal and medical establishments had restored their professional status by controlling the credentials and standards of their respective practices. Unlike medicine and law—except for those of certain denominations—there are no clerical credentials, licensing, or control over the practice of the ministry. In effect, religion is functioning in a free market while law and medicine operate in a monopolistic situation.[56]

Finney's theology also demonstrated the democratic tenor of the time. The cultural consensus and dominant religious trend emerging from the first Great Awakening was a Calvinism that stressed a conversion process initiated and controlled by God. Yet Calvinism as the dominant religious and cultural consensus could not effectively cope with the vast number of democratic, social, and economic changes, and it faded fast after 1800. In its place arose a new consensus, an evangelical Arminianism, which could better deal with a more democratically reordered society. People were now sovereign in politics and in the marketplace. So why not in religion? Finney rejected predestination and said that people could choose God without waiting for God to first choose them. In fact, "Finney was more Arminian than John Wesley." Wesley argued that humans could respond positively to divine overtures but only after God had prepared the heart. Finney discarded this requirement.[57]

Finney's revivals and others of the Second Great Awakening coincided with other developments in American culture—the rise of literacy and the consumer culture. With more people able to read, the evangelicals jumped into the publishing business. In particular, the American Tract Society distributed Bibles and other forms of Christian literature. Their prime vehicles for this activity were the colporteurs who performed numerous tasks. They sold Bibles, served as missionaries, set up libraries, preached to congregations, and organized Sunday schools. Like the itinerate evangelists, they embodied the democratic and entrepreneurial spirit of the age. They functioned as free spirits and took advantage of the emerging commercial economy.[58]

Winners and Losers

In the religious marketplace of early national America there were winners and losers. And success or failure depended on how religious bodies adjusted to the new democratic and populist environment. The mainline denominations—that is the Congregationalists, Presbyterians, and Episcopalians—came out of the Revolutionary era as the largest religious bodies. Yet they declined because they did not adapt to the free market religious economy. At their peril, they ignored the democratic and populist tidal wave that was sweeping America. The Methodists and Baptists benefited the most from the democratic and populist trends. In 1800, the Methodists and Baptists were small in number. By 1850, they had become the largest Protestant groups because they adjusted to the new democratic climate.

For a religious body to grow it must have an adequate supply of ministers. That the mainline denominations required a minister to have certain educational credentials caused two problems—there arose a shortage of ministers and the educated clergy did not appeal to the common people. Conversely, the Methodists used circuit riders and the Baptists uneducated clergy to meet their ministerial needs. In both cases, these ministers were ill paid, poorly educated, and could relate to the common people. Both of these denominations fervently embraced revivalism, which struck a strong cord with democracy and the market economy. The Arminian theology of the Methodists, with its focus on human choice, was at home in democratic America. While the Baptists were still officially Calvinistic, in practice this was often played down. But the most democratic aspect of Baptist church life was its congregational church polity, which situated power in the local congregation. Along this line, the Methodists were officially quite hierarchical, but in practice on the local level considerable autonomy rested with the people.[59]

Revivalism closely paralleled the dominant social and political norms of early national America and thus contributed to the Christianization of the nation. Appealing to all ranks of society and emphasizing human choice, they were democratic. In that the same message was preached to all and everyone had an equal opportunity to respond, the revivals were egalitarian. The sermons had a populist appeal in that they often came from an uneducated clergy in a simple, direct language. Being highly individualistic, revivalism was liberal in the nineteenth-century meaning of the term. Along with all of this, however, the revivals presented a picture of God and the Christian life that harmonized with the view depicted in the more traditional churches.[60]

Arminianism

Early national American society also put its stamp on theology and values. While not necessarily originating in America, the major theological trends—Arminianism, perfectionism, postmillennialism, and the commonsense tradition—were nurtured by the culture of the new nation. Arminianism originated with Jacob Arminius (1560-1609) in the Netherlands and was given a fuller expression by John Wesley (1703-1791) in England and the Methodists in America. According to Mark Noll, it held that "God gave prevenient grace (a grace coming before full salvation) to all people so that original sin could be overcome and all could make a free choice for God." As developed by Wesley and the Methodists, Arminianism also came to include "a belief in Christian perfection, or that it was possible for believers to be liberated from all known sin."[61]

Arminianism in America evolved gradually. The Methodists, of course, had accepted free will at an early stage. The Great Awakening embraced predestination but set in motion forces that would subvert it. By the Second Awakening, the doctrine had either been watered down or repudiated. Most evangelists held to either an Arminianized Calvinism—that is, a Calvinism so modified that it resembled Arminianism—or rejected predestination. Key to this development was the New Haven theology of Nathaniel W. Taylor (1786-1858). He said that human beings will certainly sin, but they still have "power to the contrary." By means of the original sin, humankind lost its righteousness but this sin did not destroy his or her free agency. Sin and depravity result from moral choice, not from an inherited tendency to do evil. On the issue of free will, this shift modified Calvinism nearly beyond recognition.[62]

Orthodox Calvinism ran counter to the individualistic, democratic, and optimistic impulses of early nineteenth-century America. It offered salvation to the few, while Arminianism offered it to all. Calvinism had an aristocratic tone, while Arminianism was more democratic. Calvinism could not stand in its original form. So as noted earlier, Finney and other revivalists would carry their rejection of Calvinism much further. With little subtlety, Finney asserted the role of human choice in salvation and morals. Turning to God is an individual choice. God requires humankind to do this and he will not do it for them. "It must be your voluntary act."[63] In respect to morals, people have a great capability. "The will is free and...sin and holiness are voluntary acts of the mind." In sum, evangelical theology had to be adjusted to suit the tastes of a people drunk on self-determinism, individualism, and optimism.[64]

Perfectionism and Social Reform

Early national America abounded with optimism. Standards of living had improved markedly over the preceding century: scientific discoveries increased, technological advances became noticeable, and economic conditions rose visibly. Consequently, in the early nineteenth century, Americans firmly believed in a kind of progress that could be advanced by education, government, technology and science, and by the efforts of individual and community action. Related to these developments are several secular intellectual currents, especially the doctrine of progress. But so were two Christian beliefs—perfectionism and postmillennialism—and a number of reform movements spawned by them.[65]

Closely related to Arminianism is the belief in perfectionism. The doctrine of perfectionism can be regarded as a religious affirmation of several secular trends in early nineteenth-century America: the contemporary beliefs in optimism, progress, and democratic individualism. Perfectionism places a strong emphasis on Christian holiness, contending that the believer through God's grace can achieve and maintain a moral perfection in this life. In its modern manifestation, perfectionism nearly always lays stress on a post-conversion experience of God. The quest for perfection has been an important goal throughout Judeo-Christian history. With variations in regard to the degree and chronology of perfection of the Christian life, many individuals and groups normally regarded as within the context of orthodoxy have embraced this doctrine. In addition, perfectionism has been expressed in many forms by bodies on the fringes of Christianity.[66]

Movements embracing perfectionism more or less within the mainstream included the Methodist church and Phoebe Worrall Palmer, revivalism—especially Finney and what became known as Oberlin Theology—and several humanitarian movements containing religious overtones (e.g., abolitionism, temperance, and the peace movement). In fact, the reform impulse in the United States received its strongest support from the revivalism that swept the country in the 1820s and 1830s. Russel Nye says evangelical revivalism spawned two beliefs: perfectionism—the belief "that American life could be reformed and rearranged" to meet the moral standards "God had set down for the perfect society"—and that "saved or perfected Christians" must make their salvation complete, apply their religion to life, and make their piety practical. Salvation, therefore, was not the end but rather "the beginning of a useful life." Thus, the evangelical religion made social reform a moral imperative.[67]

Evangelicals attempted to transform society by supporting several reform movements and by forming voluntary associations to help the unfortunate and poor. For example, they established hospitals, orphanages, and schools; reformed prisons and mental institutions; passed laws against dueling; and supported abolitionist and temperance societies. But individual morality primarily drove their approach to social problems, not a broad vision of social justice.[68]

If social evil resulted from individual sin and selfishness, then progress came from reforming individuals by religious conversion. The reformer, then, was obligated to convert the nation rather than to attempt to legislate it into benevolence. (Such would be unheard of in the age of Jackson.) While exceptions existed, most evangelicals viewed social problems as a breakdown of personal morality and thus could be treated in terms of pietism and perfectionism. Many social and economic injustices, prejudices, and discriminatory institutions were imbedded in American culture. Revivalism and church discipline could correct these problems, many evangelicals insisted. All Christians believed in keeping the Ten Commandments. Evangelicals, however, tended to focus on keeping the Sabbath, dancing, and modifying excessive male behavior—gambling, drunkenness, and brawling.[69]

Most evangelicals believed that social reform would grow naturally from the behavior of converted individuals. Employing revivalism, however, to convert individuals who, in turn, would then reform society had its limitations. By the 1830s, "the dream of a moral Christian society, transformed outwardly by the voluntary efforts of inwardly converted people, began to collapse," writes Mark Noll. Two failures—the treatment of the Cherokee Indians and slavery—contributed to the demise of this individualized approach to social problems. Many Cherokees had been converted and Americanized. Despite a Supreme Court decision in their favor, the Jackson administration yielded to the desire of white lust for territory and they were forced to give up their land and move west. Slavery became an intractable problem for the nation, including evangelicals. Many blacks had been converted and the number of African American churches grew dramatically. Northern evangelicals denounced slavery from the pulpit. But their counterparts in the South, employing a literal interpretation of Scripture, defended the peculiar institution with equal vigor. The churches—especially the Baptists and Methodists who vigorously promoted revivalism—could not reconcile their differences and thus split over slavery.[70]

Evangelical Christians did not have a corner on perfectionism. By mid-century, perfectionism also had a secular face. Many Americans desired to improve the quality of their lives. On how to improve your life, Sylvester Graham offered all kinds of advice—eat high fiber food, exercise, exclude all stimulants, and avoid excessive sex. Mary Gove Nichols saw hydropathy—a method of bathing and drinking water—as the key to life. For others the secret to happiness rested in phrenology, the practice of determining one's personality by the shape of their head. Others believed life could be restructured through utopian communities.[71]

Millennialism

If individuals could be perfect, why not society? The optimism of nineteenth-century America spilled over into the way evangelicals viewed Christ's return. Millennialism, in its generic usage, is concerned with the future of the human community on earth and with the chronology of coming events, just as history is involved with the study of the record of the past. In particular, the American millennial look into the future relates to the Second Coming of Christ and a period of earthly bliss or progress.[72]

Individuals and groups who believed in a millennium were deeply divided in early national America, as they have been throughout much of history. The various types are difficult to categorize. Perhaps the simplest way is to place them in two categories whose names vary. The most common terms are pre- and postmillennialism.

The progressives, also called millennialists or postmillennialists, assumed that the kingdoms of this world will eventually become those of Christ, and that through the endeavors of Christians the world will get better and better until it is finally worthy to receive Christ at his Second Coming. This view projected an optimistic view of the future and increasingly came to be equated with the idea of progress.[73]

Postmillennialism held sway until the late nineteenth century. At first it maintained an evangelical orientation, believing that the gradual improvements would be the fruit of human efforts and the work of the Holy Spirit. In fact, postmillennialism forged a link with another nineteenth-century movement—perfectionism. Christian perfectionism places a strong emphasis on holiness, contending that the believer through God's grace can achieve and maintain a moral perfection in this life.[74] Both postmillennialism and perfectionism promoted evangelicalism, morality, and a better quality of life.

But a different type of postmillennialism also came to the forefront. In earlier years, Protestants believed that the coming millennium could be inaugurated by such spiritual efforts as prayer and evangelism. As the nineteenth century progressed, many Americans linked the moral and national aspirations of America with the kingdom of God.[75] They believed that God was on America's side. This new postmillennialism justified America's conquest of the West. Religious leaders saw the advances in learning, the arts, science, morality, and religion as signs that the millennium was coming. As a means to advance this Christian commonwealth in the United States, postmillennialism promoted a wide variety of reform efforts. But as time went on, the religious impulses declined and a more secular millennium developed.[76]

The second group also has several names: pessimists, millenarians or, most commonly, premillennialists. Adherents of this view expected a divine intervention to establish a divinely ruled state, after evil had reached its fullest extent in the world at large. Since trials and tribulations would increase before the return of Christ, premillennialists tended to see any negative event as a sign that the world was growing worse and thus evidence that the end was near.[77] Though premillennialism had its proponents throughout the eighteenth and first half of the nineteenth centuries, postmillennialism overshadowed it and held the day.

Scottish Common Sense Philosophy

From about 1780 to 1820, the common people overthrew the intellectual authority of the educated elites. This precipitated a crisis of authority in early America, especially in religion. Everyone now had the right to think for themselves. The private interpretation of the Bible abounded. "Every man his own interpreter," became the cry. "No creed but the Bible," declared the Christian, or Disciples of Christ, movement.[78] Behind this line of thinking existed a philosophy—the Scottish Philosophy of Common Sense. The influence of this philosophy on American evangelicalism, however implicit, has been tremendous. While few in the current evangelical community are even aware of it, Common Sense or Scottish Realism—as it is called—has shaped the thinking of many evangelicals, especially their interpretation of Scripture.[79]

Most Americans rejected the more skeptical or radical interpretations of the Enlightenment. But a form of the Enlightenment, known as Scottish "common sense," exerted a widespread influence in the late eighteenth century. Developed largely by Francis Hutcheson (1694-1746) and Thomas Reid (1710-1796), common sense attempted to negate both the skepticism of David Hume (1711-1796) and the idealism of George Berkeley (1685-1753). It argued that common people could acquire an accurate knowledge of the real world by means of a responsible use of their senses. Humankind's physical senses could discover truth about the outside world through an empirical and inductive study. But only an innate "moral sense" common to all people allowed for intuitive knowledge of the basic principles of morality.[80] The key to Common Sense was its "appeal to universal (common) experience (or sense)." People now believed they could "see the truth—moral, physical, social—with greater clarity than in previous generations."[81]

In early America, many people, not just the evangelicals, bought heavily into Scottish Realism. From about 1780 to 1820, the nation was in transition. It had rejected many of the pillars that had supported traditional British society—an inherited monarchy, social hierarchy, an established church, and centuries of tradition and history. Something had to replace these props, so founders of the nation such as Jefferson and Madison turned to Common Sense. This Scottish philosophy helped them justify the American Revolution, establish new rules for social order and stability, and further the cause of the Christian faith without support from an established church. Moreover, Scottish Realism helped the nations' leaders secure a solid moral foundation for the new republic. People feared that public morals would be corrupted in the absence of an established church and social hierarchy. In regard to many public issues—e.g., following demagogues, political infighting, and ignoring debts—there existed a consensus between evangelicals and those less explicit in their Christian faith. To this list church leaders added declining church attendance and failure to observe the Sabbath.[82]

Evangelicals Embrace Common Sense

While most American thinkers embraced a form of Scottish Realism during the antebellum period, evangelicals were its strongest advocates. This had not always been the case. The Puritans generally rejected the concept of a natural moral sense. But during the Revolutionary era, most religious leaders acknowledged that the authority of Scripture had to be grounded on human perceptions of the external world. Such thinking made its way into the colleges. John Witherspoon (1723-1794) introduced it at Princeton where it flourished for over a century. Other evangelical educational leaders—including Timothy Dwight (1752-1817) and Nathaniel Taylor (1786-1858) at Yale—brought it to their respective institutions.[83]

Complementing the methodological emphasis of Common Sense are the scientific methods of Francis Bacon, which argued that "truths about consciousness, the world, or religion must be built by strict induction from irreducible facts of experience." Such an approach to the world encouraged many people, including evangelicals, to see religion and nearly everything else in scientific terms. Thus, Newton's work in the physical sciences became a model for most areas of human inquiry.[84]

Evangelicals gravitated more toward the Common Sense approach than to Bacon's inductive method. But the inquiry moved in the same direction. Unlike Locke who believed the mind was a blank slate, Scottish Realism said that God had installed in the mind the capacity to know right from wrong and true from false. This often fostered a literal approach to Scripture. The Bible is plain and it means exactly what it says. Trained theologians are not needed to interpret it. This interpretation of Scripture complemented the democratic and populist mood of antebellum America.[85]

During early national America, not all evangelicals bought into the Common Sense and literal approach to the Bible. It was more pronounced among the anti-formalist groups (Baptist, Methodists, and Disciples of Christ). Even during this time, however, embracing Scottish Realism and Baconianism would not place one outside of the intellectual mainstream. Such would come after the Civil War when Common Sense and Bacon's methods were no longer in vogue. In the late nineteenth century, many evangelicals refused to abandon Scottish Realism long after the rest of the intellectual world had. So they found themselves as outsiders in the world of thought.[86]

Some Cultural Trends

By the mid-eighteenth century, the future contours of American evangelicalism became discernable. And these outlines closely connected with American culture, that is, both were individualistic, populist, pragmatic and embraced the spirit of liberty. Evangelical preaching had acquired its peculiar characteristics—extemporaneous as opposed to written, intended to impact both the emotions and the intellect, and calling on individuals to make a decision for Christ. Even before the Revolutionary War, most American evangelicals embraced a republican view of politics. They distrusted centralized political power and desired a system of checks and balances in government. Dominating their political agenda was their belief in liberty, rule by law, and natural rights. Along with most Americans, evangelicals were pre-democratic, but their view of republicanism included many democratic principles.[87]

These early years also saw evangelicals develop a relationship with society that has largely persisted to the present. First and foremost, evangelicalism was and still is a spiritual renewal movement. Evangelicals concerned themselves with political, social, economic, and intellectual developments primarily as such issues interacted with the Christian faith. Despite their focus on spiritual matters, they did not withdraw from the world. The early evangelicals, however, did not maintain a worldview that encouraged the transformation of institutional structures. Changing individuals and creating Christian communities came first. Thus, the evangelical approach to social change tended to be individualistic and *ad hoc*. In the world of the mind, the early evangelicals set the tone for the future. On the whole, they tended to neglect the pursuit of rigorous intellectual activity. And somewhat related, the early evangelicals often trivialized the great matters of the faith by marketing the gospel as if it were a secular commodity.[88]

From about 1795 to 1835, white evangelical Protestantism grew by leaps and bounds. During this period, evangelicalism was the dominant moral force and its ethic significantly shaped the nation. This does not mean that every aspect of American life reflected evangelical values. Rather, to a considerable degree the public morals and manners of antebellum America bore the stamp of evangelicalism. The evangelicals achieved much. They took a variety of

Protestant groups with different beliefs and practices and created a cultural consensus. In North America, only in overwhelmingly Catholic Quebec did a comparable situation exist. "After the mid-1830s, however, the situation in the United States was reversed. Political circumstances and social forces...began to exert more influence on the churches than the churches did on the nation," notes Noll.[89] And the direction of cultural influence reached enormous proportions in the late twentieth century.

That the cultural influence flowed away from the church was due in a large part to the increased secularization that took place after the Civil War. Secularization, as defined by George Marsden, is "the removal of some area of human activity from the domain, or significant influence, of organized or traditional religion." Groups antagonistic to traditional religion promote secularization for a variety of reasons. Such a situation developed in Europe. But in America, secularization has traveled down a different path. Christianity has helped to promote it. The Constitution, while disestablishing religion, was friendly to it. In turn, Protestantism has been friendly to secularization, often applying a layer of Christianity to the government, economic system, and many aspects of culture. Thus, much accommodation went on under the veneer of Christianity

Notes

1. Martin E. Marty, *Righteous Empire: The Protestant Experience in America* (New York: Dial Press, 1970); Curtis D. Johnson, *Redeeming America: Evangelicals and the Road to Civil War* (Chicago: Ivan Dee, 1993), 3, 4 (quote); John D. Woodbridge, Mark A. Noll, Nathan O. Hatch, *The Gospel in America: Themes in the Story of Evangelicals* (Grand Rapids: Zondervan, 1979), 216.
2. Robert T. Handy, *The Protestant Quest for a Christian America, 1830-1930* (Philadelphia: Fortress Press, 1967), 10, 11; Johnson, *Redeeming America*, 4; Marty, *Righteous Empire*, 38.
3. Alexis de Tocqueville, *Democracy in America* (New York: Alfred A. Knopf, 1945), 1:303.
4. Henry F. May, *Protestant Churches and Industrial America* (New York: Harper and Brothers, 1949), 91 (quote); Johnson, *Redeeming America*, 10, 11; Sidney E. Mead, *The Lively Experiment* (New York: Harper and Row, 1963), 142.
5. Jerry Falwell, *Listen America* (New York: Doubleday, 1980), 50.
6. Tim LaHaye, *The Battle for the Mind* (Old Tappan, NJ: Revell, 1977), 36 (quote); Kathleen Fox, "Praise the Lord (And Howard Dean, Too)," *Newsweek* (9 February 2004): 13 (quote) See Stephen Mansfield, *The Faith of George W. Bush* (New York: Penguin, 2003).
7. Peter Marshall and David Manuel, *The Light and the Glory* (Grand Rapids: Revell, 1977), 16-26 (quote on 16). See also Peter Marshall and David Manuel, *From Sea to Shining Sea* (Grand Rapids: Fleming H. Revell, 1993).
8. G. Aiken Taylor, "Francis Schaeffer: America's Underpinnings," *The Presbyterian Journal* 2 (March 1983): 7, 8 (quote). See also Francis A. Schaeffer, *How Should We Then Live?* (Old Tappan, NJ: Revell, 1976), 109, 110, 124, 218, 220-22.
9. Robert Linder and Richard Pierard, *Twilight of the Saints: Biblical Christianity and Civil Religion in America* (Downers Grove, IL: InterVarsity Press, 1978), 21.

10. See Robert N. Bellah, *The Broken Covenant: American Civil Religion in Time of Trial* (New York: Seabury Press, 1975); Elwyn A. Smith, ed., *The Religion of the Republic* (Philadelphia: Fortress Press, 1971); Catherine L. Albanese, *Sons of the Fathers: The Civil Religion of the American Revolution* (Philadelphia: Temple University Press, 1976); John F. Wilson, *Public Religion in American Culture* (Philadelphia: Temple University Press, 1979); Cushing Strout, *The New Heavens and New Earth* (New York: Harper and Row, 1974); Dick Anthony and Thomas Robbins, "Spiritual Innovation and the Crisis of American Civil Religion," *Daedalus* 111, 1 (1982): 215-34; John Murray Cuddihy, *No Offense: Civil Religion and Protestant Taste* (New York: Seabury Press, 1978).

11. Robert D. Linder, "Civil Religion in Historical Perspective: The Reality That Underlies the Concept," *Journal of Church and State,* 17, 3 (1975): 412-14; Linder and Pierard, *Twilight of the Saints*, 54, 55; Christopher Highley and John N. King, eds., *John Foxe and His World* (Aldershot, UK: Ashgate, 2002); Richard T. Hughes, *Myths America Lives By* (Urbana: University of Illinois Press, 2004), 20-23.

12. Edmund S. Morgan, *The Puritan Dilemma: The Story of John Winthrop* (Boston: Little and Brown, 1958), 69-83, quote on 69; Linder and Pierard, *Twilight of the Saints*, 58-60; Richard Kyle, *The Last Days Are Here Again* (Grand Rapids: Baker, 1998), 80, 81; James A. Morone, *Hellfire Nation: The Politics of Sin in American History* (New Haven, CT: Yale University Press, 2003), 34-54; George Marsden, "America's Christian Origins: Puritan New England as a Case Study," in *John Calvin: His Influence in the Western World,* ed. W. Stanford Reid (Grand Rapids: Zondervan, 1982), 241-60; Christopher M. Beam, "Millennialism and American Nationalism, 1740-1800," *Journal of Presbyterian History* 54 (spring 1976): 182-99; Hughes, *Myths America Lives By*, 28-30.

13. Linder and Pierard, *Twilight of the Saints*, 61, 62 (quote on 61); Conrad Cherry, ed., *God's New Israel* (Englewood Cliffs, NJ: Prentice-Hall, 1971), 1-3; Lefferts A. Loetscher, *The Problem of Christian Unity in Early Nineteenth-America* (Philadelphia: Fortress Press, 1969), 16; Hughes, *Myths America Lives By*, 106-08.

14. Ernest Lee Tuveson, *Redeemer Nation: The Idea of America's Millennial Role* (Chicago: University of Chicago Press, 1968), 91, 157 (quotes); Loetscher, *The Problem of Christian Unity*, 15; Hughes, *Myths America Lives By*, 107, 108, 110 (quote).

15. Kyle, *The Last Days Are Here Again,* 80, 81; Nathan O. Hatch, "The Origins of Civil Millennialism in America: Recent Studies," in *Reckoning with the Past*, ed. D. G. Hart (Grand Rapids: Baker, 1995), 98; Robert C. Fuller, *Naming the Antichrist* (New York: Oxford University Press, 1995), 68-70; Jon Butler, *Awash in a Sea of Faith: Christianizing the American People* (Cambridge, MA: Harvard University Press, 1990), 164-224; Ruth H. Bloch, *Visionary Republic: Millennial Themes in American Thought, 1756-1800* (New York: Cambridge University Press, 1985); Melvin B. Endy, Jr., "Just War, Holy War, and Millennialism in Revolutionary America," *William and Mary Quarterly* 3, 1 (1985): 3-25; Hughes, *Myths America Lives By*, 98-100.

16. Robert Clouse, "The New Christian Right, America, and the Kingdom of God," *Christian Scholar's Review* 12 (1983): 6, 72, 73; Dawn Glanz, "The American West as Millennial Kingdom," in *The Apocalyptic Vision in America*, ed. Lois Parkinson Zamora (Bowling Green, OH: Bowling Green University Popular Press, 1982), 141; James H. Moorhead, "The Erosion of Postmillennialism in American Thought, 1865-1925," *Church History* 53, 1 (1984): 62-72; Kyle, *The Last Days Are Here Again*, 81; Hughes, *Myths America Lives By*, 107, 108.

17. Tuveson, *Redeemer Nation*, 128, 129, 137; James H. Moorhead, *World Without God: Mainstream Protestant Visions of the Last Things, 1880-1925* (Bloomington: Indiana University Press, 1999), 91-96; James H. Moorhead, "The Erosion of Postmillennialism in American Religious Thought, 1865-1925," *Church History* 53, 1 (1984): 61-77; James G. Moseley, *A Cultural History of Religion in America* (Westport, CT: Greenwood Press, 1981), 51-66; Hughes, *Myths America Lives By*, 133.

18. Mark A. Noll, "The American Revolution and Protestant Evangelicalism," *Journal of Interdisciplinary History* 23, 3 (1993): 617, 618, 630, 631; Linder and Pierard, *Twilight of the Saints*, 69, 70.

19. Linder and Pierard, *Twilight of the Saints*, 69, 70 (quote on 69); Noll, "The American Revolution and Protestant Evangelicalism," 617, 618, 630, 631; Timothy L. Smith, "Protestant Schooling and American Nationality, 1800-1850," *Journal of American History* 53 (1966-67): 679-94; Robert T. Handy, *A Christian America: Protestant Hopes and Historical Realities* (New York: Oxford University Press, 1984), 27 (quote).

20. Noll, "American Revolution and Evangelicalism," 616, (quote), 630-35; Mark Noll, *America's God* (Oxford: Oxford University Press, 2002), 73-92; Steven J. Keillor, *This Rebellious House: American History and the Truth of Christianity* (Downers Grove, IL: InterVarsity Press, 1996), 86-91.

21. Robert N. Bellah, "Religion and Legitmation in the American Republic," *Society* 15, 4 (1978): 19; Strout, *The New Heavens and New Earth*,1974), 50-90; George Marsden, *Understanding Fundamentalism and Evangelicalism* (Grand Rapids: Eerdmans, 1991), 83, 86; Noll, "American Revolution and Evangelicalism," 616, 630-35.

22. Marty, *Righteous Empire*, on the first printed page preceding Contents page (quote). Woodbridge, Noll, Hatch, *The Gospel in America,* 216; Hughes, *Myths America Lives By*, 77, 78.

23. Mark A. Noll, Nathan O. Hatch, and George M. Marsden, *The Search for Christian America* (Colorado Springs: Helmers and Howard, 1989), 30, 128, 132; Mark Couvillon, "Christians in the Cause," *Christian History* 15, 2 (issue 50): 18-21; R. Laurence Moore, *Touchdown Jesus: The Mixing of Sacred and Secular in American History* (Louisville: Westminister John Knox Press, 2003), 16; Frank Lambert, *The Founding Fathers and the Place of Religion in America* (Princeton, NJ: Princeton University Press, 2003); Michael Novak, *On Two Wings: Humble Faith and Common Sense at the American Founding* (San Francisco: Encounter Books, 2002).

24. Noll, "American Revolution and Evangelicalism," 622; Noll, Hatch, Marsden, *Search for Christian America*, 31, 130, 131; Couvillon, "Christians in the Cause," 18-21; Edwin S. Gaustad, "Disciples of Reason," *Christian History*, 15, 2 (issue 50): 28-31; Edwin S. Gaustad, (San Francisco: Harper and Row, 1987), 59-109; Keillor, *Rebellious House*, 84, 85; Marty, *Righteous Empire*, 43; Moore, *Touchdown Jesus*, 17; Alf J. Mapp, Jr., *The Faiths of Our Fathers* (Lanham, MD: Rowman and Littlefield, 2003); Hughes, *Myths America Lives By*, 53-55.

25. Noll, Hatch, Marsden, *Search for Christian America*, 31, 130, 131; Gaustad, "Disciples of Reason, 28-31; Noll, "American Revolution and Evangelicalism," 622.

26. Mark Noll, *American Evangelical Christianity* (Oxford, UK: Blackwell, 2001), 185; Hughes, *Myths America Lives By*, 67, 70.

27. Noll, Hatch, Marsden, *Search for Christian America*, 24-26; Nathan O. Hatch, "The Democratization of Christianity and the Character of American Politics," in *Religion and American Politics*, ed. Mark A. Noll (New York: Oxford University Press, 1990), 101; Hughes, *Myths America Lives By*, 32.

28. Donald S. Armentrout, "Democracy and Christianity in America," in *Dictionary of Christianity in America,* ed. Daniel Reid et al. (Downers Grove, IL: InterVarsity Press, 1990), 348.
29. Ibid., 349.
30. Alice Felt Tyler, *Freedom's Ferment* (New York: Harper Torchbooks, 1962), 5-7. See Joel H. Silbey, *Martin Van Buren and the Emergence of American Popular Politics* (Lanham, MD: Rowman and Littlefield, 2005).
31. Mark Noll, *A History of Christianity in the United States and Canada* (Grand Rapids: Eerdmans, 1992), 115, 116; Moseley, *A Cultural History of Religion,* 39, 40; Robert N. Bellah, "Religion and Legitimation in the Early American Republic," *Society* 15, 4 (1978): 16-23; George M. Thomas, *Revivalism and Cultural Change* (Chicago: University of Chicago Press, 1989), 89-92.
32. George Marsden, *Religion and American Culture* (New York: Harcourt Brace, 1990), 29; Mark A. Noll, *The Old Religion in a New World* (Grand Rapids: Eerdmans, 2002), 51-58; Moseley, *A Cultural History of Religion,* 47; Edwin Scott Gaustad, *The Great Awakening in New England* (Chicago: Quadrangle Paperbacks, 1968); Gordon S. Wood, "Religion and the American Revolution," in *New Directions in American Religious History,* ed. Harry Stout and D. G. Hart (New York: Oxford University Press, 1997), 173-205; Thomas, *Revivalism and Cultural Change,* 89-92.
33. Tyler, *Freedom's Ferment,* 11.
34. Hatch, "The Democratization of Christianity," 108, 109 (quote); Butler, *Awash in A Sea of Faith,* 206-24, 257-88; Hatch, "Evangelicalism as a Democratic Movement," 71-82.
35. Daniel Walker Howe, "The Evangelical Movement and Political Culture in the North During the Second Party System," *Journal of American History* 77, 4 (1991), 1217.
36. Robert Booth Fowler, Allen D. Hertzke, and Laura R. Olson, *Religion and Politics in America* (Boulder, CO: Westview Press, 1990), 24; Jean V. Matthews, *Toward A New Society: American Thought and Culture 1800-1830* (Boston: Twayne Publishers, 1991), 31.
37. Sydney E. Ahlstrom, *A Religious History of the American People* (New Haven, CT: Yale University Press, 1972), 385 (quote); Nathan O. Hatch, "Evangelicalism as a Democratic Movement," *Reformed Journal* (October 1984): 11; Matthews, *Toward A New Society,* 43.
38. Hatch, "Evangelicalism as a Democratic Movement,"11; Nathan O. Hatch, "Evangelicalism as a Democratic Movement," in *Evangelicalism and Modern America,* ed. George Marsden (Grand Rapids: Eerdmans, 1984), 71-73; Roger Finke and Rodney Stark, *The Churching of America 1776-1990* (New Brunswick, NJ: Rutgers University Press, 1992), 17, 18; Moore, *Touchdown Jesus,* 22.
39. Mark A. Noll, *The Scandal of the Evangelical Mind* (Grand Rapids: Eerdmans, 1994), 12, (quote) 64; Hatch, "Evangelicalism as a Democratic Movement," 13; Richard Hofstadter, *Anti-Intellectualism in American Life* (New York: Vintage Books, 1963), 47-50.
40. Bruce Shelley, *Evangelicalism in America* (Grand Rapids: Eerdmans, 1967), 46.
41. William Warren Sweet, *Revivalism in America* (Nashville: Abingdon Press, 1944), xii; Shelley, *Evangelicalism in America,* 46 (quote); Hofstadter, *Anti-Intellectualism in American Life,* 47.
42. Sweet, *Revivalism in America,* 24, 25 (quote); Noll, *Old Religion in a New World,* 51; William G. McLoughlin, "Pietism and the American Character," *American Quarterly* 17, 2, pt. 2 (1965), 169, 170.

43. R. Laurence Moore, *Selling God: American Religion in the Marketplace of Culture* (New York: Oxford University Press, 1994), 41, 50; Nathan O. Hatch, *Democratization of American Christianity* (New Haven, CT: Yale University Press, 1989), 45, 138; Hofstadter, *Anti-Intellectualism in American Life*, 68, 69, 74, 80.

44. Hatch, *Democratization of American Christianity*, 138 (quote); Nathan O. Hatch, "Millennialism and Popular Religion in the Early Republic," in *The Evangelical Tradition in America*, ed. Leonard I. Sweet (Macon, GA: Mercer University Press, 1984), 113-30.

45. Randall Balmer, *Blessed Assurance: A History of Evangelicalism* (Boston: Beacon Press, 1999), 64, 65 (quote on 64).

46. Noll, *Scandal of the Evangelical Mind*, 61 (quote).

47. Harry S. Stout, "Religion, Communications, and the Ideological Origins of the American Revolution," *William and Mary Quarterly* 34, 3 (1977): 525.

48. Harry S. Stout, "Heavenly Comet," *Christian History* 38, 2 (spring 1993): 10, 15 (quote); Stout, "Religion, Communications, and the American Revolution," 529, 530; Harry S. Stout, *The Divine Dramatist: George Whitefield and the Rise of Modern Evangelicalism* (Grand Rapids: Eerdmans, 1991); Harry S. Stout, *The New England Soul: Preaching and Religious Culture in Colonial New England* (New York: Oxford University Press, 1986); Frank Lambert, *Peddlar in Divinity: George Whitefield and Transatlantic Revivals, 1737-1770* (Princeton, NJ: Princeton University Press, 1994); Finke and Stark, *Churching of America*, 44-46; Moore, *Touchdown Jesus*, 18, 19; Mark Noll, *The Rise of Evangelicalism* (Downers Grove, IL: InterVarsity, 2003), 88, 89, 132.

49. Frank Lambert, " 'Pedlar in Divinity': George Whitefield and the Great Awakening, 1737-1747," *Journal of American History* 77, 3 (1990): 812, 813, 817, 822-26, 828, 829; Moore, *Selling God*, 41, 42; Lambert, *Pedlar in Divinity*, 52-94; Finke and Stark, *Churching of America*, 44-46; Roger Finke and Laurence R. Iannacone, "Supply-Side Explanations for Religious Change," *Annals of the American Academy of Political and Social Science* 527 (May 1993): 31, 32; Noll, *The Rise of Evangelicalism*, 107, 108.

50. Hofstadter, *Anti-Intellectualism in American Life*, 80; Noll, *Scandal of the Evangelical Mind*, 61; Hatch, "Evangelicalism as a Democratic Movement," 73; Balmer, *Blessed Assurance*, 62.

51. Willam McLoughlin, *Revivals, Awakenings, and Reform* (Chicago: University of Chicago Press, 1978), 126 (quote); Noll, *Christianity in the United States and Canada*, 174, 175; Hofstadter, *Anti-Intellectualism in American Life*, 86, 93, 94; Mark Galli, "Revival at Cane Ridge," *Christian History* 14, 1 (1995): 9-14. See Dickson D. Bruce, Jr. *And They All Sang Hallelujah: Plain-Folk Camp Meeting-Religion, 1800-1845* (Knoxville: University of Tennessee Press, 1974); Kathryn Teresa Long, "The Power of Interpretation: The Revival of 1857-58 and the Historiography of Revivalism in America," *Religion and American Culture* 4, 1 (1994): 77-105; Kathryn Teresa Long, *The Revival of 1857-58* (New York: Oxford University Press, 1998); Whitney R. Cross, *The Burned-Over District* (New York: Harper Torchbooks, 1965); Moore, *Touchdown Jesus*, 20, 21.

52. Bernard A. Weisberger, *They Gathered at the River* (New York: Octagon Books, 1979), 101-03; Johnson, *Redeeming America*, 60; Moore, *Selling God,* 50-52. Hofstadler, *Anti-Intellectualism in American Life*, 86, 92, 94; R. Laurence Moore, "Religion, Secularization, and the Shaping of the Culture Industry in Antebellum America," *American Quarterly* 41 (June 1989); 228; Moore, *Touchdown Jesus*, 20, 21; Razelle Frankl, *Televangelism: The Marketing of Popular Religion* (Carbondale: Southern Illinois University Press, 1987), 4.

53. Quote from Shelley, *Evangelicalism in America*, 47.
54. McLoughlin, *Revivals and Reform*, 126 (quote); Johnson, *Redeeming America*, 60, 61; Noll, *Christianity in the United States and Canada*, 176; Donald W. Dayton, *Discovering An Evangelical Heritage* (New York: Harper and Row, 1976), 16; Charles G. Finney, *Reflections on Revival*, comp. Donald Dayton (Minneapolis: Bethany Fellowship, 1979), 11-44; Garth M. Rosell, "Charles G. Finney: His Place in the Stream," in *The Evangelical Tradition in America*, 131-47; Donald Mathews, "The Second Great Awakening as an Organizing Process, 1780-1830: An Hypothesis," *American Quarterly* 21 (1969): 22-43; David Paul Nord, *The Evangelical Origins of Mass Media in America* (Columbus, OH: American Education in Journalism and Mass Communications, 1984), 2-25.
55. Hofstadler, *Anti-Intellectualism in American Life*, 34, 84, 85, 92, 93 (quote on 93); Weisberger, *They Gathered at the River*, 94; Moore, *Touchdown Jesus*, 20, 21.
56. Hatch, *Democratization of American Christianity*, 16.
57. Noll, *Christianity in the United States and Canada*, 177 (quote), 177; Richard Kyle, *The Religious Fringe: A History of Alternative Religions in America* (Downers Grove, Il: InterVarsity Press, 1993), 54; McLoughlin, *Revivals and Reform*, 98, 113; Charles Finney, *Finney's Systematic Theology*, ed. J. H. Fairchild (Minneapolis: Bethany Fellowship, 1976).
58. Balmer, *Blessed Assurance*, 65, 66.
59. Finke and Stark, *Churching of America*, 54-108; Noll, *Christianity in the United States and Canada*, 171-74, 178-80; Timothy L. Smith, *Revivalism and Social Reform* (Baltimore, MD: Johns Hopkins University Press, 1980), 80, 92; Fowler, Hertzke, Olson, *Religion and Politics in America*, 24; Weisberger, *They Gathered at the River*, 48, 53.
60. Noll, *Old Religion in a New World*, 63.
61. Noll, *America's God*, 563 (quotes); Dayton, *Discovering An Evangelical Heritage*, 17.
62. McLoughlin, *Revivals and Reform*, 114-21; Shelley, *Evangelicalism in America*, 47, 48; Noll, *America's God*, 277-81, 297-99; Ahlstrom, *Religious History*, 419-21.
63. Quote from Shelley, *Evangelicalism in America*, 48; Dayton, *Discovering An Evangelical Heritage*, 17; Noll, *America's God*, 253-329.
64. Quote from McLoughlin, *Revivals and Reform*, 125; Sweet, *Revivalism in America*, 128; Balmer, *Blessed Assurance*, 58.
65. Rush Welter, "The Idea of Progress in America," *Journal of the History of Ideas* 14 (1955): 401-15; Russel Blaine Nye, *Society and Culture in America, 1830-1860* (New York: Harper Torchbooks, 1974), 22-30.
66. William G. McLoughlin Jr., *Modern Revivalism* (New York: Ronald Press, 1959), 102-03; Shelley, *Evangelicalism in America*, 49; Nye, *Society and Culture*, 36, 289-92; Larry Shelton, "Perfectionism, " in *Evangelical Dictionary of Theology*, ed. Walter A. Elwell (Grand Rapids: Baker, 1984), 843; Timothy L. Smith, "Righteousness and Hope: Christian Holiness and the Millennial Vision in America, 1800-1900," *American Quarterly* 31, 1 (1979): 22,23.
67. Nye, *Society and Culture*, 36 (quote). See also Timothy L. Smith, *Revivalism and Social Reform* (Baltimore, MD: Johns Hopkins Press, 1980); Dayton, *Discovering and Evangelical Heritage*, 15-20; Morone, *Hellfire Nation*, 144-168, 281-317.
68. Robert Booth Fowler, Allen D. Hertzke, and Laura R. Olson, *Religion and Politics in America* (Boulder, CO: Westview Press, 1999), 18; Nye, *Society and Culture*, 36.
69. McLoughlin, *Modern Revivalism*, 106, 107; Nye, *Society and Culture*, 36; Smith, *Revivalism and Social Reform*, 225-36; Johnson, *Redeeming America*, 90, 91; David O. Moberg, *The Great Reversal: Evangelism and Social Concern* (Philadelphia: Lippincott, 1977), 28-30.

70. Noll, *Old Religion in a New World*, 104-08 (quote on 104); Keillor, *Rebellious House*, 136-73; Stephen R. Haynes, *Noah's Curse: The Biblical Justification of American Slavery* (New York: Oxford University Press, 2002); Hughes, *Myths America Lives By*, 115-17.
71. Johnson, *Redeeming America*, 112, 113; Stephen Nissenbaum, *Sex, Diet, and Debility in Jacksonsian America* (Chicago: Dorsey Press, 1980).
72. Robert G. Clouse, "The Views of the Millennium," in *Evangelical Dictionary of Theology*, 715; Catherine Albanese, *America: Religion and Religions* (Belmont, CA: Wadsworth, 1981), 275, 276; George Rosen, "Social Change and Psychopathology in the Emotional Climate of Millennial Movements," *American Behavioral Scientist* 16, 2 (1972): 153-67; Kyle, *Religious Fringe*, 55.
73. J.F.C. Harrison, *The Second Coming: Popular Millennarianism, 1780-1850* (New Brunswick, NJ: Rutgers University Press, 1979), 4-7; Tuveson, *Redeemer Nation*, 232; Smith, "Righteousness and Hope," 22-25; James H. Moorhead, "Searching for the Millennium in America," *Princeton Seminary Bulletin* 8, 2 (1987): 17-33; Kyle, *Religious Fringe*, 55, 56.
74. Smith, "Righteousness and Hope," 21-27; Nye, *Society and Culture*, 36, 289-92; McLoughlin, *Modern Revivalism*, 102, 103; Kyle, *The Last Days Are Here Again*, 79.
75. Clouse, "The New Christian Right," 6; James Allan Patterson, "Changing Images of the Beast: Apocalyptic Conspiracy Theories in American History," *Journal of the Evangelical Theological Society* 31 (December 1988): 445; Ruth H. Bloch, *Visionary Republic* (New York: Cambridge University Press, 1985), 103-04; Tuveson, *Redeemer Nation*, 125-31; Kyle, *The Last Days Are Here Again*, 81; Melvin B. Endy, Jr., "Just War, Holy War, and Millennialism in Revolutionary America," *William and Mary Quarterly* 3, 1 (1985): 3-25.
76. Clouse, "New Christian Right," 6-7; Fuller, *Naming the Antichrist*, 72,73; Dawn Glanz, "The American West as Millennial Kingdom," in *The Apocalyptic Vision in America*, ed. Lois Parkinson Zamora (Bowling Green, OH: Bowling Green University Popular Press, 1982), 141; Albanese, *America,* 426-27; Moorhead, "The Erosion of Postmillennialism in American Religious Thought," 62-72; James H. Moorhead, "Between Progress and Apocalypse: A Reassessment of Millennialism in American Religious Thought, 1800-1880," *Journal of American History* 71, 3 (1984): 526-27; Tuveson, *Redeemer Nation*, 131, 162, 163; Jean B. Quandt, "Religion and Social Thought: The Secularization of Postmillennialism, *American Quarterly* 25 (October 1973): 391-92; Kyle, *The Last Days are Here Again*, 81; Moorhead, *World Without End*, 97-123.
77. Harrison, *Second Coming*, 4-6; Tuveson, *Redeemer Nation*, 232; Albanese, *America*, 276-77; William Martin, "Waiting for the End," *Atlantic* (June 1982): 31-32; Kyle, *Religious Fringe*, 56.
78. Nathan O. Hatch, "Sola Scriptura and Novus Ordo Seclorum," in *The Bible in America*, ed. Nathan O. Hatch and Mark A. Noll (Oxford: Oxford University Press, 1982), 64, 70, 71 (quotes on 71).
79. Mark A. Noll, "Common Sense Traditions and American Evangelical Thought," *American Quarterly* 37 (summer 1985): 224, 225; Harriet A. Harris, *Fundamentalism and Evangelicals* (Oxford: Clarendon Press, 1998), 96-130; George M. Marsden, *Fundamentalism and American Culture* (New York: Oxford University Press, 1980), 7, 16-18, 20, 23, 28, 55-56, 221; Marsden, *Religion and American Culture*, 58,59.
80. Sydney E. Ahlstrom, "The Scottish Philosophy and American Theology," *Church History* 24, 3 (1955): 260, 261; Richard W. Pointer, "Scottish Realism," in *Dictio-*

nary of Christianity in America, 1061; Noll, "Common Sense Traditions," 220, 221; Noll, *America's God,* 102,103; Henry May, *The Enlightenment in America* (New York: Oxford University Press, 1978), 342-46.

81. Noll, *Christianity in the United States and Canada,* 154 (quote); Marsden, *Fundamentalism and Evangelicalism,* 192, 193.

82. Noll, *Scandal of the Evangelical Mind,* 86, 87; Noll, *Christianity in the United States and Canada,* 154, 155; Noll, *America's God,* 110, 111; Ahlstrom, "Scottish Philosophy and American Theology," 267.

83. May, *Enlightenment in America,* 341-50; Noll, *Christianity in the United States and Canada,* 156; Marsden, *Fundamentalism and Evangelicalism,* 128, 129; Marsden, *Fundamentalism and American Culture,* 16-18.

84. Noll, "Common Sense Traditions," 222, 223 (quote). See Theodore Dwight Bozeman, *Protestants in an Age of Science: The Baconian Ideal and Antebellum Religious Thought* (Chapel Hill: University of North Carolina Press, 1977); Herbert Hovenkamp, *Science and Religion in America 1800-1860* (Philadelphia: University of Pennsylvania Press, 1978); George M. Marsden, "Everyone One's Own Interpreter?: The Bible, Science, and Authority in Mid-Nineteenth-Century America," in *The Bible in America,* 81-84.

85. Johnson, *Redeeming America,* 32,33; Hatch, *Democratization of American Christianity,* 45; Marsden, *Fundamentalism and American Culture,* 58; Marsden, *Fundamentalism and Evangelicalism,* 128, 129.

86. Noll, "Common Sense Tradition," 223, 226, 227; Marsden, "Everyone One's Own Interpreter," 94, 95.

87. Noll, *The Rise of Evangelicalism,* 132, 133, 185,186.

88. Ibid., 233-36.

89. Noll, *Old Religion in a New World,* 108 (quote); Noll, *Christianity in the United States and Canada,* 243.

3

Cracks in the "Evangelical Empire"

In the mid-nineteenth century, it could be said that "evangelical Christians ran the show in the United States."[1] The Second Great Awakening ushered in a period of evangelical cultural ascendancy—one that hung on until the end of the century. The public values and morals of the nation bore the stamp of evangelical Christianity. So at the dawn of the twentieth century, evangelicalism in America appeared to be vigorous and prosperous. Church attendance remained high, many beautiful church edifices had been erected, revivalism was still going strong, and missionary activity soared to great heights. Evangelicals actively pursued many social reforms—especially temperance, which was seen as necessary for a Christian civilization. In fact, the Progressive movement itself owed much to this evangelical impulse.

This evangelical cultural dominance touched most areas of society—so much so that few Protestants would have questioned whether America was a Christian nation. And this was a time when *Protestant* and *evangelical* were nearly synonymous terms. At the turn of the century, Protestantism had not yet divided into two mutually hostile groups—the modernists and fundamentalists. In 1892, no less an authority than the Supreme Court in one of its cases declared the United States "is a Christian nation."[2]

Fueled by the United States' growing economic power in the late nineteenth century, American nationalism, civilization, and Christianity became nearly indistinguishable. "Surely to be a Christian and an Anglo-Saxon, and an American in this generation is to stand on the very mountain-top of privilege."[3] Such words came not from an archconservative but from Josiah Strong, a leader of the Home Missionary movement. Revivalist Samuel Porter Jones asserted that "we have the most advanced civilization in the world today" and that "God has given us the greatest country the sun shines on."[4]

American Protestantism moved into the twentieth century with great confidence. Protestants believed that America (with Britain's help) was God's chosen vessel to Christianize and civilize the world. Evangelicals had their differences, but they saw themselves as part of a great crusade spreading the blessings of Christianity and civilization throughout the globe. Utterly convinced that America was a Christian civilization and of Anglo-Saxon cultural superiority, evangelicals believed victory—even global dominance—to be close at hand. To most evangelicals Christianization, Americanization, and civilization were one and the same. Despite separation of church and state, religion and nationalism lived in an intimate relationship. And most evangelicals were oblivious as to how much their faith had become a religion of culture.[5]

A head count would also indicate that evangelical Protestantism was riding high and well adapted to the popular ideals of nineteenth-century American life. By 1890, the Methodists and Baptists were numerically and theologically the most dominant of the Protestant bodies. The Presbyterians were third, with the Christians and Disciples of Christ and Congregationalists following. These mainline denominations made up about 80 percent of American Protestantism and approximately 55 percent of the total religious population.[6]

While these bodies differed over specific doctrinal points, many threads unified them into a "Protestant empire." Ideologically, they had deep roots in either the Reformed or Arminian traditions. Revivalism, which made a conversion experience the essential mark of a true Christian, had made an imprint on these groups. These denominations found themselves in almost complete agreement with America's nationalism and political and economic systems—that is, democracy and capitalism. On most moral issues—gambling, dancing, drunkenness, smoking, profanity, Sabbath observance, and the frequency of divorce—evangelical Protestantism maintained a more or less unified front.[7]

"To permeate society with the leaven of the Christian religion—this was the focus of Protestant energy and a source of Protestant unity despite diversity and tension," notes Robert Handy. This Protestant dominance must not be exaggerated, however. Protestantism should be seen as more of a culture than as a set of religious doctrines or behavioral codes that most people practiced. Many Protestants went to theaters, drank alcoholic beverages, and had sex outside of marriage—all against the advice of their clergy. Rather, Protestantism represented the dominant cultural values.[8]

Tears in the Social Structure

At first glance, evangelical Protestantism was riding high. In the sense of being dominated by Protestantism, about 1910 American culture in many ways resembled that of 1860. But appearances can be deceptive. Beneath the surface lurked tremendous problems and challenges. So serious were they that the days of the "evangelical empire" were numbered. In fact, Robert Handy has described this loss of Protestant cultural ascendancy in the 1920s as the "second disestablishment" of religion.[9]

The maintenance of this Protestant cultural dominance demanded a broad popular base—one that was Anglo-Saxon and Protestant. And all of this was changing after the Civil War, which can be viewed as a watershed between the old and new America. By general consensus, modern America is said to have emerged sometime between 1865 and World War I, the years when industry, the telegraph, and the railroads developed extensively and when the national government became secure in its relationship to the governments of the various states. During this period, the American people became much more heterogeneous. The advent of modern science drastically altered the intellectual climate, and the quickening pace of industrialization created new centers of power in national life.[10]

An obvious contrast between the old and new America was the changing composition of the population. Prior to the Civil War, most Americans were of Northern or Western European stock and except for the Irish immigrants, overwhelmingly Protestant. In the late nineteenth century great influxes of people came to America from Southern, Central, and Eastern Europe. These individuals were not as easily assimilated into the American culture as were immigrants from Northern and Western Europe. Moreover, many of these immigrants brought with them their Roman Catholic, Eastern Orthodox, or Jewish faiths. This demographic revolution produced by immigration had a heavy impact on the spiritual self- consciousness of the American people.[11]

Many Americans reacted to this massive influx with fear, hostility, and prejudice. The late nineteenth and early twentieth centuries were not a happy time for ethnic and racial minorities in the United States. Segregation had a legal basis in the Supreme Court's *Plessy v. Ferguson* decision. Racist prejudice was the standard attitude toward the Chinese. The Bolshevik Revolution aroused the fear that Eastern European immigrants would bring communism with them.

American nativist impulses perhaps climaxed during this period. The Ku Klux Klan was organized in 1915 and reached its peak membership in 1923. Americans believed that they were economically and socially threatened by various minorities. Such an influx, they believed, would bring an end to Protestant Anglo-Saxon dominance. After the war, such attitudes led to severe restrictions, culminating in the Johnson-Reed Act of 1924, which based immigration quotas on proportions of the U.S. population as it had been in 1890. These measures directly lashed out at the growth of Jewish, Catholic, and Orthodox communities, and Eastern religions from India and China. Thus, the flow of non-Protestant religions from other lands slowed considerably, not to be revived until after World War II.[12]

Another development of the post-Civil War era that became a permanent feature of American life was a marked shift in the center of power. Prior to the war, the agrarian democracy envisioned by Thomas Jefferson still dominated, although even then the lure of the city had begun to attract individuals of spirit and ambition. Within a generation after the Civil War, the United States was transformed from a predominately agricultural to a manufacturing nation.

By 1890, the factory had outdistanced the farm as the country's chief producer of wealth, and by 1920 the population's center of gravity had shifted decisively to the cities.[13]

For religion this urban trend had two particularly devastating and related consequences. First, large segments of the new urban population—whether migrants from the country to the city or immigrants from Europe—had little contact with the Protestant churches. In fact, many were Catholic, Jewish, or Eastern Orthodox. Second, in respect to religious affiliation, urban growth created a serious cleavage in the urban population. While those able to afford churches were well churched, people who could not were either unchurched or set up alternative religions. In fact, some of the unchurched even regarded church people as their economic oppressors. All of this resulted in a dramatic exodus of Protestant churches from the growing areas of American cities, one that revealed both serious problems in the crumbling Protestant establishment and an increased movement toward religious pluralism.[14]

Intellectual Challenges

Another difference between the old and new America was a dramatic change in the intellectual climate. Geology, pioneered by Charles Lyell (1797-1875), presented a version of the origin and history of the earth that seemed to conflict with the Genesis story. Lyell challenged the biblical account on geological grounds because of the records that the rocks preserved. Needless to say, controversy ensued. And the matter did not stop with geology—in part because the fossil records and geological estimates of the earth's great age made developmental theories of biological evolution increasingly plausible.

Yet the greatest challenge to traditional Christianity and the chief symbol of the new intellectual revolution was the new biology, as set forth by Charles Darwin (1809-1882). Darwin unquestionably became the nineteenth century's Newton, and his theory of evolution through natural selection became the century's cardinal idea. The idea of evolution did not begin with Darwin, of course, and it was to be carried even further by others. The writings of Herbert Spencer (1820-1903) carried the implications of evolutionary thinking into social theory. The doctrine of evolution became a unifying philosophical principle that was applied to all phenomena—social structures, economic developments, race relations, and the growth of nations.[15]

With evolutionary ideas penetrating every realm of thought, a new history began to be written, based on the application of evolutionary theories of learning to the past. In turn, this new historical understanding bolstered the developing "higher criticism" of the Bible, first in Germany and then in Britain and America. Higher criticism studies Scripture from the standpoint of literature, as if the Bible were any other ancient book whose credentials and accuracy had to pass the test of historical methods. This approach resulted in conclusions that shook orthodoxy. Among other things, the critics generally agreed that Moses did not write the first five books of the Bible, that the apostle John did not write the Gospel of John and, of course, that the life of Jesus was different from the story portrayed in the Gospels.[16]

The years after 1830 also witnessed an extensive development of the social sciences. Before the nineteenth century, nearly all efforts to analyze the social environment were restricted to history, economics, and philosophy. The first of the new social sciences was sociology, originated by Auguste Comte (1798-1857) and elaborated by Herbert Spencer. Next came the founding of anthropology, and about 1870 psychology was broken off from philosophy and cultivated as a separate science. After the beginning of the twentieth century, psychologists divided into a number of conflicting schools, with behaviorism and psychoanalysis the two major ones. Behaviorism, originating in the work of the Russian Ivan Pavlov (1856-1939), is an attempt to study the human being as a purely physiological organism—that is, reducing all human behavior to a series of physical responses. Psychoanalysis, founded by the Austrian Sigmund Freud (1856-1939), interprets human behavior mainly in terms of the subconscious or unconscious mind.[17]

These new social sciences maintained some assumptions about human behavior and existence that conflicted with orthodoxy. Yet they did not present such an immediate challenge to Christianity as did the new sciences, the new approach to history, and higher criticism. The social impact of the social sciences—especially psychology—on religion would be tremendous in the post-World War II era. In fact, psychology blended with Eastern religions produced many of the psycho-religions and self-help groups that sprang up during the 1970s and 1980s.[18]

Religious Responses

Religious groups in late nineteenth-century America faced an onslaught of challenges—cultural diversity, migrations, new religions, industrialization, urbanization, and the new intellectual currents. How did they respond? They reacted in a variety of ways. Sometimes they ignored these challenges. But most religious bodies alternated between accommodating and resisting the emerging modern world. Existing sects (e.g., Mennonite groups), whether in America or migrating in, usually remained withdrawn religious bodies. Language barriers or the their subculture helped to insulate them from the broader society. So by and large they ignored or resisted many of the new social and intellectual trends and did not undergo many changes.

Occultic, metaphysical, and other such fringe groups—which were outsiders already—appeared to move in two directions, sometimes simultaneously. Some clung to their traditional beliefs as if the new science did not exist. Other such bodies utilized "pseudoscience" to give empirical evidence to their beliefs. Some new groups, such as Christian Science, came into being claiming to be scientific. In fact, as R. Laurence Moore notes, "virtually every new

American religion of the late nineteenth and early twentieth centuries has offered to prove itself by empirical and objective standards."[19] This statement would also apply to several new evangelical movements.

These evangelicals also moved in both directions. They created new sectarian bodies from the mainline denominations. Rather than accommodate their faith to the world, they chose to resist the new intellectual currents, even if it meant separating from the mainline denominations and establishing new religious bodies. Examples of this option include groups associated with the fundamentalist, holiness, and Pentecostal movements. But many of these sectarian groups sought to prove themselves empirically. For example, Pentecostals believed that healings and tongues-speaking overtly demonstrated the operation of the Holy Spirit. Fundamentalists sought to "prove" the Christian faith by scientific claims.[20]

Theological liberalism offers an example of the accommodation response. According to Bruce Shelley, Protestant liberalism "engaged a problem as old as Christianity itself: how do Christians make their faith meaningful in a new world of thought without distorting or destroying the gospel? The Apostle Paul tried and succeeded. The early Gnostics tried and failed." Many individuals in the mainline churches were faced with a difficult choice. They could hang onto evangelicalism and sacrifice current standards of intellectual respectability. If they were to retain intellectual respectability, it seemed they must either abandon Christianity or modify it to meet the standards of the day. For many the latter choice seemed the only option—but at a price. Liberalism, it would seem, replaced evangelicalism as the consensus by 1930 and became the mainstream.[21]

This movement had two names, *liberalism* and *modernism*, both reflecting its two primary emphases. The movement was liberal in that it stressed freedom from tradition and modern in its focus on adjustment to the modern world. While the movement encompassed a wide variety, some idea of its outlook can be gained by considering three of its methods for saving the Christian faith from the modern intellectual onslaught. First, liberals responded to intellectual challenges by deifying the historical process. This meant that God revealed himself in history and was incarnate in the development of humanity. Liberals felt that the old orthodox Christian idea of God somewhere beyond the universe was unacceptable to the modern mind. So they stressed divine immanence, the idea that God dwells in the world and works through the natural processes. Liberals believed the kingdom of Christ to be the continuing manifestation of the power of God to alter human relationships. To them the Bible was not an encyclopedia of dogma, but a record of the religious experience of an ancient people.[22]

To a large extent, the second and third strategies of liberalism separated Christianity from the intellectual arena. Thus, the liberals sheltered important aspects of the Christian heritage from the challenge of modern thought. The liberals emphasized the ethical component of Christianity. The crucial test for the Christian faith was lifestyle, not doctrine. Liberals reasoned that while traditional theology might collapse before the blistering blasts of modern criticism, the ethics of Jesus would survive. The practical outcome of such ethical emphases came in several varieties, but social concern in the form of the Social Gospel was the most prominent.

The third approach, common to the liberal defense of Christianity, was the belief that religious feelings went to the very core of Christianity. As in their emphasis on ethics, liberals contrasted religious feelings with the religion of reason, dogma, or some literal interpretations of the Bible. Historical criticism and science could not challenge a religion of feelings and intuition, something residing outside the confines of reason. Liberal Christians followed the Romantic and liberal sentiments of their day by allowing science to reign freely in its own domain, while insisting on a realm of religious truth that science could not touch.[23]

In the next two chapters, our concern is with evangelicalism from the Civil War to World War II. How evangelicals dealt with the challenges of the modern world will be noted in some detail, but at this point an overview is in order. The evangelical paradox becomes evident. Conservative Protestants both accommodated and resisted key aspects of the modern America.

For most of the late nineteenth century, evangelicals were oblivious to the impact of American society on them, and instead believed themselves to be in control of American culture. They affirmed the new industrial and capitalistic economic order. America's rise to power both economically and politically was part of God's design to civilize, Americanize, and Christianize the world—so many believed. Evangelicals jumped on the patriotic bandwagon in many ways—supporting American nationalism, the Spanish-American War, World War I, and the anti-communist paranoia following the Bolshevik Revolution. On the whole, they also shared in the hostile American attitudes toward the influx of immigrants and discrimination against blacks.

Still, the evangelicals resisted a number of cultural trends. They responded to the new intellectual challenges toward the Christian faith in a variety of ways—some vigorously defended the historic faith, others separated from the mainstream denominations and created their own movements. And after the terrible denominational conflicts of the 1920s, many evangelicals retreated into their own subculture and rebuilt their own institutions while largely ignoring national affairs.

The New Economic Order

The market economy and the industrial revolution began in America well before the Civil War. In colonial America, the British imposed a number of commercial restrictions, which were a hangover of the old mercantilist policies that prevailed in Europe. Such measures grated on the colonists, ran counter to their spirit of liberty and individualism, and gradually came to an end. Evangelical Christianity and its revivals assisted in this matter. They promoted free choice not only in religion but also in other aspects of life, including the economy. Thus, early national America provided a fertile soil for the growth of both Christianity and the market economy. The industrial revolution also made great strides in early national America. By 1840, the northern cities were bustling with new factories and urban growth. Still, in many ways the America of 1860 would have been recognizable to one living in 1800. The same cannot be said for the America of 1900.

The years following the Civil War witnessed an industrial explosion. The old industries continued to expand and the new industries grew by leaps and bounds. Most important were oil, steel, electricity, railroads, meat-packing, flour, telegraph, telephone, and the automobile. Prior to the Civil War, most industry had been located in the Northeast. It now spread west. America had great resources—a large nation, abundant coal and mineral deposits, fertile land, a mild climate, an adequate labor force swelled by immigrants, innovative business leaders, and a government eager to promote business. By 1900, America had become an industrial giant, even outstripping Great Britain. While agriculture would remain strong, never again would America be predominately an agricultural nation.[24]

The nature of business also changed. Previously, single proprietors, partners, or small companies prevailed. Large-scale production now necessitated a change in business organization. Business monopolies such as pools, trusts, holding companies, and huge corporations dominated the economic scene and crowded out smaller businesses. As a result of business consolidations, 1 percent of the corporations controlled over 33 percent of the nations' productivity. The concentration of economic power thus became a raging issue that continued throughout the twentieth century.

All of these economic changes created a new ruling class. The middle classes—represented by agrarian interests, merchants, professionals, and small manufacturers—declined and were replaced by the masters of the giant corporations. Indeed, America had a new ruling class and wealth became the indispensable ingredient for power and prestige. The successful businessman became the new American hero and "business thinking" became the dominant mode of thought and action. Previously, at various times the national leaders had been the clergy, pioneers, patriots, and statesmen. In the late nineteenth century, the businessman led society and occupied a position analogous to that of the professional athlete or actor/actress in the early twenty-first century.[25]

How did the Protestant churches respond to these economic changes? Did they embrace or challenge the new economic realities? It must be remembered that until the 1920s no clear line separated the evangelical and mainline Protestants. At best, in the late nineteenth century, one could categorize them as the more liberal or orthodox Protestants. And for that matter, there existed little difference in how they responded to the new economic order. Advocates of the Social Gospel did take a different approach, but evangelicals could be found in their ranks. Even those Protestants who focused on the salvation of souls had a social conscience, though their approach might be different from that of the more liberal Protestants.[26]

Embracing Capitalism: Before the Civil War

While there was no standard Protestant response to the new economic developments, on the whole they embraced the market economy. This marriage began well before the Civil War and has continued strong thereafter; and it has not been a marriage of convenience for evangelical Protestantism and capitalism have much in common. Both rest on the pillars of individualism, free choice, and voluntarism. Both must persuade people to buy their product. Prior to the early nineteenth century, the voluntary basis of both the American religious and economic systems were unique to the world and must be seen as a key to the success of both.[27]

In antebellum America, evangelicalism and capitalism shared common values and complemented each other. Separation of church and state gave rise to voluntarism in religion. The lack of government restraints did the same for the economy. Prior to the Civil War, "evangelicals came to assume the God-given character of liberal political economy," notes Mark Noll. In this context, liberal meant "the tradition of individualism associated with John Locke and Adam Smith." The dominant assumptions about economic life emphasized "the freedom of individuals from hierarchical restraint and the formation of community upon unfettered choices of free individuals joined by contract."[28]

Calvinism fostered many middle-class values, which had both religious and business implications—hard work, thrift, self-discipline, self-help as the way to wealth, and even the Christian duty to prosper. Such themes frequented the sermons of the antebellum preachers. Revivalism, fueled by the shift from Calvinism to Arminianism, emphasized the personal freedom and responsibility to acquire salvation—a viewpoint basic to the market economy predicated on individual initiative.[29] By the mid-nineteenth century, "nothing less than a coherent theory of "Christian capitalism" had developed to give sweeping religious and moral sanction to the existing economic order."[30]

Embracing Capitalism: Post-Civil War

After the Civil War, Protestantism and capitalism continued to complement each other. As before the war, religious leaders did not set out to make religion a commodity. But in the competitive religious market, Protestantism had to expand or decline. So embracing a business mentality may have been inevitable. For years the ministers preached an individualistic gospel intended to save souls. Their message now acquired a material dimension and it was applied to the world of big business.[31] Should the government become involved in economic matters? Over this question, Protestants disagreed. But most came down on the conservative side of the question and opposed government intervention.[32] As the government was not to interfere in religious matters, it should not regulate the economy.

This new Protestant ethic merged with Social Darwinism and produced what Henry May has described as "a school of political economy, which might be labeled as clerical laissez-faire."[33] Social Darwinism is the application of Charles Darwin's laws of evolution and natural selection among species to human society. As only the strongest survive in nature, so only the fittest individuals flourish in society and in business. Success came, it was believed, through hard work, thrift, and acquisitiveness—all traditional Protestant virtues. And failure was equally deserved. It came from laziness, carelessness, stupidity, and perhaps even moral weakness. The state should not interfere in this process by rescuing the weak. Indeed, laissez-faire teaching had a firm grip on the Protestant mind and they generally "found the prevailing individualistic social and economic philosophy entirely satisfactory."[34]

For the most part, the American version of the free enterprise system seemed to work. Incredible wealth was made during the Gilded Age. For this and other reasons, most Protestants embraced the new economic order. But all was not well. Many people fell between the cracks of the system and did not share in the nations' wealth. There were serous economic and social problems—crowded urban slums, long work hours, starvation wages, child labor, work-related accidents and illnesses, and periodic unemployment. And evangelicals were not oblivious to these developments.

Not until late in the nineteenth century, however, did they advocate any significant overhaul of the capitalistic order. Prior to that time, most Protestants assumed that the nation's social and economic problems could be remedied in a piecemeal fashion—e.g., hard work, moral virtue, rescue missions, and Christian charity. Because they believed poverty and other social problems to be the result of sin and vice, they could be handled by the older personal ethic. The seventeenth-century Puritan ethic, indeed, had survived with little change into the nineteenth century. Yet it is a myth to say that prior to 1890 evangelicals did not have a social conscience or attempt to alleviate social misery. They engaged in a number of genuine social and humanitarian programs and did not limit themselves to the salvation of souls.[35]

But while they attacked specific problems, they did not seriously critique the system. The free enterprise system—most evangelicals believed—could be humanized, perhaps even Christianized. There were no inherent evils in the system. Great inequities in wealth could be reduced by Christian stewardship, not by modifying the American version of free enterprise. Labor problems could be solved if employers were fair and workers exhibited patience, not by governmental interference. The evils of capitalism, most Protestants believed, were not inherent in the operation of the market economy but temporary glitches.

Along with most Americans, evangelicals saw their economic system as benevolent and that it could be guided by good Christian people.[36]

The Gospel of Wealth

The Gospel of Wealth can be viewed as an attempt either to sanctify laissez-faire economics or to temper the harsh realities of Social Darwinism. Andrew Carnegie saw three sacred laws as indispensable for progress—private property, free competition, and the free accumulation of wealth. Sometimes these laws are hard on individuals but they are best for "the race" because they insure "the survival of the fittest" and a material development that benefits all. If these laws are violated, the material level of all of society will decline. Most important were Carnegie's views regarding the "sacredness of property." Such ideas implied that capitalism was divinely ordained and rested on the commonly held perception of America as a chosen Christian nation. He tempered these views by insisting that a person's wealth should be distributed in ways to benefit society. But indiscriminate charity would only serve to make individuals lazy. Carnegie's views harmonized with similar longstanding Protestant values—the "stewardship of time, money, and talent."[37]

A number of prominent Protestant ministers gave the Gospel of Wealth a Christian twist and effectively propagated it. Best known were Phillips Brooks (1835-1893), Henry Ward Beecher (1813-1887), and Russell Conwell (1843-1925). Both Brooks and Beecher questioned whether poverty existed in America and if so, it had only one cause—sin. And the government had no business alleviating this poverty. To do so would be un-American, said Beecher. "God has intended the great to be great, and the little to be little." Beecher believed that the creation of wealth and genuine Christianity were compatible and closely linked. He sanctified the acquisition of both individual and national wealth, believing both came from God. Such riches, however, had to be used responsibly and for noble purposes. [38]

Most eloquent was Russell Conwell, a Baptist minister who delivered his lecture "Acres of Diamonds" over 6,000 times nationwide. The central theme of Conwell's lecture was that everyone has the Christian responsibility to become wealthy and to use it for the cause of Christ. He echoed Carnegie's contention that the rich were to be wise stewards. But unlike Carnegie, Conwell said that wealth was available to all—there were "acres of diamonds" in everyone's backyard.[39] When asked why he encouraged people to get wealth instead of preaching the gospel, Conwell replied, "Because to make money honestly is to preach the gospel."[40]

The views of Carnegie, Beecher, and Conwell rested on a transformed interpretation of the covenant and America as a chosen nation. Previously the covenant related to America as a nation and to its moral example. The new twist now connected the covenant with both individuals and the nation. God chose the rich for material blessings and privilege because they were righteous. Conversely, the poor were in poverty because God had cursed them for their immorality and laziness.

America as a nation, however, was not left out of God's plans. America had been expanding economically and geographically and needed an explanation for this imperialism. Since God blessed the righteous and cursed the wicked, it only stood to reason that America deserved its growing wealth. Moreover, when the United States expanded economically it should not be viewed as imperialism but as an attempt to improve humankind. And of great importance, while the government and military supported this global economic expansion, it came largely from the private sector.

By the late nineteenth century, many Protestants had indeed sacralized capitalism as they had the nation itself and many aspects of American culture. They believed that God had ordained capitalism and even who would succeed or fail on the battlefield of economic competition. Of course God selected the winners or losers because of their virtue or sinfulness.[41]

Consumerism Emerges

In his book, *An All-Consuming Century*, Gary Cross has described the rise of the consumer society in twentieth-century America. While twentieth-century America has been dominated by consumerism, the roots of this problem go back to the eighteenth century and the means for its implementation can be found in the late nineteenth century. The industrial revolution produced more than the population could afford or consume. Overproduction became the norm, not an exception. A huge gap existed between production and consumption. So something had to be done. People had to be encouraged to buy more and be given the means to do so. The industrialists had to prime the pump of consumption, to increase demand to match production. They realized that they had to teach consumption as a way of life.[42]

Over the years, the manufacturers came up with a number of devices to reshape American economic tastes—credit buying, money-back guarantees, mail order purchasing, and brand names. And most important, they advertised. "Until the late nineteenth century, advertising had been mainly informational." Advertisements were rather dull, usually telling people about prices and the availability of products. Pictures and catchy jingles did not exist. Advertising now took a new twist; it began to persuade people that they needed a particular commodity. Desire was now being created. People were learning to be consumers. Advertisements convinced people of the need to shave on a daily basis, to eat breakfast food, to smoke cigarettes, and to brush their teeth daily. "Early advertising successfully introduced an expansive array of new products and services." Advertising was now teaching people to be consumers and in doing so shaped an ethos that would carry down to the present.[43]

Consumerism and the Churches

What does evangelicalism have to do with all of this? To say that Protestantism caused consumerism would be a tremendous overstatement. Protestants did not cause the new trend of consumerism and they could not control it. They did embrace it, nevertheless. Still, conservative Protestants did not buy into consumerism any more than did their liberal cousins. Both groups fell equally into this trap. The men who preached the Gospel of Wealth, however, gave it a boost. Their sanctification of wealth naturally encouraged the ethos of consumption. As with many aspects of culture, evangelicals had an ambivalent relationship with consumerism. On one hand, evangelicals bought into it and offered little serious critique of the new economic system. On the other, their concept of stewardship helped to take the rough edges off of the crass consumer ethic.[44]

Evangelical Protestants may not have caused consumerism, but they contributed to its rise. Their values of free choice and individualism resonated with the new consumer ethic. Revivalism sanctified choice and opened people up to conversion—not only to the Christian faith but also to many new products, brands, and experiences. Revivalism stressed the emotional and nonrational as did the new approach to advertising. Conversion had now been secularized. As R. Lawrence Moore demonstrates, Christianity had been associated with a consumer culture throughout its history. Jesus had to chase the money-changers from the temple. Merchants flocked to medieval cathedrals and in America peddlers gathered on the fringes of revival meetings.[45]

In the late nineteenth and early twentieth centuries, several Protestant businessmen vigorously promoted the new advertising and consumerism. John Wanamaker (1838-1922), a supporter of Dwight L. Moody and the Sunday School Movement, owned the nation's largest department store and "was pleased that he could translate luxuries into commodities or necessities more rapidly than any other merchant." Asa G. Candler, a devout Methodist, promoted Coca-Cola "with something like evangelistic zeal," and concluded "sales meetings with a group singing of 'Onward Christian Soldiers.'" As a result, Coca-Cola became one of the first products to be widely advertised. Christmas and Easter became heavily commercialized with little objection from the evangelical community. In fact, Wanamaker was at the forefront of this movement.[46]

Two values now clashed—the new consumer ethic and traditional Protestant morals. The new consumer culture exalted acquisition, consumption, leisure, indulgence, impulsive spending, and self-gratification. Along with politics and religion, desire had indeed been democratized. The old Protestant ethic—hard work, frugality, self-denial, self-discipline, civic responsibility, and plain living—were being pushed aside. Advertising now sought "to liberate the middle class from the tyranny of Puritanism...and to convince Americans that desiring, purchasing, and enjoying material goods were salutary rather than sinful," notes Gary Scott Smith. What was once a sin now became acceptable and even desirable.[47]

Evangelicals registered few objections to the new advertisements, except for those regarding cigarettes and alcohol. Evangelical preachers often criticized the new ethic of consumption and self-indulgence. But they were reluctant to attack the structure of the American economy because thousands of successful businessmen financially supported many of the religious enterprises—missions, churches, parachurches, and revivals. What set evangelicals apart from the mainstream culture was their emphasis on stewardship. Possessions were a trust from God and they should be used for his work. So in the end, they Christianized most aspects of money—making money, saving money, and spending money.[48] Consumer capitalism was a giant that evangelicals could not tame.

Moody and the Business World

A host of evangelists paraded across the late nineteenth century landscape, the most prominent by far being Dwight L. Moody (1837-1899). He was to his generation what Finney had been to the pre-Civil War era. Moody, in fact, built on many of the trends initiated by Finney, but his message and methods did not spark controversy as did those of his predecessor. Moody arose from simple beginnings and became a successful shoe salesman before turning to evangelism. He was a homely, self-made, and self-educated man whose approach to revivalism mirrored his background and the culture of the day. He conducted urban revivals in a business-like manner and preached a simple gospel message that appealed to his Victorian middle-class audiences.[49]

Finney, Beecher, and several other preachers conducted revivals in urban areas. The "prayer meeting revival of 1857-58" can be viewed as an urban phenomenon supported by businessmen and related to the changes taking place in technology and mass communications—cheap penny newspapers, installing the Atlantic cable, and a national telegraph system.[50] But it was left for Moody to systematize urban evangelism. He galvanized into religious action church people in cities of millions—London, Chicago, New York, Philadelphia, and Boston. Moody began his urban ministry by working in the Chicago YMCA. After some preaching in smaller areas, he teamed up with singer Ira Sankey and they went to London, where they became a huge success. They returned to America as heroes and launched their massive urban evangelistic campaigns.[51]

Moody epitomized the business climate of the Gilded Age. "The business of conducting revivals is an appropriate term for Moody," states Winthrop Hudson. Corporate America could not have run a revival any better than did Moody. Not only did he look like a businessman, but he preached like a salesman of salvation—a simple, direct, and sentimental message. He organized his revivals like a corporate CEO, leaving little to chance. There were committees for everything—prayer, finances, Bible study, visitation, music, ushering, tickets, and an executive committee to supervise the other committees. Moreover, Moody advertised extensively, utilizing the most current methods of his day. One critic said that it was undignified to advertise religious services. Moody replied that "he thought it more undignified to preach to empty pews." All of this took money. Where did it come from? Moody usually took no collections at his revivals. Rather, he successfully solicited "money, more money" from the wealthy corporate interests of his day.[52]

That Moody could raise considerable sums from the business community, tells us something about his era and his social ethic. According to Thomas Askew, "The list of Moody's sponsors reads like a roster of tycoons": Henry Field, John Wanamaker, J. P. Morgan, Cyrus McCormick, George and J. F. Armour, Cornelius Vanderbilt II, Amos Lawrence, and Joseph Story, to name a few. The social and labor unrest due to crowded urban areas and terrible working conditions made the business community nervous. They hoped that Moody's simple message would improve the morals of the "unchurched masses" in the cities.[53]

While Moody engaged in helping the poor and the downtrodden, he maintained a conservative social ethic. He believed that such social problems could be corrected by converting individuals and improving their morals. "Society could only be reformed by the moral and spiritual regeneration of individuals and that all political, social, and economic reform must be an appendage of revivals," writes William McLoughlin. Like most Protestants of his day, he distanced himself from any serious discussion of the structural ills of society. At times he criticized the greed and selfishness of the business community. But on the whole, he did not attack the rich and powerful who supported his crusades and he usually supported the Republican candidates for political office.[54]

Moody's lack of a social message can be attributed to several sources—the prevailing laissez faire attitude of his day, the usual evangelical emphasis on individualism plus his embrace of premillennialism. Both Finney and Moody engaged in a piece-meal approach to social problems. Both could blame individuals for the social ills of their day. But there was one big difference. Being a postmillennialist, Finney believed the millennium to be at hand and that perhaps more efforts regarding evangelism and social reform would usher it in. By the 1870s, Moody was preaching the doctrine of premillennialism, which believed that the world would get worse and worse until Christ returned to commence the millennium. After the Civil War, conservative Protestants began to question whether the reform efforts of the day could actually improve society. So Moody believed that the world's problems could not be solved until Christ returned.[55]

Moody took a business-like approach to evangelism, but in the pulpit he spoke to the common people in a simple, easy to understand language. Some educated preachers have trouble translating their theology into a message for the people. Moody had no such handicap. His education ended at age thirteen and he never attempted to become an ordained or licensed clergyman. When asked about his theology, he replied, "My theology! I didn't know I had any. I wish you would tell me what my theology is."[56] "Preaching was not an exercise of mind, but an arrow of common sense shot to the heart.... No theology was needed, only a straightforward appeal."[57]

What theology he had could be summed up in the "Three R's": Ruin by Sin, Redemption by Christ, and Regeneration by the Holy Ghost. Saving souls was his mission. "I looked upon this world as a wrecked vessel," he said. And "God has given me a lifeboat and said to me, Moody save all you can."[58] Sydney Ahlstrom summed up his message as a "simple and relatively innocuous blend of American optimism and evangelical Arminianism."[59]

Moody was not a sensationalist like Finney before him or Billy Sunday who came after. But the democratization of Christianity, which began earlier in the century, found a home in the person and message of Moody. Also, he was pragmatic to the core. On commenting about his methods of evangelism, he once said, "it makes no difference how you get a man to God, provided you get him there."[60]

Despite hobnobbing with some of the wealthiest men in America and conducting years of successful revivals, Moody was a man of modest means and he died with little wealth. The same could not be said for his contemporary, the evangelist Sam Jones (1847-1906). He paved the way for the twentieth-century evangelists in two ways. He accumulated considerable wealth and by his antics from the pulpit turned revivalism into a form of entertainment.[61]

Some Social Concern

On the whole, evangelical Protestants embraced the prevailing American economic dogmas of the 1870s and 1880s—success-oriented competitive individualism, free enterprise economics, resistance to government regulation of the production and distribution of wealth, and extreme fear of socialism. Moreover, most evangelicals believed that hard work was the best cure for poverty. Such views were in the mainstream of American social thought during the Gilded Age. Being closely identified with American culture, evangelicals naturally accepted such ideas. But lest one be left with a lopsided impression, it must be noted that until the 1890s evangelicals did exhibit a vigorous social concern.[62]

Thanks to the doctrines of postmillennialism and perfectionism, evangelicals believed the world could be significantly improved. The pillar of the evangelical social conscience consisted of individual acts of charity. Evangelical social concern, however, went beyond individual impulses. Organized efforts including church programs and inner city missions substantially aided the poor. Prior to the rise of the Social Gospel, evangelicals with a holiness orientation took the Protestant lead in this regard. Some evangelicals went beyond organized kindness and even promoted social and moral legislation related to the anti-slavery and temperance movements. The indifference on the part of evangelicals toward poverty and other social issues came after 1890. Many developments pushed evangelicalism in this direction—migrations, urban problems, the rise of premillennialism, intense nationalism, a preoccupation with personal vices, and the fundamentalist reaction to theological liberalism and the Social Gospel.[63]

The Perfectionist Impulse

Not until the 1920s did the Protestant big tent split into two warring factions, the modernists and fundamentalists. These divisions, however, did not come overnight. They had been developing for about fifty years. A number of Protestant groups grew dissatisfied with the direction of nineteenth-century America—urbanism, industrialism, consumerism, increased wealth, a tidal wave of migrations, and many intellectual challenges to the historic Christian faith. When religious groups disapprove of mainstream society and religion, they often split forming sectarian bodies. While not separating, other dissenters formed movements within the mainstream religion.

A host of such movements developed in the nineteenth century. Many fall outside the framework of historic Christianity—for example, Mormonism, the Shakers, Oneida Perfectionists, Jehovah's Witnesses, and Christian Science. But at least four are in the evangelical category—the holiness movement, dispensationalism, Pentecostalism, and fundamentalism. All of these movements have reacted with displeasure at the direction of nineteenth-century America. Dispensationalism, Pentecostalism, and fundamentalism have had their greatest impact in the twentieth century and will be treated in that context. The holiness movement, as demonstrated in the Wesleyan and Reformed traditions, developed in the nineteenth century.

The basic notion of going on to Christian perfection was not new with John Wesley (1703-1791) or the holiness movement. It is as old as Christianity itself. The desire to follow Christ's call "Be perfect, therefore, as your heavenly Father is perfect" (Mt. 5:48) has caused many divisions within Christianity. Monks, nuns, and many groups have harkened to this call. In the late nineteenth century, the perfectionist impulse resulted in the "holiness churches." These churches made the drive for holiness or perfection their primary emphasis. One result of this drive was separation from Christians who did not make perfection a major priority. Therefore, in the holiness movement the drive for perfection produced a separatist tendency that reached explosive proportions in the last years of the nineteenth century.[64]

In the modern sense, the perfectionist impulse originated with John Wesley, who believed that Christ's admonition to be perfect was to be taken literally. Sanctification, or moral growth, could be both instantaneous and progressive. From the time of conversion, said Wesley, the will is progressively freed from the grip of sin. Still, corrupt impulses continued until eliminated by an instantaneous second work of grace. The result would not be sinless perfection but the ability to overcome selfish or sinful desires.[65]

These ideas arrived in America by the early nineteenth century. Here they were nourished by conditions in American society and by several individuals and movements. The early nineteenth century was generally an optimistic time. Arminianism—which had displaced the more gloomy Calvinism—gave people the freedom to approach God for both salvation and sanctification. Jacksonian democracy encouraged people to make choices in politics and religion. Revivals created a hunger for holiness. Vinson Synan draws parallels between the ethical ideals of Henry David Thoreau and Ralph Waldo Emerson and the early holiness movement. In doing so, he views holiness as a kind of "evangelical transcendentalism." Religious leaders preached a postmillennialism that pointed to a golden age here on earth and inspired people to work for a perfect society. By the 1840s, perfectionism had become "one of the central themes of American social, intellectual, and religious life." And it prompted a number of reform movements intended to perfect American life—temperance, anti-masonry, women's rights, and the abolition of slavery.[66]

After the Civil War, liberalism contributed to the perfectionist impulse. Rather than doctrine, the liberals emphasized the ethical aspect of Christianity. This form of holiness could be generated by human efforts. The holiness movement can be seen as a mirror image of this modernist theme: "the stress on morality." Unlike liberalism, however, the holiness movement did not emphasize innate human goodness as the key to morality. Instead, its members asserted "that nothing less than a dramatic work of the Holy Spirit could cleanse the heart of sin." The increasing wealth within American society and the churches in particular also played a role. Holiness groups, often of the lower social classes, objected to this trend and formed their own denominations.[67]

The holiness movement in the late nineteenth century can be seen from the vantage point of specific religious traditions. But in a more general sense, it can be viewed from three perspectives. It can be seen as a continuation of the perfectionist impulse from the early nineteenth century—for example, the work of Phoebe Palmer and Charles Finney, Oberlin Theology, several humanitarian movements, and even postmillennialism. Two, as evangelicals became disillusioned with the course of American society, they turned inward and sought the perfection of a "subjective inner kingdom." Last, the holiness movement represents an expression of populism—it was driven largely by the common people, not the elite.[68]

Methodist Holiness

Methodists in America built on Wesley's doctrine of sanctification, but they tended to compress it into three stages—the unconverted, converted, and entire sanctification. Phoebe Worrall Palmer (1807-1874)—the leading proponent of Methodist sanctification before the Civil War—blended revivalism with Wesleyan perfectionism. Her altar call for sanctification consisted of three steps: "consecrating oneself entirely to God; believing God keeps his promise to sanctify; and witnessing to what God has done."[69] Sanctification did not come through a gradual struggle with sin but by means of an instantaneous experience, which she regarded as a second conversion. She also modified Wesley's doctrine by linking this "second blessing, as it came to be known, with the baptism of the Holy Spirit." Several holiness denominations—the Free and Wesleyan Methodists, the Church of the Nazarene, and the Salvation Army—adopted her theology.[70]

Despite much displeasure, prior to the Civil War most holiness bodies remained within mainstream Methodism. The exceptions were the Wesleyan and Free Methodists who broke in 1843 and 1860, respectively. By the mid-1870s, however, serious problems emerged. Once a plain living people, the Methodists now acquired a measure of wealth. They began to dress fashionably and build large churches with choirs and instrumental music. More troubling was the change in lifestyle. Church members began to dance, attend theaters, play cards, and cease attending revivals. Tremendous differences arose over culture and lifestyle. At first, the dissenters formed a church within a church—the holiness associations—and church leaders struggled to keep them within the denomination. In these circles, however, a separatistic "come-outer" movement began to arise. Between 1880 and 1895, some 100,000 dissidents broke from the church and formed a number of sectarian organizations. The largest of these were the Church of the Nazarene and the Pilgrim Holiness Church. Some non-Methodist denominations—the Church of God (Anderson, Indiana), the Salvation Army, Brethren in Christ, and others—adopted the Methodist view of sanctification.[71]

Reformed Holiness

Does Methodism have a corner on holiness? No! While not as pronounced as in Wesleyanism, the Reformed tradition has its holiness impulse. The Congregationalists, Presbyterians, Baptists, and other groups were inspired by a non-Wesleyan or Reformed brand of holiness. The Reformed tradition takes a dimmer view of human nature than does Arminianism, which believes that Christ's death has endowed people with the ability to turn to God. The Reformed holiness variety encouraged a second moment of grace, but it did not have the same results as it did with Methodism. It believed sin to be inbred in human nature, so it could never be eradicated. The second blessing, it insisted, could empower the will to embrace godliness—not purify the heart.[72]

The Reformed version of holiness flowed from two sources—Oberlin Perfectionsim and the Keswick Higher Life Movement. Two successive presidents at Oberlin College—Asa Mahan (1799-1889) and Charles G. Finney—largely framed the doctrine of Oberlin Perfectionism. This doctrine said that perfection of the will is available to every Christian after conversion. Finney blended this Wesleyan perfectionism with his "new measures" revivalism and took it to the Congregationalists and Presbyterians. He differed from the Methodists, however, in that he tended to see the "second conversion" as more gradual than instantaneous and a more perfect obedience to moral law than as submission to divine law. Of importance, unlike private holiness this Oberlin theology advocated social reform and Oberlin College became a hotbed of Christian activism.[73]

The second stream of Reformed holiness took its name from a conference held in Keswick, England. The Methodists did not dominate these meetings so Calvinism colored their approach toward holiness. Rather than eradicate the inclination toward sin in the believer as the Arminians contended, the Keswick teachers taught that the second work of grace suppressed it. The sinful nature still exists but it need not have power over the believer. And this second blessing did not purify the heart as much as it empowered the believer to serve God and humanity. In the 1880s and 1890s, this Keswick teaching crossed the Atlantic to be voiced at the celebrated Northfield Conferences organized by Dwight Moody. From this source, this "somewhat de-Wesleyanized version of holiness" spread rapidly among evangelicals. It found a home among the "Calvinistic oriented premillennialists," including some prominent dispensationalists—C. I. Scofield, R. A. Torrey, A. J. Gordon, and Harry A. Ironside. When combined with John Nelson Darby's dispensational premillennialism, the Keswick version of holiness became a pillar of American evangelicalism in the early twentieth century.[74]

The White Man's Burden

The years from the Civil War to World War I saw a dramatic increase in Protestant missions. Prompted by Moody's revivals, the primary motive for this surge was spiritual. Many people had been won to the Lord by the nineteenth-century revivals, and sincere people desired to spread the gospel throughout the world. A number of societies arose to implement this impulse. After the Second Great Awakening, state, regional, and national mission societies spearheaded the effort. By the end of the century, three new movements led the charge to win the world for Christ—faith missions, Bible institutes, and the Student Volunteer Movement.[75]

Even this worthy endeavor cannot be divorced from secular events, especially the more vigorous role that America began to play in global affairs. By the end of the century, the United States had become an economic giant. Foreign trade had increased and businessmen desired foreign markets. So

America's foreign policy became more aggressive—negotiating trade agreements, establishing naval bases, and encroaching upon the Hawaiian Islands. The new temper contributed to the Spanish-American War and the imperialism that followed. After this war, the United States acquired Puerto Rico, Guam, the Philippines, other Pacific islands and built the Panama Canal. Meanwhile, America also dominated areas of the Caribbean and began to intervene in China. This territorial expansion and aggressive foreign policy became known as "dollar diplomacy." Americans, including political and religious leaders, were divided over this imperialism. A majority appeared to sanction it, but a substantial minority—including evangelicals such as William Jennings Bryan (1860-1925)—opposed this expansion.[76]

From 1830 to 1880, most missionary sermons urged obedience to Christ's Great Commission—"go and make disciples of all nations."(Mt. 28:18-20). But late in the century, a secondary motive gained importance: the spread of Christian or Anglo-Saxon civilization. Nurtured by American nationalism and a sense of Manifest Destiny, many equated Western, especially American civilization with Christianity. At first, both evangelical and liberal Protestants pushed the idea of Christianity furthering civilization. As time went on, however, liberals promoted it more than evangelicals. Spearheading this effort was Josiah Strong (1847-1916), a champion of both missions and social reform. In his 1885 best-selling book, *Our Country*, he saw Anglo-Saxon civilization as God's instrument to redeem the world. The Anglo-Saxon race had two great principles to offer the world—"civil liberty" (the love of liberty) and "spiritual Christianity." The world's future depended on the adoption of these ideas, and it was America's job—primarily through missionary efforts—to spread such beliefs. This rhetoric by Strong and others spurred the advance of missions.[77]

Like many of his contemporaries, Strong held to what would now be regarded as racist views, namely, the superiority of the Anglo-Saxon race. Relying on Social Darwinist beliefs, he believed this notion to be a proven scientific fact. He clearly saw the Anglo-Saxon civilizations as morally and materially supreme. Other civilizations were either past their prime, decadent, or uncivilized. They had been surpassed by this vigorous Anglo-Saxon Protestant civilization. He did not, however, relegate Anglo-Saxon to a racial strain or define it in terms of blood. Rather, he defined Anglo-Saxon as a tradition of liberty and spirituality. Other peoples could adopt these values. And as Rudyard Kipling said, it was "the white man's burden," to lift up such peoples.[78]

Entering the New Century

How did evangelicals enter the twentieth century? Was the "evangelical empire" still intact? Or, as Douglas Frank puts it, did they enter the twentieth century as "less than conquerors?" Actually, one could make a case for both interpretations. On the surface, evangelical Protestantism was still vigorous.

Church numbers were strong. Beautiful churches had been built. The late nineteenth century must be regarded as the great age of Protestant missions. Protestantism had not yet split into two mutually hostile camps—the liberals and fundamentalists. Of great importance, evangelical Protestantism still dominated the cultural scene. American values bore the stamp of this Anglo-Saxon Protestant ascendancy. The political, cultural, religious, and intellectual leaders of the nation were largely of a Northern European Protestant stock, and they propagated public morals compatible with their background.

But appearances can be deceptive. The "evangelical empire" had developed serious cracks. Its dominance assumed an Anglo-Saxon Protestant population. But this went by the wayside. In the late nineteenth century, migrations had changed America into a diverse pluralistic society. There existed strong cultural and religious alternatives to Anglo-Saxon Protestantism. Evangelical Protestant cultural values also had a rural, small-town ethos. This was also becoming a thing of the past. With industrialization, Americans moved from the country to the city where they often became unchurched and abandoned their Protestant morals.

Industrialization also brought great wealth to America, and on the whole, evangelicals bought into the capitalism and consumerism of the age. Perhaps of greater importance, Protestantism experienced serious intellectual challenges from science and higher criticism. Protestants struggled with these new intellectual currents, but on the whole, their disagreements were papered over until the 1920s. Not all Protestants accepted the flow of American culture. So even before the great rupture of the 1920s a number of dissident movements arose—the holiness movement, Pentecostalism, dispensationalism, and fundamentalism.

Prior to the Civil War, evangelical Protestantism largely set the tone for American culture. After mid-century, the opposite occurred—Protestantism became thoroughly Americanized. Unfortunately, most evangelicals were not aware of what had happened. They had come to believe that American and Christian values were one and the same. But in the years to come, they would be painfully aware of the unreality of this situation. The "evangelical empire," had some serious cracks, but had not ruptured in two. And when it did, evangelical Protestantism could not hope to maintain its cultural dominance.

Notes

1.   Douglas W. Frank, *Less Than Conquerors* (Grand Rapids: Eerdmans, 1986), 2.
2.   *Church of the Holy Trinity v. United States*, 143 U.S. as quoted by Joseph Tussman, ed., *The Supreme Court on Church and State* (New York: Oxford University Press, 1962), 41.
3.   Ernest Lee Tuveson, *Redeemer Nation* (Chicago: University of Chicago Press, 1968), 137 (quote); Josiah Strong, *The New Era, or The Coming Kingdom* (New York: Baker and Taylor, 1893), 354.

4. Quoted in William G. McLoughlin, Jr., *Modern Revivalism* (New York: Ronald Press, 1959), 310.
5. Robert Handy, *A Christian America: Protestant Hopes and Realities* (New York: Oxford University Press, 1984), 99, 101,105,117, 123.
6. Edwin Scott Gaustad, *Historical Atlas of Religion in America* (New York: Harper and Row, 1976), 44; Sydney E. Ahlstrom, *A Religious History of the American People* (New Haven, CT: Yale University Press, 1972), 843.
7. Sidney E. Mead, *The Lively Experiment* (New York: Harper and Row, 1963), 156, 157; Ahlstrom, *Religious History*, 843-46; Handy, *Christian America*, 120, 121.
8. Robert T. Handy, *The Protestant Quest for a Christian America, 1830-1930* (Philadelphia: Fortress Press, 1967), 16 (quote); R. Laurence Moore, *Touchdown Jesus: The Mixing of Sacred and Secular in American History* (Louisville: Westminster John Knox Press, 2003), 31-34.
9. George Marsden, *Religion and American Culture* (New York: Harcourt Brace, 1990), 98; Handy, *Christian America*, 159-84 (quote is the chapter title).
10. Richard Brown, *The Transformation of American Life 1600-1865* (New York: Hill and Wang, 1976), 4; Thomas C. Cochran and William Miller, *The Age of Enterprise*, rev. ed. (New York: Harper and Row, 1961); Samuel P. Hays, *The Response to Industrialism, 1885-1914* (Chicago: University of Chicago Press, 1957); Allan Nevins, *The Emergence of Modern America* (Chicago: Quadrangle Books, 1971); Robert Walker, *Life in the Age of Enterprise* (New York: Capricorn Books, 1971).
11. Ahlstrom, *Religious History*, 789; Catherine Albanese, *America: Religions and Religion* (Belmont, CA: Wadsworth, 1981), 197, 205-10; Marcus Lee Hanson, *The Immigrant in American History* (Cambridge, MA: Harvard University Press, 1948); Maldwyn A. Jones, *American Immigration* (Chicago: University of Chicago Press, 1960); Philip Taylor, *The Distant Magnet: European Emigration to the U.S.A.* (New York: Harper and Row, 1971); Oscar Handlin, *The Uprooted* (New York: Grosset and Dunlap, 1951).
12. Mark Noll et al., eds., *Eerdman's Handbook to Christianity in America* (Grand Rapids: Eerdmans, 1983), 374; Handlin, *The Uprooted*, 186-300; John Higham, *Strangers in the Land: Patterns of American Nativitism, 1860-1925* (New York: Atheneum, 1971), 131-57, 234-63; Stuart C. Miller, *The Unwelcome Immigrant: The American Image of the Chinese, 1785-1882* (Berkeley: University of California Press, 1969); C. Vann Woodward, *The Strange Career of Jim Crow*, 3rd ed. (New York: Oxford University Press, 1974).
13. Winthrop S. Hudson and John Corrigan, *Religion in America*, 6th ed. (Upper Saddle River, NJ: Prentice Hall, 1999), 210, 211; Dennis Cashman, *America in the Gilded Age* (New York: New York University Press, 1984); 10-46, 110-42; Robert H. Walker, *Life in the Age of Enterprise, 1865-1900* (New York: Capricorn Books, 1971); Zane Miller, *Urbanization of Modern America* (New York: Harcourt Brace, 1973), 25-145; Constance McLaughlin Green, *The Rise of Urban America* (New York: Harper and Row, 1965), 85-106.
14. Ahlstrom, *Religious History*, 738.
15. Ahlstrom, *Religious History,* 210; Mary Bednarowski, *American Religion* (Englewood Cliffs, NJ: Prentice Hall, 1984), 38-39; Cynthia Eagle Russett, *Darwin in America: The Intellectual Response, 1865-1912* (San Francisco: W.H. Freeman, 1976), 1-43, 89-110; Bert James Loewenberg, *Darwinism Comes to America, 1859-1900* (Philadelphia: Fortress, 1969).
16. R. K. Harrison, "Higher Criticism," in *Evangelical Dictionary of Theology*, ed. Walter A. Elwell (Grand Rapids: Baker Books, 1984), 511-12; Bruce Shelley, *Church History in Plain Language* (Waco: TX: Word Books, 1982), 240.

17. Roland N. Stromberg, *An Intellectual History of Modern Europe*, 2nd ed. (Englewood Cliffs, NJ: Prentice Hall, 1975), 375-78.
18. Richard Kyle, *The Religious Fringe: A History of Alternative Religions In America* (Downers Grove: IL: InterVarsity Press, 1993), 102, 103.
19. R. Laurence Moore, *In Search of White Crows* (New York: Oxford University Press, 1977), 235.
20. Ahlstrom, *Religious History*, 805-24, 827, 840; R. Laurence Moore, *Religious Outsiders and the Making of Americans* (New York: Oxford University Press, 1986); Arthur M. Schlesinger Sr., *A Critical Period in American Religion, 1875-1900* (Philadelphia: Fortress Press), 11-14; Roger Robins, "A. J. Tomlinson: Plainfolk Modernist," in *Portraits of a Generation: Early Pentecostal Leaders*, ed. James R. Goff, Jr. and Grant Wacker (Fayetteville, AR: University of Arkansas Press, 2002), 347, 348.
21. Shelley, *Church History in Plain Language*, 416 (quote); Kenneth Cauthen, *The Impact of American Religious Liberalism* (New York: Harper and Row, 1962), 4-17; William R. Hutchison, *The Modernist Impulse in American Protestantism* (Cambridge, MA: Harvard University Press, 1976).
22. Noll, *Christianity in America*, 322; Cauthen, *Impact of American Religious Liberalism*, 209-220; Hutchison, *Modernist Impulse*, 76-110.
23. Noll, *Christianity in America*, 322-23; Cauthen, *Impact of Religious Liberalism*, 209-20; Ahlstrom, *Religious History*, 779-80; Hutchison, *Modernist Impulse*, 74
24. Thomas A. Askew and Peter W. Spellman, *The Churches and the American Experience* (Grand Rapids: Baker Books, 1984), 154,155; Ray Ginger, *Age of Excess*, 2nd ed. (Prospect Heights, IL: Waveland Press, 1975), 36-54; Glenn Porter, "Industrialization and the Rise of Big Business," in *The Gilded Age*, ed. Charles W. Calhoun (Wilmington, DE: SR Books, 1996), 1-18; Robert Higgs, *The Transformation of the American Economy, 1865-1914* (New York: John Wiley, 1971); Ray Ginger, *Age of Excess* (Prospect Heights, IL: Waveland Press, 1989), 19-54.
25. Askew, *Churches and the American Experience*, 155-57; Robert H. Wiebe, *The Search for Order 1877-1920* (New York: Hill and Wang, 1967), 27-30; Alan T. Trachtenberg, *The Incorporation of America: Culture and Society in the Gilded Age* (New York: Hill and Wang, 1982); Matthew Josephson, *The Robber Barons* (New York: Harcourt Brace, 1962).
26. George Marsden, "The Gospel of Wealth, the Social Gospel, and the Salvation of Souls in Nineteenth-Century America," *Fides et Historia* 5, 1 (spring 1973): 12-14.
27. Mark A. Noll, "Introduction," in *God and Mammon: Protestants, Money, and the Market, 1790-1860*, ed. Mark A. Noll (New York: Oxford University Press, 2001), 18; Daniel Walker Howe, "Charles Sellers, the Market Revolution, and the Shaping of Identity in Whig-Jacksonian America," in *God and Mammon*, 63; Charles Sellers, *The Market Revolution: Jacksonian American, 1815-1846* (New York: Oxford University Press, 1991); George Thomas, *Revivalism and Cultural Change: Christianity, Nation Building, and the Market in Nineteenth Century United States* (Chicago: University of Chicago Press, 1989); Roger Finke and Rodney Stark, *The Churching of America 1776-1990* (New Brunswick, NJ: Rutgers University Press, 1992), 54-108; Stuart Bruchey, *Enterprise: The Dynamic Economy of a Free People* (Cambridge, MA: Harvard University Press, 1990).
28. Mark A. Noll, *The Scandal of the Evangelical Mind* (Grand Rapids: Eerdmans, 1994), 75 (quote). See Mark A. Noll, *America's God* (New York: Oxford University Press, 2002), 565.
29. Richard W. Pointer, "Philadelphia Presbyterians, Capitalism, and the Morality of Economic Success," in *God and Mammon*, 172; R. Laurence Moore, *Selling God:*

American Religion in the Marketplace of Culture (New York: Oxford University Press, 1994), 177; George M. Thomas, *Revivalism and Cultural Change* (Chicago: University of Chicago Press, 1989), 67-70; Steven J. Keillor, *This Rebellious House* (Downers Grove, IL: InterVarsity Press, 1996), 158.

30. Pointer, "Presbyterians, Capitalism, and Economic Success," 172.

31. Moore, *Selling God,* 119; Martin E. Marty, *Righteous Empire: The Protestant Experience in America* (New York: Dial Press, 1970), 149; Roger Finke and Laurence R. Iannaccone, "Supply-Explanations for Religious Change," *Annals of the American Academy of Political and Social Science* 527 (May 1993): 29-33; Keillor, *Rebellious House*, 158.

32. Robin Klay and John Lunn with Michael S. Hamilton, "American Evangelicalism and the National Economy, 1870-1997," in *More Money, More Ministry*, ed. Larry Eskridge and Mark A. Noll (Grand Rapids: Eerdmans, 2000) 22, 23; Henry F. May, *Protestant Churches and Industrial America* (New York: Harper Torchbook, 1967).

33. May, *Protestant Churches and Industrial America*, 14 (quote); Mead, *Lively Experiment,* 150.

34. Handy, *Christian America*, 66.

35. Marsden, "The Gospel of Wealth," 14, 15; Handy, *Christian America*, 137; Meade, *Lively Experiment*, 159; Timothy L. Smith, *Revivalism and Social Reform* (Baltimore, MD: Johns Hopkins University Press, 1980), Frank, *Less Than Conquerors*, 131,132.

36. Frank, *Less Than Conquers,* 35, 36; Marsden, "The Gospel of Wealth," 17, 18; Mead, *Lively Experiment,* 139.

37. Hudson, *Religion in America*, 297-99 (quotes); J. C. Brown, "Social Darwinism," in *Dictionary of Christianity in America*, ed. Daniel G. Reid et al. (Downers Grove, IL: InterVarsity, 1990), 1238, 1239; Meade, *Lively Experiment*, 158,159; Andrew Carnegie, "Wealth," in *The Role of Religion in American Life: An Interpretative Historical Anthology,* ed. Robert Mathisen (Dubuque, IA: Kendall/Hunt, 1994), 168, 173; Richard T. Hughes, *Myths America Lives By* (Urbana: University Illinois Press, 2004), 131, 132.

38. Marty, *Righteous Empire,* 150 (quote); Winthrop Hudson, *The Great Tradition of the American Churches* (New York: Harper and Row, 1953), 181; Meade, *Lively Experiment*, 160; Hughes, *Myths America Lives By*, 129, 130; Henry Ward Beecher, "The Tendencies of American Progress," in *God's New Israel: Religious Interpretation of American Destiny,* rev. ed., ed. Conrad Cherry (Chapel Hill: University of North Carolina Press, 1998), 237, 242, 245.

39. Hudson, *Great Tradition of American Churches,* 180-83; R. R. Conwell, *Acres of Diamonds,* (New York: Harper and Brothers, 1890); A. R. Burr, *Russell Conwell and His Work* (Philadelphia: John C. Winston, 1917); Hughes, *Myths America Lives By*, 129.

40. Conwell, *Acres of Diamonds*, quoted in *Sources of the American Mind: A Collection of Documents and Texts in American History,* 2 vols., ed. Loren Baritz (New York: John Wiley and Sons, 1966), 2: 41; Hudson, *Great Tradition of the American Churches*, 180-86.

41. The material in the last three paragraphs has been drawn from Hughes, *Myths America Lives By*, 130, 134, 135; James Oliver Robertson, *American Myth, American Reality* (New York: Hill and Wang, 1980), 372; Emily S. Rosenberg, *Spreading the American Dream: American Economic and Cultural Expansion, 1890-1995* (New York: Hill and Wang, 1982), 22.

42. Gary Cross, *An All-Consuming Century* (New York: Columbia University Press, 2000); Rodney Clapp, "Why the Devil Takes Visa," *Christianity Today* (October

1996): 24; William Leach, *Land of Desire: Merchants, Power, and the Rise of a New American Culture* (New York: Pantheon Books, 1993).

43. Clapp, "Devil Takes Visa," 24, 25 (quotes). See Richard Wightman Fox and T. J. Jackson Lears, eds., *The Culture of Consumption: Critical Essays in American Cultural History, 1880-1930* (New York: Pantheon Books, 1983); Daniel Horowitz, *The Morality of Spending: Attitudes Toward Consumer Society in America, 1875-1940* (Baltimore, MD: Johns Hopkins Press, 1985).

44. Gary Scott Smith, "Evangelicals Confront Corporate Capitalism: Advertising, Consumerism, Stewardship, and Spirituality, 1880-1930," in *More Money, More Ministry*, 53, 56-58, 79; Clapp, "Devil Takes Visa," 24, 25; Leigh Eric Schmidt, *Consumer Rites: The Buying and Selling of American Holidays* (Princeton, NJ: Princeton University Press, 1995), 14.

45. Moore, *Selling God*, 5-10; Finke and Stark, *Churching of America*, 59-106.

46. Clapp, "Devil Takes Visa," 23 (quotes); Smith, "Evangelicals Confront Capitalism," 45, 55; Frank Presbrey, *The History and Development of Advertising* (New York: Greenwood Press, 1969), 330-36; Schmidt, *Consumer Rites*, 159-67; Colleen McDannell, *Material Christianity: Religion and Popular Culture in America* (New Haven, CT: Yale University Press, 1995); Moore, *Selling God*, 205; Leigh Eric Schmidt, "The Easter Parade: Piety, Fashion, and Display" in *Religion in American History*, ed. Jon Butler and Harry S. Stout (New York: Oxford University Press, 1998), 346-65.

47. Smith, "Evangelicals Confront Capitalism,"39, 40,41,58,62,72,78,79 (quote on 41).

48. Frank, *Less Than Conquers,* 40-46, 123-29; Leach, *Land of Desire,* 197-209, 214, 220; Smith, "Evangelicals Confront Capitalism," 39, 40, 58, 62, 72, 78, 79.

49. Marsden, *Religion and American Culture*, 115, 116; George M. Marsden, *Fundamentalism and American Culture* (New York: Oxford University Press), 32, 33; J. F. Findlay, *Dwight L. Moody: American Evangelist, 1837-1899* (Grand Rapids: Baker Books, 1973), 40-53; Razelle Frankl, *Televangelism: The Marketing of Popular Religion* (Carbondale: Southern Illinois University Press, 1987), 4; Bruce J. Evensen, *God's Man for the Gilded Age: D. L. Moody and the Rise of Mass Evangelism* (New York: Oxford University Press, 2003).

50. Kathryn Teresa Long, *The Revival of 1857-58* (New York: Oxford University Press, 1998); Kathryn Long, "The Power of Interpretation: The Revival of 1857-58 and the Historiography of Revivalism in America," *Religion and American Culture* 4, 1 (winter 1994): 77-105; William G. McLoughlin, *Revivals, Awakenings, and Reform* (Chicago: University of Chicago Press, 1978), 141, 142; Kathryn T. Long, "Turning…Piety into Hard Cash: The Marketing of Nineteenth-Century Revivalism," in *God and Mammon*, 237.

51. Bernard A. Weisberger, *They Gathered at the River: The Story of the Great Revivalists and Their Impact upon Religion in America* (New York: Octagon Books, 1979), 176, 206, 217; Findlay, *Moody*, 54-82.

52. Hudson, *Religion in America,* 228, 229 (quotes); Findlay, *Moody*, 192-225; Frank, *Less Than Conquers*, 169; Moore, *Selling God*, 186; Evensen, *God's Man for the Gilded Age*.

53. Askew, *Churches and the American Experience*, 131, 132 (quotes); Findlay, *Moody*, 201, 202; Charles E. Hambrick-Stowe, "Sanctified Business: Historical Perspectives on Financing Revivals of Religion," in *More Money, More Ministry*, 89, 92.

54. William G. McLoughlin, Jr., *Modern Revivalism* (New York: Ronald Press, 1959), 169, 170 (quotes); Askew, *Churches and the American Experience*, 131, 132; Marsden, *Fundamentalism and American Culture*, 36; McLoughlin, *Revivals, Awakenings and Reform*, 143; Richard Hofstadter, *Anti-Intellectualism in American Life* (New York: Vintage Book, 1963), 110, 111.

55. Richard Kyle, *The Last Days Are Here Again: A History of the End Times* (Grand Rapids: Baker Books, 1998), 104, 105; McLoughlin, *Modern Revivalism*, 256, 257; Timothy Weber, *Living in the Shadow of the Second Coming*, rev. ed. (Chicago: University of Chicago Press, 1987), 32, 33; Stanley N. Gundry, *Love Them In: The Proclamation Theology of D. L. Moody* (Chicago: Moody Press, 1976), 180, 181; Russell Chandler, *Doomsday* (Ann Arbor, MI: Servant, 1993), 104, 106; Martin E. Marty, *Righteous Empire.*

56. Quoted in Askew, *Churches and the American Experience*, 131.

57. Weisberger, *They Gathered at the* River, 212 (quote).

58. Quoted in George M. Marsden, *Understanding Fundamentalism and Evangelicalism* (Grand Rapids: Eerdmans, 1991), 21; Gundry, *Love Them In*, 87-130.

59. Ahlstrom, *Religious History*, 745 (quote).

60. Quoted in Hofstadter, *Anti-Intellectualism in American Life*, 85.

61. Hambrick-Stowe, "Sanctified Business," 93, 97; McLoughlin, *Modern Revivalism*, 282-346; Weisberger, *They Gathered at the River,* 233-35, 241-42.

62. Marsden, "Gospel of Wealth," 14, 17, 18; Marsden, *Fundamentalism and American Culture,* 80-85.

63. Smith, *Revivalism and Social Reform*, 148-77; Marsden, "Gospel of Wealth," 14, 17, 18; Marsden, *Fundamentalism and Evangelicalism*, 233-35, 241-42; Richard V. Pierard, *The Unequal Yoke: Evangelical Christianity and Political Conservatism* (Philadelphia: Lippincott, 1970), 29-33; David O. Moberg, *The Great Reversal* (Philadelphia: Lippincott, 1977).

64. J. Gordon Melton, *The Encyclopedia of American Religions*, 2 vols. (Wilmington, NC: McGrath, 1978), 1:199; Edwin Scott Gaustad, *Historical Atlas of Religion in America* (New York: Harper and Row, 1976), 122; Vinson Synan, *The Holiness-Pentecostal Movement in the United States* (Grand Rapids: Eerdmans, 1971), 53; Frederick A. Norwood, *The Story of American Methodism* (Nashville: Abingdon, 1974), 292-94.

65. Grant Wacker, "The Holiness Movement," in *Eerdmans' Handbook to Christianity in America*, 332; Colin W. Williams, *John Wesley's Theology Today* (Nashville: Abingdon, 1960), 167-90; Robert G. Tuttle, *John Wesley, His Life and Theology* (Grand Rapids: Zondervan, 1978); Paul A. Mickey, *Essentials of Wesleyan Theology* (Grand Rapids: Zondervan, 1980).

66. Synan, *Holiness-Pentecostal Movement*, 28 (quotes); Askew, *Churches and the American Experience*, 135.

67. Noll, *Christianity in America*, 331, 332 (quotes); Hudson, *Religion in America,* 332; Timothy L. Smith, "Righteousness and Hope: Christian Holiness and the Millennial Vision in America, 1800-1900," *American Quarterly* 31, 1 (1979): 21-45.

68. Mark A. Noll, *A History of Christianity in the United States and Canada* (Grand Rapids: Eerdmans, 1992), 380, 381 (quote); Frank, *Less Than Conquerors*, 118-23.

69. Charles E. White, "Phoebe Worrall Palmer," in *Dictionary of Christianity in America*, 860, 861 (quotes). See Harold E. Raser, *Phoebe Palmer: Her Life and Thought* (Lewiston, NY: Edwin Mellen Press, 1987).

70. Wacker, "Holiness Movement," 333 (quotes); Norwood, *American Methodism,* 294-301.

71. Hudson, *Religion in America*, 332, 333; Wacker, "Holiness Movement," 333 334; Norwood, *American Methodism*, 292-301; Melvin E. Dieter, *The Holiness Revival of the Nineteenth Century* (Metuchen, NJ: Scarecrow Press, 1980); Harold E. Raser, "Holiness Movement," in *Dictionary of Christianity in America*, 543-46; Ahlstrom, *Religious History*, 817.

72. Wacker, "Holiness Movement," 334; Raser, "Holiness Movement," 544, 545; Norwood, *American Methodism*, 292-301.
73. Roger J. Green, "Oberlin Theology," in *Dictionary of Christianity in America*, 834; Donald W. Dayton, *Discovering an Evangelical Heritage* (New York: Harper and Row, 1976), 15-24; Charles Finney, *Finney's Systematic Theology* (Minneapolis: Bethany Fellowship, 1976), 12-31; Raser, "Holiness Movement," 544.
74. Frank, *Less Than Conquerers*, 114 (quotes); Raser, "Holiness Movement," 546; Bruce L. Shelley, "Keswick Movement," in *Dictionary of Christianity in America*, 612, 613; Wacker, "Holiness Movement," 334, 335; John D. Woodbridge, Mark A. Noll, and Nathan O. Hatch, *The Gospel in America: Themes in the Story of America's Evangelicals* (Grand Rapids: Zondervan, 1979), 74; D. G. Hart, *That Old-time Religion in Modern America: Evangelical Protestantism in the Twentieth Century* (Chicago: Ivan R. Dee, 2002), 74.
75. Askew, *Churches and the American Experience*, 168; B. Harder, "The Student Volunteer Movement for Foreign Missions and Its Contribution to 20th Century Missions," *Missiology* 8 (1980): 141-154; George M. Marsden, *Understanding Fundamentalism and Evangelicalism* (Grand Rapids: Eerdmans, 1991), 23.
76. Robert H. Wiebe, *The Search for Order* (New York: Hill and Wang: 1967), 224-48; Lewis L. Gould, *The Spanish-American War and President McKinley* (Lawrence: University Press of Kansas, 1982); Hudson, *Religion in America,* 308, 309; Foster Rhea Dulles, *America's Rise to World Power* (New York: Harper Torchbooks, 1963); Sean Dennis Cashman, *America in the Gilded Age* (New York: New York University Press, 1984), 312-30; Nell Painter, *Standing at Armageddon* (New York: Norton, 1987), 141-50.
77. Hudson, *Religion in America,* 310, 311 (quote); Josiah Strong, *Our Country: Its Possible Future and Its Present Crisis,* ed. Jurgen Herbst (Cambridge, MA: Harvard University Press, 1963), 201-3, 205, 210, 212, 215-18, 252-56; Marsden, *Religion and American Culture,* 116, 117; Harvie M. Conn, "Evangelical Foreign Missions," in *Dictionary of Christianity in America*, 752; Stephen Neill, *A History of Christian Missions* (New York: Penguin Books, 1964), 322-96; Hughes, *Myths America Lives By*, 133, 134.
78. Painter, *Standing at Armageddon*, 149-62; Hudson, *Religion in America*, 310, 311; Strong, *Our Country*, 201-3; 205, 210, 212, 215-18, 252-56; Marsden, *Religion and American Culture*, 116, 117; Hughes, *Myths America Lives By*, 133, 134.

4

From Mainline to Sideline: Evangelicalism in Retreat

Mainstream American culture: Should evangelical Protestants love it or leave it? From the late nineteenth to the mid-twentieth century, they did both. And they often had a difficult time deciding which to do. But in the end, evangelicals largely withdrew from the cultural mainstream. Evangelical Protestantism entered the twentieth century riding high. Its proponents were some of the most respected people in the country. The presidential elections of 1896 and 1900 told part of the story. The Republican and Democratic candidates, McKinley and Bryan, were both devout Protestants of the evangelical stripe. The next fifty years saw a reversal of this position. By the mid-twentieth century, evangelical Protestants were cultural outsiders—sometimes despised and ridiculed and usually viewed as culturally and intellectually backward. How did this situation develop? This chapter tells part of the story.

The Big Picture

The events of the late nineteenth and the first half of the twentieth centuries set the stage for this evangelical transformation. As noted previously, the late nineteenth century set in motion many developments that made evangelicals uneasy with the direction of American society. Included were industrialism, urbanization, immigration, and intellectual challenges to orthodox Christianity. All of this and more continued into the twentieth century. The problems of the time set in motion a reform movement usually called Progressivism. This era spanned roughly the first two decades of the twentieth century. Many evangelicals contributed to Progressivism, especially to the Prohibition movement. But evangelicals also reacted to aspects of the Progressivism, especially the Social Gospel, and they retreated from social concern.

In one area—the surge of patriotism connected with the Spanish-American War, World War I, and the Red Scare—evangelicals usually supported the flow of American society. In fact, many evangelicals could be described as hyper patriots. They usually supported the war efforts, attacked all things German, linked socialism and labor unions with communism, and generally equated 100 percent Americanism—meaning white, Protestant, and patriotic—with Christianity. In fact, divisions within Protestantism had been brewing for years and without the patriotic surge associated with World War I, the battle probably would have erupted sooner than it did.

Politically, the 1920s saw the nation retreat into a conservative era. Twenty years of reform, idealism, and the war to end all wars had burnt people out. America elected some of its most conservative presidents, Harding and Coolidge. Socially, however, America was not very conservative. The roaring twenties witnessed a cutting loose from the old Victorian moral standards. The twenties also saw a continuation of economic growth, featuring consumerism, speculation, mass production, and mass communication. In this context, a Protestant intramural fight broke out, fracturing what was left of its unity. As several scholars point out, this Protestant unity has been exaggerated. There had always been divisions within Protestant ranks. What really existed had been a Protestant culture.[1] But this terrible religious battle divided Protestantism into liberal and fundamentalist camps. And without even the myth of a Protestant unity, the vision of a "Christian America" could no longer be sustained.

When confronted with the modern world, religious groups can do one of three things. They can adjust their beliefs to conform more to societies' norms. A second alternative is to move more in a sectarian direction, choosing to remain separate and pure rather than dominate or influence the wider culture. For the most part, evangelicalism chose this alternative from the late twenties to the 1960s. A third choice is neither to accommodate one's faith nor give up the hope of cultural dominance. Rather, a religious group must battle for their values in the public arena. After the 1960s, many evangelicals adopted this alternative.[2]

Since the late nineteenth century, many evangelicals were becoming disillusioned with the direction of American society. The old sectarian, populist, and democratic spirit had once again reared its head. American democracy places a high premium on the dispersal of power. In such a society when religious groups disapprove of spiritual and moral trends, they can separate and form their own bodies. This is especially true when the religious norms appear to be dictated by the elite. So a number of new religious movements with a populist spirit arose in protest of what they perceived to be wrong with the direction of Protestantism. Four of these movements—the holiness movement, dispensationalism, Pentecostalism, and fundamentalism—all with a populist orientation can be regarded as evangelical.[3] Because the holiness movement took shape in the nineteenth century, it has already been noted. While dispensationalism, Pentecostalism, and fundamentalism have their roots in the nineteenth century, they acquired a clear identity during the early twentieth century.

During the 1920s, evangelicals failed in their attempt to shape Protestantism and lost control of the northern mainline denominations. In the process, they suffered a public relations defeat, appearing to be backward and obstructionist. Consequently, the fundamentalists—as they now identified themselves—largely withdrew from the public arena until the 1960s. Never before or since has evangelicalism been less visible. But appearances can be deceptive. The fundamentalists may have retreated but they were not inactive. They worked overtime to build religious institutions—mission societies, colleges, publishing houses, radio networks, and new denominations—to conform to their vision of the historic Christian faith. In doing so, they laid the basis for the evangelical resurgence of the 1970s.[4]

During the Depression years, fundamentalists suffered along with the rest of America and had to tighten their belts. Still, they experienced considerable growth and did not suffer numerical losses as did the mainline denominations. As for World War II, except for the peace churches, evangelicals supported the war effort. In the 1940s, evangelicals showed signs of moving out of their religious self-confinement. Evangelicals who formed the National Association of Evangelicals (NAE) began to chafe at fundamentalism's combativeness and anti-intellectualism. Then Billy Graham began his career in 1944. While he largely conformed to the fundamentalist image until 1957, he was becoming the voice of moderate evangelicalism.

Reaction to the Social Gospel

The concern here is not so much with the Social Gospel per se but with the evangelical response to it. Still, some description of the Social Gospel would be in order. The term *Social Gospel* did not come into use until early in the twentieth century, but its roots can be found in earlier movements and developments. The Second Great Awakening spawned many reform movements, which continued throughout the nineteenth century. Protestants of many stripes had a concern for the unfortunate. The postmillennial doctrine of the coming kingdom, while declining in the late nineteenth century, still inspired Christians to work for the improvement of American society. With many Protestants, the vision of a Christian America continued strong and became the primary motive for most advocates of the Social Gospel. The Social Gospel also has much continuity with theological liberalism and must be regarded as a subset of this movement.[5]

First and foremost, the social gospel must be seen as a response to the conditions of the Gilded Age. Industrialism had brought great wealth to America, but everyone did not share in this prosperity. Around the turn of the century, 10 percent of the population owned 90 percent of the nation's wealth. Many poverty stricken people were crowded into urban slums. Rising prices for what they bought and falling prices for what they sold put farmers in a terrible squeeze. Industrial workers worked for a pittance in awful conditions. America's contradictory economic policy favored the wealthy industrialists. On one hand, it advocated a hands-off policy, which gave big business the freedom to exploit both workers and consumers alike. Unregulated capitalism became an excuse for unrestrained greed. On the other hand, the government protected America's industries from foreign competition and granted many favors to the rich and powerful.[6]

In response to such conditions, a powerful reform movement began to emerge in the 1870s and 1880s. Known as social Christianity at this time, Protestants of both a liberal and conservative bent attempted to help the downtrodden. As time went on, however, differences emerged between these two types of social concern. Conservatives paid serious attention to the problems of the age, but they sought individual, spiritual, and ethical solutions. They rejected structural reforms as inconsistent with personal freedom. Examples of this approach would be rescue missions, the Salvation Army, and the Volunteers of America. Martin Marty describes these differences as the "private" party of evangelicalism and the "public" party of liberalism. The former regarded individual salvation as the answer to the nation's problems, while the latter supplemented revivalism with public or political solutions.[7]

When the Social Gospel first appeared, it criticized this old evangelical individualism. For the age of big business and sprawling urbanism, this personal ethic was inadequate. Social gospel advocates argued for a new social ethic and structural reforms—changes in the law, government policy, and institutions. A second difference emerged: theology. While evangelicals could be found in the Social Gospel movement, most advocates of this new social ethic identified with liberal theology—divine immanence, the historic development of Scripture, the ethic of Jesus rather than his supernatural acts, and an evolutionary approach to civilization.[8]

Early advocates of social Christianity included Washington Gladden (1836-1918), Josiah Strong (1847-1921), and Charles M. Sheldon (1857-1946), who wrote *In His Steps: What Would Jesus Do.* The movement, however, did not take off until the first two decades of the twentieth century. The environment of the early twentieth century produced a cluster of reforms—including women's suffrage, prohibition, pacifism, attempts to curtail political corruption, the direct election of senators, and improvements for rural life. In this context the Social Gospel and Progressivism had a close linkage, despite having differences over specific issues. In respect to lasting influence, the outstanding prophet of the Social Gospel movement was Walter Rauschenbusch (1861-1918). His 1907 book, *Christianity and the Social Crisis,* thrust him and the social gospel into the national spotlight.[9]

For the conservatives and advocates of the Social Gospel alike, the goal was a Christian America. But the emphasis was different. For most of the nineteenth century, concern for improving civilization was secondary to the spiritual or religious mission. With the liberals the reverse became true. "The complete Christianization of all life is what we pray and work for..." stated Washington Gladden.[10] As time went on, however, achieving this goal rested more on human efforts than on divine activity. The classic Social Gospel, as represented by Rauschenbusch, did not explicitly deny the validity of specific Christian doctrines. Instead, it minimized them. Evangelicalism argued that conversion must come first with good works coming as a necessary result. The liberals were more pragmatic, moving directly to good works and the ethic of Jesus, while largely ignoring conversion and the supernatural aspects of Christianity. Indeed, the test of Christianity was its good works.[11]

George Marsden notes two stages in the "Great Reversal,"—that is, evangelicalism's abandonment of social concern. The preparatory stage came from 1865 to 1900. The holiness movement with its turning inward and emphasis on personal piety helped to pave the way. More important was the rise of dispensationalism. This new doctrine drew sharp lines between the Old and New Testaments, between law and spirit, and promoted premillennialism. A corporate social ethic is most readily found in the Old Testament. Even the ethic of Jesus is for another dispensation, say the dispensationalists. Premillennialism argues that the world is growing worse, not better as postmillennialism contends. And the dispensationalists saw this confirmed by current events. As a result of the holiness movement and dispensationalism, many evangelicals adopted a more "private" approach to Christianity.[12]

But it took more than the holiness movement and dispensationalism to diminish evangelicalism's support for social programs. Marsden dates the second stage of the "Great Reversal" from 1900 to 1930. During this time— except for Prohibition—evangelicals either abandoned or relegated social concern to the backburner. These years saw the rise of theological liberalism and the Social Gospel with its focus on social programs, not regenerating souls. Evangelicals saw this reversal of priorities as tantamount to abandoning the gospel. So when they turned "their heavy artillery against liberal theology, the Social Gospel was among the prime targets."[13]

Evangelicalism: Southern Style

To this point, little has been said about evangelicalism in the South—in part because it has undergone few changes. Evangelicalism did not originate in the South. It was imported from the North via the First and Second Great Awakenings.[14] Once adapted to southern culture, however, evangelicalism has experienced less change in the South than elsewhere. Throughout the nineteenth century, evangelicalism must be regarded as the dominant cultural influence in America—a fact that would change after the turn of the century. But as a cultural force in the South—except for some urban areas— evangelicalism has continued to rule.

This dominance, indeed, has helped to lay the basis for the evangelical resurgence that began in the 1970s. Look at the key individuals and organizations driving popular evangelicalism since that time. They are often from the South or have a southern outlook. Examples are television preachers such as Jerry Falwell, Oral Roberts, Jim Bakker, Pat Robertson, Billy Graham, Jimmy Swaggart, and James Robison and institutions such as the Moral Majority and the Christian Coalition.[15]

Why has this occurred? In part, Southern evangelicals did not encounter the same cultural challenges as did their cousins in the North. And when they did arrive, Southerners had a theology to insulate themselves from such threats. The flood of immigrants that hit the northern cities did not materialize in the South. So except for the blacks, the South remained Protestant and largely of English, Irish, Scottish, and Scotch-Irish descent. Because industrialization lagged behind in the South, that region did not encounter serious urbanization problems. Of even greater importance, theological liberalism did not take hold in the South. As a result, southern evangelicals did not face the same intellectual challenges as did their northern counterparts.[16]

Against such threats, two ideas fortified Southern evangelicalism. Before the Civil War, they had already developed the doctrine of the "spirituality of the church." When it became apparent that the issue of slavery was going to disrupt religious life, leaders suggested that the church should "confine itself to making good Christians" and not concern itself with societal and political matters, which it could not control. This continued after the war and the churches focused on revivalism and converting souls. In support of both slavery and then segregation, southern preachers defended these practices on biblical grounds—usually by applying literal examples from Scripture to the black race. Though the Social Gospel made a few inroads in the South, Southerners believed social problems could be solved better by individual conversion than by religious social engineering. Consequently, they emphasized an individual moral code—which forbade alcoholic beverages, smoking, gambling, theater attendance, and cosmetics for women.[17]

After the Civil War, Southerners adopted the notion of the "lost cause." This belief contended that the South had fought for an ideal civilization, which they regarded as a Christian civilization, and that losing the war could not negate that ideal. This southern way of life had been "morally and spiritually superior to the Yankee civilization, (and) could be preserved in the hearts and minds of the people." So maintaining this ideal civilization meant hanging on to the past with all of its religious implications—namely preserving the revivalist evangelicalism of the mid-nineteenth century. They looked with disdain upon the Yankee civilization with its industrial and urban problems and its embrace of theological liberalism. And they wanted none of it. Thus, the characteristics of mid-nineteenth-century evangelicalism with its focus on biblical authority, revivalism, and individual morals has remained strong in the South throughout most of the twentieth century.[18]

The civil rights movement of the 1960s and its accompanying legislation significantly changed the South. The "Jim Crow" line could not be maintained legally. These developments, in addition to the pressures of economic growth and urbanization, have created "the New South." But evangelicalism is still dominant in the South and has been expanding throughout the nation. Southern Baptist congregations can be found in most parts of the country. Southern televangelists are now national figures. Country music, which has been incorporated in many gospel hymns, has a national audience. Evangelicalism never became a subculture in the South as it did in the North. It remained the dominant culture and is now exporting its ethos and religion to other areas. Continuing a process that began with World War I, Southerners have transferred their loyalty from the Confederacy to the United States and have become some of the nations' most fervent patriots—a characteristic found in modern evangelicalism.[19]

Dispensationalism: Its Origins

Not liking what they saw in late nineteenth-century America, many evangelicals began to retreat from mainstream culture. Dispensational premillennialism was one such movement. It began to gain strength in the 1870s and 1880s and since then has become a bedrock theology of fundamentalism. More than any other doctrine, premillennialism has fostered an interest in end of the world thinking and the "any moment" second coming of Jesus Christ. Dispensationsalism also emphasizes that God has dealt differently with humankind through a series of ages or dispensations. Classic dispensationalism divided history into epochs—usually seven. We are currently living in the sixth dispensation—the church age.[20]

Among many evangelicals today, dispensationalism is synonymous with biblical truth. They know of no other approach to Scripture. Where did it come from? Among theological systems, it is rather recent. Its exact origins are shrouded in mystery. But there can be no question that John Nelson Darby (1800-1882) became its foremost advocate. Born into an Anglo-Irish family, Darby graduated from Trinity College. Ordained three years later, he served in the Church of Ireland. Uneasy about the established church, however, Darby joined the Plymouth Brethren, a separatist sect with an interest in prophecy. As a member of this group, Darby systemized dispensationalism and spread its major principles throughout the English-speaking world.[21]

While not dominant, premillennialism had been around for a long time. It usually came in the form of historicist premillennialism—a view that tied the events predicted in the book of Revelation to a timetable. Now Darby came along with a new type of premillennialism. Dispensational premillennialism belonged to the futurist school, which held that, except for the first few chapters, Revelation foretells developments taking place in the last days. In taking this position, Darby said that no event stood in the way of Christ's return. This teaching of the imminent return of Christ "proved to be one of the greatest attractions of dispensational theology."[22]

Beyond the futuristic approach to prophecy, Darby's theology stood on two principles—his doctrine of the church and his method of interpreting the Bible. He sharply separated Israel and the church, insisting that God has a different plan for each. Moreover, Darby interpreted the prophetic passages with a rigid literalism.[23]

Building on these principals, Darby developed an exact scheme for end-time events. Christians are currently living in the "Great Parenthesis," the period between the crucifixion and the rapture. The next event on God's calendar is the secret rapture. Believers will rise to meet Christ in the air. Then the horrors described in Revelation will take place, including the tribulation, the reign of Antichrist, and Armageddon. At this point, Christ will return to set up his thousand-year rule. After the millennium, Satan will be defeated and the final judgment will take place.

The Rise of Dispensationalism

The last half of the nineteenth century witnessed the decline of postmillennialism. In 1860, the majority of American Protestants embraced postmillennialism, but by the early twentieth century it had largely disappeared. In part, this change occurred because many evangelicals defected to the growing premillennial ranks. Several factors contributed to the erosion of postmillennialism. Evangelical postmillennialism had gradually acquired a secular character. Previously, evangelicals had seen God and humanity as working hand in hand to usher in the thousand-year golden age. Some Protestants now began to equate the kingdom of God with America; others came under the influence of the new biblical criticism associated with theological liberalism. These new biblical studies undercut the supernaturalness of the Christian faith, including the apocalyptic elements of Daniel and Revelation and the second coming of Christ.[24]

Changing conditions in the late nineteenth and early twentieth centuries also tarnished postmillennialism. Postmillennialism rests on the premise that the world will get better. The Civil War, the decline of evangelicalism, a flood of immigrants, the influx of Catholicism, and the outbreak of World War I cast a shadow across this optimistic outlook. In the eyes of many, the situation was getting worse and worse. Under these circumstances postmillennialism became less believable.[25]

Individuals and institutions also contributed to the rise of dispensationalism. Between 1859 and 1872, Darby traveled extensively in the United States teaching his distinctive dispensationalism. He won many prominent ministers and laypersons to his teachings, especially in Presbyterian and Baptist circles. By the 1870s, Moody was preaching the premillennial return of Christ. Nearly every evangelist after Moody followed in Darby's train. Included would be

Billy Sunday, Reuben Torrey, W. J. Erdman, J. Wilbur Chapman, and George Needham. A number of leaders in the evangelical missions movement also embraced Darbyism. Among them were A. B. Simpson, who founded the Christian and Missionary Alliance, and Robert Speer of Presbyterian missions.[26]

Moody and his successors established networks to promote dispensational premillennialism. A number of Bible schools sprang up, at least fifty that spread the dispensational message—the most prominent being Chicago's Moody Bible Institute, the Bible Institute of Los Angeles (Biola), and Northwestern Bible Training School of Minneapolis. A number of evangelical magazines also promoted dispensationalism. Among the institutions spreading dispensationalism, the Bible conferences loomed large. At a series of Bible conferences from about 1875 to 1900, the dispensationalists encountered other conservative evangelicals and won many converts to their cause. By addressing issues other than eschatology these meetings forged the new premillennialism into a protodenominational movement with larger doctrinal concerns and much energy.[27]

Dispensationalism Takes Hold

In the last half of the nineteenth century, evangelical Protestantism came under an attack from several quarters—liberal theology, Darwinism, and the Social Gospel. In such a climate, the evangelicals circled their wagons and sought allies. At first the new premillennialists were suspect. Most evangelicals did not embrace their teaching of a secret rapture at any moment. But the dispensationalists did staunchly uphold the basic Christian beliefs. So the evangelical mainstream gradually welcomed the new premillennialists into their ranks—a step that did much to legitimize their eschatology. And eventually the dispensationalists won over many evangelicals to their belief in a secret rapture.[28]

By the early twentieth century, dispensationalism had caught on in a big way among American evangelicals. Cyrus Ingerson Scofield (1843-1921) had much to do with this development. His enduring legacy rests on *The Scofield Reference Bible*—published in 1909, expanded in 1917, and revised in 1967. Sales of this Bible total about 10 million. The Scofield Bible immediately became the standard of dispensationalism, and for over ninety years has been a major vehicle for distributing dispensational ideas.[29]

Scofield's *Reference Bible* packages dispensationalism in an attractive format. It provides paragraphing, cross-references, and notes to the King James Bible that reflect Darby's dispensationalism. Unlike most commentators, who put some distance between the biblical text and their notes, Scofield placed his notes and the biblical text on the same page.[30] As a result, his comments often acquired the authority of Scripture. *The Scofield Reference Bible* has been "subtly but powerfully influential in spreading (Darby's) views among hundreds of thousands who have regularly read that Bible and who often have been unaware of the distinction between the ancient text and the Scofield interpretation." Readers often fail to remember where they first encountered a particular idea—in Scofield's notes or the biblical text.[31]

During the first fifty years of the twentieth century, the world stood at the brink of Armageddon. The talk of wars and rumors of wars made a particularly deep impression at this time. "All our present peace plans will end in the most awful wars and conflicts this old world ever saw," said Reuben A. Torrey in 1913.[32]

These years after 1914 gave dispensationalism a tremendous boost. This era witnessed tragedy after tragedy. But "things were never better for American premillennialism."[33] The basic prophecies of the early dispensationalists in the nineteenth century began to take concrete form in the early twentieth century. In the eyes of the dispensationalists, world war, the return of the Jews to Palestine, the Russian Revolution, the redrawing of the European map, and the rise of totalitarianism were all predicted in Scripture. Indeed, most of the major themes so conspicuous in modern popular dispensationalism had taken shape before World War II, the only exceptions being the threat of nuclear annihilation and control of the masses by the Antichrist through television and computers.[34]

The apparent fulfillment of ancient biblical prophecies enabled dispensationalism to take solid root in the evangelical subculture. Within premillennialism the tenet of an any moment rapture had prevailed over the posttribulationists. In Pentecostalism and early fundamentalism, premillennialism had taken hold. Further, the modernist-fundamentalist conflict of the 1920s fragmented many denominations. What emerged was a separatist fundamentalism with its own churches, schools, mission agencies, and publishing houses. Dispensationalism thus had a subculture and a substantial institutional structure to perpetuate itself.[35]

Pentecostalism: Its Roots and Traditions

Pentecostalism is a mass religious movement, perhaps the largest of the twentieth century. Along with its more recent outgrowth, neo-Pentecostalism or the charismatic movement, Pentecostalism is the most significant of the new or innovative religious movements in the twentieth century, even being designated as the "Third Force in Christendom." No one knows just how large the movement is, but from inauspicious beginnings at the turn of the century Pentecostalism claimed more than 500 million global adherents by the end of the century.[36]

Rising from humble origins, Pentecostal and charismatic individuals have become leading figures on Christian television. Examples include Oral Roberts, Kathryn Kuhlman, Pat Robertson, Rex Humbard, Jim Bakker, Jimmy Swaggart, Kenneth Copeland, and Kenneth Hagin. Some have either reached the highest levels of the American government or aspired to these offices. Pat

Robertson sought the presidency in 1988; James Watt was Ronald Reagan's Secretary of the Interior; and John Ashcroft served as George W. Bush's Attorney General.

The distinguishing mark of Pentecostalism is a religious experience, usually called the Pentecostal experience, which entails receiving the gift of speaking in an unknown tongue as a sign of the baptism of the Holy Spirit. In Pentecostalism, this baptism usually comes as an experience subsequent to conversion and is regarded as the Holy Spirit's coming to dwell in an individual believer. From the idea of this baptism of the Holy Spirit and speaking in tongues emerged the belief in the current operation of the gifts of the Holy Spirit manifested in the New Testament church. Grant Wacker regards such experiences as evidence of Pentecostalism's primitive impulse, which he defines as a "longing for direct contact with the divine."[37]

The practice of speaking in tongues has occurred periodically through church history. Most people probably associate it with modern Pentecostalism, which was born in Kansas at the turn of the twentieth century. As Wacker notes, Pentecostalism appears to have developed from the confluence of several religious traditions, the most important being the holiness movement. Tongues-speaking and faith healing—the hallmarks of Pentecostalism—may be seen as a radicalization of the holiness doctrine of the "second blessing," or entire sanctification. Individuals in the holiness tradition found it hard to demonstrate empirically that they had received the second blessing, but Pentecostals could point to tongues-speaking as evidence of the reception of the Holy Spirit. This ability to provide a tangible expression of the indwelling of the Holy Spirit gave Pentecostalism its great impetus.[38]

Many holiness people believed that attaching tongues to Holy Ghost baptism had biblical warrant. But it should not be forgotten that speaking in tongues erupted on the American scene at a time when many religious groups felt the need to validate empirically their beliefs and experiences. Faith healing should also be seen in this context. In an age when science challenged Christianity, tongues-speaking and faith healing were seen as "signs and wonders" to bolster Christian faith.

A second tradition also emphasized a second life-changing experience following conversion. It was not defined "as a moment of purification" freeing one from sin, but as "an enduement of power" that enables the believer to serve God. Growing from the work of Finney and others in the Reformed tradition, this power was often called the higher Christian life. By the end of the century, however, this second experience came to be known as the baptism of the Holy Spirit. A third tradition was that of dispensational premillennialism with its emphasis on the any moment secret return of Christ. Pentecostals fervently believed that they were living in the last days, evidenced by the outpouring of the Holy Spirit.[39]

Fourth is a new theology of faith healing, one that departed from historic Christian teachings. Previously, Christians prayed for healing and elders anointed the sick. This new teaching insisted that "Christ's atonement provides physical healing just as it provides spiritual healing." A. B. Simpson of the Christian and Missionary Alliance and John Alexander Dowie, an early faith healer, popularized this idea. A fifth tradition influencing Pentecostalism was the desire for "the restoration of the power and miracles of the New Testament church." Many people believed that the former rain of the book of Acts would be complemented by a latter rain—a final outpouring of the Holy Spirit in the last days as predicted in the book of Joel. Assisted by those who saw these manifestations of the Holy Spirit as signs of Christ's imminent return, these various forces came together by 1900 to form the Pentecostal tradition.[40]

Pentecostalism: Social Factors

Pentecostalism cannot be explained solely as a social phenomenon. Nevertheless, social factors played a major role in shaping this new religious movement. Strong doses of populism propelled many of the new religious movements—the holiness movement, Pentecostalism, dispensationalism, and fundamentalism. All of these movements rejected modernism and its elite culture. They also advocated separation from the world and a strict lifestyle. But the populist impulse reached greater proportions in Pentecostalism than in any other mass movement.

From a general perspective, Pentecostalism may be seen as a small segment of a widespread, long-term protest against the whole thrust of "modernity": the modern urban-industrial capitalistic society. Pentecostalism arose at the end of a century in which science and technology, through urbanization and industrialization, had significantly changed all aspects of life. Accompanying these revolutions in the means of production was the growth of large, impersonal social institutions. Moreover, these revolutions facilitated both social and geographic mobility, allowing vast numbers of people to move from continent to continent, from farm to city and from one lifestyle to another.[41]

Pentecostalism made its strongest appeal to those who had difficulty coping with these massive changes, especially to individuals in the lower echelons of society. The poverty of the early Pentecostals has been exaggerated. Recent studies have shown that they came more from the blue-collar class than from the truly destitute segments of society. Still, the movement thrived with lower- and lower-middle-class people.[42]

These individuals were disappointed; their worldly hopes had repeatedly been frustrated. Pentecostal meetings, which were with charged emotion, provided a real sense of relief from oppressive, frustrating, and even bewildering social circumstances. In these meetings, individuals who were otherwise poor, uneducated, and powerless experienced a sense of power that provided compensation for their status in life. Because of its supernatural source, they regarded such an experience as "real power," greater than the power of the rich and worldly.[43]

Two other social factors characterized early Pentecostalism—racial diversity and significant roles for women. And both ran counter to the social norms of the day. Pentecostal congregations, especially those on the West Coast, contained a smorgasbord of ethnic and racial groups: Anglo-Saxon whites, African-Americans, Asians, Hispanics, and European immigrants. Thus conversion to early Pentecostalism also entailed a change in social attitudes. As time went on, however, Pentecostalism became more segregated. The modern day has seen a reversal of this trend. Pentecostalism has also afforded women prominent leadership roles. While Pentecostals have not pursued a feminist agenda, their belief in the Holy Spirit's direct inspiration has overridden scriptural injunctions (e.g., 1 Timothy 2:12) prohibiting women from speaking in church. When the Spirit prompts a woman to speak, she is not expected to be silent, and obviously gifted women have become some of Pentecostalism's best-known leaders.[44]

Pentecostalism also reacted to the modern world's emphasis on science and reason. The late nineteenth century was a time of great advances in science and technology. Liberalism regarded itself as supremely rational and insisted that religion must conform to the dictates of reason. While other religious reactionaries rejected the major premises of modernism, they still attempted to prove themselves as rational and scientific. Fundamentalism was based on Baconian science and Scottish Common Sense philosophy. The protofundamentalists at Princeton rigorously and rationally defended the historic Christian faith. In counting their dispensations, the dispensationalists appeared to be exact and precise.[45] The Pentecostals even saw tongues and physical healings as empirical verification of the Holy Spirit's work.

Pentecostalism, however, represented a more fully developed and irrational reaction to modern theology and culture. In ignoring the importance of all history since the early church and in believing that a new Apostolic Age was dawning, Pentecostalism was radically ahistorical contends Wacker. It reached back into history and resurrected the "models of primitive Christian ecstasy and enthusiasm," notes Martin Marty. At first this surge of emotion and display of the gifts of the Spirit were spontaneous and fluid. While not relinquishing this spontaneity, the Pentecostal primitivism and emphasis on the work of the Holy Spirit became doctrine. Pentecostals often belittled theology because they regarded it as cold and dead. But they did believe in what they regarded as biblical truth—especially when it was presented by strong charismatic personalities in a fiery manner.[46]

In many ways Pentecostalism represents the mirror image of modernity. Marty lists a number of ways in which they differ. The liberal churches encouraged cooperation and union while the Pentecostals "advocated a 'come-outism' and propagated new sects." Modernity rests on rationalism while Pentecostals "followed charismatic emotionalism." The modernists interpreted events by means of "theological naturalism, but the Pentecostals were raging supernaturalists." The mainstream churches insisted on manners and decorum; "the Pentecostals were often unmannered and indecorous in their eruptive worship." Modern medicine was making progress in healing at the time Pentecostals turned to miraculous healings. Such descriptions are stereotypes, but they do present a reasonable comparison between Pentecostalism and liberal Protestantism as they developed in the early twentieth century.[47]

Pentecostalism: Its Early Development

Pentecostalism is usually traced to the ministry of an itinerant holiness faith healer, Charles Fox Parham (1873-1929). While teaching from the book of Acts at a Bible school in Topeka, Kansas, one of his students spoke in tongues. The experience of glossolalia soon swept the school and Parham insisted that tongues-speaking was the initial, physical evidence of the baptism of the Holy Spirit. This notion became the central belief of modern Pentecostalism. When tongues-speaking became a regular practice is a matter of debate, but this 1901 event in Topeka is usually seen as the beginning of the modern tradition.[48]

Parham preached his message throughout the Midwest, but the decisive event occurred when he went to Houston, Texas. Here a young African American hotel waiter and holiness minister named William J. Seymour (1870-1922) came under his influence. Seymour moved to Los Angeles where his preaching sparked the most famous event in modern Pentecostal history—the 1906 Auza Street revival. This event ignited Pentecostalism's early growth and its message caught fire and spread across the United States.[49]

Coming under the influence of the Auza revival, from 1906 to 1911, several Wesleyan sects joined the new Pentecostal movement. Based in the South and Southeast, they include the predominately African American Church of God in Christ, the Church of God (Cleveland, Tennessee), and the Pentecostal Holiness Church. By 1914, the Pentecostal message had spread to the lower Midwest. Here members of the Christian and Missionary Alliance with a Pentecostal orientation joined Parham's followers to form the Assemblies of God, the largest Pentecostal denomination.[50]

Pentecostalism has produced many schisms. In less than a hundred years, the movement has spawned more than 300 denominations and organizations in the United States alone. These divisions have come over a variety of reasons—doctrine, excessive emotionalism, lifestyle issues, and because charismatic individuals have just gone their own way. Pentecostals have quarreled over the nature of sanctification. Building on the holiness movement, some have argued for a three-step process: conversion, sanctification, and then the baptism of the Holy Spirit. Others have said that sanctification is gradual thus compressing the process into two steps. One significant controversy concerned the Trinity. Some Pentecostals argued that the apostles baptized only "in Jesus name," and adopted a Jesus-Unitarian theology. This "Jesus-Only," "Oneness" or "Jesus-Name" doctrine has produced the bitterest and most entrenched schism in Pentecostalism. An example of a charismatic individual going her own way is Aimee Semple McPherson (1890-1944). She had a ministry in the Assemblies of God and then launched the Foursquare Gospel Church, incorporated in 1927.[51]

Popular Religions Have an Appeal

In the last two chapters, we have seen three new religious teachings take hold—the holiness movement, dispensationalism, and Pentecostalism. These movements did not come from the top. They never made much of an impression at the nations' elite universities and divinity schools. Rather, they came from the ordinary people and were propelled by popular preaching and writing, which appealed more to the heart than to the mind. Few of their proponents had the benefit of formal education or any significant theological training. Still, these individuals instinctively understood the psychology of popular religion and mastered the techniques of mass communication. In doing so, they have had a tremendous appeal and influenced millions of people through the twentieth century, far more than have the elite church leaders.[52]

These new teachings represented a populist counterattack against modernist theology and its accompanying worldview. In response to the great problems of life, the liberal elites offered political, pragmatic, scientific, and social solutions. The holiness advocates, dispensationalists, and Pentecostals countered with supernatural answers. Rather than give natural explanations, these evangelicals argued that only a divine intervention could solve human problems. In contending this, they upheld the supernatural component of the historic Christian faith.

These movements registered their specific appeals. To many evangelicals, society seemed to be going in the wrong direction. Dispensational premillennialism had an answer for this situation. The world indeed would get worse and worse until Christ returns to set things right. In an age of science and reason, dispensationalism had its own rational appeal. It broke history into neat dispensations and appeared to be exact and "scientific." But it also had its simplicity. Despite being rather complex, it made things appear black and white and put most issues in tidy categories. Very important, dispensationalism returned the Bible and its plain meaning to the people. Consistent with its populist appeal, dispensationalism insisted on a literal interpretation of Scripture. Its greatest attraction, however, was its ability to relate the prophetic passages of the Bible to current events. Dispensationalists claim that the prophetic passages of Daniel and Revelation are being unfolded in the present. They have in effect turned parts of the Bible into "Christian tea leaves" and in so doing have captivated the interest of millions. Nearly everyone—including evangelicals—is curious about the future, and dispensationalism satisfies this need.[53]

The holiness movement and Pentecostalism took a different tact. While their proponents did not ignore theology, doctrine had little to do with their appeal. The holiness advocates counted on the direct action of the Holy Spirit to perfect individuals who would, in turn, work to bring about a better society. They sought a "deeper work of grace" that would allow them to live the "victorious life." Pentecostalism above all was emotional and pragmatic. Through its various gifts, the Holy Spirit worked in the lives of people producing what appeared to be miraculous results. People could feel and see the works of the Spirit, and this is what counted.

None of these three evangelical movements gained any respect in academic or elite circles. But their advocates could not care less for they had more practical results than any elite theology in the twentieth century. The same could be said for a number of movements not related to evangelicalism. The Jehovah's Witnesses, Church of the Latter Day Saints (Mormons), and Seventh-Day Adventists all had belief systems different from mainstream Christianity. But they have a dynamic populist appeal that has attracted millions.[54]

Fundamentalism: Some Interpretations

Fundamentalism is a complex movement that developed in the early twentieth century in defense of the historic Protestant faith. By the 1920s, fundamentalism had its present name and was a self-conscious movement. It has been defined as a social movement, the religious aspect of the urban-rural conflict that took place in late nineteenth century. From this perspective, along with other social groups, fundamentalism struggled to maintain America's rural ethos. This way of life was rapidly passing, so fundamentalism is seen as a cultural lag—that is, resistance from rural minded, semi-educated Protestants to immigration, urbanization, and modern thought.[55]

Others have viewed fundamentalism from an intellectual perspective. Some regard it as a form of anti-intellectualism growing out of revivalism. Conversely, others say it is a form of intellectualism but one different from that of its detractors and current intellectual trends. Still, Ernest Sandeen sees fundamentalism as growing out of the alliance between the Calvinist orthodoxy of Princeton Seminary and dispensational premillennialism.[56]

While these social and intellectual interpretations have validity, fundamentalism combines several elements. George Marsden defines it as "militantly anti-modernist Protestant evangelicalism." It is a strident revolt against several aspects of the modern world. While fundamentalism has much in common with a number of related traditions—revivalism, the holiness movement, dispensationalism, Calvinist confessionalism, and pietism—its militancy sets it apart.[57]

Most important, fundamentalism rejects the religious and intellectual assumptions of modernism, which it regards as compromising orthodox Protestantism. Fundamentalism should be primarily interpreted as an attempt to protect the basic Christian doctrines from the eroding influence of theological modernism. But fundamentalism is also uneasy with many social conditions, especially urbanization and the growing immigrant Catholic population. The "Christian America" that they envision rests on a white Protestant cultural consensus. And they saw this America receding before their very eyes.

Harriet A. Harris regards fundamentalism as an "extremist element of evangelicalism." Separatism is its most distinguishing feature, setting it apart not only from American culture but even from its evangelical cousins. She believes the word *fundamentalism* can be used in three ways. It can refer to the fundamentalist mentality, which can be found in segments of contemporary evangelicalism. While such evangelicals may not embrace all elements of fundamentalism, they think like fundamentalists—in black and white terms, believe in conspiracies, close their minds to opposing ideas, and evidence hostility toward the educated elite. Two, fundamentalism refers to the historic movement of the 1920s. Three, fundamentalism designates modern groups or individuals who self-consciously employ the term and separate from culture.[58]

The Buildup to Fundamentalism

Fundamentalism's roots go back to the last quarter of the nineteenth century. As mentioned previously, after the Civil War a number of intellectual and cultural trends challenged the dominance of evangelical Protestantism. Protestants responded differently to these challenges. Nearly all of them disliked the immigrant invasion and intensified their Americanism. But they had contrasting reactions to modern science and theology. Many Protestants adjusted to these new intellectual currents by adopting the "New Theology," which accepted evolutionary thought, higher criticism, and modernized traditional Christian doctrine.

Others were uneasy about these trends. Dispensational premillennialism and the holiness movement began to gain steam during these years. To increase confidence in Scripture, theologians such as Benjamin Warfield and Archibald Hodge of Princeton Seminary countered with the doctrine of biblical inerrancy. Revivalists like Moody preached the old-time gospel and organized many Bible conferences to promote traditional beliefs. Still, other Protestants advanced historic evangelical doctrines through missions, Bible institutes, and summer conferences. While these responses to modernism were generally conciliatory, they did lay the basis for a more fully developed fundamentalism. Of great importance, before 1900, conservative coalitions—which would spearhead the future fundamentalist attack against modernism—began to take shape.[59]

During the first two decades of the twentieth century, conservative Protestants continued to consolidate their forces, to articulate what was essential to the Christian faith, and to specify the issues over which they would do battle. Such a desire prompted many conservative evangelicals from America and Britain to compile a series of twelve volumes called *The Fundamentals* (1910-15). These booklets identified the enemies of historic Christianity and society—socialism, Romanism, Christian Science, atheism, spiritualism, Mormonism, modern philosophy, and more. But above all, they regarded modern thought—liberal theology, German higher criticism, Darwinism, and the naturalistic interpretations of the Christian faith—as undermining biblical authority and the supernatural basis of Christianity. The *Fundamentals* covered a range of subjects and on the whole they were fair, polite, and well reasoned.[60]

This moderate defense of the faith did not last long. Conservative evangelicals had been articulating the non-negotiable Christian doctrines since the 1878 Niagara Bible Conference. From this conference flowed the "Niagara Creed," which spelled out fourteen "fundamentals of the faith." By the early twentieth century, the list of fundamentals became less comprehensive. In 1910, the General Assembly of the Northern Presbyterian Church affirmed five essential doctrines which they deemed as under attack: the inerrancy of Scripture, the virgin birth of Christ, his substitutionary atonement, Christ's bodily resurrection, and the historicity of miracles. These doctrines were reaffirmed in 1916 and 1923, and by this time many regarded them basic to Christianity itself.[61]

Other conservative Protestants drew up their lists. Following in the train of the Bible conferences, premillennial Baptists and independents led by William B. Riley organized the World's Christian Fundamentals Association in 1919. These premillennialists issued several faith statements, which slightly modified the doctrines set forth by the Presbyterians. Miracles were replaced with the resurrection and Christ's Second Coming; the deity of Christ was put in place of the virgin birth; and premillennialism was added.[62]

Fundamentalism and the Cultural Crisis

The fundamentalist modernist controversy, which erupted in the 1920s, was grounded primarily in theological differences. By this time, the battle lines were drawn. But social issues should not be ignored. They helped to fuel the crisis. America had been drifting from its Protestant moral vision for years. World War I, however, temporarily papered over the many social cracks. It brought the nation together in a surge of patriotism. One hundred percent Americanism swept the country and was the order of the day. Anything less was tantamount to treason. Except for the peace churches, evangelical Protestants backed the war. Many agreed with Billy Sundays' words, "Christianity and Patriotism are synonymous terms," and "hell and traitors are synonymous." Such conservatives had nothing on the more liberal Protestants (or Catholics for that matter). Except for a more sophisticated style, they were equally patriotic and staunchly backed the war effort. Rather than the crude patriotism evidenced by some evangelicals, the liberals had a deeper theological reasoning. They saw God working through democratic civilization, especially the American version. Thus, the war "to make the world safe for democracy" became a sacred cause.[63]

World War I ended abruptly but the intense patriotism that drove the nation did not. Most Protestants continued to closely link Christianity with Americanism and viewed the events of the 1920s in such a light. The "war to end all wars" left the world in shambles and embittered many people. The successful 1917 Bolshevik Revolution in Russia made communism a reality, not just a theory. This event when combined with labor unrest and a series of bombings in the United States ignited the "Red Scare." In 1919, the fears of communist infiltration and uprisings gripped the nation. While only marginally related to the churches, most Protestants regarded anything resembling socialism as un-American and opposed to Christianity.[64]

The old racism occasioned several other disruptions. The notion that God had ordained America to be a nation of white Anglo-Saxon Protestants died hard. The horror of Asian immigrants inspired the fear of the "Yellow Peril." In using language that combined racial and religious antagonisms, both politicians and clergy fueled tensions. They envisioned a Christian America, which ruled out Asians and other unwelcome people. The revival of the Ku Klux Klan had more direct religious connections. Despite being denounced by both liberals and conservatives alike, the Klan claimed to be Protestant. Best known for its hatred of African Americans, the Klan also evidenced antagonisms toward Jews, Catholics, and non-northern Europeans in general. The Klan can be regarded as an extreme of a tendency found in American culture and Protestantism in general. Millions of Americans, including conservative Protestants, feared the end of Anglo-Saxon dominance and the economic threat of the immigrants. In the 1920s these sentiments culminated in the form of laws to restrict immigration.[65]

The war accelerated the secularization trend that had been growing in America for some time. Conservative Protestants fought to maintain the Victorian morals of the past. Despite the passage of Prohibition, this was a losing battle. The 1920s—often called the roaring twenties—saw a sea change in respect to morals. Previously, one would not mention sex in polite company. Tabloid newspapers now headlined sensational stories. Freudianism encouraged the open expression of sex, and both men and women spoke openly of sex. Movies glorified sex stars. Women now smoked in public and wore short skirts called the flappers. The automobile gave young people mobility and the rumble seat became the place for night maneuvers. Dancing, which Protestants considered a taboo, now became a common aspect of the social scene. Conservative Protestants reacted strongly to these social trends, believing that they signaled the end of the Christian civilization in America. Such a perception fueled their determination to resist modernization and all that it entailed.[66]

Billy Sunday and His Times

The years from 1890 to 1920 witnessed many changes in American society and the buildup to the fundamentalist and modernist confrontation. Billy Sunday's (1862-1935) career straddled these years and it reflected the apprehensions of the Anglo-Saxon Protestant middle classes. Like many evangelicals (and Americans for that matter), he was fighting a rear guard action against the forces of the modern world. He strongly displayed many of the characteristics of the evangelical subculture—populist, pragmatic, patriotic, xenophobic, macho, intolerant, and anti-intellectual. Sunday stood at the center of the cultural confusion of his day and demonstrated some of the more pugnacious qualities of the developing fundamentalist culture.

Born on a farm in Iowa, Billy Sunday was in his own words "a country rube." Receiving little formal education, he began his career as a major league baseball player in 1883. He received Christ three years later, and in 1891 he walked away from a successful baseball career to devote his life to a full-time Christian ministry. At first he worked at the YMCA and then took a position as an advance man with the evangelist J. Wilbur Chapman. As an apprentice to Chapman, Sunday learned the revival profession. Despite no training and little knowledge of theology, the Presbyterian Church ordained him in 1903. (They reasoned that "God has used him to win more souls to Christ than all of us combined, and must have ordained him...") From 1900 to 1920, Sunday was immensely popular, at first preaching in small towns and then moving up to the nation's major cities, where he staged massive crusades.[67]

Until the ministry of Billy Graham, no American preached to more people or registered more decisions for Christ than Sunday. He conducted almost 300 revivals in his forty-year career, preaching to millions with nearly 600,000 coming forward. These "trail-hitters," as he called them, did not have to make agonizing decisions or go to a counseling room. Shaking Sunday's hand signified their commitment to Christ and a new life. His great success can be attributed to two facts—his dramatic sermons and an efficient organization.[68]

Sunday's Message and Methods

Following in the path of Whitefield and Finney, Sunday turned the sermon into a dramatic performance; only he was much more flamboyant. While theatrical, Whitefield and Finney projected some dignity. Moody lacked their flare, but his sentimentality attracted many. Sam Jones (1874-1906)—the Methodist evangelist who was dubbed the "Moody of the South"—more closely set an example for Sunday. Like Jones, Sunday used blunt, crude, homespun language, which many regarded as irreverent. His funny stories, impassioned gestures, and flamboyant antics—leaping around his revival plat-form like an acrobat and waving the American flag while standing on top of the pulpit—attracted the press and made him a household name. Sunday would rage against the Devil by pounding the pulpit and smashing chairs. Gradually, he would shed his coat, vest, and tie and finally roll up his sleeves. Every sermon was an impassioned performance—and the crowds loved it.[69]

Sunday's sermons expressed his populism, pragmatism, Americanism, xe-nophobia, anti-intellectualism, and macho attitude. In respect to theology, he said: "I don't know any more about theology than a jack rabbit knows about ping-pong, but I'm on my way to glory."[70] He summed up his doctrine in ten words: "With Christ you are saved, without him you are lost." For him theol-ogy consisted of a simple choice between heaven and hell. "You are going to live forever in heaven or...hell. There's no other place—just the two. It is for you to decide." Sunday had no time for modern learning and in expressing his disap-proval of it, evidenced a deep-seated anti-intellectualism. He heaped a brutal invective upon higher criticism and that "bastard theory of evolution."[71] He had little time for higher education. "Thousands of college graduates are going as fast as they can straight to hell." Or as he said elsewhere, "When the Word of God says one thing and scholarship says another, scholarship can go to hell."[72]

Sunday's message can also be seen as an Americanized fundamentalism with a masculine overtone fit for the Teddy Roosevelt era. Along with the birth of Jesus Christ, he regarded the discovery of America as one of the greatest events in history. "We are citizens of the greatest country in the world and we will admit it," he declared. Sunday upheld the stereotype of the 100 percent pure American, which he believed could be proved both scientifically and intuitively. Immigrants he did not like, unless they would "assimilate our ways and conditions." Most criminals, he believed, were foreign born. "America has become the backyard in which Europe is dumping its paupers and crimi-nals." As with most Americans, Sunday's intolerance and xenophobia increased after the start of World War I and it carried over into the reactionary years after the war. During this time, revivalism generally reflected the atmosphere of the "Red Scare" and the immigration restriction laws.[73]

One hundred percent Christianity and Americanism also entailed a strong dose of masculinity, said Sunday. In expressing such opinions, not even Teddy Roosevelt insisted on so much militant masculinity. Sunday bragged about his ability to fight: "I'm still pretty handy with my dukes." Like Jones, he preached an aggressive, masculine, and muscular Christianity. Sunday told his audiences that the church needed fighting men of God, not "sponge-col-umned, mushy-fisted, jelly-spined...Christians." Sunday also took a muscular view of Christ. Jesus "was no dough-faced, lick-spittle proposition. Jesus was the greatest scrapper that ever lived." In making such statements, Sunday was paving the way for Bruce Barton's book, *The Man Nobody Knows,* which portrayed Christ as a real go-getter.[74]

In many ways, Sunday's attitude toward social problems mirrored those of most evangelicals of the day. His career peaked during the Progressive era. Was Sunday a reformer? To some extent, both liberals and conservatives believed he was in their camp, and to some extent he was. Sunday hated "booze" and he staunchly supported Prohibition, and he deserves some credit for its passage. What about capital versus labor, one of the great issues of the day? He criticized both the employers and laborers for the existing problems and in doing so pleased the middle class. But he gave spiritual and individualistic answers to this problem, as he did to most issues. If the owners and workers would only love each other, the problems would end. His criticisms of big business, however, were few and he did not suggest a social ethic demanding the regulation of industry. In part, this attitude developed because the business community supported his crusades.[75]

Little has been said about Sunday's organization, but this must be seen as a second key to his success. His wife, Helen Amelia Thompson, had remarkable organizational talents. She selected the cities where he was to preach, made the pre-campaign arrangements, and organized the crusades themselves. Sunday's revival methods were a refinement of those of his predecessors in the profession. So efficient was his organization that one observer compared it to that of the United States Steel Company and Standard Oil. His revival party consisted of more than twenty experts who focused on some aspect of the crusade—advance men, research assistants to help him gather material for sermons, liaison men between his crusades and the churches, pianists, and choir leaders. He even had a cook, housekeeper, and personal masseur. In having such an organization, Sunday reflected the mentality of the day. Though he lived until 1935, his popularity and success declined after 1920. Mass evangelism required a broad Protestant cooperation and this ended with the modernist-fundamentalist controversy and cultural upheaval of the 1920s.[76]

Establishmentarian or Sectarian?

On the eve of the modernist-fundamentalist conflict of the 1920s and for part of the decade, evangelicals were undecided as to the course of action they should take. Should they be establishmentarian—that is, struggle to maintain the de facto evangelical Protestant establishment that had prevailed for much of the nineteenth century? Or should they be sectarian? Should they give up in their attempt to establish a Christian civilization and retreat into their subculture? Even their view of America was ambivalent. Was it Babylon or the New Israel?

During the nineteenth century, evangelical Protestants endeavored to make America a Christian nation. This Christianization was to come by persuasion and voluntary means. Being dominant, evangelical Protestantism became the carrier of culture. In this process, religion and culture became so intermixed as to make them indistinguishable. Instead of Protestantism driving the culture, the opposite occurred and evangelical Protestantism became a culture religion. And this acculturation occurred so subtly that most Protestant leaders were unaware that it had happened. Consequently, in the mind of many, American civilization and Christianity were one and the same.[77] As the century progressed, however, American civilization became more secular and most Protestants responded by blessing "its manifestations—such as materialism, capitalism, and nationalism—with Christian symbolism."[78]

In blessing American culture with Christian symbols, however, evangelicals were paradoxical. On one hand, they did not like the direction society was taking—especially the breakdown of Victorian morals, the influx of immigrants, the problems associated with enforcing Prohibition, and the challenges of modern thought. So they were determined to arrest these trends in both society and the churches. They began to fight these modern developments, and in the early stages, they did not surrender their desire to Christianize America. In part, this accounts for their militancy. But after many defeats, the fundamentalists (as they were now called) began to rethink their strategy. Failing to arrest the development of what they regarded as apostasy in their denominations, they went their own way and attempted to create pure churches. They called for some disengagement with society, but not completely so because even in retreat they retained an allegiance to many aspects of the American system—namely, its nationalism and economic system.[79]

The Battle Erupts in the Churches

The battle over the direction of Protestantism had been brewing for several decades. Thanks to the cultural crisis of the 1920s, the Protestant intramural fight broke out. By now the fundamentalist forces were strong because they had been growing for some time. At the heart of this conservative coalition stood the dispensationalists who had promoted their teachings through Bible institutes, Bible conferences, the *Scofield Reference Bible*, and revival meetings. They infused this coalition with a militancy, a premillennial worldview that saw civilization declining, and a populist appeal. When combined with the intellectual rigor of the Princeton apologists, a formidable coalition came into being. The holiness tradition as modified by the Keswick teachings (Victorious Life movement) contributed to this coalition. While the fundamentalists rejected Pentecostalism, most Pentecostals embraced the various faith statements set forth by the fundamentalists.[80]

In 1920, Curtis Lee Laws first used the term *fundamentalist* in the Baptist *Watchman-Examiner*. The term then popped up in the twenties to identify those who were vigorously defending the historic faith. During the 1920s and early 1930s, the fundamentalists did battle in two arenas—in several denominations and the public schools. Several denominations witnessed struggles between the fundamentalists and modernists for control of the denominational machinery, but the fiercest battles occurred in the Northern Baptist

Convention and (northern) Presbyterian Church U.S.A. In these denominations the fundamentalists and modernist forces were about equal in strength.
Among other groups, the balance of power rested with one contending faction
or the other so the struggles were less intense. In the South, by contrast, little
controversy occurred because evangelicalism was intertwined with the conservative southern culture.[81]

Harry Emerson Fosdick (1878-1969), a Baptist preacher filling a Presbyterian pulpit, fueled the flames with his 1922 sermon entitled, "Shall the fundamentalists Win?" This sermon and its published version irritated the
fundamentalists by its overt modernism. They then called for investigations of
Baptist institutions and for a binding statement of faith, which they hoped
would force liberals out of the denomination. The modernists, however, out-
maneuvered the fundamentalists by presenting their case as a violation of
Baptist "soul liberty." Even the Baptist Bible Union—which was organized in
1923 to wage uncompromising war on modernism—failed to unseat the liberals. In this struggle, the moderates held the balance of power and the liberals
convinced them to support the policies of toleration and inclusiveness—not
exclusion as the fundamentalists desired.[82]

An ecclesiastical war also erupted in the Northern Presbyterian Church in
the 1920s. J. Gresham Machen (1881-1937), a professor at Princeton Theological Seminary, wrote *Christianity and Liberalism* (1923) in which he contended that because of its radically different assumptions liberalism really was
not Christian. Rather, it must be regarded as an entirely different religion—
one with a faith in human beings while dressed in Christian symbols. The
liberals responded with the Auburn Affirmation, which distinguished between
the facts of the faith and the theological theories used to explain them. They
also called for toleration on doctrinal issues. By 1927, the General Assembly
voted that the essentials were no longer a binding test of faith. The last straw
for the conservatives came when Princeton Seminary, the traditional bastion
of Calvinist theology, was reorganized to reflect this theological diversity.
Led by Machen, the fundamentalists withdrew and formed Westminster Theological Seminary in 1929 and eventually a new church, the Orthodox Presbyterian Church.[83]

Did We Come From Humans or Monkeys?

By the mid-1920s, the fundamentalists took their battle into the public
arena. From their perspective, something had gone wrong with American life
since World War I. The culprit behind the nations' problems, they believed,
was evolution. The materialistic and naturalistic assumptions underpinning
evolution had undercut the supernatural worldview embraced by most Americans, especially the conservatives. In fact, many Americans believed that modern science not only conflicted with historic Christianity, but also undermined
the moral order. Some Christians attempted to bridge the gap between natural-

ism and supernaturalism by means of theistic evolution. But even this type of evolution was to be feared, said the fundamentalists. So they regarded it as their mission to arrest evolution. If evolution was to be stopped, this had to be done in the public schools. The battle with modernism thus moved to the classroom and the courtroom.[84]

The World's Christian Fundamentals Association and the Anti-evolution League succeeded in passing legislation to ban the teaching of evolution in several states. The courtroom battle, however, took place in Dayton, Tennessee. Into the fray against evolution came William Jennings Bryan (1860-1925), the three-time Democratic candidate for president and a great orator. Coming together in the person of Bryan were the forces of the evangelical faith and democratic populism.[85]

Among other issues, fundamentalism can be viewed as a populist revolt against the educated elite, who promoted evolution. The populist impulse suggested that nothing, including evolution, was beyond the grasp of the common person. And by using their common sense, they accepted the biblical account rather than that of the educated elite. Ordinary people might defer to the experts in some areas, but other subjects—social mores, public education, and the interpretation of Scripture—were within the understanding of the average person. "The Fundamentalists' complete confidence in ordinary people, however, carried within it…a scorn for advanced learning and often for scholarship in general," notes Frank Szasz.[86]

In Bryan's mind, teaching of evolution in the schools was a rejection of popular democracy. "What right have the evolutionists—a relatively small percentage of the population—to teach at public expense a so called scientific interpretation of the Bible when orthodox Christians are not permitted to teach an orthodox interpretation of the Bible?" Or in another place, "They have no right to demand pay for teaching that which the parents and the taxpayers do not want taught. The hand that writes the paycheck rules the school."[87]

The Monkey Trial

The confrontation over evolution came to a head in the Scopes Trial or "Monkey Trial" as it was often called. Like a number of southern states, Tennessee had passed legislation outlawing the teaching of biological human evolution. The American Civil Liberties Union persuaded John Scopes (1900-1970), a young high school teacher in Dayton to challenge the law. They then provided him with the services of a famous trial lawyer, Clarence Darrow (1857-1938). The prosecution accepted the services of another prominent American, William Jennings Bryan, who had been crusading against evolution. These two contestants reinforced the image of the fundamentalist–modernist controversy as a rural versus urban struggle. Darrow, who was urbane and sophisticated, represented modern culture. Bryan, speaking for the populist and agrarian interests, could be stereotyped as a country bumpkin. Even the setting of rural Tennessee fit the image.[88]

The trial drew some of the widest media attention in history and captured the interest of the public. This was the age of jazz, media generated crazes, new styles of dress for women, and suggestive movies. Reporters flocked to Dayton and the trial—unfolding more like a prizefight or a camp meeting—did not disappoint. In dramatic fashion, it lasted for two weeks and became a national event. Scopes was found guilty and given a token fine. But the big event came when Darrow cross-examined Bryan. With teaching Sunday school as his only theological credential, the judge allowed Bryan to serve as an expert witness regarding the Bible.[89]

For the fundamentalist cause, the results were tragic. Darrow had consulted with some of the nation's top scientists and theologians and subjected Bryan to a brutal cross-examination, which attacked the authority of Scripture and Christianity as a supernatural religion. Bryan knew next to nothing about science, other religions, and his knowledge of Scripture bordered on simplicity. His answers thus demonstrated how much he and fundamentalism were out of sync with modern thinking. The media picked up on this and its portrayal of fundamentalists as ignorant hicks and country rubes discredited the movement for years.[90] As one critic said, "thank the inscrutable gods for Harding, even for Coolidge.... The President of the United States may be an ass, but he at least doesn't believe that the earth is square, and that witches should be put to death, and that Jonah swallowed the whale."[91]

Bryan did not realize how badly he had done. The Great Commoner died five days later, putting an end to the ridicule of his critics. Remembering his achievements, the nation mourned. But fundamentalism did not do as well. It pulled back from the public arena, receiving national attention only when involved in strange incidents such as the disappearance of Aimee Semple McPherson (who was not a fundamentalist in any strict sense). The fundamentalists did rally for the presidential election of 1928 to help defeat the Catholic Al Smith. But this was their last hurrah for some time.[92]

The Image of Defeat

The fundamentalists failed in their two crusades—to take control of the denominations and to stop the teaching of evolution in the public schools. These setbacks had two major consequences. They created the image of defeat and caused the fundamentalists to become increasingly separated and alienated from society. Fundamentalism had been on the offensive for much of the 1920s, but now it was on the defensive. The significance of the Scopes Trial is that fundamentalism appeared to be ignorant and intolerant, and thus became subject to ridicule in the public arena.[93]

The defeat of Al Smith, notwithstanding, national events did not go their way. In the election of 1928, Anglo-Saxon civilization was at stake, so the fundamentalists believed. Being wet (opponent of Prohibition) and Catholic, Smith had to be defeated. But his defeat came for several reasons (a booming economy being one), not just the efforts of the fundamentalists. The lifestyle changes of the roaring twenties severely shook the perception of America as a white, Anglo-Saxon civilization with a special calling from God. The election of Franklin D. Roosevelt and the repeal of the Eighteenth Amendment (Prohibition) compounded the fundamentalists' grievances. These events appeared to seal the victory of urban culture and secularism.[94]

Roosevelt's New Deal also did not set well with conservative Protestants, who regarded big government as an enemy to be resisted. In fact, many believed the Depression to be God's judgment for the social excesses of the twenties. With the New Deal, the government began to take more responsibility for the welfare of American citizens. The church, in turn, took less, and during the 1930s Christians exerted less influence on the nation than before. Actually, a new society was developing—one characterized by cultural pluralism, a pragmatic approach to politics, and a less inhibited lifestyle.[95]

The image of fundamentalism's defeat is in part due to the difficulties encountered by Protestantism in general. Liberal Protestants and the old Protestant middle class also supported Prohibition as a way to defend the older culture. So its repeal was a setback for a wide slice of Protestantism, not just the fundamentalists. But this defeat connected more with the image of fundamentalism than it did with the liberal Protestants. Mainline Protestantism experienced a decline at this time, so much so that it has been described as "the American religious depression." Mainline Protestantism, however, was not all of American religion. The fundamentalists and other conservative denominations—Pentecostal and holiness bodies—were regrouping and rebuilding. They actually experienced considerable growth during the 1930s. And Protestantism in the South remained overwhelmingly conservative.[96]

Down But Not Out: Rebuilding the Institutions

The image of a defeated fundamentalism did not conform to reality. Yes, it did become more separatist, divisive, and alienated. Fundamentalists lost control of the mainline denominations but could not get along with each other. So they continued to separate, forming denominations from previous splits. Many fundamentalists stayed within the mainline denominations, but the more militant decided that "come-outism" was their only option. In 1932, militant Baptists broke from the Northern Baptist Convention and formed the General Association of Regular Baptists. More moderate fundamentalists stayed in the Northern Baptist Convention until 1947 when they organized the Conservative Baptist Association. Fundamentalists in the Presbyterian Church (USA) left and founded the Orthodox Presbyterian Church in 1936. But they had differences over the millennium and two years later, the Bible Presbyterian Church was formed. In the South during the 1930s, the controversial Frank

Norris established the World Baptist Fellowship, which by the late 1940s split into the Baptist Bible Fellowship. Other denominational divisions occurred and thousands of independent Baptist and Bible churches were established in the decades of the thirties and forties.[97]

Creating new denominations was only one aspect of the fundamentalist response to the defeats they suffered. Denominations and nondenominational churches need institutional support in order to thrive. And fundamentalists had no desire to associate with those whom they believed had compromised the faith, so they established their own schools, mission agencies, magazines, summer conferences, and publishing houses. In doing so, they created a separate but dynamic subculture, which thrived while mainline Protestantism experienced a decline in the 1930s.[98]

This subculture was loosely constructed for many of these new institutions were nondenominational. Of these institutions, the Bible institutes loomed most important. They became the major coordinating agency of the movement. They provided services—educating pastors, missionaries, school superintendents, and lay workers—previously provided by the denominations. Another important institution were the summer Bible conferences. Such conferences at a resort became a unique form of vacation—blending recreation, fellowship, and biblical teaching from leading fundamentalist preachers in a camp-meeting atmosphere. Despite losing control of the denominations, fundamentalists did not lose interest in missions. Rather, they turned to independent missions, either supporting them or founding new ones. The fundamentalists even engaged in a form of ecumenism. To provide fundamentalists an alternative to the World Council of Christian Churches, militants led by Carl McIntire established the American Council of Christian Churches in 1941. One year later, more moderate fundamentalists founded the less separatistic National Association of Evangelicals.[99] Such institutions provided the basis for the evangelical revival in the post-World War II era.

Taking to the Air

Throughout its history, evangelicals have not shied away from innovative methods to promote the gospel. In fact, they have often been at the forefront in utilizing new methods and technology. Fundamentalists have been described as "moderns, but not modernists,"—meaning that they would not let their embrace of science or technology extinguish the old-time gospel.[100] With the rise of commercial radio in the 1920s, the fundamentalists wasted no time in utilizing this new medium to spread the gospel message.

The fundamentalists, however, were not the only religious group using the radio to propagate their ideas. Mainline liberals, Catholics, and some extremists also took to the airwaves. Some of these fringe individuals and groups preached anti-Catholic and anti-government sermons. As a result, the government classified such messages as "propaganda," and set up a regulatory apparatus. The major broadcasting companies (CBS and NBC) allotted free airtime to mainline religious bodies. Such steps were designed to insure "safe" religious programming. Being sectarian and often controversial, the fundamentalist preachers were not given this free time.[101]

But the fundamentalists were not driven from the air. Radio stations needed customers so they sold airtime to the fundamentalists. These regulations were a blessing in disguise. They forced the fundamentalists to raise money for airtime, and having a long history of being entrepreneurs the fundamentalists met the challenge. In doing so, they produced programs that attracted large audiences and they learned the art of soliciting money. Fundamentalists utilized advertising, large choirs, current music, and dramatic sermons to garner the attention of a radio audience. Conversely, the mainline Protestants were lulled to sleep by favorable regulations and free radio time. When these benefits came to an end, they lacked the skills to compete for a radio audience. As in other areas, the evangelicals outdistanced mainline Protestants because of their popular appeal and entrepreneurial spirit.[102]

One of the earliest revivalists to use radio was Paul Rader (1879-1938). A rugged individualist with an athletic background, Rader served as a pastor, a revivalist, and a radio preacher. During the 1920s and 1930s, he set the direction that many radio preachers would follow. He exuded a manly image, a salesman's confidence, and made his revivals "unlike a church meeting as much as possible." He advertised extensively, used jazzy band numbers and pranced around the stage proclaiming a clear fundamentalist message.[103] Aimee Semple McPherson (1890-1944)—a Pentecostal evangelist and the founder of the Foursquare Gospel Church—led a tumultuous private life but also pioneered the use of radio. Her revival meetings, which were broadcast on radio, were "spectacles of entertainment, music, and emotion-rousing preaching." A flamboyant person, McPherson had the ability to draw and hold a crowd—a necessary quality for a radio revivalist.[104]

Most successful of the radio evangelists was Charles Fuller (1887-1969). From modest beginnings in 1925, his "Old Fashioned Revival Hour" became the most widely heard religious program in the nation. For decades his services were broadcast around the nation and the world and helped to lay the basis for other ministries—especially establishing Fuller Seminary, launching Billy Graham's career, and forging a wider evangelical coalition. While avoiding the excesses of some revivalists, Fuller's broadcasts were with a live audience but tailored to reach the listeners in "radioland." Other individuals who successfully ventured into the early use of radio include Donald Gray Barnhouse's "Bible Study Hour," Martin R. DeHaan's "Radio Bible Class," and Walter Maier of the Lutheran Church, Missouri Synod. The most influential radio station was Chicago's WMBI, operated by Moody Bible Institute.[105]

On the whole, the fundamentalist venture in national broadcasting was tremendously successful. By 1948, over 1,600 fundamentalist programs were being broadcast each week. What is the significance of such figures? They provide some measure of conservative Protestantism's strength during the 1930s and 1940s. Such figures seem to contradict the image of a declining movement. Moreover, as Quentin Schultze argues, religious radio helped to create "a national evangelical identity, locating and promoting symbolic leaders, and legitimizing particular values and attitudes." Of great importance, the "electric church" of the later twentieth century grew out of the successes of the earlier radio ministry.[106] For better or for worse, television has forged an image of evangelicalism and has introduced millions of people to the evangelical faith. Evangelicals have indeed mastered the use of the media, and in part this can be traced back to the radio evangelists.

Separation and Militancy

The evangelicals entered the twentieth century a respected people, largely indistinguishable from other Protestants who formed the nation's dominant faith. Protestantism had not yet divided into two clashing groups—the fundamentalists and modernists. But by mid-century the fundamentalists felt besieged and despised. Rather than have their ideas and values dominate society, they had become a cognitive minority. Their beliefs and worldview were out of sync with those of most Americans. How did this happen? Their defeats in the 1920s forced them to retreat and retrench. The fundamentalists put their vision to dominate American culture on the backburner and developed an elaborate subculture of institutions, free from the taint of modernism. Rather than reform Protestantism and American society, fundamentalism opted out for a pure church, one free from worldly influences. They developed a fortress mentality and condemned worldliness.[107]

During the second quarter of the twentieth century, fundamentalists intensified their dualistic worldview. Their us-versus-them theology became essentially Manichean: it viewed the world in black and white terms and as a battleground between absolute good and evil. This 100-percent mindset scorned compromises and ambiguities—for if the battle is between God and Satan the issues are crystal clear and no compromises can be made. Such a mentality led fundamentalists to separate from the "apostate" denominations and to adopt an alienated "faithful remnant" posture toward culture. It also infused the movement with a militancy toward modernism on an ideological level. As George Marsden and others have noted, militancy is fundamentalism's most distinguishing mark. Fundamentalists were a "contentious lot," and militancy and confrontation became sacred duties.[108]

Fundamentalism drew its militancy and rationale for separation largely from premillennial dispensationalism. Dispensationalism said that Christians were living in the church age, the last age in world history. During this dispensation the world would get worse. Fundamentalists saw current events—World War I, the Depression, modernism, the New Deal, and the apostasy of the churches—as confirming this decline. The world situation could not be reversed until the Second Coming of Jesus Christ, which would usher in the Kingdom of God. And until then, the "true church" could do only two things— witness to unbelievers and be a faithful remnant separate from the world. The Social Gospel and other human efforts to improve society are to no avail.[109]

Dispensationalism, however, was not the only source for fundamentalist separation. The populist strand of American culture, with its emphasis on local control and dislike of centralized bureaucracies, contributed to the separationist impulse. In part, the rise of independent churches is related to this impulse. During the 1920s and 1930s—especially in the universities and mainline denominations—evangelical views were being displaced by the expertise of the intellectual elite. This development alienated the fundamentalists who responded with anti-intellectual and populist attacks against the knowledge of "experts." Also, the holiness movement contained a powerful come-outer spirit. Beyond any institutional tendencies, there are personal factors. Throughout American history there have been the many charismatic religious leaders who have departed from a particular church and taken people with them. Moreover, individuals have separated because of some unpleasant personal experience.[110]

A Macho Attitude

Related to fundamentalism's militancy is its machismo spirit. In many ways, the nickname "fighting fundamentalists" fits quite well. They certainly obeyed the admonition of Jude, verse three: "Earnestly contend for the faith which was once delivered unto the saints." Fundamentalists prized a combative and aggressive spirit. Evangelists such as Sunday and Rader, who had athletic backgrounds, pushed the masculine theme and equated Christianity and Jesus with "real manhood." Fundamentalists believed that the liberals had presented Christ as soft, weak, and effeminate. In his best selling book, *The Man Nobody Knows,* Bruce Barton portrayed Christ as a masculine Savior, a manual laborer, and an outdoorsman who preferred the company of men. Most fundamentalists probably would have agreed with Barton's perspective. Also, fundamentalist preachers often acquired pugnacious and macho nicknames—"Texas Tornado," "Duke," "Fighting Bob," "The Cowboy Evangelist," "The Railroad Evangelist," and the like. In fundamentalist circles, browbeating from the pulpit became a common practice. Such militant and macho attitudes contributed to the growing dictatorial spirit within fundamentalist ranks.[111]

The other side of this macho spirit is fundamentalism's reactionary attitude toward women. During the 1920s, women had acquired the right to vote and Victorian morals were breaking down. Consequently, this was a time that many middle-class people, not just the fundamentalists, voiced concern about the changing role of women. Before World War I, women had been arrested for profanity, smoking in public, and for wearing shorts or slacks. Within a decade such restrictions were on the way out. So no wonder the flappers (dresses reaching the knees) caused a stir. Feminism and women's rights caused even more problems for the fundamentalists. Such trends conflicted with the Victorian norms that the fundamentalists believed to be the biblical ideal for the family and society. In fact, it is estimated that the fundamentalists opposed women's suffrage by a margin of ten to one.[112]

To compound the problem among fundamentalists, some churches were allowing women into the ministry. John R. Rice's book—*Bobbed Hair, Bossy Wives and Women Preachers*—captures the fundamentalist spirit. He condemns the "modern, masculine, pants-wearing, cigarette-smoking, bobbed-haired woman" for their lifestyle and says that by preaching to mixed audiences they are violating "the command of God..." But women were so indispensable to the work of the church, the fundamentalists could not do without their services. So fundamentalism's public image did not always match reality. In fact, except for the role of ordained ministers, thousands of fundamentalist women were active in some form of ministry. Despite the rhetoric of its leaders, fundamentalism offered women more opportunities for Christian service than did the mainline churches. In fact, fundamentalist Bible schools enrolled more women than did the liberal seminaries.[113]

Conspiracies and a Restrictive Lifestyle

Conspiratorial thinking also characterized the fundamentalist mindset. Earlier secret plots—believed to be related to the Masons, slave uprisings, international financiers, and Jews—became imbedded in fundamentalist thinking. Dispensationalism contributed to this paranoid tendency. Its followers interpreted the events following World War I as the fulfillment of prophecy, namely, the Bolshevik Revolution, the Red Scare, the cultural conflict of the 1920s, and the apostasy of liberalism. They saw Christian America fighting against an array of sinister, secret, and evil forces. The dispensational Bible teacher Arno C. Gaebelein (1861-1945) promoted such conspiracy theories with great vigor. His 1933 publication, *The Conflict of the Ages,* traced such sinister forces and plots from ancient Babylon through Karl Marx to the Bolshevik Revolution. This book was well received in fundamentalist circles.[114]

Such a conspiratorial mentality spilled over into fundamentalist politics. In general, the fundamentalists viewed Roosevelt's New Deal with great suspicion, regarding any form of government intervention to alleviate social problems as akin to communism and an intrusion into local affairs. In fact, many saw the New deal as preparation for the one world government and rule of the Antichrist. They interpreted the Depression from a spiritual perspective, as the fulfillment of prophecy and God's judgment on America. In the elections of the 1930s, they generally supported Roosevelt's opponents. Previously, evangelicals had voted for both Democratic and Republican candidates. But they tended to support candidates who appealed to their individualistic and pietistic inclinations. The New Deal pushed them further in this direction and, except for the South, locked them into the Republican Party.[115]

The 1920s and 1930s witnessed the rise of several demagogues, most visible being Huey Long and Charles E. Coughlin. Some of these demagogues had fundamentalist connections. Most militant was the premillennialist Gerald B. Winrod (1898-1957). In the 1920s, he resisted the spread of evolutionary teaching in the schools, and in the 1930s he fought Roosevelt's "Jewish New Deal." After a trip to Germany, he came to admire Hitler and manifested a strong anti-Semitism. By means of his *Defender Magazine,* he reached over a hundred thousand homes and fed a huge audience with fear, bigotry, as well as dispensational theology, anti-communism, and rugged individualism. The thinking of Winrod and the Disciples of Christ minister Gerald L. K. Smith helped to pave the way for a number of right-wing extremists after World War II. Included are the McCarthyites, John Birchers, and fundamentalists such as Billy James Hargis and Carl McIntire.[116]

On the level of lifestyle, fundamentalists also resisted the prevailing direction of American culture. Traditionally, evangelicals had protested a number of behavioral issues—drunkenness, fighting, gambling, Sabbath breaking, dancing and more. But the roaring twenties and the breakdown of Victorian morals intensified their resistance. Fundamentalists now worked to restore the moral values held by evangelicals in the nineteenth century. In doing so, they reflected influences from the Wesleyan holiness movement and Keswick (or Victorious Life) spirituality. These movements emphasized personal piety, which came through Christians surrendering themselves to God.[117]

On the whole, fundamentalist conduct codes were not as restrictive as those of the holiness or Keswick movements. They did have much in common, however. They both separated from a world that they regarded as hostile to their worldview and values. In doing so, they built their own institutions—denominations, missions, colleges, and publishing houses—as shelters from society. The fundamentalists endeavored to tighten up behavioral standards, which they believed had declined in recent decades. The taboo list would include profanity, use of alcohol, smoking, dancing, theater attendance, popular music, cards, gambling, sex outside of marriage, and work on the Sabbath. Ministers encouraged women to dress modestly and use makeup sparingly. Secular amusements were feared because they might keep people from church. Even novel reading raised some eyebrows. Where these moral standards could be enforced, such as at Christian colleges, they became behavioral codes.[118]

Flowing with the Culture

George Marsden has described fundamentalism's relationship with American culture as "paradoxical." Yes, the "fighting fundamentalists" could be confrontational and resistant to American society. They have been described as evangelicals who are mad at somebody. But they also had a softer side, one more accommodating to culture. The source of fundamentalism's paradoxical behavior stems from its two roots: nineteenth-century revivalism and piety and the humiliating defeat of the 1920s. In the nineteenth century, evangelicalism was not alienated from society. It was mainstream and evangelicals were insiders. Such a position predisposed them to be more accommodating and less confrontational. Fundamentalism's revivalistic heritage had encouraged its followers to pursue their highest goal, winning souls for Christ. As a result, they never completely gave up upon America. But their failure to defeat the forces of modernism embittered them. Instead of a respected segment of society, they had become a beleaguered and ridiculed minority. Herein lies the source of their polemical and confrontational behavior.[119]

In respect to religious beliefs and lifestyle, fundamentalism has been at odds with modern America. In most other respects, however, they have been thoroughly acculturated and this was evident even in the 1920s and 1930s— the time when evangelicalism had withdrawn more from American society than at any time before or since. Most obvious was fundamentalism's allegiance to the American political and economic system. America remained in their mind the world's last and great hope. The funds for missions and other Christian enterprises came largely from America. Its recent deficiencies, however, had to be corrected, and this would not come by remedying societies' structural flaws but by converting souls. The New Deal, not withstanding, America still had the best political system, but it had to be safeguarded from "Satanic" socialism and communism. In maintaining such political views, the fundamentalists were not that out of sync with the attitudes of many non-evangelical, conservative Americans.[120]

In respect to the American economic system, the fundamentalists were most at home. Traditionally, evangelicals have believed that God would bless hard work and individual initiative. As a result, they have been inclined toward the principles of a free and unregulated market. The first half of the twentieth century saw no exception to this trend. Most fundamentalists opposed the New Deal, and they even raised objections to the less intrusive Progressive reforms, which preceded the major changes of the Roosevelt era.[121]

The fundamentalists objected to many areas of mass culture. The glaring exception to this trend, however, was fundamentalism's embrace of mass consumerism and the methods of the business community. Though militantly anti-modernist in theology, the fundamentalists drank deeply at the springs of the new business culture—urbanism, mechanization, mass production and marketing, advertising, and efficiency. As we have seen earlier, they were at the forefront in respect to utilizing the radio. In *The Man Nobody Knows*, Bruce Barton not only depicted Christ as a masculine Savior, but he also portrayed him as the model corporate executive and master salesman. Again, many fundamentalists would have agreed with this picture.[122]

Going back to at least Moody, the evangelicals have enjoyed a cozy relationship with big business, which has often been the patron of Christian enterprises. On a more personal level, evangelicalism's embrace of consumerism that began after the Civil War did not abate with the emergence of fundamentalism. Like most Americans, the fundamentalists were oblivious to the subtle changes that consumerism had brought to their lives. So blinded by America's business successes, they easily swallowed the materialistic assumptions of their age and even managed to Christianize them. On a more ecclesiastical level, the churches emulated the business ethos and methods. After all, as one evangelist said, "soul-winning is big business."[123]

The Legacy of Fundamentalism

During the first half of the twentieth century, evangelicalism underwent tremendous changes, ones that helped to shape the movement down to the present. Evangelicalism entered the century apparently in a strong position. It had shaped American culture for much of the nineteenth century. By 1940, it had a different look, resembling a minority that commanded little respect in American society. Both of these images are misleading. Around 1900, evangelicalism was not as strong as it appeared, serious problems were looming on the horizon, and evangelicalism did not weather the ecclesiastical and cultural wars intact. These conflicts fragmented Protestantism and evangelicalism largely went underground. But things were not as bad as they seemed. The fundamentalists rebuilt their institutions and established a vigorous subculture. These actions laid the foundation for the evangelical comeback in the 1950s. Without these institutions, evangelicalism could not play the vigorous role in American society that it currently does.

Nineteenth-century evangelicalism became successful because of its popular appeal. Revivalist preachers packaged Christianity in a way that attracted the masses. Throughout the first half of the twentieth century, evangelicalism continued to have a populist base. The major evangelical movements—the holiness impulse, Pentecostalism, dispensationalism, and fundamentalism—all arose from the people, not the elite. In their different ways, these movements represent a revolt against modernity and the ideas of the educated elite. The holiness people turned inward; Pentecostalism emphasized the experiential element; dispensationalism put everything into a neat box; and fundamentalism responded in a militant manner. While these movements had their rational component, they succeeded because of their populist appeal. During the inter-war years, conservative Protestantism grew while its more liberal denominations declined, largely because the former mounted a popular appeal while the latter did not.

Fundamentalism maintained a hate-love relationship with American culture. It responded to modernity with a great deal of ambivalence. In its bid to capture the denominations and curtail the teaching of evolution, fundamentalism suffered humiliating defeats. Fundamentalists became angry at many things and many people. They lost the denominational wars because the moderate fundamentalists did not side with them. Because of the Scopes trial, the media portrayed the fundamentalists as ignorant and bigoted. The lifestyle changes of the roaring twenties greatly disturbed them. Urban areas teeming with Catholic immigrants and blacks from the South frightened the fundamentalists and many other Americans. They regarded modernist theology as heresy and new scientific theories with great suspicion. And Roosevelt's New Deal would open the door to the one world government and the rise of the "man of sin," so they believed.

What then did the fundamentalists like about American culture? While they resisted American culture, they did not withdraw as did the Amish. The fundamentalists were intensely patriotic. Most important, they embraced the business ethos and American capitalism with little serious criticism. Most regarded the free enterprise system as biblical and resented attempts to regulate it. Fundamentalists did not hesitate to employ the latest business methods and technology—radio, advertising, and public relations—to promote the gospel. This limited their ability to any future serious critique of materialism, consumerism, and the excesses of American capitalism.

The fundamentalist mentality has had a great impact. In the twenty-first century, many evangelicals run from the fundamentalist label. Only the militant separatists, such as those connected with Bob Jones University, employ the term as a badge of pride. The fundamentalist mindset, however, has had a tremendous influence in evangelical circles. Many people who would deny being fundamentalists, think like fundamentalists. They are "one-hundred percenters"; they see the world in black and white terms. So there is no room for ambiguity or compromise. Such people often have a populist mindset, regarding the educated elite with great suspicion. And they accept only a literal interpretation of the Bible, which they often equate with the inerrancy of Scripture.

Notes

1. R. Laurence Moore, *Touchdown Jesus: The Mixing of Sacred and Secular in American History* (Louisville: Westminister John Knox Press, 2003), 33, 34, 46, 47.
2. George M. Marsden, *Religion and American Culture* (New York: Harcourt Brace, 1990), 168, 169.
3. Nathan O. Hatch, *The Democratization of American Society* (New Haven, CT: Yale University Press, 1989), 213, 214.
4. Mark Noll and Lyman Kellstedt, "The Changing face of Evangelicalism," *Pro Ecclesia* 4, 2: 149; Mark Noll, *American Evangelicalism* (Oxford: Blackwell, 2001), 16-18. See also Joel A. Carpenter, "Fundamentalist Institutions and the Rise of Evangelical Protestantism, 1929-1942," *Church History* 49, 1 (1980): 62-75; Joel A. Carpenter, *Revive Us Again* (New York: Oxford University Press, 1997).
5. Robert T. Handy, *A Christian America: Protestant Hopes and Historic Realities* (New York: Oxford University Press, 1984), 135, 136; Sydney E. Ahlstrom, *A*

Religious History of the American People (New Haven, CT: Yale University Press, 1972), 786; R. C. White and C. H. Hopkins, *The Social Gospel: Religion and Reform in Changing America* (Philadelphia: Temple University Press, 1976); Robert T. Handy, ed., *The Social Gospel* (New York: Oxford University Press, 1966); Martin E. Marty, *Righteous Empire: The Protestant Experience in America* (New York: Dial Press, 1970), 204.

6. Grant Wacker, "The Social Gospel," in *Eerdmans's Handbook to Christianity in America*, ed. Mark Noll et al. (Grand Rapids: Eerdmans, 1983), 318, 319; Winthrop S. Hudson and John Corrigan, *Religion in America*, 6th ed. (Upper Saddle River, NJ: Prentice Hall, 1999), 300-02.

7. Handy, *Christian America*, 135-37; Wacker, "Social Gospel," 318, 319; Robert T. Handy, "Social Gospel Movement," in *Dictionary of Christianity in America*, ed. Daniel G. Reid et al. (Downers Grove, IL: InterVarsity Press, 1990), 1104; White and Hopkins, *Social Gospel*, 6-12; George M. Marsden, *Understanding Fundamentalism and Evangelicalism* (Grand Rapids: Eerdmans, 1991), 28-30; Marty, *Righteous Empire,* 177,178; James E. Moseley, *A Cultural History of Religion in America* (Westport, CT: Greenwood Press, 1981), 84.

8. Wacker, "Social Gospel," 319; Handy, *Christian America*, 137; Ahlstrom, *Religious History*, 788; White and Hopkins, *Social Gospel*, 31-35; Thomas A. Askew and Peter W. Spellman, *The Churches and the American Experience* (Grand Rapids: Baker Books, 1984), 164, 165; Sidney E. Mead, *The Lively Experiment* (New York: Harper and Row, 1963), 182.

9. Ferenc Morton Szasz, *The Divided Mind of Protestant America, 1880-1930* (Tuscaloosa: University of Alabama Press, 1982), 43; Wacker, "Social Gospel," 320; White and Hopkins, *Social Gospel,* 179-89; Donald C. Swift, *Religion and the American Experience* (Armonk, NY: M.E. Sharpe, 1998), 216-219; Askew, *Churches and the American Experience*, 164,165; Martin E. Marty, *Modern American Religion: The Irony of It All, 1893-1919* (Chicago: University of Chicago Press, 1986), 288-93; Winthrop Hudson, *The Great Tradition of the American Churches* (New York: Harper Torchbooks, 1953), 241, 242.

10. Quoted in Handy, *Christian America*, 140; Robert T. Handy, *The Protestant Quest for a Christian America 1830-1930* (Philadelphia: Fortress Press, 1967), 16, 17.

11. Szasz, *Divided Mind*, 46; Handy, *Christian America*, 139-41; George Marsden, *Fundamentalism and American Culture* (New York: Oxford University Press, 1980), 92.

12. Marsden, *Fundamentalism and American Culture*, 86-89; George Marsden, "The Gospel of Wealth, the Social Gospel, and the Salvation of Souls in Nineteenth-Century America," *Fides et Historia* 5, 1 (1973): 18, 19; James H. Moorhead, "The Erosion of Postmillennialism in American Religious Thought, 1865-1925," *Church History* 53, 1 (1984): 61-77; James H. Moorhead, *World Without End: Mainstream American Protestant Visions of the Last Things, 1880-1925* (Bloomington: Indiana University Press, 1999), 170-96; Jean B. Quandt, "Religion and Social Thought: The Secularization of Postmillennialism," *American Quarterly* 25 (October 1973): 390-409; David O. Moberg, *The Great Reversal: Evangelism and Social Concern* (Philadelphia: Lippincott, 1977).

13. Marsden, *Fundamentalism and American Culture*, 90,91 (quote); Marsden, "The Gospel of Wealth," 17; Szasz, *Divided Mind, 55-58;* Askew, *Churches and the American Experience*, 166; Marsden, *Understanding Fundamentalism*, 39-44; Carpenter, *Revive Us Again*, 118, 119; James A. Morone, *Hellfire Nation* (New Haven, CT: Yale University Press, 2003), 337.

14. See Donald G. Mathews, *Religion in the Old South* (Chicago: University of Chicago Press, 1977).

15. See Mark A. Shibley, *Resurgent Evangelicalism in the United States* (Columbia: University of South Carolina Press, 1996), 2, 10, 20.

16. Peter W. Williams, *America's Religions: Traditions and Cultures* (Urbana: University of Illinois Press, 1998), 266, 267; Ahlstrom, *Religious History*, 728; Shibley, *Resurgent Evangelicalism*, 17.

17. Hudson, *Religion in America*, 218 (quote); Williams, *America's Religions*, 269; Stephen R. Haynes, *Noah's Curse: The Biblical Justification of American Slavery* (New York: Oxford University Press, 2002); Laura L. Mitchell, "Original Sin: Slavery and the Biblical Curse of Ham," *Books and Culture* (July/August 2003): 28, 29; Paul Harvey, *Freedom's Coming: Religious Culture and the Shaping of the South from the Civil War through the Civil Rights Era* (Chapel Hill: University of North Carolina Press, 2005).

18. Marsden, *Religion and American Culture*, 169 (quote); Williams, *America's Religions*, 271; Charles Reagan Wilson, *Baptized in Blood: The Religion of the Lost Cause, 1865-1920* (Athens: University of Georgia Press, 1980); Shibley, *Resurgent Evangelicalism*, 14; William R. Glass, *Strangers in Zion: Fundamentalists in the South, 1900-1950* (Macon, GA: Mercer University Press, 2001).

19. Shibley, *Resurgent Evangelicalism*, 14, 15; Williams, *America's Religions*, 273, 274; Ahlstrom, *Religious History*, 728; Marsden, *Religion and American Culture*, 177; Earl and Merle Black, *The Rise of Southern Republicans* (Cambridge, MA: Harvard University Press, 2002).

20. Clarence B. Bass, *Backgrounds to Dispensationalism* (Grand Rapids: Eerdmans, 1960), 19-23; Charles C. Ryrie, *Dispensationalism Today* (Chicago: Moody Press, 1965), 22-47. See also Timothy P. Weber, *On the Road to Armageddon: How Evangelicals Became Israel's Best Friend* (Grand Rapids: Baker Books, 2004).

21. Timothy P. Weber, *Living in the Shadow of the Second Coming* (New York: Oxford University Press, 1979), 22; Bass, *Backgrounds to Dispensationalism*, 17, 18. For more information on Darby and the Plymouth Brethren, see Harold H. Rowdon, *The Origins of the Plymouth Brethren* (London: Pickering and Inglis, 1967); F. Roy Coad, *History of the Brethren Movement* (Grand Rapids: Eerdmans, 1968); George T. Stokes, "John Nelson Darby," *Contemporary Review* 48 (October 1885): 537-52: Henry M. King, " The Plymouth Brethren," *Baptist Review* 3 (1881): 438-65; Thomas Corskery, "The Plymouth Brethren," *Princeton Review*, n.s. 1 (1872): 48-77.

22. Ernest R. Sandeen, *The Roots of Fundamentalism* (Chicago: University of Chicago Press, 1970), 59, 60, 63, quote on 64; Weber, *Living in the Shadow of the Second Coming*, 14, 15; Richard G. Kyle, *The Last Days Are Here Again: A History of the End Times* (Grand Rapids: Baker Books, 1998), 73,74.

23. Bass, *Backgrounds to Dispensationalism*, 129; Kyle, *The Last Days Are Here Again*, 74.

24. Moorhead, "Erosion of Postmillennialism," 63-75; Moorhead, *World Without End*, 2-30; Robert G. Clouse, "The New Christian Right, America, and the Kingdom of God," *Christian Scholars Review* 12 (1983): 6-8; Kyle, *The Last Days Are Here Again*, 102.

25. Weber, *Living in the Shadow of the Second Coming*, 41, 42; Kyle, *The Last Days Are Here Again*, 102.

26. Jon R. Stone, *A Guide to the End of the World: Popular Eschatology in America* (New York: Garland, 1993), 34; Sandeen, *Roots of Fundamentalism*, 74-76; Kyle, *The Last Days Are Here Again*, 104,105; Weber, *Living in the Shadow*, 32, 33;

Russell Chandler, *Doomsday* (Ann Arbor, MI: Servant, 1993), 104, 106; Marsden, *Fundamentalism and American Culture*, 46, 47; Stanley N. Gundry, *Love Them In: The Proclamation Theology of D. L. Moody* (Chicago: Moody Press, 1976), 180, 181.

27. Paul Boyer, *When Time Shall Be No More* (Cambridge, MA: Harvard University Press, 1992), 92; Weber, *Living in the Shadow*, 26-28, 33, 34; William V. Trollinger Jr., *God's Empire: William Bell Riley and Midwestern Fundamentalism* (Madison: University of Wisconsin Press, 1990), 84; Marsden, *Fundamentalism and American Culture*, 32-39; C. Norman Kraus, *Dispensationalism in America: Its Rise and Development* (Chicago: Moody Press, 1965), 71-80; Stone, *Guide to the End of the World*, 47, 48; Douglas W. Frank, *Less Than Conquerors* (Grand Rapids: Eerdmans, 1986), 69, 75.

28. Weber, *Living in the Shadow*, 27-42; Marsden, *Fundamentalism and American Culture*, 124, 125; Sandeen, *Roots of Fundamentalism*, 162-64; Frank, *Less Than Conquerors*, 92, 93; Kyle, *The Last Days Are Here Again*, 105, 106.

29. J. Gordon Melton, *The American Encyclopedia of Religions*, 2 vols. (Wilmington, NC: McGrath, 1978), 1:416, 417; Boyer, *When Time Shall Be No More*, 97, 98; C. W. Whiteman, "Scofield Reference Bible," in *Dictionary of Christianity in America*, 1058; Robert C. Fuller, *Naming the Antichrist* (New York: Oxford University Press, 1995), 125.

30. Sandeen, *Roots of Fundamentalism*, 222; Boyer, *When Time Shall Be No More*, 98; Chandler, *Doomsday*, 106; Kyle, *The Last Days Are Here Again*, 106, 107.

31. Sandeen, *Roots of Fundamentalism*, 222 (quote); Stanley J. Grenz, *The Millennial Maze* (Downers Grove, IL: InterVarsity, 1992), 93.

32. Reuben A. Torrey, *The Return of the Lord Jesus* (Los Angeles: Bible Institute, 1913), 89.

33. Weber, *Living in the Shadow*, 105.

34. Boyer, *When Time Shall Be No More*, 102; Sandeen, *Roots of Fundamentalism*, 224-26.

35. Carpenter, "Fundamentalist Institutions," 62-75; Timothy P. Weber, "Happily at the Edge of the Abyss: Popular Premillennialism in America," *Ex Auditu* 6 (1991): 90; Marsden, *Fundamentalism and American Culture*, 192-95; Sandeen, *Roots of the Fundamentalism*, 219-22.

36. For general information on Pentecostalism, see Walter J. Hollenweger, *The Pentecostals* (Minneapolis: Augsburg, Publishing House, 1972); Vinson Synan, *The Holiness-Pentecostal Movement in the United States* (Grand Rapids: Eerdmans, 1971); John Thomas Nichol, *The Pentecostals* (Plainfield, NJ: Logos International, 1966); Jessyca Russell Gaver, *Pentecostalism* (New York: Award Books, 1971); Robert Mapes Anderson, *The Vision of the Disinherited: The Making of American Pentecostalism* (New York: Oxford University Press, 1979); Vinson Synan, ed., *Aspects of the Pentecostal-Charismatic Origins* (Plainfield , NJ: Logos International, 1975); James R. Goff Jr. and Grant Wacker, "Introduction," in *Portraits of a Generation: Early Pentecostal Leaders*, ed. James R. Goff and Grant Wacker (Fayetteville, AR: University of Arkansas Press, 2002), xi, xii.

37. Grant Wacker, *Heaven Below: Early Pentecostalism and American Culture* (Cambridge, MA: Harvard University Press, 2001), 12 (quote); Melton, *Encyclopedia of American Religions*, 1:243-44; Dennis J. Bennett, "The Gifts of the Holy Spirit," in *The Charismatic Movement*, ed. Michael P. Hamilton (Grand Rapids: Eerdmans, 1975), 16-20.

38. James N. Lapsley and John N. Simpson, "Speaking in Tongues," *The Princeton Seminary Bulletin* 58 (February 1965): 6,7; Synan, *Holiness-Pentecostal Move-*

ment, 122; Grant Wacker, "The Pentecostal Movement," in *Christianity in America*, 336, 337; Donald W. Dayton, *Theological Roots of Pentecostalism* (Grand Rapids: Francis Asbury Press, 1987), 38-54; Anderson, *Vision of the Disinherited*, 47-61; John D. Woodbridge, Mark A. Noll, and Nathan O. Hatch, *The Gospel in America: Themes in the Story of American Evangelicals* (Grand Rapids: Zondervan, 1979), 73-75; Wacker, *Heaven Below*, 1-8; Goff and Wacker, "Introduction," xi, xii.

39. Wacker, "Pentecostal Movement," 336 (quote); Anderson, *Vision of the Disinherited,* 93-97.

40. Wacker, "Pentecostal Movement," 336, 337 (quotes); Dayton, *Roots of Pentecostalism*, 115-37, 143-67; Raymond J. Cunningham, " From Holiness to Healing: The Faith Cure in America 1872-1892," *Church History* 43, 4 (December 1974): 499-513.

41. Anderson, *Vision of the Disinherited*, 223, 224; Bryan Wilson, *Religious Sects* (New York: McGraw-Hill, 1970), 72, 73; Roger Robins, "A. J. Tomlinson: Plainfolk Modernist," in *Portraits of a Generation*, 347, 348, 350-52.

42. See Wacker, *Heaven Below*, and Anderson, *Vision of the Disinherited* for different positions regarding the social status of the early Pentecostals. James R. Goeff, "Thomas Hampton Gourley: Defining the Boundaries," in *Portraits of a Generation*, 143,144.

43. Anderson, *Vision of the Disinherited*, 114,115; Wilson, *Religious Sects*, 70-72; Wacker, *Heaven Below*, 197-216.

44. Roger G. Robins, "Pentecostal Movement," in *Dictionary of Christianity in America*, 888; Nichol, *The Pentecostals*, 123-36; Synan, *Holiness-Pentecostal Movement*, 188; David G. Roebuck, "Loose Women," *Christian History* 27, 2 (issue 58): 38,39; Wacker, *Heaven Below*, 158-76.

45. Martin E. Marty, *Modern American Religion: The Irony of It All, 1893-1919* (Chicago: University of Chicago Press, 1986), 238.

46. Marty, *The Irony of It All*, 236 (quote); Robins, "Pentecostal Movement, 888; Williams, *America's Religions*, 261.

47. Marty, *The Irony of It All*, 238, 239 (quote); George M. Marsden, *Understanding Fundamentalism and Evangelicalism* (Grand Rapids: Eerdmans, 1991), 43; Marsden, *Religion and American Culture*, 157.

48. Ted Olsen, "American Pentecost," *Christian History* 27, 2 (issue 58): 10-13; Nichol, *The Pentecostals*, 25-39; Wacker, "Pentecostal Movement," 337; Robins, "Pentecostal Movement," 886.

49. Frank Bartleman, *Azusa Street* (Plainfield, NJ: Logos International, 1980); Synan, *Holiness-Pentecostal Movement*, 95-116; Nichol, *The Pentecostals*, 32-39; Wacker, "Pentecostal Movement," 337, 338; Robins, "Pentecostal Movement," 888; Olsen, "American Pentecost," 13-15; Hollenweger, *The Pentecostals*, 47-59.

50. Synan, *Holiness-Pentecostal Movement*, 117-39;Wacker, "Pentecostal Movement," 338; Robins, "Pentecostal Movement," 888; Vinson Synan, *The Old-Time Power: A History of the Pentecostal Holiness Church* (Franklin Springs, GA: Advocate Press, 1973).

51. Richard Kyle, *The Religious Fringe: A History of Alternative Religions in America* (Downers Grove, IL: InterVarsity Press, 1993), 154, 164-66; Wacker, "Pentecostal Movement," 338; Robins, "Pentecostal Movement," 889, 890; James R. Goff, Jr., "Pentecostal Quilt," *Christian History* 27, (issue 58): 18, 19; Kenneth Hill, "Dividing Over Oneness," *Christian History* 27, 2 (issue 58): 21; Edith L. Blumhoffer, "Sister," *Christian History* 27, 2 (issue 58): 31-34; Anderson, *Vision of the Disinherited*, 153-94.

52. Mark A. Noll, *The Old Religion in a New World* (Grand Rapids: Eerdmans, 2002), 144, 196; Nathan O. Hatch, *The Democratization of American Christianity* (New Haven, CT: Yale University Press, 1989), 214; Carpenter, *Revive Us Again*, 35, 36.

53. Mark A. Noll, *The Scandal of the Evangelical Mind* (Grand Rapids: Eerdmans, 1994), 119,120; D. G. Hart, *That Old- Time Religion in Modern America: Evangelicalism in the Twentieth Century* (Chicago: Ivan R. Dee, 2002), 35; Kyle, *The Last Days Are Here Again*, 136, 137.

54. Noll, *Old Religion in a New World*, 197, 198.

55. For examples of this social interpretation, see Stewart G. Cole, *The History of Fundamentalism* (New York: (New York: R. R. Smith, 1931); H. Richard Niebuhr, "Fundamentalism," in *Encyclopedia of Social Sciences*, vol. 1 (New York: Macmillan, 1937), 526, 527; William Leuchtenburg, *The Perils of Prosperity: 1914-1932* (Chicago: University of Chicago Press, 1958); George E. Mowry, *The Urban Nation: 1920-1960* (New York: Hill and Wang, 1965). Marty does not take this approach but he does note the social aspects of fundamentalism. See Martin E. Marty, "Fundamentalism as a Social Phenomenon," *Review and Expositor* 19, 1 (1982): 19-29.

56. See Richard Hofstadler, *Anti-Intellectualism in American Life* (New York: Vintage Books, 1963); Ernest R. Sandeen, *The Roots of Fundamentalism* (Chicago: University of Chicago Press, 1970); Timothy Weber, "Fundamentalism," in *Dictionary of Christianity in America*, 462; Ernest R. Sandeen, "Fundamentalism and American Identity," *The Annals of the American Academy of Political and Social Science* 387 (January, 1970): 56-65; LeRoy Moore, Jr., "Another Look at Fundamentalism: A Response to Ernest R. Sandeen," *Church History* 37, 2 (1968): 195-202.

57. Marsden, *Fundamentalism and American Culture*, 4 (quote); George Marsden, "Fundamentalism as an American Phenomenon: A Comparison with English Evangelicalism," *Church History* 46, 2 (1977): 215, 225.

58. Harriet A. Harris, *Fundamentalism and Evangelicals* (Oxford: Clarendon Press, 1998), 17.

59. Marsden, *Fundamentalism and American Culture*, 43-102; Weber, "Fundamentalism," 462; Harris, *Fundamentalism and Evangelicals*, 22-25; Timothy P. Weber, "The Two-Edged Sword: The Fundamentalist Use of the Bible," in *The Bible in America*, ed. Nathan O. Hatch and Mark A. Noll (New York: Oxford University Press, 1982), 101-17.

60. Marsden, *Fundamentalism and American Culture*, 118-23; C. T. McIntire, "Fundamentalism," in *Evangelical Dictionary of Theology*, ed. Walter A. Elwell (Grand Rapids: Baker Book House, 1984), 435; Weber, "Fundamentalism," 463; Harris, *Fundamentalism and Evangelicals*, 25-28; Sydney E. Ahlstrom, "Continental Influence on American Christian Thought Since World War I," *Church History* 37 (1958): 256-73; Sandeen, *The Roots of Funamentalism*, 132-61; Bert James Loewenberg, *Darwinsim Comes to America 1859-1900* (Philadelphia: Fortress Press, 1969).

61. McIntire, "Fundamentalism," 433; Weber, "Fundamentalism," 463; Marsden, *Fundamentalism and American Culture*, 46; Szasz, *Divided Mind*, 74-76; Sandeen, *Roots of Fundamentalism*, 188-207; D. G. Hart, "Right Jabs and Left Hooks," *Christian History* 16, 3 (issue 55): 23-25.

62. Weber, "Fundamentalism," 463; McIntire, "Fundamentalism," 433; Marsden, *Fundamentalism and American Culture*, 152, 158; Szasz, *Divided Mind*, 80-82; Trollinger, *God's Empire*.

63. Marsden, *Understanding Fundamentalism and Evangelicalism*, 51, 52 (quotes); Marty, *The Irony of It All*, 298-316; Marsden, *Religion and American Culture*, 177, 178; Askew, *Churches and the American Experience*, 179, 180; Marsden, *Fundamentalism and American Culture*, 142-52; Hudson, *Religion in America*, 353.

64. Martin E. Marty, *Modern American Religion: The Noise of Conflict 1919-1941* (Chicago: University of Chicago Press, 1991), 59, 60; Marsden, *Understanding Fundamentalism and Evangelicalism*, 53, 54; Marsden, *Fundamentalism and American Culture*, 141-45; Arthur M. Schlesinger, Jr., *The Crisis of the Old Order* (Boston: Houghton Mifflin, 1957), 4, 101, 166; Frederick Lewis Allen, *Only Yesterday* (New York: Harper and Row, 1931), 38-62; Ellis W. Hawley, *The Great War and the Search for a Modern Order* (Prospect Heights, IL: Waveland Press, 1997), 38-40.

65. Marty, *The Noise of Conflict*, 62-64; Marsden, *Understanding Fundamentalism and Evangelicalism*, 54, 55; Swift, *Religion and the American Experience*, 227, 228; Marsden, *Fundamentalism and American Culture*, 153-64; Hawley, *Great War and Search for Order*, 103-06; Leuchtenburg, *Perils of Prosperity*, 204-15; Glen Jeansonne, *Transformation and Reaction: America 1921-1945* (New York: Harper and Row, 1994), 36-42.

66. Marsden, *Understanding Fundamentalism and Evangelicalism*, 55, 56; Allen, *Only Yesterday*, 73-101; Michael L. Kurtz, *The Challenging of America 1920-1945* (Arlington Heights, IL: Forum Press, 1986), 31-50; Leuchtenburg, *Perils of Prosperity*, 158-77; Jeansonne, *Transformation and Reaction*, 54-73.

67. Elijah P. Brown, *The Real Billy Sunday* (Dayton, OH: Otterbein Press, 1914), 200 (quote); William T. Ellis, *Billy Sunday, The Man and His Message* (Philadelphia: John C. Winston Co., 1936), 487-88; W. G. McLoughlin, Jr., *Billy Sunday Was His Name* (Chicago: University of Chicago Press, 1955); Robert F. Martin, *Hero of the Heartland: Billy Sunday and the Transformation of American Society* (Bloomington: Indiana University Press, 2002).

68. William McLoughlin, Jr., *Modern Revivalism* (New York: Ronald Press, 1959), 415, 416; Lyle W. Dorset, "William (Billy) Ashley Sunday," in *Dictionary of Christianity in America*, 1146; William G. McLoughlin, *Revivals, Awakenings, and Reform* (Chicago: University of Chicago Press, 1978), 146.

69. Bernard A. Weisberger, *They Gathered at the River: The Story of the Great Revivalists and Their Impact Upon Religion in America* (New York: Octagon Books, 1979), 247; McLoughlin, *Modern Revivalism*, 426,427; McLoughlin, *Revivals, Awakenings, and Reform*, 147; Robert R. Mathisen, "Samuel (Sam) Porter Jones," in *Dictionary of Christianity in America*, 602.

70. Marty, *The Irony of It All*, 217 (quote).

71. McLoughlin, *Modern Revivalism*, 409, 411 (quotes).

72. McLoughlin, *Billy Sunday*, 125, 132, 138 (quotes); Richard Hofstadter, *Anti-Intellectualism in American Life* (New York: Random House, 1963), 122.

73. McLoughlin, *Modern Revivalism*, 433, quotes on 435, 444; Weisberger, *They Gathered at the River*, 243, 250; Marty, *The Noise of the Conflict*, 74.

74. McLoughlin, *Modern Revivalism*, 427 (quotes); Weisberger, *They Gathered at the River*, 248; Ellis, *Billy Sunday*, 204, 205; Tony Ladd and James A. Mathisen, *Muscular Christianity* (Grand Rapids: Baker Books, 1999), 77-94. See also Guy Lewis, "The Muscular Christianity Movement," *Journal of Health, Physical Education, Recreation* (May 1966): 27, 28, 42; William E. Winn, "Tom Brown's Schooldays and the Development of Muscular Christianity," *Church History* 29, 1 (1960): 364-73; Guy Lewis, "The Muscular Christianity Movement," *Johper* 37 (May 1966): 27,28, 42; Clifford Putney, *Muscular Christianity: Manhood and Sports in Protestant America, 1880-1920* (Cambridge, MA: Harvard University Press, 2001); Margaret Bendroth, "Why Women Loved Billy Sunday: Urban Revivalism and Popular Entertainment in Early Twentieth-Century American Culture," *Religion and American Culture* 14, 2 (summer 2004): 251-71.

75. McLoughlin, *Modern Revivalism,* 400, 402, 411, 435-37; Weisberger, *They Gathered at the River*, 262, 263.
76. McLoughlin, *Modern Revivalism*, 420-24; Dorset, "Billy Sunday," 1146; Weisberger, *They Gathered at the River,* 250-53; Joel Carpenter, "Billy Sunday," in *Christianity in America*, 372.
77. Handy, *Christian America,* 182; Hudson, *The Great Tradition of the American Churches,* 201, 202.
78. Marsden, *Fundamentalism and American Culture*, 49 (quote).
79. Handy, *Christian America*, 182; Marsden, *Fundamentalism and American Culture*, 49, 124, 141, 183; Marty, *The Noise of the Conflict*, 174.
80. Marsden, *Understanding Fundamentalism and Evangelicalism*, 57; Marsden, *Fundamentalism and American Culture,* 72-80; Szasz, *Divided Mind*, 72-74.
81. Szasz, *Divided Mind*, 102-05; Marsden, *Understanding Fundamentalism and Evangelicalism*, 57,58; Askew, *Churches and the American Experience*, 186.
82. Marsden, *Understanding Fundamentalism and Evangelicalism*, 58, 59; Ahlstrom, *Religious History*, 911,912; Weber, "Fundamentalism," 463; George W. Dollar, *A History of Fundamentalism in America* (Greenville, SC: Bob Jones University Press, 1973), 162-72; Szasz, *Divided Mind*, 94-106.
83. George M. Marsden, "J. Gresham Machen, History and Truth," *Westminster Theological Journal* 42 (1979): 157-75; D. G. Hart, *Defending the Faith: J. Gresham Machen and the Crisis of Conservative Protestantism in Modern America* (Baltimore, MD: Johns Hopkins University Press, 1994); Weber, "Fundamentalism," 464, 465.
84. Szasz, *Divided Mind*, 126-30; Ahlstrom, *Religious History*, 910; Cynthia Eagle Russett, *Darwin in America: The Intellectual Response* 1865-1912 (San Francisco: Freeman, 1976), 38-43; Marty, *The Noise of Conflict*, 188.
85. Hofstadtler, *Anti-Intellectualism in American Life*, 128, Szasz, *Divided Mind*, 118, 132, 133; Dollar, *Fundamentalism in America*, 159-62.
86. Szasz, *Divided Mind*, 134 (quote); Hofstadler, *Anti-Intellectualism in American Life*, 130; Mark A. Noll, *The Scandal of the Evangelical Mind* (Grand Rapids: Eerdmans, 1994), 114-39.
87. Hofstadtler, *Anti-Intellectualism in American Life*, 128, 129 (quotes); Szasz, *Divided Mind*, 132, 133.
88. Marsden, *Religion and American Culture,* 184, 185; Szasz, *Divided Mind*, 110-16, 118-20; David Goetz, "The Monkey Trial," *Christian History* 16, 3 (issue 55): 25-25.
89. Ahlstrom, *Religious History*, 909; Harris, *Fundamentalism and Evangelicals*, 32, 33; Szasz, *Divided Mind*, 120, 121; Marsden, *Religion and American Culture*, 185; Marsden, *Fundamentalism and American Culture*, 184-86.
90. Harris, *Fundamentalism and Evangelicals*, 33, 34; Szasz, *Divided Mind*, 121; Marsden, *Understanding Fundamentalism and Evangelicalism*, 60; Marsden, *Religion and American Culture*, 185, 186; Marsden, *Fundamentalism and American Culture*, 187, 186; Randall Balmer and Lauren F. Winter, *Protestantism in America* (New York: Columbia University Press, 2002), 64; Moore, *Touchdown Jesus*, 131.
91. Quoted in Henry May, *The Discontent of the Intellectuals: A Problem of the Twenties* (Chicago: Rand McNally, 1963), 29.
92. Marsden, *Understanding Fundamentalism and Evangelicalism*, 60; Szasz, *Divided Mind*, 122,123; Balmer, *Protestantism in America*, 64; Moore, *Touchdown Jesus*, 132.
93. Marsden, *Religion and American Culture*, 186, 187; Joel Carpenter, "From Fundamentalism to the New Evangelical Coalition," in *Evangelicalism and Modern America*, ed. George Marsden (Grand Rapids: Eerdmans, 1984), 4; Balmer, *Protestantism in America*, 64; Swift, *Religion and the American Experience*, 237.

94. Swift, *Religion and the American Experience*, 237, 238; Noll, *Christianity in America*, 404, 405; Leuchtenburg, *The Perils of Prosperity*, 158-77.

95. Carpenter, *Revive Us Again*, 100, 101; Swift, *Religion and the American Experience*, 238; Noll, *Christianity in America*, 405; Hostadler, *Anti-Intellectualism in American Life*, 131.

96. Robert T. Handy, "The American Religious Depression, 1925-1935," *Church History* 29 (1960): 2-16; Frederick Allen, *Since Yesterday 1929-1939* (New York: Harper and Row, 1940); Marsden, *Religion and American Culture*, 187; Marty, *The Noise of the Conflict*, 253, 254; Swift, *Religion and the American Experience*, 238.

97. Carpenter, *Revive Us Again*, 15, 43-46; Mark A. Noll, *A History of Christianity in the United States and Canada* (Grand Rapids: Eerdmans, 1992), 385; Weber, "Fundamentalism," 464; McIntire, "Fundamentalism," 434; Marty, *Righteous Empire*, 218-20; Ahlstrom, *Religious History*, 912-15; Carpenter, "From Fundamentalism to the New Evangelical Coalition," 5, 6; Barry Hankins, *God's Rascal: J. Frank Norris and the Beginnings of Southern Fundamentalism* (Lexington: University of Kentucky Press, 1996).

98. Handy, "American Religious Depression," 2-16; Carpenter, "From Fundamentalism to New Evangelical Coalition," 6; Noll, *Christianity in America*, 407; Carpenter, "Fundamentalist Institutions," 66-69; Carpenter, *Revive us Again*, 22-30.

99. Carpenter, "Fundamentalist Institutions," 65-67; Weber, "Fundamentalism," 464; Carpenter, *Revive Us Again*, 18, 29, 30, 55, 74, 75; Hart, *That Old-Time Religion*, 49, 58.

100. Tona J. Hangen, *Redeeming the Dial: Radio, Religion, and Popular Culture in America* (Chapel Hill: University of North Carolina Press, 2002), 10 (quote).

101. Quentin J. Schultze, "Evangelical Radio and the Rise of the Electronic Church, 1921-1948," *Journal of Broadcasting and Electronic Media* 3, 32 (1988): 292-94; Carpenter, "Fundamentalist Institutions," 70, 71; Douglas Carl Abrams, *Selling the Old-Time Religion: American Fundamentalists and Mass Culture, 1920-1940* (Athens: University of Georgia Press, 2001), 58, 59; Spencer Miller, Jr., "Radio and Religion," *The Annals of the American Academy of Political and Social Science* 177 (January 1955): 135-40; Dave Berkman, "Long Before Falwell: Early Radio and Religion—As Reported by the Nation's Periodical Press," *Journal of Popular Culture* 21 (spring 1988): 1-11.

102. R. Laurence Moore, *Selling God: American Religion in the Marketplace of Culture* (New York: Oxford University Press, 1994), 292-94; Schultze, "Evangelical Radio," 295-97; Carpenter, "Fundamentalist Institutions," 70, 71; Roger Finke and Laurence R. Iannoccone, "Supply-Side Explanations for Religious Change," *Annals of the American Academy of Political and Social Science* 527 (May 1953): 27-39; Charles M. Crowe, "Religion on the Air," *The Christian Century* 23 (August 1944): 973-75.

103. Hangen, *Redeeming the Dial*, 37, 38 (quote), 48-53; Carpenter, *Revive us Again*, 129,130.

104. Hangen, *Redeeming the Dial*, 62, 63 (quote), 64; Abrams, *Selling the Old-Time Religion*, 114, 115; Matthew A. Sutton, "Between the Refrigerator and the Wildfire: Aimee Semple McPherson, Pentecostalism, and the Fundamentalist-Modernist Controversy," *Church History* 72, 1 (2003): 159-88.

105. Schultze, " Evangelical Radio," 293-97; Carpenter, "Fundamentalist Institutions," 71; Hangen, *Redeeming the Dial*, 80-94; Carpenter, *Revive Us Again*, 129,130; Abrams, *Selling the Old-*Time *Religion*, 34-38.

106. Schultze, "Evangelical Radio," 290, 302 (quote); Hangen, *Redeeming the Dial*, 16-19.

107. Balmer, *Protestantism in America*, 64, 65; Hart, *That Old-Time Religion*, 44; James Davison Hunter, *American Evangelicalism* (New Brunswick, NJ: Rutgers University Press, 1983), 39, 40.

108. Hofstadtler, *Anti-Intellectualism in American Life*, 135; Balmer, *Protestantism in America*, 65; Carpenter, "From Fundamentalism to the New Evangelical Coalition," 4, 5; Carpenter, *Revive Us Again*, 66; Marsden, *Fundamentalism and American Culture*, 4; Ernest R. Sandeen, "Fundamentalism and American Identity, *Annals of the American Academy of Political and Social Science* 387 (January 1970), 60-62.

109. Marsden, *Understanding Fundamentalism and Evangelicalism*, 100, 101; Hart, *That Old-Time Religion*, 34-40; Carpenter, *Revive Us Again*, 49, 50; Noll, *Scandal of the Evangelical Mind*, 118-20.

110. Carpenter, *Revive Us Again*, 37, 49-52; Noll, *Scandal of the Evangelical Mind*, 119.

111. Carpenter, *Revive Us Again*, 66, 67; McLoughlin, *Modern Revivalism*, 427, 449; Weisberger, *They Gathered at the River*, 248, 249; Ladd, *Muscular Christianity*, 77-86; Abrams, *Selling the Old-Time Religion*, 42, 43.

112. Abrams, *Selling the Old-Time Religion*, 102-110; Balmer, *Protestantism in America*, 65; Steven J. Keillor, *This Rebellious House* (Downers Grove, IL: InterVarsity Press, 1996), 187-95.

113. Carpenter, *Revive Us Again*, 67 (quote); Abrams, *Selling the Old-Time Religion*, 105, 110-15; John R. Rice, *Bobbed Hair, Bossy Wives and Women Preachers* (Wheaton, IL: Sword of the Lord, 1941), 65, 77; Balmer, *Protestantism in America*, 65; Noll, *American Evangelicalism*, 90-92.

114. Marsden, *Fundamentalism and American Culture*, 141-70, 184-92, 206-11; Carpenter, *Revive Us Again*, 103; Hart, *That Old-Time Religion*, 100-02; Paul T. Coughlin, *Secrets, Plots and Hidden Agendas* (Downers Grove, IL: InterVarsity Press, 1999), 26-28.

115. Hart, *That Old-Time Religion*, 101, 102; Richard Hofstadter, *The Paranoid Style in American Politics and Other Essays* (New York: Vintage Books, 1967), 29; Robert Booth Fowler, Allen D. Hertzke, and Laura R. Olson, *Religion and Politics in America*, 2nd ed. (Boulder, CO: Westview Press, 1999), 25, 26.

116. Ahlstrom, *Religious History*, 926-28; Hart, *That Old-Time Religion*, 102-04; Carpenter, *Revive Us Again*, 102, 103; Hofstadter, *Anti-Intellectualism in American Life*, 131, 132; Swift, *Religion and the American Experience*, 239, 240.

117. Abrams, *Selling the Old-Time Religion*, 65; Hart, *That Old-Time Religion*, 74, 75; David D. Bundy, "Victorious Christian Life," in *Dictionary of Christianity in America*, 1124.

118. Abrams, *Selling the Old-Time Religion*, 65-79; Hart, *That Old-Time Religion*, 73-75.

119. Marsden, *Understanding Fundamentalism and Evangelicalism*, 110, 111; Carpenter, *Revive us Again*, 76; Carpenter, "From Fundamentalism to the New Evangelical Coalition," 9.

120. Marty, *The Noise of the Conflict*, 174; Hart, *That Old-Time Religion*, 110, 111.

121. Abrams, *Selling the Old-Time Religion*, 1-4; Hart, *That Old-Time Religion*, 106,107; Hofstadter, *Anti-Intellectualism in American Life*, 131, 132.

122. Abrams, *Selling the Old-Time Religion*, 1-6; Hudson, *Religion in America*, 354,355; Warren I. Susman, *Culture as History: The Transformation of American Society in the Twentieth Century* (New York: Pantheon Books, 1984), 130-32; Cross, *An All-Consuming Century*, 17-65.

123. Abrams, *Selling the Old-Time Religion*, 12-22 (quote on 13); Hudson, *Religion in America*, 354, 355; Peter Dobkin Hall, "Moving Targets: Evangelicalism and the Transformation of American Economic Life, 1870-1920," in *More Money, More Ministry*, ed. Larry Eskridge and Mark A. Noll (Grand Rapids: Eerdmans, 2000), 168, 169.

5

Reaction and Renewal

Evangelicals have often maintained a hate-love attitude toward American society. Still, in the years following World War II this paradoxical relationship became more obvious. The separatist fundamentalists continued to challenge American society in a range of ways. More moderate evangelicals, however, began to engage society. They maintained their theological orthodoxy, and they had few doctrinal differences with the fundamentalists. Evangelicals, nevertheless, began to distance themselves from their more belligerent and anti-intellectual fundamentalist cousins.

The paradox does not end here. Both the fundamentalists and the evangelicals bought heavily into the affluent society, which developed after World War II. Like most Americans, they succumbed to materialism. In some other areas, the fundamentalists-evangelicals continued the trends begun in the nineteenth century. Whether operating their businesses or running church organizations, they employed efficient methods, the latest media technologies, and bold advertising. For their preaching and music they took a page from the most entertaining secular sources.

While still confronting many social trends—abortion, sexual permissiveness, homosexuality, pornography, drugs, gambling, and feminism—except for the strictest fundamentalists, most evangelicals progressively caved in to the norms of society. Previously, they forbade movies but television made this impractical. Evangelicals now advised people which movies to watch and which not to watch. Jazz and rock music were previously prohibited. By the last twenty years of the century, the evangelicals had Christianized such music. Except for going to church on Sunday, Sabbath observance was a thing of the past. After church, evangelicals often went to the shopping mall or watched the ball game. The megachurches adapted to society in nearly every conceivable way and did all they could not to resemble a church. Evangelicals replaced serious biblical teaching and prophetic preaching with feel good and how to do it sermons. Church growth, indeed, came by conforming to society, not resisting it.

The way evangelicals view the end of world presents a particular paradox. Postmillennialism had seriously declined and some evangelicals were amillennialists, but most embraced the premillennial position. Premillennialism sees the world getting worse and worse until Christ returns to set up the millennium. But most premillennialists act like postmillennialists: they are working to change America for the better. They can be very critical of America, but they have not given up on the nation. It is still God's chosen instrument for reaching the world. Together, the sales of Hal Lindsey's *The Late Great Planet Earth* and Tim LaHaye's *Left Behind* series have reached 100,000,000. One can thus assume that millions of people have embraced the premillennial-pretribulational position regarding the end of time. In spite of believing that the world will end in the not too distant future, many of these people drive expensive cars and have invested heavily in this late great planet, including long-term real estate ventures.[1]

The Happy Fifties

Such trends have their roots in nineteenth-century evangelical practices. But the events of the 1950s set the stage for many later twentieth-century developments. Many people, including numerous evangelicals, regard the 1950s and early 1960s as a golden age—a time when Christian values prevailed. If this perception is correct, it has two causes. First, America experienced a booming prosperity, one that significantly shaped the nations' social, economic, and physical landscape. Second, the Cold War and the struggle with communism created much anxiety. These forces helped forge two post-World War II characteristics—a self-satisfied society and a national purpose. But this consumer society and patriotism also had the effect of blinding the nation to some of the problems that would explode in the 1960s.[2]

The prosperity of the 1950s and early 1960s dwarfed anything that had preceded it, even the economic surge of the 1920s. This economic expansion was much sounder and wider spread than that of thirty years earlier and would continue for almost twenty years. There occurred an explosion in science and technology, including breakthroughs in medicine, electronics, military research, and the space program. Socially, the most striking development centered on the extension of a middle-class lifestyle. The key to understanding the American character of the postwar era concerns the expansion of prosperity to millions of people, pushing them into the ranks of the middle class. The middle-class culture became absorbed with consumer goods. Fueled by credit, middle-class people could now afford automobiles and television—the two commodities that did the most to shape middle-class culture. The automobile gave Americans mobility and created the suburbs. The impact of television was pervasive, becoming the most important source for news and entertainment.[3]

Forces of both continuity and change were active in post-World War II America. Historians have tended to focus on the enormous change, ignoring the fact that such forces had already been active for much of the twentieth century. During the 1960s, many elements in American society exploded; thus this period is often seen as a revolutionary decade, a watershed in American society. Such observations are essentially true. But the 1960s were also a time when the "chickens came home to roost." This turbulent decade served as a catalyst to forces already in motion. Long-term economic, moral, theological and cultural processes were brought to a crisis point by rapid social change and the tremendous economic expansion that Americans had experienced and carelessly enjoyed during the affluent years following World War II.[4]

The 1950s are generally seen as a conservative and affluent period. A popular president, Dwight Eisenhower, presided over the peak of a postwar economic boom. The friendly policies of this administration helped to promote a decade of industrial growth. Middle America shared in this prosperity, enjoying a steady rise in living standards. The Soviet Union had the bomb; Japanese and European economies were recovering from the war. Still, America was not yet seriously challenged either economically or militarily. Not surprisingly, the prevailing mood was complacency. Nevertheless, in the late 1950s, many premonitory signs could be seen on the horizon. Certain attitudes and interests of the 1950s presaged the secularizing theologies of the 1960s. A group of young poets, artists, and writers known as the "beats"—or "beatniks" by their critics—decried the homogenized middle-class society. The unrest in the black community in the late 1950s was a sign of what was to come. President Eisenhower's speech concerning the growing power of the "the military-industrial complex" gave hints of the next decades radical protests.[5]

The Revival of Mainline and Civil Religion

During the 1950s, evangelicalism experienced a revival. But it was not alone. Mainline Protestantism, Catholicism, and even a version of civil religion also staged a comeback. Religion, indeed, prospered in the late 1940s and 1950s. Why? Three words—anxiety, prosperity, and mobility—summarize the causes of this revival. During this time, Americans were an anxious lot. They had just come out of the Depression, which they feared would return, only to go through World War II. This terrible war ended with a mushroom-shaped cloud, which ushered the world into the atomic age. The world then jumped into the Cold War with the Soviet Union, a potent enemy with nuclear weapons. If this was not bad enough, in Korea the Cold War became a hot war. Meanwhile, we turned on ourselves. Senator Joe McCarthy launched a witch-hunt intended to root out the so-called communists in the government and society. Anxiety and insecurity drove Americans back to religion, but prosperity also helped. Donations rose, enabling Protestants to erect church buildings and to launch new programs. This prosperity enabled Americans to become more mobile. They bought automobiles in record numbers and moved to the suburbs, thus creating a suburban Christianity. Such a Christianity often became privatized and blinded church members to the plight of people in the cities.[6]

Unprecedented numbers of Americans were evincing an interest in religion. Polls confirmed this impression. Two out of three attended some kind of religious service at least once a month. Nineteen out of twenty believed in God. Nine out of ten claimed to engage in some kind of prayer; six of seven believed the Bible to be divinely inspired; and three out of four hoped for life after death. Much of this religious interest, however, tended to be shallow and very general. Americans favored some kind of "religion-in-general" and saw God as the kindly "man upstairs," notes Martin Marty. This type of religion blended well with the humanitarian and secular values of the immediate postwar era, namely, democracy, individualism, capitalism, anti-communism, and patriotism. As through much of its history, America was both very religious and secular at the same time, and Americans often could not tell the difference. Or as Richard Hughes puts it, "many Americans confused religion in general with the Christian faith and therefore imagined that America was still a Christian nation..."[7]

Accompanying this general religiosity was a revival of civil religion. Dwight Eisenhower became president in 1953, and he symbolized American spiritual values and patriotic moralism. The nation's capitol saw special church services and prayer breakfasts, which members of the Eisenhower administration often attended. Eisenhower's famous quote captured the religious mood and provides some justification for the spiritual outlook of the time: "Our government makes no sense, unless it is founded in a deeply felt religious faith—and I don't care what it is." Like many Americans, Eisenhower was a "very fervent believer in a very vague religion," notes William Miller.[8]

But this "piety on the Potomac" was not limited to the executive branch of government. It spilled on to Congress, who took steps to extend the nineteenth-century's de facto establishment of religion. In 1954, they added the words "under God" to the Pledge of Allegiance. This phrase, of course, was subject to many meanings. Fundamentalists later used it to reinforce their notion that America was a Christian nation. Humanists could go along with this expression of national loyalty and the general religiosity contained therein. Since 1865, American coins have had printed on them the statement "In God We Trust." In 1956, Congress elevated this semi-official phrase to the nation's official motto. Americans in general equated this revival of religion with patriotic Americanism, a strident anti-communism, and a sense of American righteousness.[9]

During the 1950s, both mainline Protestants and Catholics expressed this general faith in faith. Most famous was Norman Vincent Peale (1898-1993), an inspirationalist and New York Protestant preacher who attained great fame.

His book, *The Power of Positive Thinking* (1952), became a run-away best seller. He preached a gospel of peace of mind and faith in human capabilities. His book contained many steps for success, but it came down to self-confidence: "Believe in yourself! Have faith in your abilities!" Peale's human potential approach to religion has come down to us today through Robert Schuler's ministry. Not to be left out, during the 1950s, the Catholics also had their own tremendously popular priest—Bishop Fulton J. Sheen (1895-1979). Well educated and scholarly, Sheen addressed popular and practical subjects. His blend of common sense and patriotism appealed to millions of Americans of all faiths. And his phenomenal success on radio and television paved the way for future religious broadcasting.[10]

From Fundamentalism to Evangelicalism

Fundamentalism acquired a different identity during the 1930s. Previously, fundamentalists were people within the denominations who took a stand for the orthodox faith and rejected the new theological trends. After the defeats of the 1920s, many of them became more belligerent and narrowed their doctrine and religious associations. For example, to the essentials of the Christian faith they added the doctrine of Christ's premillennial Second Coming. Fundamentalists tended to judge a person's spiritual condition by their adherence to certain doctrines and social practices. And they severed relations with those who did not conform to these standards or whom they regarded as too moderate. In the mind of many, they developed a paranoid style. Fundamentalists, indeed, had a penchant for conspiratorial theories. They saw many events as signs of Christ's return or perhaps a communist conspiracy. As a result, they became identified with anti-intellectualism, extremism, and combativeness.[11]

Many moderate evangelicals desired to distance themselves from this brand of fundamentalism. They wanted to free themselves from the intellectual and cultural straightjacket that fundamentalism had placed them in. Led by Harold J. Ockenga , Bernard Ramm, and Carl F. Henry, they faulted fundamentalism for its divisiveness, anti-intellectualism, lack of social concern, and uncritical acceptance of conservative political and economic policies. Edward J. Carnell leveled a broadside at fundamentalism for its failure to engage modern intellectual thought. Desiring to achieve intellectual respectability, Charles Fuller funded the establishment of Fuller Theological Seminary in 1947. A score of other evangelical seminaries were also founded. As a format for addressing current religious issues, other evangelicals began a new magazine— *Christianity Today* (1956). Neo-evangelicalism, as many called it, established a number of parachurch ministries—Youth for Christ, Campus Crusade for Christ, and Young Life. At the center of this evangelical resurgence and the symbol for the movement was Billy Graham (1918-)—a subject that will be noted in more detail later.[12]

These moderate evangelicals felt the need to be organized. Since 1908 the Federal Council of Churches (FCC) represented mainstream Protestantism, but by the 1930s many conservatives had become increasingly uncomfortable with this organization. So in 1941, fundamentalist separatists led by Carl McIntire (1906-2002) formed the American Council of Christian Churches (ACCC) to counter the FCC. The confrontational nature of McIntire's organization, primarily to attack the FCC, disturbed many moderate evangelicals. These evangelicals believed that a Christian organization should be more positive, less belligerent, and more inclusive. Thus, in 1942, they began a new organization—the National Association of Evangelicals (NAE). They avoided such confrontational terms as *fundamentalist* or *modernist,* and came to be called neo-evangelicals or just evangelicals. This organization signaled the start of a new evangelical coalition—one that upheld the orthodox faith but desired to reenter the mainstream of American life. In doing so, it saw itself as reviving nineteenth-century evangelical Protestantism and bringing a national spiritual renewal.[13]

This new organization grew because of several factors. The NAE accepted a number of groups previously influenced by fundamentalism, but still estranged from it because of some doctrinal differences. For example, a number of holiness-pentecostal denominations had embraced dispensational premillennialism and considered themselves to be "fundamental." But because of the tongues-speaking issue, the fundamentalists would not accept them. Some of them joined the NAE. Two, evangelicalism assimilated a number of European ethnic communities, especially the Christian Reformed Church, which infused the movement with considerable intellectual vigor. It provided evangelicalism with several publishers (Eerdmans, Baker, and Zondervan), which became primary outlets for evangelical scholars.[14]

Other like-minded groups continued to form this new evangelical coalition, gradually building up a broad constituency. Some of these denominations formally joined the NAE, others just shared similar beliefs and values. Because it had its own distinct identity, the Southern Baptist Convention—the largest Protestant body in America—did not become a formal member. While many black Protestants had a radically different history and their members do not call themselves evangelicals, they have shared convictions and values with white evangelicals. Other bodies that were evangelical in their outlook and practices include Mennonites, many Lutherans, and several holiness bodies, especially the Christian Missionary Alliance and Nazarenes. In fact, this evangelical coalition has grown so broad that it is difficult to define exactly what an evangelical is or to draw a line between evangelicalism and other Protestants.[15]

These neo-evangelicals also underwent intellectual changes. They broadened their horizons by tapping into the ideas of British evangelicals. Thanks to the efforts of the British InterVarsity Press and fellowship, British evangelicals gained intellectual respectability. American evangelicals began to cross the Atlantic for their graduate training and in America many more began to read the works of British evangelical scholars, especially F. F. Bruce, James I. Packer, and John R. W. Stott. The greatest British influence on American evangelicalism, however, came not from an evangelical but from C. S. Lewis. His books experienced a phenomenal reception in America because many evangelicals were seeking an expression of the Christian faith that contained intellectual substance and beauty.[16]

In yet another way, many evangelicals broke out of fundamentalism's intellectual straightjacket. During the 1930s, dispensational premillennialism was taught in most fundamentalist and Pentecostal churches. Believing that the world will end in the near future with Christ's return, dispensationalists view the surrounding culture negatively and regard social services as a useless activity. Their negative attitude toward the churches prompted them to adopt a separatist attitude toward other religious institutions. In attempting to free themselves from this negativism, many evangelicals moved away from dispensationalism.[17]

Rather than promote this relatively recent and narrow theological innovation, they aligned themselves with more traditional Christian orthodoxies—Calvinism, Lutheranism, Anabaptism, Anglicanism, or Wesleyan-Arminianism. Carl Henry's *Uneasy Conscience of Modern Fundamentalism* (1947) attacked fundamentalism for regarding personal piety as a substitute for social concern. In addition, the Bible colleges and popular preachers promoted an anti-intellectualism that became associated with dispensational fundamentalism. This embarrassed the neo-evangelicals and encouraged them to distance themselves from the fundamentalists.[18]

To establish a new movement is not what the evangelicals initially intended. They set out to reform fundamentalism, not to break from it. In George Marsden's words, they "were not breaking away entirely from original fundamentalism since original fundamentalism included the defense of the very orthodoxy they were attempting to recover." In taking this position, the evangelicals placed themselves in somewhat of an "ecclesiastical no man's land between two warring sides," the fundamentalists and the liberals. In effect, they were redrawing the line between the fundamentalists and secular society and in doing so placed themselves in the middle. Since the evangelicals agreed with the fundamentalists in respect to the essentials of the faith, this middle position was not ideological but social. The real issue centered on this question: Were the fundamentalist churches and associations going to be inclusive or exclusive?[19]

The Fundamentalist Response

How did the militant fundamentalists respond to the development of neo-evangelicalism? They did not like it. They viewed the neo-evangelicals as compromisers and defectors who had sold out the faith. They had minimized essential Christian doctrines and associated with people from apostate denominations. Despite tensions, however, strict separatists such as Bob Jones, Sr. (1883-1968) and John R. Rice (1895-1980) maintained connections with the NAE into the 1950s. But these issues came to a head during Billy Graham's 1957 New York City crusade. Graham had been moving away from separatist fundamentalism and began associating with the respectable centers of American life. In his New York crusade, he accepted the sponsorship of the local Protestant Council of Churches—which was dominated by mainline Protestants—and Catholics in the work of evangelism. This infuriated the fundamentalists, who regarded separation from apostasy as an essential Christian doctrine. It cost Graham the support of the ACCC, of Bob Jones University, and of Rice, who edited the fundamentalist newspaper *The Sword of the Lord*.[20]

The fundamentalists boycotted the Graham crusade and avoided any institutions that had been contaminated by the neo-evangelicals. In the aftermath of the Graham crusade, the division between fundamentalists and neo-evangelicals became clearer. Strict ecclesiastical separation became a mark of the fundamentalists, and their former allies went by the name of *evangelicals*. Bob Jones derisively described these evangelicals as "fudgymentalists," and insisted that Scripture demanded two types of separation, ecclesiastical and personal. While some evangelicals may personally separate from sin, they certainly ignore ecclesiastical separation. Because of this failure, he questioned whether they believed in Scripture as the Word of God.[21]

Viewing the evangelicals weak-kneed and heretical, the fundamentalists began to see them as more compromising than even the liberals. They "do more harm to the cause of the Gospel and the purity of the Church than the liberals themselves," noted Carl McIntire. As time went on, both the fundamentalists and evangelicals continued to uphold the orthodox Christian faith, but differences in lifestyle and response to the world increased. The fundamentalists remained committed to resisting the beliefs and lifestyle of the modern world at all costs. To compromise in either would be disastrous. Conversely, the evangelicals were becoming very middle class and culturally mainstream.[22]

This refusal to compromise has continued to create divisions within the fundamentalist movement. When they disagree with each other, they do not negotiate the differences but create new organizations. After all, each group regards themselves as the "true Bible believers," as the defenders of the "true faith." As a result, like evangelicalism, fundamentalism is a loose coalition not bound to any one person or organization. While its numbers may not be large, it has continued to have a significant impact, especially in politics—a subject that will be noted later. To a large extent, fundamentalism's influence has continued because its mentality—its way of thinking in uncompromising black and white terms—has penetrated the evangelical subculture.[23]

Fundamentalism's assault on liberalism and neo-evangelicalism had political overtones. On the whole, from the election of Hoover in 1928 to the early 1970s, conservative Protestants tended not to participate in politics. The exception was fundamentalism's militant opposition toward communism. In this crusade, they were in sync with the national mood of the late 1940s and 1950s. The Cold War was in full swing. Communism had taken over Eastern Europe, China had fallen, Americans had fought communism in Korea, and other areas of Southeast Asia were being threatened. In this context, nearly all religious groups adopted a strong anti-communist stance. Moreover, the McCarthy witch-hunts made the notion of internal conspiracies seem plausible. Being patriotic and prone to believe conspiracy theories, the fundamentalists became caught up in all of this. And they targeted their religious opponents, the liberals and evangelicals alike as less than patriotic.[24]

In the early 1950s, Carl McIntire of the ACCC, Edgar Bundy of the Church of America, and Billy James Hargis of the Christian Crusade led the charge against the perceived communist infiltration of the churches. They focused their guns on the National Council of Churches (NCC) and World Council of Churches (WCC). They regarded these liberal organizations as apostate, un-American, and procommunist. The logic of these fundamentalists was simple: "liberalism is socialism and socialism is the first phase of communism." McIntire and Hargis used the radio to spread their anti-communist message. They regarded it as their duty as both Christians and patriotic Americans to fight atheistic communism and to root out the "Red clergy." While the liberal Protestants were the primary object of this fundamentalist assault, McIntire tended to lump everything on his left together. Beginning with the conservative magazine *Christianity Today* and its editor, Carl Henry, he accused the evangelicals of being "soft" on communism.[25]

The Revival of Revivalism

The 1920s and 1930s witnessed a decline in revivalism for reasons that are not always clear. Billy Sunday's emotional antics from the pulpit may have soured some people on revivalism. Sinclair Lewis's 1927 novel, *Elmer Gantry,* created a negative image of evangelists that lasted for years. Gantry was a scam artist who used the pulpit as a means to bilk the faithful out of money. During the 1920s and 1930s, liberal Protestants saw revivalism as a tool of the fundamentalists and thus had little use for it. They regarded educational institutions and social agencies (YMCA, YWCA, Sunday school, universities, etc.)—not conversion— as the best means to Christianize America. The decline of revivalism, said William Warren Sweet, was because rugged individualism and emotionalism—the staples of revivalism—were not in vogue.[26]

During the 1950s, mainline Protestantism and civil religion experienced a revival. So did evangelical Protestantism, largely for the same reasons—Cold War anxiety, prosperity, and mobility—plus the catalyst of Billy Graham. The mainline revival, however, slowed down and these churches went into a decline during the last forty years of the twentieth century. Not so with evangelicalism. The 1960s and 1970s saw an explosion of two religious types—the evangelical faith and alternative religions. New religions arose, old ones were resurrected, and Eastern religions poured into America. But even they tapered off or took new forms less alien to America.[27]

Evangelicalism, nevertheless, continued strong into the twenty-first century and shows no sign of numerically declining. In fact, with the election to the presidency of Jimmy Carter, an avowed evangelical, *Newsweek* declared 1976 to be the year of the evangelical. The largest and most vigorous religious institutions in the last fifty years have been related to evangelical Protestantism. Thanks to this cumulative surge in religion, William McLoughlin has described the years after 1960 as "The Fourth Great Awakening." He has also characterized the rise of pietistic religion during this time as "the third force in Christendom." For the most part, this pietistic religion has been evangelical in its orientation.[28]

Billy Graham and Revivalism

The greatest impact of these religious developments came from the evangelicals and the linchpin of this evangelical revival was Billy Graham. The surge of modern evangelicalism has many facets—the charismatic movement, the church growth movement, the health and wealth gospel, the seeker sensitive movement, parachurch organizations, and megachurches—but no one individual or organization overshadows Billy Graham and his evangelistic association. He has preached to more people in history, well over 1 million in person plus countless numbers by means of radio and television. While many evangelists have been tarnished by scandals or lavish lifestyles, Graham has not gone down this path. He remains one of the most respected public figures of his time and the most influential evangelical of the twentieth century. Except for some hard-core fundamentalists, he has been well received by most Christians—evangelicals, liberals, Catholics, and Orthodox.[29]

Billy Graham is a product of his time and culture. Born in North Carolina into a Presbyterian family, he was raised in a pietistic evangelical atmosphere. Converted in 1936, he attended Bob Jones University, Florida Bible Institute, and graduated from Wheaton College in 1943. After a short pastorate, Graham became a traveling evangelist for Youth for Christ. In this capacity he made several evangelistic trips to England, one with Cliff Barrows. From 1947 to 1951, Graham also served as president of Northwestern Bible College in Minneapolis. Graham's evangelistic efforts took off during his 1949 evangelistic campaign in Los Angeles. Here several local celebrities were converted and he gained the attention of William Randolph Hearst, who instructed his news people to "puff Graham." The evangelist thus gained national attention, appearing on the front pages of *Life, Time,* and *Newsweek* magazines. In 1950, he founded the Billy Graham Evangelistic Association and began airing the "The Hour of Decision."[30]

In several ways, Graham's early ministry reflected the emerging neo-evangelicalism of the 1950s. He expressed distaste for the "fumbling fundamentalists" who feuded with each other and had retreated into sectarianism and intolerance. As noted, the big break came with his 1957 New York crusade. But his early message mirrored the conservative political stance maintained by most Americans. He mixed religion and politics and few of his supporters would question this approach. During the 1950s, evangelicals were not politically active, but they did believe that spiritual religion had the power to shape the behavior and policies of the nation. And if these policies received proper guidance, they would result in a conservative course of action: a limited government with few social programs, a strong military, and stanch opposition to communism.[31]

Graham's conservatism and anti-communism appealed to many. Not unlike the messages of Peale and Sheen, Graham's sermons linked Christianity and patriotism. America's survival depended on its market economy, military strength, and the personal commitment of individuals to Christ. If Americans did not turn to biblical Christianity, God would punish the nation and it would not fulfill its divinely appointed mission. This would be disastrous for the world because "America is truly the last bulwark of Christian civilization," said Graham. "If America falls, Western culture will disintegrate." At this stage of his ministry, he closely coupled Christianity and Americanism: "If you would be a true patriot, then become a Christian. If you would be a loyal American, then become a loyal Christian."[32]

For Graham, during the 1950s and 1960s, many clouds dotted the horizon. He saw the United States as "falling apart at the seams." Graham criticized government deficit spending, immorality in high places, give-away foreign aid programs, the influence of "big labor and pinks and lavenders" in Washington. He regarded communism as Satanic and saw it infiltrating the government, schools, and churches. For examples of the "deadly work" of communism, he cited the "betrayals" at Yalta and Potsdam, the ineffective war in Korea, and the bungling of the United Nations. Graham firmly believed that civilization was living in the last days and that America's only hope was a great revival, which could purge the nation. The most "effective weapon against communism today is a born-again Christian," not guns and bullets.[33]

These patriotic themes did not consume all of Graham's preaching. The centerpiece of his message was the cross of Christ and the necessity for a personal faith in Christ. At the beginning of his ministry, he made this declaration: "I made a commitment never to preach again without being sure that the Gospel was as complete and clear as possible, centering on Christ's sacrificial death for our sins on the Cross and His resurrection from the dead for our salvation."[34] He preached against the sins that have traditionally received the most attention in the evangelical subculture—sexual immorality, excessive use of alcohol, the breakdown of the family, and the decline of national moral standards. While he did not feature social sins or those relating to the pride of life, he did address such issues—greed, misuse of wealth, disregard for the poor, and egotism.[35]

Actually as Graham grew older, his political and social message matured. The catalyst for this was the resignation of Richard Nixon. Graham had contacts with all American presidents and close relationships with several conservative political leaders—especially Richard Nixon. In fact, he came close to endorsing Nixon in his 1960 run against Kennedy. Referring to Kennedy, Graham said, "This is a time of world tensions and I don't think it is the time to experiment with novices."[36]

Later, Nixon spoke at Graham rallies and the evangelist felt free to give him political advice. Nixon, however, exploited his relationship with Graham and the president's resignation embarrassed Graham and sobered him. To be sure, he continued to go to the usual prayer breakfasts and make calls at the White House, but he became more guarded in his relationships with political leaders. More than that, he toned down his patriotic messages and his anti-communist rhetoric, made several visits to communist countries, and developed a stronger social consciousness. In fact, Graham desegregated his meetings in 1953 and compiled a credible record regarding race relations.[37]

Graham's phenomenal success can be attributed to several factors. First and foremost he steadfastly preached the gospel in a simple language that could be understood by all. Graham could shift ground on several issues and he often tailored his message to suit his conservative constituency. For example, he castigated communism during the peak of the Cold War and let up when the threat diminished. Nevertheless, the centerpiece of his message—faith in the atoning work of Christ—remained firm.[38]

But personal and organizational factors also come into play. Graham is an effective speaker and a charismatic figure who attracts millions of people to his crusades and broadcasts. Moreover, unlike many evangelists his personal life has not been tainted by scandal. Following in the path of the great evangelists from Whitefield on down, Graham has utilized the most current methods of communication and organization. His crusades demonstrate state of the art organization—advance preparation, advertising, prayer groups, follow up teams, committees for nearly everything, and cooperation from the local churches. The crusades also feature appealing music and testimonies from well-known or local people. "The glorious Gospel of Jesus Christ," is the "miracle drug that can heal the ills of the world," said Graham. And the Graham team often functioned as if it were a business corporation marketing such a drug. Madison Avenue and the Holy Spirit were often in close cooperation and at times it is difficult to tell them apart.[39]

The Impact of Revivalism

From the First Great Awakening to the present, revivalism has been a staple of American evangelicalism. In the mind of many people, the answer to America's problems—whether they be political, moral, social, or economic—has been a spiritual revival. Whether revivalism has actually addressed such critical issues is subject to debate.

Evangelicalism, nevertheless, has had its strengths and weaknesses. American religion is perhaps the most dynamic in the world, and evangelical Protestantism may be the most vigorous aspect of this development. Church attendance is high, billions of dollars go for religious activities, and cathedral-like edifices abound. Revivalism, it would seem, has energized American evangelicalism and inspired many worthwhile religious activities. But it has its down side. Evangelicalism— perhaps more than other aspect of American religion—has often been superficial, materialistic, and subject to the demands of popular culture.

From its beginnings in the eighteenth century, evangelicalism in the form of revivalism has had a close affinity with American culture. The pillars of American culture—self-reliant individualism, progress, free choice, democracy, the market economy, voluntarism, progress, and perfectibility—have harmonized with revivalism. The revivalist presented the gospel in an attractive popular form, but the individual had to accept or reject it. In pursuing the goal of saving souls, revivalism has blurred the distinctions between denominations, tamed many quarreling sectarian groups, and forged a form of Protestant unity.[40]

Revivalism has been remarkably sensitive to the winds of popular culture and has adapted its methods and even some aspects of its message to suit the changes in American culture. In doing such, revivalism's methods and message have become thoroughly populist. The revivalist has had to be a colorful and persuasive embodiment of his or her culture. But in doing so, the revivalist secularized the Christian message. He or she has so closely linked the gospel to American culture that the two have become nearly indistinguishable. Americanism and Christianity became synonymous. Rather than a state church, we now have an Americanized Christianity.[41]

In appealing to the average person, the revivalist has reduced the gospel to a few essentials and in the process has "dumbed down" the Christian message. This indeed is often what the audience desired. Being sufficiently enthralled by the evangelist's dynamic presentation, the audience has failed to notice his or her inconsistencies and contradictions. The result is often an abbreviated gospel devoid of the complexities that confronts the Christian throughout life. Moreover, revival preaching usually lacks a serious social message. The social ills of society will be solved if enough individuals are converted to Christ. Individuals need a change of heart and that comes through regeneration, not legislation.[42]

Despite many negatives, revivalism has been a tremendous shot in the arm to the evangelical faith and American religion in general. Revivalism has encouraged millions of people to dedicate themselves to the cause of Christ and to flesh out this commitment in tangible ways—missions, Christian education, social services, etc. In some instances, especially the first half of the nineteenth century, revivalism had a major impact on the public values of American culture. Without revivalism, the evangelical faith would be much different, and probably a weaker force in American religion.[43]

Evangelicals and the Parachurches

A parachurch may be defined as an association of Christians working outside of the denominational structure for some specific ministry or purpose. American religion rests on the denominational structure of the church. This religious type assumes that the "true church" cannot be identified with any single ecclesiastical structure. It requires religious toleration, the separation of church and state and religious pluralism. Such an environment allows no one religious group to dominate but requires them to cooperate and compete with each other in the market of culture. Such pluralistic and competing conditions, however, have produced more than sects and denominations. They have also given birth to the parachurch.[44]

The parachurch, or special purpose groups as Robert Wuthnow calls them, has existed throughout Christian history. Orders approved by the Catholic Church have operated from the earliest years of the church. When the Reformation fragmented the Catholic monopoly over Western religion, denominations sprang up. Eventually, this pluralism produced many special purpose groups or parachurches—some within the denominational structures but many independent of such control. Very few, however, have been associated with the liberal Protestant denominations or have had a liberal orientation. Most have been related to evangelical Protestantism in America. In part, this is because evangelicalism has aggressively sought to convert individuals and Christianize American culture.[45]

Special purpose groups, within the denominations and across denominational lines, have characterized American religion since at least the nineteenth century. In fact, parachurch organizations have been the driving force behind many efforts to reform American society—abolition societies, temperance organizations, educational institutions, mission agencies, and humanitarian efforts. Some examples include the following: the American Tract Society (1823), American Sunday School Union (1824), American Educational Society (1826), American Temperance Union (1836), Women's Christian Temperance Union (1874), Anti-Saloon League (1895), Young Men's Christian Association (1844), and Salvation Army (1865).[46]

The Parachurch Explosion

While special purpose groups have been numerous in American history, the twentieth century has seen an explosion of parachurch organizations. Two general trends—the changes in American religion and the characteristics of special purpose groups—have fostered this development. In respect to American religion, five factors are important. First, the separation of church and state has made religion a voluntary activity, a situation ready made for parachurch organizations. This situation fostered the growth of many special purpose groups in the nineteenth century, but religious pluralism produced by religious disestablishment has increased in the twentieth century.

Second, denominationalism is currently in decline. People care little for theology. Thus, the belief systems that once marked denominational boundaries have been blurred beyond recognition. Consequently, we now have a homogenized version of mainstream or evangelical Protestantism. While the gap is still significant, even Catholicism and conservative Protestantism have now moved closer together, especially in regard to some social issues. This decline of denominationalism also connects with the fragmentation of American life. Increasingly, Americans tend to do religion with no overarching theological or historic framework. They do religion a la carte.[47]

Next and closely related is the weakening of denominational loyalties. People attend the churches that are convenient or meet their personal and family needs. Intermarriage between members of different denominations is common today. Many people are satisfied with a generic evangelicalism. Four, by its very nature, evangelicalism tends to be transdenominational in character, exhibiting qualities found in many denominations. When "shorn of certain denominational particularities (such as the mode of baptism) or cultural distinctions (such as ethnic origins)," there may be little difference between various groups. Such a condition lends itself to the growth of parachurch ministries.[48]

Five, and of considerable importance, during the 1920s and 1930s the fundamentalists lost the struggle for control of the denominational structures. The modernists now ran the denominational agencies, which the fundamentalists could not support. So they started their own independent parachurch organizations to fulfill their mission objectives. The parachurch structures thus became vehicles for Christian service and protest against liberal Protestantism. And since that time, both evangelicals and fundamentalists have relied heavily on special purpose groups to carry out what they believed to be their Christian mandate. The NAE even took steps to accommodate the parachurch structure. Moreover, beginning in the 1960s, the charismatic movement swept through evangelical Christianity. This movement, with its charismatic leaders and lack of denominational affiliations, added hundreds of parachurch groups to those already created by the fundamentalists and evangelicals.[49]

Parachurch groups have also grown because of the way they function. First, they focus on a specific purpose and thus become more specialized. They usually do not emphasize worship or instruction as would a local church. This fits well with the professionalization trend among religious workers—counselors, educators, youth workers, music ministry, etc. Next, special purpose groups are run like a business corporation—highly organized and top down. Unlike many churches, they allow very little democratic participation in the organization's decisions. In fact, many parachurchs are one person shows and guard their financial records from any outside scrutiny.[50]

Third, special purpose groups have more efficient methods for raising funds. Churches pass the plate. Parachurch groups aggressively seek out money. They have full-time fund-raisers, appeals on television, direct mailing lists, endowments, and large contributors. Parachurch organizations are locked into the mindset that "more net income…translates directly into more ministry."[51] Four, as the state has expanded its activities into education and social welfare or outlawed such activities as prayer in the schools, many evangelicals have resented this intrusion. In response, they have created special purpose groups to fulfill Christian objectives. In particular, a number of parachurch organizations have political influence as their primary objective. They lobby members of the legislature to enact laws favorable to Christian values.[52]

Next, many parachurch groups, especially those engaged in youth work, have thoroughly accommodated themselves to American culture. While they may preach the old-fashioned gospel, they are in tune with the youth culture. For example, during the peak of the Cold War, Youth for Christ appealed directly to the patriotic spirit of the nation. Military heroes were commonplace at their meetings. And these youth groups did not ignore the pop culture. Rallies were a Christianized form of entertainment, tailored for the youth. The music was lively, celebrities gave their testimonies, and the leaders dressed in the latest styles.[53]

Parachurches: Successes and Failures

Robert Wuthnow contends that the structure of American religion is changing. It is moving from the denomination to the special purpose group. For tax purposes, the IRA registers over 800 of these bodies as religious groups. In comparison, given the broad criteria for a denomination, there are about 1,200 in America. If more standard criteria are used, there are only about 200 denominations. Not using IRS figures, Bruce Shelley estimates that including a host of smaller bodies, the number of special purpose ministries could reach 10,000. But beyond these numbers, many parachurch organizations dwarf comparable agencies within the major denominations. World Vision, Campus Crusade, Feed the Children, Billy Graham Evangelistic Association, Promise Keepers, Young Life, The Navigators, InterVarsity Christian Fellowship and others have budgets and structures that surpass those of many denominations.[54]

For much of the nation's history, parachurch groups have been in sync with America's consumer society, entrepreneur spirit, and frontier mentality. If you have a spiritual need, don't turn to an existing religious organization. Start another one! These special purpose organizations have achieved much. They have evangelized millions, taken the gospel to foreign nations, fed the poor, served as surrogate parents for juveniles, sheltered the homeless, facilitated reform movements, and much more. Through the years, they have represented an important and dynamic aspect of the evangelical subculture.

But special purpose groups have also caused some concern. Being outside of the denominational structures, they have been subject to few restraints. In particular, the financial practices of parachurch groups have had no oversight. The financial scandals associated with Jim Bakker and Jimmy Swaggart plus some lavish living by other charismatic leaders have caused great concern. This has led to the formation of The Evangelical Council for Financial Accountability, an agency to oversee the financial activities of evangelical organizations. Some parachurch groups have joined the council, but others have not. Special purpose groups have also had little respect for traditional Christianity. They have also tended to be insular and autonomous, not looking beyond their own agency or cooperating with other groups. Moreover, they have been inclined to be faddish and infatuated with anything new.[55]

Pentecostalism: The Middle Years

Pentecostalism must be seen as an aspect of the post-World War II revival. From its origins in the early twentieth century to the 1940s, Pentecostal groups were isolated from the rest of American Christianity and from each other. The low point came after World War I. The Pentecostals considered themselves to be fundamental. They embraced not only the historic Christian faith but also dispensational teachings including the premillennial rapture. So the Pentecostal psyche was shattered when the fundamentalists refused to admit Pentecostal churches into their organization.[56]

Such a condition prevailed until the 1940s when things began to change. The years from about 1940 to the 1960s can be viewed as a time of transition. Pentecostalism changed from a movement with sectarian characteristics to one with denominational traits. It moved from the old Pentecostalism to neo-Pentecostalism (also called the charismatic movement).

Before the 1940s, the fundamentalists took a very dim view of Pentecostalism. To distance themselves from the "fanatical glossolalics" (tongues-speakers), the Church of the Nazarene deleted the word *Pentecostal* from its official title. Oswald Chambers of the British Keswick movement labeled the "Tongues Movement" as a "Satanic Counterfeit." At their 1928 convention, American fundamentalists condemned Pentecostalism as fanatical and unscriptural, regarding it as "a real menace to the churches and a real injury to the same testimony of Fundamental Christians."[57]

With the beginning of the more moderate National Association of Evangelicals in 1942, things began to change for the Pentecostals. Internally, Pentecostal leaders began to question their isolation. Externally, the neo-evangelicals were less rigid doctrinally and more accepting of other religious groups. To join their organization, they only required denominations to affirm a general statement of faith embracing historic Christianity. So in 1943 a number of major Pentecostal denominations joined the NAE.[58]

What factors allowed the Pentecostals to be accepted by mainstream evangelicalism? These reasons are more a matter of speculation than certainty. First, evangelicals adopted a less rigid stance in regard to Pentecostalism. In the process of joining the NAE, one Pentecostal commented: "We were not asked to compromise one iota of our distinctive Pentecostal testimony."[59] Next, despite having some pacifist inclinations, Pentecostal chaplains served with distinction in World War II—a step that improved their patriotic image during the Cold War years. Third, the advances that Pentecostals made in respect to foreign missions commended them to other evangelicals. Lastly, leading Pentecostals condemned fanaticism and exclusivism within their ranks, and in doing so they became more accepting of other evangelicals. While they regarded their Pentecostal distinctives as important, they could live with other evangelicals who rejected them.[60]

Such changes in Pentecostalism signaled a move from sectarian to denominational traits. The sect erects barriers between it and the world; it is narrow, exclusive, and demands high standards from its adherents. It also lacks a highly developed institutional structure. Conversely, the denomination has made more compromises with the world and is at home in society. It is more inclusive; requires less from its followers and has an institutional structure to support its many activities.[61]

Increasingly, in the years after World War II, Pentecostals became more respectable—socially, economically, and intellectually. They began to erect beautiful sanctuaries, publish journals, and establish educational institutions. They also developed associations uniting Pentecostals, namely, the Pentecostal Fellowship of North America. Of importance, their worship services became more restrained with less emotional outbursts.[62]

But the movement from sect to denomination produces tensions. Not all Pentecostals liked the direction the movement was taking. Dissent voices regarded these changes as unacceptable compromises with the world. They saw more organized worship services as restraining the spirit; large sanctuaries as displays of wealth; and increased intellectual activities as cooling the fires of revivalism that had produced the movement. In sum, the critics believed Pentecostalism had abandoned many of the historic Pentecostal practices. Thus, in good sectarian fashion, protest groups arose and broke from the larger Pentecostal denominations in order to restore Pentecostalism to its pristine purity. The best known of these split offs was the New Order of the Latter Rain, which came into existence in 1947.[63]

These middle years witnessed an emphasis on healing. From the mid-1940s to the early 1960s, many sawdust trail-healing tent evangelists paraded across the American religious scene. The best known was Oral Roberts (b. 1918). But other colorful figures include A. A. Allen, William Freeman, Tommy Hicks, O. L. Jaggers, and Gordon Lindsay. Kathryn Kuhlman and Rex Humbard came a little later and are not as directly related to the Pentecostal healing ministry.[64]

The Pentecostal churches had always emphasized the doctrine of divine healing, but it was not practiced on a regular basis. After World War II, however, the practice of praying for the sick surged in a way not seen previously. The healing evangelists believed that people came to Christ primarily because of his healing ministry. Moreover, as they contended, the Great Commission included the command to heal the sick. As such, it is a vehicle to reach the masses in heathen lands. Pentecostals referred to healing as "deliverance evangelism." Just as God desires all to be saved, he wants everyone to be healthy. The healing evangelists, indeed, had the burden of proclaiming this message.[65]

Oral Roberts and Pentecostalism

With the exception of Billy Graham, Oral Roberts was the best-known evangelist during the 1950s and 1960s. His career illustrates the transition from the old Pentecostalism to the charismatic movement. Born in Oklahoma to a struggling Pentecostal preacher, Roberts grew up in poverty during the Depression years. As a teenager, he experienced both a conversion and a dramatic healing from tuberculosis. After this, he prepared himself to be a Pentecostal preacher and was ordained in the Pentecostal Holiness Church. For the next twelve years, he served as a pastor and evangelist in Pentecostal circles.[66]

Roberts was like a host of other tent evangelists and became its leading practitioner. Riding a surge of interest in healing and Pentecostal ecumenism, after World War II Roberts launched an independent healing ministry. He conducted huge tent revivals and developed groundbreaking methods for mass mailing methods. Like the other faith healers, he claimed that God had given him miraculous powers, especially a "word of knowledge" about the hidden aspects of people's lives and their illnesses. Also, like other faith healers Roberts distributed clothes anointed with prayer, which supposedly had the power to heal.[67]

While not fully identified with the faith movement that arose in charismatic circles during the 1970s, Roberts seemed to have influenced it. In addition to evangelistic messages and performing healings, he preached that success and prosperity were attainable by faith. He developed the "seed faith" principle, which contended that giving to God (and by implication to Roberts' ministry) was like planting the seeds of prosperity. God would increase your gift many times over and prosperity would be yours. In fact, he offered to pray that any gift given to his ministry would be returned "in its entirety from a totally unexpected source."[68] As George Marsden notes, "Roberts' message amounted to a mix of revivalist Protestantism, Pentecostalism, and a poor person's version of Norman Vincent Peale's 'power of positive thinking'. Each proclaimed a gospel of success."[69]

Among the poorer and less educated classes, Roberts' ministry became tremendously successful. Fueled by this response, in the 1950s and 1960s he built up a large financial empire. In 1954, he began to televise his healing crusades, a step which gained him much fame and influence. But healing revivalism declined in the late 1950s and Roberts adapted his ministry to the changing times. And in doing so, he began to move toward the evangelical mainstream and greater social respectability.[70]

Supported by Roberts, in 1951, Demos Shakarian—a wealthy California businessman—founded the Full Gospel Businessmen's Fellowship International, an instrument to bring Pentecostal teachings to mainstream evangelicals. Roberts built Oral Roberts University, which opened its doors in 1965. To this, he later added graduate programs, a medical school, and a hospital. The late 1960s saw dramatic changes in his ministry. In 1968, he stopped holding crusades. In 1967, he discontinued his television programs, but two years later he began a series of television specials featuring well-known celebrities. Roberts left the Pentecostal Holiness Church in 1968 and became an ordained Methodist minister. The late 1960s saw Roberts de-emphasize some extreme Pentecostal views and he became a leading figure in the emerging charismatic movement.[71]

As the twentieth century wound down, Roberts' image suffered for several reasons. As his institutional commitments grew, his need for money increased greatly. As a result he resorted to some questionable and distasteful methods to increase financial support. And some of this money found its way into his pockets. By the late 1980s, his empire was valued at around $500,000,000. Compounding his image as a money grabber, Roberts began to associate with some of the more radical leaders of the faith movement.[72]

These problems, not withstanding, Roberts has made many significant contributions to American religion. In addition to the institutions that he has founded, he brought the message regarding the gifts of the Holy Spirit to mainstream Christianity. He played an indispensable role in transmitting the old Pentecostalism into the charismatic movement. His media innovations—especially presenting the Christian message in an entertainment format—promoted the explosion of religious television. While he believed in divine healing, he did not discount the medical profession. In doing so, he helped to facilitate an interaction between people of faith and the medical community.[73]

During these middle years, Pentecostalism maintained a paradoxical relationship with American religion and culture. On one hand, their peculiar distinctives—tongues-speaking, faith healing, and exuberant worship—set them outside the mainstream of American religion. These practices drew a line between them and non-charismatic Christians. The baptism of the Holy Spirit and the accompanying tongues-speaking presented a stumbling block to other Christians. On the other hand, Pentecostalism was at home with American religion and culture. According to Martin Marty, "American religion has been characteristically...experiential, affective, emotive, practical, personal, activist, and behavioral in intent and expression." And so has Pentecostalism. In fact, during the 1960s Pentecostalism and American society took steps toward each other. The Pentecostals became more mainstream while American society became more experiential, subjective, and less cognitive in its outlook.[74]

The Old Paradox in a New Setting

Since early national America, evangelicalism has had a paradoxical relationship with American culture. These tensions have become more evident in the years after the 1960s. The story of evangelicalism since that time has been one of reaction and accommodation. Demonstrating counter cultural characteristics, evangelicals have reacted strongly to and resisted many developments in modern American society—cultural pluralism, Supreme Court decisions that legalized abortion and banned prayer from the schools, a more open attitude toward sex, pornography, feminism, and homosexuality. And with the rise of the Religious Right, these issues are seriously contested in the political arena.

Conversely, evangelical Protestants have blended aspects of American culture and Christianity to the extent that the two are nearly indistinguishable. Numerous evangelicals have indiscriminately swallowed American nationalism, believing that the United States is a Christian nation with a divinely called mission. While this is not a new concept, many evangelicals regard it as their duty to restore America to its Christian ways. Since the 1960s, American culture has emphasized the experiential and subjective modes of life, and so has evangelical Christianity.

In modern America, consumerism has reached ridiculous heights—a characteristic that is evident in the megachurches and the way evangelicals market their faith. In addition, the evangelical community has become as high tech as any aspect of society. These subjects will be addressed in future chapters of this book. But before proceeding further, the social changes to which evangelicals have responded must be described. To a large extent, these changes occurred in the 1960s and early 1970s.

Society in Change

The years from the election of John F. Kennedy in 1960 to 1975, when Gerald Ford inaugurated the bicentennial era, were tumultuous and traumatic. According to Sydney Ahlstrom, "never before in the nation's history have so many Americans expressed revolutionary intentions and actively participated in efforts to alter the shape of American civilization in almost every imaginable aspect"—from religion to the political process, from art to the economic order, from health to diplomacy. These years were a watershed in American history. American society was severely shaken and in many ways permanently transformed.[75]

Urbanization, science and technology brought much of this change. Rampant, unregulated urban and industrial growth had begun to create difficulties with which American political and fiscal practices could not cope. Technological and scientific advances had seemed to have no bounds. In face of sensational scientific achievements, dramatized by the moon landing and heart transplants, transcendent reality had faded from view. Consequently, for many the idea of the supernatural had lost its force.[76]

Theodore Roszak speaks of the impact of technology on society, particularly its role in creating a counterculture. The advance of science and technology, along with urban growth, depersonalized human relationships, created a thirst for community and intimacy that for some could be quenched in several ways—small groups within the church and the secular community and some alternative religions. The great emphasis on science, technology and cold rationality caused a backlash. A shift in epistemology, our way of learning, could be detected. Research and cognitive methods began to be replaced by experience and intuition. Such means of acquiring truth are, of course, central to the evangelical subculture and many fringe religions.[77]

The 1960s also witnessed drastic alternations in social and political relations. Most important, the situation that had long supported Protestant dominance and white Anglo-Saxon Protestant (WASP) ascendancy in American life came under serious challenge. Cracks in the Protestant establishment had been visible by the turn of the century, but they now opened into gaping fissures. Immigration patterns brought many new voters who repudiated this Protestant ascendancy. In 1961, the Protestant lock on the presidency ended, and a Roman Catholic entered the White House. This, combined with the ending of the Counter-Reformation by Vatican II, drastically altered the old Protestant-Catholic relationships.[78]

What the voters did not do the Supreme Court accomplished. In the 1950s and 1960s, the Supreme Court removed crucial legal supports from the power structure of the white Protestant establishment. Segregation became illegal. The court supported the principle of one person, one vote. Also, the court outlawed the use of Christian ceremonies in the public schools. In a series of decisions, the court declared America to be a religious nation. While this may have been consistent with the developing cultural pluralism, it was not the Christian America that many envisioned.[79]

Of great importance were the protest movements. Black America, first through the vehicle of the civil rights movement and later under the banner of Black Power, began to demand an end to the historic inequalities that had characterized African Americans' existence. Though not as violent and divisive as the civil rights and antiwar movements, feminism and environmentalism challenged some of the most fundamental assumptions of Western culture: that men dominated women and that humanity could act with impunity toward nature. In particular, *Roe v. Wade* (1973), which permitted abortion on demand, gave women control over their bodies but it outraged conservatives.[80]

President Lyndon Johnson's decision to escalate the Vietnam War provided the supreme catalyst for all of these challenges to the American system. Cynicism toward the political establishment erupted into violence. Some saw the war's escalation as the betrayal of a political promise. Others believed that the war would be used as an excuse for the government to avoid implementing civil rights. Among the youth there developed a level of hostile feeling toward the establishment that was probably unique in America's history. College students and others agitated for nearly half a decade. To cap off this period, America experienced a series of traumas: Watergate, the resignation of President Nixon, and the collapse of the American-backed regime in Vietnam.[81]

All of these developments, writes Ron Enroth, helped to foster an apocalyptic mentality in American society at large. This mood was very strong in both secular and religious sectors during the 1960s and 1970s. "The invention of the atomic bomb began the...apocalyptic mood." The widespread concern with environmental pollution was a manifestation of the apocalyptic mindset. Apocalypticism was political as well. During the 1960s and 1970s, many believed "that the American government [was] beyond reforming and must be destroyed totally in order for something new and better to take its place." While such an apocalyptic mood could be discerned in many groups, "it was perhaps the strongest in counterculture" and the evangelical subculture. Evangelical publishers cranked out books on this subject right and left, with Hal Lindsey's *Late Great Planet Earth* topping the list.[82]

Cultural Pluralism and the Third Disestablishment

The 1960s marked a turning point in American life. The confluence of so many widespread changes led Martin Marty to speak of a "seismic shift" in the nation's religious landscape.[83] Sydney Ahlstrom regarded the 1960s as a time when the "old foundations of national confidence, patriotic idealism, moral traditionalism, and even of historic Judeo-Christian theism were awash. Presuppositions that had held firm for centuries—even millennia—were being widely questioned."[84]

Robert Bellah defines civil religion as a complex of symbolic meanings that many Americans share and that unite them in a moral community.[85] The upheaval and turbulence, the emergence of many sects and cults, and the deep sense of disillusionment in the 1960s had a shattering effect on civil religion. To many the United States was no longer a beacon of hope to the world. The image of America as the chosen nation, the new Israel, had been smashed. The old public faith that once unified Americans around national values and purpose was deemed by many to be hollow and deceitful.

Polls indicated that church attendance declined during the 1960s, and more and more Americans believed that religion was losing its importance. As a consequence, the terms *post-Protestant* and even *post-Christian* were used to describe American society. These phrases are not misleading or simplistic if they are used to point out that other forces have displaced Protestantism, and even Christianity in the broader sense, as the primary definer of cultural values and behavior patterns in the nation.[86]

Religious pluralism has a long history in America. Despite a de facto Protestant establishment that lasted well into the twentieth century, American religion has not been monolithic. In addition to Catholicism, Eastern Orthodoxy, Judaism, and Eastern religions, the religious landscape has been dotted with many other marginal religions. Nevertheless, for over a hundred years, such pluralism had little impact on American culture. As Roof and McKinney write, "In self perception, if not in fact, the United States was a white country in which Protestant Christianity set the norms of religious observance and moral conduct." WASP influence "shaped much of public life."[87]

The Constitution of 1789 legally disestablished religion on a national level. As a result, pluralism has been around for a while. But it did not pose much of a problem throughout most of the nation's religious history. So long as a common core of Protestant values could be taken for granted, religious pluralism had much less of an impact.[88] All of this began to change during the twentieth century. After World War I, the old WASP order was challenged by a growing pluralism. Protestantism now had to accommodate other faiths. Robert Handy speaks of these developments during the 1920s and 1930s as a "second disestablishment." From the 1920s to the 1960s, the United States had become, in Will Herberg's words, a "Protestant-Catholic-Jewish" country.[89]

Yet not until the 1960s did the realities of an extended pluralism become apparent. Cultural pluralism had mushroomed. Immigrants from Asia and Latin America poured in, expanding America's cultural horizons. The ease of travel and communication also played a role; Americans traveled abroad much more. Middle-class Americans had been in the military all over the world. Foreign students with appreciation for other religions came to North America in droves.[90]

The extended pluralism was moral as well as cultural. As American culture became more secular and rational, diversity in moral values and lifestyle also increased. The liberal consensus had been shattered by the 1960s, and thereafter religion lost much of its strength as an integrative influence in America. America no longer had a moral core. When a moral core still existed, pluralism in morals had not seemed so threatening. Now lacking a common religious culture, groups contend with each other for power and influence. The debate over morals and values has crystallized around two camps: moral traditionalists versus those advocating a more libertarian and secular position.[91]

The controversy over values is centered in two basic social institutions: the family and the school. Throughout the 1970s, conservatives generally opposed the Equal Rights Amendment and the extension of legal rights to homosexuals, while favoring a ban on abortion. In the schools, they supported prayer in the classroom and condemned the teaching of evolution and the use of "humanist" textbooks. These conservatives seek to turn the country around and to restore a Christian America. Meanwhile, secularists push for greater openness, insisting that individuals are fully capable of choosing for themselves what to believe and how to make moral choices. On the surface, the secularists appear to be more accommodating and less dogmatic than the conservatives. Yet many of them pursue their values—racial and gender equality, the ERA, affirmative action, freedom of choice in respect to abortion—with the same vigor and intolerance that conservatives manifest. As a consequence, America since the 1970s has been morally polarized.[92]

Religious Responses

There have been four major religious developments in America since the 1960s: the rise of new religions, the decline of liberalism, the revival of conservative religion, and privatization of religion. Only the last two concern this study, but all four sprang from the same cultural milieu and are connected. In fact, while their beliefs may be dramatically different, the fringe religions and conservative ones often manifest many of the same characteristics.[93]

A resurgence of conservative religion began in the 1970s, in part as a reaction to the developments of the 1960s. The churches that grew since the late 1960s were virtually all conservative—Protestant evangelical and fundamentalist, neo-Pentecostal, Seventh-day Adventist, Jehovah's Witness, Mormon, and Orthodox Jewish bodies. Though these groups have obvious theological differences, they all manifest in various degrees what Dean M. Kelley calls "traits of straitness": demanding, absolutist beliefs, social and moral conformity, and a missionary spirit.[94]

The emergence of the "electronic church," with its vast network of television programming, popular preachers, and broad-based support, can be seen as a new form of conservative religion. Moreover, the politicization of religious conservatism, the rise of the Religious Right, and the formation of organizations like the Moral Majority and Christian Coalition can be seen as new religious developments.[95]

The fringe religions and conservative groups—especially the evangelicals—share several important characteristics. Both sought authority in a world of intellectual chaos. Both groups placed a heavy emphasis on religious experience. Further, both reacted to the mainline religions and to the pluralization and secularization of society. The new religions and the conservative groups attracted people who were disconnected with the chaos of pluralism: the hallmark of modernity. People sought authoritative teachings instead of the babble of ideological voices that tend to cancel one another out. Such individuals were also intolerant of moral pluralism—the many competing claims to values and to definitions of right and wrong.[96]

However, people sought to satisfy their cravings for intellectual and moral authority not through abstract propositions, but through experience. Mainstream modern religiosity has seldom ministered to the thirst for experience, but the new religions and much of evangelicalism—especially the charismatics— have emphasized experiential dimensions of faith. Public opinion polls have noted a surge toward experiential religion. With few exceptions, fringe religions minister to this need. The "born again" experience is basic to evangelicalism. According Gallop polls in the 1970s, one out of three Americans had been "born again." Some evangelical groups also emphasize other experiences such as tongues-speaking and fervent feelings of devotion.[97]

The growth of the new religions and the conservative bodies accompanied the decline of liberalism. As noted by Wade Roof and William McKinney, during the 1960s and 1970s, "religion was flourishing on the right and left fringes but languishing in the center." In quest of their own spiritual pursuits and in rebellion against old authorities, many young, well-educated people turned to meditation techniques and mystical faiths. In a world out of kilter, the turn inward in quest of self-enlightenment seemed the correct thing to do. On the other extreme, many conservative faiths, "seeking to restore the traditional ways of believing and behaving were prospering as well." Against the new faiths of the young were the old faiths of history. Yet both the new religions and conservative faiths rode the crest of a tide of experiential faith that swept the country.[98]

Life-changing religious experiences are normally private and personal. The trend toward greater individualism in religious choice and practice—the privatization of faith—is important in modern history. Historically, individualism has been an important value in American culture, and in contemporary society basic psychological and social transformations have made it more so. That religion remains a matter of personal choice or preference has deep roots in American history. This religious individualism has been reinforced, of course, by cultural pluralism, political democracy, and capitalism.[99]

A new voluntarism arose in the 1970s and 1980s. While this voluntarism embraced many of the older themes of individualism found in America, it differed substantially. Previously, individualism had usually rested within the context of a religious and cultural consensus and thus had a certain direction. As the old cultural and religious consensus of the Eisenhower years unraveled, the value system within the country shifted dramatically. In the 1960s, support for public piety and patriotism no longer held. Life in the modern world had become fragmented. As the American way of life lost its idealism, the deep-seated quest for personal fulfillment gained momentum. Many Americans could not find wholeness and meaning in the institutions and values of the prevailing society. So they turned inward.[100]

As Thomas Luckmann points out, religion has become "invisible," a private affair, something to be worked out within the confines of an individual's

life experiences. Each person is expected to fashion, from the available resources, a system of sacred meanings and values in accord with personal needs
and preference.[101] According to Wade Roof, such a privatized religion knows
little of communal forms and needs little institutional support. While it may
provide meaning for the individual believer, "it is not a shared faith."[102]

This quest for fulfillment as a matter of individual experience had implications for all segments of American religion, but especially the new religions,
spiritual therapies, and evangelical groups. Most individuals in the conservative religious bodies considered personal fulfillment to be a consequence of
Christian salvation, something to be acquired only by faith in the life and
death of Jesus Christ. Whether fundamentalist, evangelical, neo-Pentecostal,
or holiness Christians, they stressed the continuing and personal benefits of
their faith. Even many within the liberal mainstream sought personal fulfillment, often through spiritual therapies. Growing numbers of both laity and
clergy took part in workshops on personal growth and meditation techniques.
Many charismatics within Catholicism and liberal Protestantism placed a high
priority on spiritual growth. Since the 1960s and 1970s, the political and
social climate has changed considerably. Nevertheless, the themes of personal
freedom and individual fulfillment gained strength in the 1980s and 1990s
because the baby boomers carried them into mainstream culture.[103]

How have the evangelicals and fundamentalists responded to the cultural
trends of the modern era? The evangelical mainstream and the moderate fundamentalist bodies have a paradoxical relationship with American society. Except for some moral issues related to abortion, sexual promiscuity, and
homosexuality they reflect an accommodating posture. Once rigid and hostile
toward society, Protestant conservatism has generally become more culture af-
firming. Today only the most separatistic fundamentalists are on the fringes of
American religion. Vastly different from the "holy rollers" and "fighting fundies"
of the earlier twentieth century, contemporary evangelicals take an intellectual
stance more consistent with modern rationality and tend to maintain behavior
that is in good taste. And they reflect the social trends found in most of American religious bodies. Moreover, any religious movement that represents a
powerful political block cannot be dismissed as a marginal phenomenon.[104]

Evangelicalism Since the Mid-1960s: An Overview

The major aspects of modern evangelicalism will be covered in separate
chapters. A partial list will include its political involvement, economic ideas,
the church growth movement, seeker-sensitive Christianity, the rise of the
megachurches, charismatic movement, the health and wealth gospel, changes
in worship, and the positive thinking movement. But at this point, a brief
overview of evangelicalism in the late twentieth century would be in order. In
general, however, the trends have been toward increased acculturation, numerical success, considerable diversity, and increased political involvement.

In the late twentieth century, evangelicalism has become increasingly diverse—so much that the movement may have lost its coherence. Breaking out of its fundamentalist straightjacket, evangelism now incorporates a wide range of groups. Yet it has retained most of its key distinctives: a reliance on the authority of Scripture (despite no unanimity in its interpretation), an emphasis on conversion, and the centrality of the death of Christ.[105] Evangelicals even have a better relationship with Catholicism. They once regarded Catholicism as a great enemy and the Pope as Antichrist. The two are now in agreement over many social issues.

In recent years, evangelicals have been most visible in the political areas. The years following World War II saw them focus on the "great evil" of communism, deeming it as a "Satanic conspiracy." When the Cold War thawed and communism eventually collapsed, however, evangelicals had to find a new enemy. And being inclined to conspiracy thinking, they did not have far to look. Liberalism was on a decline so it became less of a problem. Secular humanism loomed large in the evangelical mind, even though these fears were considerably exaggerated.

In removing prayer from the schools and making abortion legal, the courts handed the evangelicals more issues to combat. The teaching of evolution in the schools soured the evangelicals even further. As American culture became more diverse and the family began to unravel, multiculturalism and family issues came to the forefront. To combat many of these problems, evangelicals—largely in the form of the Religious Right—became increasing politically active and now represent a potent force in American politics.

For much of the twentieth century, evangelicalism in the form of fundamentalism lacked social and intellectual respect. With the election of Jimmy Carter and 1976 being declared the year of the evangelical, evangelicals came out of the closet, so to speak. Several factors caused this rise to respectability. Numerically, evangelicalism has experienced great success. Evangelicals are the fastest growing segment of American religion. Clearly, along with Catholicism and mainline Protestantism, they represent a "third force" in American religion. Intellectually, many evangelicals have moved toward respectability. With evangelicals getting advanced degrees and publishers putting out their scholarly work, the evangelical mind experienced a renewal.[106] Once relegated to the backwater of American society, evangelicalism now has numerical, economic, and political strength and can no longer be ignored. It is a significant force in American society.

Evangelical churches and organizations have grown tremendously in the postwar era largely because they have been populist and pragmatic to the core. What do the people want? Will it work? The answers to these two questions have driven evangelicalism for most of its existence. Throughout its history, evangelicalism has sensed the heartbeat of American culture and has adapted its approach to religion—if not its message and morals—to accommodate culture.

These adjustments have come in the areas of preaching, promoting Christian activities, finances, worship, music, utilizing the latest technology, and more. But in late twentieth century, the acculturation of evangelicalism reached even greater proportions. Evangelicals uncritically embraced American nationalism, the market economy, political conservatism, rampant consumerism, and an emotional approach to religion.

While they have retained the core of the gospel, many evangelicals have adjusted their values and secondary beliefs to American culture. For example, while having roots in the past, the health and wealth gospel and the positive thinking movement reflect more secular trends than biblical principles. Also, the widespread evangelical adherence to conservative political values stems, to a large extent, from American individualism, suspicion of big government, and the belief that God has chosen America for a special mission.

This combination of strictness and accommodation may be a key to the numerical success of evangelicalism. In resisting certain contemporary moral and intellectual trends, to some extent evangelicals have maintained what Dean Kelley has described as strict and absolute values. But in other ways, they are the most acculturated segment of American religion. By maintaining some measure of their values, they have not made the mistake of liberal Protestantism—namely, abandoning the historic Christian faith. Conversely, in catering to popular tastes and blurring the line between entertainment and religion, evangelicalism has attracted large numbers of people, especially the youth. In this combination of strictness and accommodation, evangelicalism may have the best of both worlds. But it has paid a stiff price. In many ways, without even knowing it, evangelicalism has simply Americanized the Christian faith and Christianized secular society. In doing so, many evangelicals are in danger of trivializing Christianity.

Notes

1. See Richard Kyle, *The Last Days Are Here Again: A History of the End of Times* (Grand Rapids: Baker Books, 1998); Robert G. Clouse, Robert N. Hosack, and Richard V. Pierard, *The New Millennium Manual: A Once and Future Guide* (Grand Rapids: Baker Books, 1999); Timothy P. Weber, *On The Road to Armageddon: How Evangelicals Became Israel's Best Friend* (Grand Rapids: Baker Books, 2004).

2. William H. Chafe, *The Unfinished Journey: America Since World War II* (New York: Oxford University Press, 1999), 97-100, 105-10, 112-22; Paul S. Boyer, *Promises to Keep: The United States Since World War II* (Boston: Houghton Mifflin, 1999), 50-63, 116-26; Alan Brinkley, *The Unfinished Nation*, vol.2, 3rd ed. (New York: McGraw-Hill), 875, 876.

3. John Edward Wilz, *Democracy Challenged: The United States Since World War II* (New York: Harper and Row, 1990), 113-25; Brinkley, *Unfinished Nation*, 875-94; Boyer, *Promises to Keep,* 116-28; Chafe, *Unfinished Nation*, 112-22.

4. Richard Kyle, *The Religious Fringe: A History of Alternative Religions in America* (Downers Grove, IL: InterVarsity Press, 1993), 182, 183; Sydney E. Ahlstrom, *A Religious History of the American People* (New Haven, CT: Yale University Press, 1972), 1091; Barbara Hargrove, *Religion for a Dislocated Generation* (Valley Forge, PA: Judson Press, 1980), 16-22.

5. Sydney Ahlstrom, "The Traumatic Years: American Religion and Culture in the 60s and 70s," *Theology Today* 36, 4 (1980): 507, 510. The late 1950s foreshadowed the upheaval of the 1960s. See Morris Dickstein, *Gates of Eden: American Culture in the Sixties* (New York: Harper and Row, 1977); Peter Clecak, "Culture and Politics in the Sixties," *Dissent* 24 (fall 1977), 440; Ronald B. Flowers, *Religion in Strange Times: The 1960s and 1970s* (Macon, GA: Mercer University Press, 1984), 15; Martin E. Marty, *Modern America: Under God, Indivisible 1941-1960* (Chicago: University of Chicago Press, 1996), 277-93.

6. Robert S. Ellwood, *1950: Crossroads of American Religious Life* (Louisville: Westminster John Knox Press, 2000), 8-15, 75-97; Marty, *Under God, Indivisible*, 354-63; Winthrop S. Hudson and John S. Corrigan, *Religion in America*, 6th ed. (Upper Saddle River, NJ: Prentice Hall, 1999), 360, 361; Mark Noll et al. eds. *Eerdmans Handbook to Christianity In America* (Grand Rapids: Eerdmans, 1983), 430-32.

7. Quoted in George Marsden, *Religion and American Culture* (New York: Harcourt Brace, 1990), 213-15; Martin E. Marty, *The Shape of American Religion* (New York: Harper and Row, 1958), 31-40; Jackson W. Carroll, Douglas W. Johnson, and Martin E. Marty, *Religion in America: 1950 to the Present* (New York: Harper and Row, 1979), 18-27; Marty, *Under God, Indivisible,* 277-93; Ellwood, *1950: Crossroads of Life*, 99-119; Douglas T. Miller, "Popular Religion of the 1950s: Norman Vincent Peale and Billy Graham," *Journal of Popular Culture* 9 (summer 1975), 66-68; Richard T. Hughes, *Myths America Lives By* (Urbana: University of Illinois Press, 2004), 172 (second quote).

8. Will Herberg, *Protestant-Catholic-Jew: An Essay in American Religious Sociology* (Garden City, NY: Doubleday, 1955), 97 (quote); Marsden, *Religion and American Culture*, 214; Ahlstrom, *Religious History*, 954; Marty, *Under God, Indivisible*, 294-332; Hughes, *Myths America Lives By*, 171; William Lee Miller, *Piety Along the Potomac: Notes on Politics and Morals in the Fifties* (Boston: Houghton Mifflin, 1964), 34 (quote).

9. Ahlstrom, *Religious History*, 954; Marsden, *Religion and American Culture*, 214; Carroll, *Religion in America*, 7; Marty, *Under God, Indivisible*, 331-32; Lee Canipe, "Under God and Anti-Communist: How the Pledge of Allegiance Got Religion in Cold War America," *Journal of Church and State* 45, 2 (spring 2003): 305-23; Hughes, *Myths America Lives By*, 171, 172.

10. Norman Vincent Peale, *The Power of Positive Thinking* (New York: Prentice-Hall, 1952), 1 (quote); Noll, *Christianity in America*, 433: Ahlstrom, *Religious History*, 956; Kathleen R. Fields, "Fulton J. Sheen," in *Dictionary of Christianity in America*, ed. Daniel Reid et al. (Downers Grove, IL: InterVarsity, 1990), 1081, 1082; Miller, "Popular Religion of the 1950s," 66-68.

11. Joel Carpenter, "From Fundamentalism to the New Evangelical Coalition," in *Evangelicalism and Modern America*, ed. George Marsden (Grand Rapids: Eerdmans, 1984), 8, 9; Timothy Weber, "Fundamentalism," in *Dictionary of Christianity in America*, 464; Marty, *Under God, Indivisible*, 434-48; Harriet A. Harris, *Fundamentalism and Evangelicals* (Oxford: Clarendon Press, 1998), 4-8; Ellwood, *1950: Crossroads of Life*, 192, 193.

12. Joel A. Carpenter, *Revive Us Again: The Reawakening of American Fundamentalism* (New York: Oxford University Press, 1997), 147-50; Weber, "Fundamentalism," 464, 465; Bruce L. Shelley, "Evangelicalism," in *Dictionary of Christianity in America*, 416; George M. Marsden, *Understanding Fundamentalism and Evangelicalism* (Grand Rapids: Eerdmans, 1991), 72, 73; Harris, *Fundamentalism and Evangelicals*, 38,39; George Marsden, *Reforming Fundamentalism: Fuller Semi-*

nary and the New Evangelicalism (Grand Rapids: Eerdmans, 1987); Jon R. Stone, *On the Boundaries of American Evangelicalism* (New York: St. Martin's Press, 1997), 9-11; D. G. Hart, *Deconstructing Evangelicalism* (Grand Rapids: Baker Books, 2004), 23-26; Timothy George, "Inventing Evangelicalism," *Christianity Today* (March 2004): 48-51.

13. Bruce Shelley, *Evangelicalism in America* (Grand Rapids: Eerdmans, 1967), 69-84; Carpenter, "From Fundamentalism to the New Evangelical Coalition," 12; Carpenter, *Revive us Again*, 150-54; Marty, *Under God, Indivisible*, 104-07; Stone, *Boundaries of Evangelicalism*, 11, 12, 14; James Davison Hunter, *American Evangelicalism: Conservative Religion and the Quandary of Modernity* (New Brunswick, NJ: Rutgers University Press, 1983), 41-43; Joel Carpenter, "The Fundamentalist Leaven and the Rise of an Evangelical United Front," in *The Evangelical Tradition in America*, ed. Leonard I. Sweet (Macon, GA: Mercer University Press, 1984), 260-63; Hart, *Deconstructing Evangelicalism*, 111-16.

14. Mark A. Noll, *American Evangelical Christianity: An Introduction* (Oxford: Blackwell Publishers, 2001), 19; Mark Noll and Lyman Kellstedt, "The Changing Face of Evangelicalism," *Pro Ecclesia* 4, 2: 152; Marsden, *Understanding Fundamentalism and Evangelicalism*, 68, 69; Harris, *Fundamentalism and Evangelicals*, 36, 37.

15. Marsden, *Understanding Fundamentalism and Evangelicalism*, 69, 70; Noll, *American Evangelical Christianity*, 19, 20; Noll and Kellstedt, "Changing Face of Evangelicalism," 154; Martin E. Marty, *A Nation of Behavers* (Chicago: University of Chicago Press, 1976), 81, 82; Carpenter, "The Fundamentalist Leaven," 267-69, 276, 281; Hart, *Deconstructing Evangelicalism*, 16-23.

16. Noll, *American Evangelical Christianity*, 19, 20; Noll and Kellstedt, "Changing Face of Evangelicalism," 152, 153; Donald G. Bloesch, *The Evangelical Renaissance* (Grand Rapids: Eerdmans, 1973), 16-18; Ellwood, *1950: Crossroads of Life*, 190.

17. George M. Marsden, *Fundamentalism and American Culture* (New York: Oxford University Press, 1980), 66-68; Marsden, *Understanding Fundamentalism and Evangelicalism*, 71, 72; Martin E. Marty, *Modern American Religion: The Noise of the Conflict 1919-1941* (Chicago: University of Chicago Press, 1991), 193-95; Mark A. Noll, *The Scandal of the Evangelical Mind* (Grand Rapids: Eerdmans, 1994), 130-38.

18. See Mildred Erickson, *The New Evangelical Theology* (Westwood, NJ: Revell, 1968); Ronald H. Nash, *The New Evangelicalism* (Grand Rapids: Zondervan, 1963); Marty, *Nation of Behavers,* 94; Timothy L. Smith, "The Evangelical Kaleidoscope and the Call to Christian Unity," *Christian Scholar's Review* 2, 15 (1986): 125-40.

19. Marsden, *Reforming Fundamentalism*, 6; (quote); Stone, *Boundaries of Evangelicalism*, 17, 18; James Davison Hunter, *Evangelicalism: The Coming Generation* (Chicago: University of Chicago Press, 1987), ix.

20. Harris, *Fundamentalism and Evangelicals*, 40, 41; Weber, "Fundamentalism," 465; Marsden, *Understanding Fundamentalism and Evangelicalism*, 73; Randall Balmer and Lauren F. Winner, *Protestantism in America* (New York: Columbia University Press, 2002), 64; Ellwood, *1950: Crossroads of Life*, 188.

21. Harris, *Fundamentalism and Evangelicals*, 41, 42; Balmer, *Protestantism in America*, 64, 65; Marsden, *Religion and American Culture*, 217, 218; Carpenter, "The Fundamentalist Leaven," 285-87.

22. Erling Jorstad, *The Politics of Doomsday: Fundamentalists in the Modern World* (Nashville: Abingdom, 1970), 159 (quote); Nancy Tatom Ammerman, *Bible Believers: Fundamentalists in the Modern World* (New Brunswick, NJ: Rutgers University Press, 1987), 24; Marty, *Nation of Behavers*, 94-96; Hunter, *American*

Evangelicalism, 44-46; Richard Quebedeaux, *The Worldly Evangelicals* (San Francisco: Harper and Row, 1978).

23. Harris, *Fundamentalism and Evangelicals*, 7, 17; Ammerman, *Bible Believers*, 24; Richard Hofstadter, *Anti-Intellectualism in American Life* (New York: Vintage Books, 1963), 133-36; Noll, *Scandal of the Evangelical Mind*, 123-26.

24. Hunter, *American Evangelicalism,* 44, 45; Marty, *Under God, Indivisible*, 366, 367; Marsden, *Religion and American Culture*, 211, 212; Noll, *American Evangelical Christianity*, 22; Jorstad, *Politics of Doomsday*, 38-59; Ellwood, *1950:Crossroads of Life*, 185-88.

25. Hunter, *American Evangelicalism*, 44, 45 (quote on 44); Marsden, *Understanding Fundamentalism and Evangelicalism*, 101, 102; Marty, *Under God, Indivisible*, 367-74, Jorstad, *Politics of Doomsday*, 38-59.

26. John D. Woodbridge, Mark A. Noll, and Nathan O. Hatch, *The Gospel in America: Themes in the Story of America's Evangelicals* (Grand Rapids: Zondervan, 1979), 155, 156; William Warren Sweet, *Revivalism in America* (New York: Scribner's, 1944).

27. Kyle, *Religious Fringe*, 203-373; Diana L. Eck, *A New Religious America* (San Francisco: Harper San Francisco, 2001); Philip Jenkins, *Mystics and Messiahs: Cults and New Religions in American History* (New York: Oxford University Press, 2000); Stephen J. Stein, *Communities of Dissent: A History of Alternative Religions in America* (New York: Oxford University Press, 2003).

28. William G. McLoughlin, *Revivals, Awakenings, and Reform* (Chicago: University of Chicago Press, 1978), 179-216; William G. McLoughlin, "Is There a Third Force in Christendom?" *Daedalus* 96, 1 (winter 1967): 58-64; Martin E. Marty, "Religion in America since Mid-Century," *Daedalus* 96 (winter 1982): 157-61.

29. Noll, *American Evangelical Christianity*, 44, 50, 51; John D. Woodbridge, "William (Billy) Frank Graham," in *Dictionary of Christianity in America*, 492; Marshall W. Fishwick, "The Blessings of Billy," in *The God Pumpers: Religion in the Electronic Age*, ed. Marshall Fishwick and Ray B. Browne (Bowling Green, OH: Bowling Green State University Press, 1987), 60. See Marshall Frady, *Billy Graham: A Parable of American Righteousness* (Boston: Little, Brown, 1979); William Martin, *A Prophet With Honor: The Billy Graham Story* (New York: William Morrow, 1991); John Pollock, *Billy Graham, Evangelist to the World* (San Francisco: Harper and Row, 1979).

30. For this general information, see Pollock, *Billy Graham*; Frady, *Billy Graham*; Martin, *A Prophet with Honor*; L. I. Sweet, "The Epic of Billy Graham," *Theology Today* 37 (1980): 85-92; Woodbridge, "William (Billy) Graham," 492; Carpenter, *Revive Us Again*, 215-26.

31. Richard V. Pierard, *The Unequal Yoke: Evangelical Christianity and Political Conservatism* (Philadelphia: Lippincott, 1970), 106-30; D. G. Hart, *That Old-Time Religion in Modern America: Evangelical Protestantism in the Twentieth Century* (Chicago: Ivan R. Dee, 2002), 86; Hudson, *Religion in America*, 362; William G. McLoughlin, *Modern Revivalism: Charles Grandison Finney to Billy Graham* (New York: Ronald Press) 482-84; Ellwood, *1950: Crossroads of Life*, 198,199.

32. Quotes from McLoughlin, *Revivals, Awakenings, and Reform,* 190; W. F. Graham, "Spiritual Inventory," ("Sermon of the Month," published by the Billy Graham Evangelistic Association, Minneapolis: 1955); Fishwick, "The Blessings of Billy," 63, 64. See also McLoughlin, *Modern Revivalism*, 511; Ellwood, *1950: Crossroads of Life*, 198-200.

33. Hudson, *Religion in America*, 362 (quotes); Richard V. Pierard, "Billy Graham and the U.S. Presidency," *Journal of Church and State* 22, (winter 1980), 109-19;

McLoughlin, *Modern Revivalism*, 482, 505, 506; William D. Apel, " The Lost World of Billy Graham," *Review of Religious Research* 20 (1979): 141-44.

34. Quote from Noll, *American Evangelical Christianity*, 53.

35. Ibid., 48.

36. *New York Times*, 21 May 1960, p. 12 (quote); Pierard, "Graham and the Presidency," 119.

37. Pierard, "Graham and the Presidency," 125-27; Noll, *American Evangelical Christianity*, 48; Fishwick, "The Blessings of Billy," 64, 65.

38. Noll, *American Evangelical Christianity*, 52, 53; Fishwick, "The Blessings of Billy," 65, 66, 71.

39. McLoughlin, *Modern Revivalism*, 513 (quote); W. F. Graham, "Three Minutes to Twelve," "Teach Us to Pray," "Why Christians Suffer," "Peace vs. Chaos" ("Sermons of the Month" published by the Billy Graham Evangelistic Association, Minneapolis, 1951, 1953; Fishwick, "The Blessings of Billy," 67-69; Miller, "Popular Religion of the 1950s," 72, 73.

40. Bernard A. Weisberger, *They Gathered at the River: Revivalists and Their Impact Upon Religion in America* (New York: Octagon Books, 1979), 18, 52; McLoughlin, *Modern Revivalism*, 523; George M. Thomas, *Revivalism and Cultural Change* (Chicago: University of Chicago Press, 1989), 62, 63, 66-69; Ellwood, *1950: Crossroads of Life*, 194, 195.

41. McLoughlin, *Modern Revivalism*, 524, 527; Weisberger, *They Gathered at the River*, 48, 49, 94; Thomas, *Revivalism and Cultural Change*, 68, 69; Razelle Frankl, *Televangelism: The Marketing of Popular Religion* (Carbondale: Southern Illinois University Press, 1987), 29, 30.

42. McLoughlin, *Modern Revivalism*, 526; Weisberger, *They Gathered at the River*, 176, 177, 217, 219; Woodbridge, *Gospel in America*, 161.

43. Woodbridge, *Gospel in America*, 160-62.

44. Sidney E. Mead, *The Lively Experiment: The Shaping of Christianity in America* (New York: Harper and Row, 1963), 103-33; Franklin H. Littell, *From State Church to Pluralism* (Garden City, NY: Doubleday, 1962), x-xx; Bruce Shelley, "Parachurch Groups," in *Dictionary of Christianity in America*, 863.

45. Robert Wuthnow, *The Restructuring of American Religion* (Princeton, NJ: Princeton University Press, 1988), 101-06; Shelley, "Parachurch Groups," 863.

46. Wuthnow, *Restructuring of American Religion*, 101-06; R. Laurence Moore, *Selling God: American Religion in the Marketplace of Culture* (New York: Oxford University Press, 1994), 20, 149, 150, 155-57, 181,182; J. Alan Youngren, "Parachurch Proliferation: The Frontier Spirit Caught in Traffic," *Christianity Today* 6 (November 1981): 38-41.

47. Wuthnow, *Restructuring of American Religion*, 113; William M. Shea, *The Lion and the Lamb: Evangelicalism and Catholics in America* (New York: Oxford University Press, 2004); Mark A. Noll and Carolyn Nystrom, *Is the Reformation Over? An Evangelical Assessment of Contemporary Roman Catholicism* (Grand Rapids: Baker Books, 2005); J. I. Packer, "Evangelicals and Catholics: The State of Play," *Books and Culture* (March/April 2005): 10, 11.

48. Michael S. Hamilton, "More Money, More Ministry: The Financing of American Evangelicalism since 1945," in *More Money, More Ministry: Money and Evangelicals in Recent North American History*, ed. Larry Eskridge and Mark A. Noll (Grand Rapids: Eerdmans, 2000), 110 (quote).

49. Carpenter, *Revive Us Again*, 54, 55, 154; Shelley, "Parachurch Groups," 864.

50. Wuthnow, *Restructuring of American Religion*, 108.

51. Hamilton, "More Money, More Ministry, 104-108 (quote 107, 108); Wuthnow, *Restructuring of American Religion*, 114, 115; Charles E. Hambrick-Stowe, "Sanctified Business: Historical Perspectives on Financing Revivals of Religion," in *More Money, More Ministry*, 81-103.

52. Wuthnow, *Restructuring of American Religion*, 114-117.

53. Bruce Shelley, "The Rise of Evangelical Youth Movements," *Fides et Historia* 18, 1 (1986): 48-50; Leslie Conrad, Jr., "Non-Denominational Youth Movements," *International Journal of Religious Education* 32, 10 (1956): 14-16; Editorial, "Has Youth for Christ Gone Fascist?" *Christian Century* 14 (November 1945): 1243, 1244.

54. Wuthnow, *Restructuring of American Religion*, 108, 109; Shelley, "Parachurch Groups, "864.

55. Shelley, "Parachurch Groups," 865; J. Alan Youngren, *Your Money/Their Ministry* (Grand Rapids: Eerdmans, 1981); Jerry E. White, *The Church and the Parachurch: An Uneasy Relationship* (Portland, OR: Multnomah Press, 1983); J. Alan Youngren, "Parachurch Church Proliferation," 38-41.

56. David Edwin Harrell, Jr. *All Things Are Possible: The Healing and Charismatic Revivals in Modern America* (Bloomington: Indiana University Press, 1975), 8, 9; Vinson Synan, *The Holiness-Pentecostal Movement in the United States* (Grand Rapids: Eerdmans, 1971), 206.

57. Carl Brumback, *Suddenly from Heaven* (Springfield, MO: Gospel Publishing, 1961), 282 (quote); Nils Bloch-Hoell, *The Pentecostal Movement* (Oslo: Universitetsforlaget, 1964), 67, 82, 120; Marty, *Under God, Indivisible*, 451, 452.

58. John Thomas Nichol, *The Pentecostals* (Plainfield, NJ: Logos, 1966), 209; Synan, *Holiness-Pentecostal Movement*, 206-08; Harrell, *All Things Are Possible*, 19.

59. Stanley Frodsham, "Fifth Annual Convention of the NAE," *Pentecostal Evangel* 10 (May 1947): 6.

60. Nichol, *Pentecostals*, 210, 211; Balmer and Winter, *Protestantism in America* 78; Jay Beaman, *Pentecostal Pacifism: The Origin, Development, and Rejection of Pacific Belief Among Pentecostals* (Hillsboro, KS: Center for Mennonite Brethren Studies, 1989).

61. For discussions regarding the sect and denomination categories, see Richard Kyle, *From Sect to Denomination: Church Types and Their Implications for Mennonite Brethren History* (Hillsboro, KS: Center for Mennonite Brethren Studies, 1985), 9-24; Calvin Redekop, "The Sect Cycle in Perspective," *The Mennonite Quarterly Review* 25, 1 (1951): 155-61; Ernest Troeltsch, *The Social Teaching of the Christian Churches*, 2 vols. (New York: Harper and Row, 1966); Bryan Wilson, *Sects and Society* (Berkeley: University of California Press, 1961); J. Milton Yinger, *Religion in the Struggle for Power* (Durham, NC: Duke University Press, 1946); Russell E. Richey, ed., *Denominationalism* (Nashville: Abingdon, 1977).

62. Nichol, *Pentecostals,* 227, 228; Synan, *Holiness-Pentecostal Movement,* 208, 209; Harrell, *All Things Are Possible*, 138-49; Grant Wacker, *Heaven Below: Early Pentecostals and American Culture* (Cambridge, MA: Harvard University Press, 2001), 7, 8.

63. Nichol, *Pentecostals,* 226-39; Synan, *Holiness-Pentecostal Movement*, 209; Marty, *A Nation of Behavers*, 111; Walter J. Hollenweger, *The Pentecostals* (Minneapolis: Augsburg Publishing House, 1977), 34, 35; Ahlstrom, *Religious History*, 822.

64. See Harrell, *All Things Are Possible*, 3-20, 190-92; Nichol, *Pentecostals*, 222, 223; Martin E. Marty, "Pentecostalism in the Context of American Piety and Practice," in *Aspects of Pentecostal-Charismatic Origins*, ed. Vinson Synan (Plainfield, NJ: Logos, 1975), 218.

65. Nichol, *Pentecostals*, 222, 223; Hollenweger, *The Pentecostals*, 38; Harrell, *All Things Are Possible*, 3-9.

66. See David Edwin Harrel, Jr. *Oral Roberts: An American Life* (Bloomington: Indiana University Press, 1985); Oral Roberts, *The Call: An Autobiography* (Garden City, NY: Doubleday, 1972); Jerry Sholes, *Give Me That Prime-Time Religion: An Insider's Report on the Oral Roberts Evangelistic Association* (New York: Hawthorn Books, 1979); James R. Goff, Jr. and Grant Wacker, " Introduction," in *Portraits of a Generation: Early Pentecostal Leaders*, ed. James R. Goff , Jr. and Grant Wacker (Fayetteville: University of Arkansas Press, 2002), xi.

67. Harrell, *All Things Are Possible*, 44-46; David Edwin Harrell, "Granville Oral Roberts," in *Dictionary of Christianity in America*, 1020; Razelle Frankl, *Television: The Marketing of Popular Religion* (Carbondale: Southern Illinois University Press, 1987), 74.

68. Harrell, *All Things Are Possible*, 43-49, 105, 158 (quote on 49); Marsden, *Religion and American Culture*, 218; Bruce Barron, "Faith Movement (Word Movement)" in *Dictionary of Christianity in America*, 426; Bruce Barron, *The Health and Wealth Gospel* (Downers Grove, IL: InterVarsity, 1987), 49, 50; Frankl, *Televangelism*, 75, 119.

69. Marsden, *Religion and American Culture*, 218, 219.

70. Marsden, *Religion and American Culture*, 218; Harrell, "Granville (Oral) Roberts," 1020; Synan, *The Holiness-Pentecostal Movement*, 209-11; Frankl, *Televangelism*, 77, 78.

71. Marsden, *Religion and American Culture*, 219; Harrell, "Granville (Oral) Roberts," 1020; Marty, "Pentecostalism in American Piety," 225, 226; Harrell, *All Things Are Possible*, 49, 51, 135, 146-49, 151-57; Synan, *Holiness-Pentecostal Movement*, 211, 212.

72. Harrell, "Granville (Oral) Roberts,"1020; Harrell, *All Things Are Possible*, 105; Randy Frame, "Did Oral Roberts Go Too Far?" *Christianity Today* 20 (February 1987): 43-45.

73. Harrell, "Granville (Oral) Roberts," 1020; Harrell, *All Things Are Possible*, 101; Hudson, *Religion in America*, 207.

74. Marty, "Pentecostalism in American Piety," 195, 215, 223 (quote); Marty, *Nation of Behavers*, 119.

75. Sydney E. Ahlstrom, "The Traumatic Years: American Religion and Culture in the 60s and 70s," *Theology Today* 36, 4 (1980): 510, 511 (quote). See also Milton Viorst, *Fire in the Streets* (New York: Simon and Schuster, 1979); Steven M. Tipon, *Getting Saved from the Sixties* (Berkeley: University of California Press, 1982); Arthur Marwick, *The Sixties* (New York: Oxford University Press, 1998); Todd Gitlin, *Sixties: Years of Hope and Days of Rage* (New York: Bantam Books, 1993); Steven J. Keillor, *This Rebellious House: American History and the Truth of Christianity* (Downers Grove, IL: InterVarsity Press, 1996), 251-75.

76. Sydney Ahlstrom, "The Radical Turn in Theology and Ethics: Why It Occurred in the 1960s," *The Annals of the American Academy of Political and Social Science* 387 (January 1970): 9, 12.

77. Theodore Roszak, *Making of a Counterculture* (Garden City, NY: Doubleday, 1969), 1-41; Theodore Roszak, *Unfinished Animal* (New York: Harper and Row, 1975), 7, 8, 14, 16, 19, 20; William Braden, *The Age of Aquarius: Technology and the Cultural Revolution* (Chicago: Quadrangle Books, 1970); Charles Reich, *The Greening of America* (New York: Random House, 1970), 17-19; Hargrove, *Religion for a Dislocated Generation*, 44, 45.

78. Ahlstrom, "The Radical Turn," 11; Ahlstrom, *Religious History*, 1091,1092.

79. Ahlstrom, "The Traumatic Years," 513; Noll, *Christianity in America*, 456, 457; Ahlstrom, "The Radical Turn," 11, 12; Ahlstrom, *Religious History*, 1091, 1092.

80. Ahlstrom, "The Traumatic Years," 513; Noll, *Christianity in America*, 554; Ahlstrom, "The Radical Turn," 11,12; Ahlstrom, *Religious History*, 1091, 1092.

81. Ahlstrom, "The Radical Turn," 12; Ahlstrom, "The Traumatic Years, 512, 513.

82. Ron Enroth, Edward E. Ericson, Jr., and C. Breckenridge Peters, *The Jesus People* (Grand Rapids: Eerdmans, 1972), 182 (quotes); Kyle, *The Last Days Are Here Again*, 115.

83. Martin E. Marty, foreword to *Understanding Church Growth and Decline, 1950-1978*, ed. Dean R. Hoge and David A. Roozen (New York: Pilgrim, 1979), 10.

84. Ahlstrom, *Religious History*, 1080.

85. Robert Bellah, *Beyond Belief* (New York: Harper and Row, 1970), 171. See Dick Anthony and Thomas Robbins, "Spiritual Innovation and the Crisis of American Civil Religion," *Daedalus* 111, 1 (1982): 215-34.

86. Kyle, *Religious Fringe*, 193, 194.

87. Wade Clark Roof and William McKinney, *American Mainline Religion* (New Brunswick, NJ: Rutgers University Press, 1987), 31, 35.

88. Ibid., 35.

89. Robert T. Handy, *A Christian America* (New York: Oxford University Press, 1984), 159-84. See also Robert T. Handy, "The American Religious Depression, 1925-1935," *Church History* 29, 1 (1960): 3-16; Will Herberg, *Protestant Catholic Jew* (Garden City, NY: Anchor, 1960).

90. Roof and McKinney, *American Mainline Religion*, 29-32, 35. See David M. Reimers, *Still the Golden Door* (New York: Columbia University Press, 1985); Eck, *A New Religious America*; Philip Jenkins, "A New Christian America," *Chronicles* (November 2001): 18, 19.

91. Roof and McKinney, *American Mainline Religion*, 29-32, 35. See Robert Wuthnow, *The Struggle for America's Soul: Evangelicals, Liberals, and Secularism* (Grand Rapids: Eerdmans, 1989; Keillor, *This Rebellious House*, 251, 252.

92. Roof and McKinney, *American Mainline Religion*, 29-32, 35. See Wuthnow, *Restructuring of American Religion*, 132-72; James Davison Hunter, *Culture Wars: The Struggle to Define America* (New York: Basic Books, 1991).

93. Kyle, *Religious Fringe*, 188.

94. See Dean Kelley, *Why Conservative Churches Are Growing* (New York: Harper and Row, 1972), 53-59; Dean M. Kelley, "Why Conservative Churches Are Still Growing," *Journal for the Scientific Study of Religion* 17, 2 (1978): 165-72; Reginald W. Bibby, "Why Conservative Churches Are Really Growing: Kelley Revisited," *Journal for the Scientific Study of Religion* 17, 2 (1978): 129-37.

95. See Gregory T. Goethals, *The TV Ritual* (Boston: Beacon Press, 1981); Paul Anthony Schwartz and James McBride, "The Moral Majority in the U.S.A. as a New Religious Movement," in *Of Gods and Men: New Religious Movements in the West*, ed. Eileen Barker (Macon, GA: Mercer University Press, 1983), 127-38; Martin E. Marty, " I Think—On the Electronic Church," *The Lutheran Standard*, 2 January 1979, pp. 11-13; Martin E. Marty, "Television is a New, Universal Religion," *Context* 15 (January 1981): 1; Jeffrey K. Hadden, "The Electronic Churches," in *Alternatives to American Mainline Churches*, ed. Joseph Fichter (Barrytown, NY: Unification Theological Seminary, 1983), 159-77.

96. Roof and McKinney, *American Mainline Religion*, 23,49.

97. Ibid.

98. Roof and McKinney, *American Mainline Religion*, 25, 49 (quotes); Wade Clark Roof, "America's Voluntary Establishment: Mainline Religion in Transition," *Religion and America*, ed. Mary Douglas and Steven M. Tipton (Boston: Beacon Press, 1982), 134-39. For more on the polarization of American religion since 1945, see

Wuthnow, *Restructuring of American Religion*; Wuthnow, *Struggle for America's Soul*; Hunter, *Culture Wars*.

99. Robert Bellah et al., *Habits of the Heart* (New York: Harper and Row, 1985), 220-25; Robert Wuthnow, *Christianity in the Twenty-first Century* (New York: Oxford University Press, 1993), 38, 39.

100. Roof and McKinney, *American Mainline Religion*, 45-47; Daniel Yankelovich, "A Crisis of Moral Legitimacy?" *Dissent* 21 (fall 1974): 526, 527. See Edwin Schur, *The Awareness Trap* (New York: McGraw-Hill, 1976); Wuthnow, *Christianity in the Twenty-first Century*, 39, 40.

101. Thomas Luckmann, *The Invisible Religion: The Problem of Religion in Modern Society* (New York: Macmillan, 1967).

102. Roof, "America's Voluntary Establishment," 132.

103. Roof and McKinney, *American Mainline Religion*, 49, 50, 62; Michael S. Hamilton and Jennifer McKinney, "Turning the Mainline Around," *Christianity Today* (August 2003): 34-40.

104. Roof and McKinney, *American Mainline Religion*, 25, 53.

105. Noll, *American Evangelical Christianity*, 24-26; Noll and Kellstedt, "The Changing Face of Evangelicalism," 155-57; Timothy L. Smith, "The Evangelical Kaleidoscope and the Call to Christian Unity," *Christian Scholar's Review* 2, 15 (1986): 125-140.

106. See Alan Wolfe, "The Opening of the Evangelical Mind, *Atlantic Monthly* (October 2000): 55-76; Michael S. Hamilton and Johanna G. Yngvason, "Patrons of the Evangelical Mind," *Christianity Today* 8 (July 2002): 42-47; Jacques Barzun, "Scholarship Versus Culture," *Atlantic Monthly* (November 1984): 93-104; James C. Turner, "Something to Be Reckoned With: The Evangelical Mind Awakens," *Commweal* 15 (January 1999): 11-13; Steve Rabey, "No Longer Left Behind," *Christianity Today* 22 (April 2002): 26-28; Michael S. Hamilton, "Reflection and Response: The Elusive Idea of Christian Scholarship," *Christian Scholars' Review* 31 (fall 2001): 13-21.

6

God is a Conservative

How do you spell God? Many evangelicals believe it is spelled GOP. They think that GOP stands for God's Only Party. Many believe that to be an evangelical is to be a Republican. About 80 to 85 percent of the evangelicals voted for George W. Bush in the 2000 election. But Karl Rove, Bush's campaign manager, estimated that 4 million evangelicals stayed at home in this election. So he made mobilization of the evangelical community the heart of the Republican strategy for Bush's reelection in 2004. This game plan worked brilliantly. In the mind of some evangelicals, not to vote for Bush in 2004 was tantamount to heresy. Prompted by the value issues, they came out in larger numbers than in 2000 and about 80 percent voted for Bush.[1]

All of this leads to the subject of this chapter, the rise of the Christian or Religious Right. Clyde Wilcox defines the Christian Right as a "social movement that attempts to mobilize evangelical Protestants and other orthodox Christians into political action." Some people prefer the broader term, *Religious Right.* This term would encompass not only conservative Protestants—who would still be the dominant element—but also conservative Catholics and Mormons. Supporters of the Christian Right praise the movement as an attempt to return America to its founding Christian principles. The opponents of the Christian Right see it as "baptizing" a political ideology in the name of Christianity.[2]

Actually, the new Christian Right should be seen as one of the two traditions emerging from the Revolutionary era that dealt with religion and politics. The Christian Right represents a tradition going back to the Puritans, which attempts to formulate the moral standards of the nation according to its vision. This conservative perspective tends to sanctify America, legitimizing its form of government, economy, and military activities. A second tradition goes back to at least Roger Williams. It recognized that even then America had deep religious and cultural divisions. So in respect to public life—once some basic standards designed to allow civilization to survive were established—explicit religion should be separate from politics. This tradition also tends to be more critical of the American political, economic, and social systems. Contemporary evangelicals have adopted both positions. Jerry Falwell, Pat Robertson, and the Christian Right represent the first tradition while Jimmy Carter upheld something resembling the second.[3]

Continuity and Discontinuity

The years since the 1960s have seen the old evangelical paradox rear its head again, especially in the political arena. In some areas of politics, the evangelicals have done a complete about-face; in others there is great continuity from the past. The discontinuity is obvious. First, from about 1925 to 1975, the evangelical community shied away from political action. The exception would be the 1928 presidential election. Here they worked hard to defeat Al Smith, the Democratic but Catholic candidate. In their attempt to stop the teaching of evolution in the public schools, the fundamentalists suffered a severe public image defeat and retreated to their subculture. Some ultra-fundamentalists became politically active, but their numbers were small. In the mid- to late 1970s, however, the evangelical community mobilized for political action, and evangelicals have been active ever since. By the early twenty-first century, they are a powerful political force, one that can be ignored only at great peril.

Second, the evangelicals have also changed their political alignment. Prior to 1970s, conservative Protestants were more likely to be Democrats than Republicans. They are now overwhelmingly Republican and represent the largest and most reliable political block in the Republican Party. The 2000 election serves as an example. George W. Bush was to run as a "compassionate conservative." Instead, he has catered to his political bases, corporate America, and the Religious Right. Why? In the New Hampshire primary, Senator McCain handily defeated him. With the critical South Carolina primary looming, Bush traveled to Bob Jones University—an ultra-fundamentalist institution—and received Bob Jones' blessing and went on to win the Republican nomination. This must not be regarded as an aberration. Today, one would have a difficult time winning the Republican nomination without support from the evangelical community. With solid backing from conservative Protestants, Bush won the presidency in the closest election in American history. Without their votes, he would have been decisively defeated.

The 2004 election provides another example of evangelicals continuing their move toward the Republican Party. Motivated by the issues of same sex marriage and abortion, evangelicals came out in droves and comprised about 53 percent of those voting. They backed Bush over Kerry by 78 to 21 percent and expected to be paid back for this support. After the election, Bush commented, "I will be your president regardless of your faith." Some evangelicals regarded this as a slap in the face. "The president could have paused to thank all those good people who poured in and gave him power again," said James

Dobson of Focus on the Family. "The GOP has been given four years to deliver on marriage and life and family, and if they fumble it...[we'll] stay at home next time."[4]

In a letter to George Bush, Bob Jones III spoke in an even more strident manner. He regarded Bush's re-election as being a " reprieve from the agenda of paganism." Jones wrote, "Don't equivocate. Put your agenda on the front burner and let it boil. You owe the liberals nothing. They despise you because they despise your Christ." In the wake of Bush's victory, Jerry Falwell re-launched his Moral Majority—now called "The Faith and Values Coalition." This organization has three objectives—to confirm pro-life Supreme Court justices; to pass a federal Marriage Amendment; and to elect in 2008 another socially, fiscally, and politically conservative president.[5]

A third paradox concerns evangelicalism's preoccupation with the end of the world and its political activism. Conservative Protestants are largely premillennialists and believe that they are living at the end of time. They interpret many events, especially those in the Middle East, as pointing toward the return of Christ. Still, they are determined to remake America according to Christian principles. In doing so, they act as if the end is not in sight, and they behave like postmillennialists. Through much of the nineteenth century, conservative Protestants were politically active and involved in many reform movements. But they were also postmillennialists, an eschatology that is more friendly to redressing society's ills. While many modern fundamentalists still embrace an implicit or residual postmillennialism, it is not an explicit doctrine but a "mixture of piety and powerful American folklore." The fundamentalist tradition is indeed torn between two traditions. On one hand, its dispensationalist theology says that the end is near and that things will get worse. On the other, they share in the Puritan heritage that sees America as the "New Israel" and a "city on a hill."[6]

How conservative Protestants view the federal government is another paradox. They do not like big government and resent its creeping influence. They are staunch advocates of states' rights, local prerogatives, and individual freedoms. Many evangelicals regard the federal government as the problem, not the solution. They regard any form of collectivism as a violation of their God-given individual rights. Still, they believe America should be a Christian civilization in a general sense. And this will come about if the central government enforces moral behavior in both some private and public matters. The standard for this action, of course, is what they believe to be biblical absolutes. Generally, liberals desire more government control over the economy while allowing for more personal liberties. Conservative Protestants, on the other hand, prefer less regulation of the economy but more controls in respect to personal moral behavior.

There exists, however, much continuity between the past evangelical political practices and those of today. According to Mark Noll, evangelicalism's legacy regarding political practices centers on four elements: "moral activism, populism, intuition, and biblicism." Evangelicals actively promoted what they believed to be moral policies and practices. Such action came from the grassroots, at times not related to ecclesiastical structures or the educated elite. And the common people did not embrace such action because of their study of history or theology. Rather, it came intuitively and through their commonsense study of the Bible. Such elements were in place before William Jennings Bryan, but they were exemplified in his career, especially in his "Cross of Gold " speech. This activist approach to politics took a vacation from the 1920s to the 1970s. Such principles, nevertheless, do not always have uniform results. This is why evangelicals often come down on different sides of political issues and why past and present evangelicals are often quite different. But their populist, moralistic, and intuitive approach is frequently the same.[7]

Continuity can also be seen in the way evangelicals communicate their political beliefs. They have always been big on the spoken word. Conservative Protestants have frequently gravitated toward the orator, whether they be preacher or politician and the line between them is often blurred. From the days of Whitefield, sermons with political action overtones have come from evangelical pulpits. Politicians indeed have often adopted the language, style, and enthusiasm of the preacher. Both preacher and politician realize that their audiences must be entertained and persuaded. So they have utilized the most advanced methods of communication for their day and railed against the powerful and privileged—even though they may be part of that social group. As a result, in both the past and present, evangelical religious and political discourse has placed style above substance. Such a focus on rhetoric, fervor, and the use of modern communications can be seen in many of the television preachers who have a not so hidden political agenda.[8]

A Brief Look at the Past

What were the past evangelical political alignments and practices? It must be remembered that the line between evangelicals and other Protestants did not clearly emerge until the 1920s. Rather, we have the evangelical type, that is, the non-liturgical, revivalist, and pietistic Protestant as opposed to the more liturgical and confessional variety. Prior to the birth of the Republican Party in the 1850s, most evangelical types gravitated toward parties (like the Whigs) that were inclined to regulate the moral life of the nation according to evangelical principles. Conversely, the liturgical types—including confessional Protestants and Catholics—advocated religious liberty and promoted the Jeffersonian notion regarding separation of church and state. They tended to be Democrats. The two types quarreled over issues such as opening public assemblies with prayer, Sunday mail delivery, and Jackson's refusal to designate a national day of prayer and fasting.[9]

Slavery not only divided the nation but it also split religious and political bodies. Drawing from several parties—including the anti-Catholic and nativist Know-Nothing Party—the Republicans explicitly opposed slavery and captured the White House in 1860. Right from the beginning, the Republicans had a strong Puritan-evangelical element determined to order national morals according to Christian principles. Opposition to slavery was the great achievement of this orientation. But anti-Catholicism and opposition to the consumption of alcohol also came out of this movement. Meanwhile, the Democrats had become the party of outsiders—namely, Catholics, Southerners and immigrants. These groups had nothing in common except their opposition to the Republicans and their inclination to push their moral vision upon the nation. The Republican tendency to build on a Protestant moral consensus can be seen in the presidential election of 1884. Their candidate James G. Blaine labeled the Democrats as the party of "Rum, Romanism, and Rebellion."[10]

The 1890s saw the decline of the traditional religious-political lineup that had held up for much of the nineteenth century. Republicans now began to recruit Catholics. Democrats sought the support of evangelicals. The major political reorientation, however, came when the evangelical William Jennings Bryan ran for president as a Democrat in 1896, 1900, and 1908. As a populist, he denounced the nation's elite power structure and enticed many lower-class Protestants from the Midwest to make a lasting home in the Democratic Party. He also brought a moral, interventionist, and reformist element into the party, much like the Republicans had practiced. This tendency carried over to Woodrow Wilson, who, while a Southerner, was a Puritan in spirit and action. His lofty vision saw America making the world safe for democracy. The traditional party patterns, however, were not entirely disrupted .The Republicans continued to build a Christian consensus and they were still overwhelmingly Protestant, but they put less emphasis on the evangelical Protestant elements. While the Democrats now courted evangelicals, they were still strongest in the South and in Catholics areas.[11]

What developed was a particular view of civilization, which everyone recognized as Christian. Actually, it was a secularized Protestant version of civilization. Secularization in America has come not by the clash between religion and the prevailing culture but by a merging of their goals. By the early twentieth century, the Democrats and Republicans both adopted this secularized Protestant vision. This era witnessed a tremendous American missionary surge, the Social Gospel, Prohibition, and other reforms, which often had religious overtones. While Prohibition was overturned by the Twenty-First Amendment, its mere passage demonstrated a Christian political consensus.[12]

Thanks to the modernist-fundamentalist conflict in the 1920s, this religious consensus fragmented and the Protestant hegemony over culture went into a nose dive. Except for the elections of 1928 and 1960—when the Democrats ran Catholics candidates—religion did not play a major role in politics.

Instead the Depression, the New Deal, and World War II placed political, economic, and international issues on the front burner.

Religious and political liberalism also forged a natural alliance. Both take a "loose" interpretation of their "sacred texts," namely, the Bible and the Constitution. Theological liberals reinterpret Scripture to conform to the modern world. They thus focus on liberal social action and the ethics of Jesus, not the historic faith and the salvation of souls. Political liberals swept aside the "strict constuctionist" approach to the Constitution and employed a "broad constructionist" method to legitimize the large government programs designed to relieve social ills.[13] Conversely, conservative Protestants continued their more or less strict and literal approach to both Scripture and the Constitution. Both of these tendencies have continued down to the present and represent a major difference between the two factions.

One can detect perhaps four periods of evangelical political involvement. First is the activist, populist approach exemplified by Bryan and so prevalent in the nineteenth century. The 1920s and 1930s can be seen as a second stage. In the 1920s, conservative Protestants battled the consumption of alcohol, the teaching of evolution in the public schools, and Catholicism. During the 1930s, they viewed the New Deal as akin to socialism, became staunchly anticommunist, and gravitated toward fascism and anti-Semitism. During the 1940s, evangelicals moderated their political views but still viewed the New Deal with suspicion and maintained great enmity toward socialism and communism. Another period would be the 1950s when Carl McIntire and Billy Hargis built on the tendencies of the twenties and thirties. This has been called the Old Christian Right and will be noted presently. Last is the "New Christian Right," which arose in the late 1970s, and will be detailed shortly.[14]

The ebb and flow of American history has shaped the political responses of evangelical Christians for over a century and a half. The issues have varied— slavery, immigration, industrialization, urbanization, the Social Gospel, prohibition, women's rights, evolution, the New Deal, socialism, and communism. Such immediate issues have provided the context for evangelical political reactions. But these responses have been largely dictated by conservative Protestantism's political inclinations—"moral activism, populism, intuition, and biblicism." The issues since the 1960s have changed. They focus on family matters, abortion, homosexuality, feminism, prayer in the schools, pornography, and same-sex marriage. The evangelical approach to these problems still centers on the above-mentioned inclinations.

The Old Christian Right and Transitional Figures

The roots the New Christian Right go back to the Protestant cultural dominance in the nineteenth century. A more immediate connection, however, can be made with the Old Christian Right. After fundamentalism's defeat in the 1920s, most evangelicals abandoned the political arena. But there were exceptions to this trend—the Old Christian Right and some transitional figures. Those classified as the Old Christian Right include Gerald B. Winrod and Gerald L. K. Smith. As noted, such men drifted into anti-Semitism and fascism. Their authoritarian and nativist ideologies represented only a small number of Christians who were swimming against the cultural tide. Such individuals were noted in chapter 4 so our attention must turn the transitional figures of the 1950s. These men—especially Carl McIntire, Verne P. Kaub, Edgar C. Bundy, and Billy Hargis—are also called the ultra-fundamentalists and bear a closer resemblance to the New Christian Right.[15]

In the 1940s, a moderate evangelical movement emerged. A number of fundamentalists, however, refused to cooperate with this movement. Their rejection of the Federal Council of Churches (FCC) and the National Association of Evangelicals (NAE) has been described. Thus, we must turn to their political activities. Erling Jorstad notes the theological foundation for these ultra-fundamentalists. It rested on their view of the Bible, how it should be interpreted, separation from the world, and their eschatology. Their Bible was verbally inspired, inerrant, and must be interpreted literally. Any interpretation based on allegory, symbol, or poetry "smacked of liberalism, and liberalism was the work of Satan." To successfully fight the "satanic triad of liberalism-socialism-communism" Christians must be separate from the world, and this included separation from Christians tainted by worldly connections. Their dispensational eschatology told them that they were living in the last days and the Battle of Armageddon loomed on the horizon.[16]

Upon these bedrock theological ideas, the ultra-fundamentalists constructed a political ideology. In doing this, they merged their theology with the political ideology of the radical right. By the late 1950s, these two streams had merged producing a far-right fundamentalism. Religious nationalism had been around since World War I. After all, Germany had been the birthplace of theological liberalism. The fundamentalists thus reasoned that Satan was directing the German war. Then, in 1917, the communists gained power in Russia. Liberalism, evolution, the German Kaiser, and Bolshevism all came from the Devil. What could be done? Only 100 percent Americanism could defeat these evils. Echoing themes from Billy Sunday, patriotism and Christianity were two sides of the same coin. To support this reasoning, they retreated to their view of American history. Only America's Christian heritage could protect the nation against the evils they faced. The Puritans and the Constitution had indeed established divinely inspired laws guaranteeing individual freedom in personal, political, and economic matters.[17]

To this nationalism, the ultra-fundamentalists added a conspiratorial mindset. Their Manichaean worldview inclined them to see everything in black and white terms and to view their perceived enemies as conspirators. They saw the struggles of the day as part of a great war—capitalism versus communism and good against evil. But their opponents were not always obvious. There existed internal enemies often dressed in sheep's clothing. In particular, McIntire and company attacked the liberal clergy, whom they viewed as a Trojan horse betraying America to communism. They were either communist dupes or outright traitors. In this attack, the fundamentalists linked arms with Joseph McCarthy who was at work ferreting out communists from the American government. Such conspiracy theories, of course, are as old as the nation itself. They rise, however, during times of stress. The failure to check communism after the end of World War II, the fall of China, the Soviets achieving nuclear parity, and the Korean War all fueled such fears.[18]

Another enemy of the ultra-fundamentalists was Roman Catholicism. McIntire declared that the "greatest enemy of freedom and liberty that the world has to face today is the Roman Catholic system." He argued that Catholicism was worse than communism. If a choice had to be made between the two, "one would be better off in a Communist society, than in a Roman Catholic fascist setup." This opposition can be seen in the 1960 election, which drew together the fundamentalists and the radical right. Kennedy's Catholicism, liberalism, elite background, and sophistication embodied what both groups viewed as an internal conspiracy. In such opposition to Kennedy, the old fundamentalist populism reared its head. Even without his Catholicism, they hated his Harvard education, his wealthy upbringing, and Boston twang. All of these elements provided a groundswell of support for Barry Goldwater in the 1964 election.[19]

Still, when the time was right, the ultra-fundamentalists put the Catholic terror on the back burner. Many of them lined up behind McCarthy's anticommunist crusade, despite the senator's Catholicism. In fact, they even ignored his domestic agenda, which they opposed. While McCarthy was a hardliner against communism, on domestic issues—such as social security, public housing, and welfare legislation—he voted with the moderate Republicans. The fundamentalists also disregarded the Catholic issue in the 1964 election. They staunchly supported Barry Goldwater, whose running mate William Miller was a Catholic. Even Goldwater's Episcopalian faith ran counter with their beliefs.[20]

In making these and other compromises, the Old Christian Right violated one of its cardinal principles—separation. While ultra-fundamentalism and the radical political right had much in common, they had their differences. The fundamentalists seemed to limit their separation to the ecclesiastical sphere. They would not contaminate themselves in churchly relationships, but they made some alliances to combat the liberal political and social agenda. Such a tendency is also evident with the New Christian Right. They have included Catholics and Mormons in their organizations because they agree on certain political and social issues.

In respect to individualism, capitalism, and limited government the Old Christian Right also baptized its political ideology. The heart of its objection to nearly every progressive legislative act was its cardinal beliefs in individual and state's rights. Both McIntire and Hargis believed that God had inspired the writers of the Constitution. And this document contained the systems of federalism and separation of powers. While they claimed not to be racists, civil rights' acts violated state's rights, which were ordained of God by virtue of being in the Constitution. Hargis argued that "God ordained segregation" and that it is "one of Nature's universal laws." In agreement, McIntire contended, "Segregation or apartheid is not sin *per se*..." The government thus had no right to tell anyone whom they must serve or hire. To do so would be an attack on one's property and a violation of the Eighth Commandment to not steal.[21]

Even more sacred was the laissez-faire free enterprise system. In the mind of the ultra-fundamentalists, God had given human beings the absolute right to own property. Thus, social security, progressive income taxes, and welfare measures violated the biblical injunction not to steal. More indirectly, they insisted that God had ordained capitalism. Acquiring wealth is not sin or greed but a sign of divine blessing. Competition, which is essential to capitalism, promotes the concept of stewardship. In a pamphlet, "Jesus, A Capitalist," the fundamentalists even say Jesus was a capitalist. The logic goes like this. Jesus was a carpenter and with no unions he had to bid for jobs against competition. "Jesus was a capitalist, preaching a doctrine of individualism which is the basis of free enterprise, and for this the religious and political hierarchies contrived his death."[22]

The Old Christian Right also used Christian and American history to bolster its support for the free enterprise system. They pointed to John Calvin's Geneva where thrift, hard work, and self-discipline were the order of the day. (They do fail to mention that for its day, Geneva had a well-developed social welfare system). Other Protestants also promoted the notions of thrift and hard work and wrote them into their creeds. As a final example, they pointed to America with its free enterprise system. As evidence that God has blessed such a system, America has become a wealthy powerful nation.[23]

The Old Christian Right was deeply rooted in the culture of its time. And its adherents responded to such developments in a manner consistent with their background. The ultra-fundamentalists were deeply populist. Many of their leaders and constituents reflected a rural background and mindset. On the whole, they were not a well-educated lot, and they scorned the educated elite of the East. Above all, they responded to two developments—a hangover from the old fundamentalist-modernist brawl and the Cold War. The ultra-fundamentalists not only defended the historic Christian faith but they added to it. They made side issues such as premillennialism and separation cardinal doctrines. While the fundamentalists feared Catholicism, this took a back seat to the communist threat, which was so widespread in the 1940s and 1950s. Extreme views need enemies. And the fundamentalists did not have far to look.

Liberalism blended into socialism, which, in turn, became the great enemy—communism. In response to these threats, the ultra-fundamentalists baptized many areas of American culture—especially its heritage and political and economic systems.

The Old Christian Right lost its steam and identity in the 1960s. With the election of Kennedy and the ultra-fundamentalists' alliance with McCarthy in the 1950s, anti-Catholicism played a reduced role in politics. The Catholics were usually staunchly anti-communist, so the fundamentalists welcomed their help in this crusade. The far secular right and the ultra-fundamentalists also moved closer together. Despite serious theological differences, they shared a similar political agenda—anti-communism, opposition to big government, and a belief in conspiracies. The Old Christian Right increased its cooperation with organizations such as the John Birch Society and We, the People. They shared information, action programs, and speakers. Patriotism indeed had become a form of religion. At times it was difficult to tell the difference between the Christian Right and the far secular right.[24]

The evangelical right, however, went into a state of disarray in the late 1960s and early 1970s. President Johnson soundly defeated Goldwater in the election of 1964. The 1960s became the decade of liberal politics and the counterculture. Some frustrated evangelicals showed their dissatisfaction by voting for George Wallace in 1968. While Nixon was a moderate Republican, many evangelicals backed him because of his public piety, ties with Billy Graham, and anti-communist credentials. Not only did his policies disappoint most fundamentalists, the Watergate scandal destroyed his presidency. Moreover, the ultra-fundamentalist leaders were not as active as in earlier decades. Some had aged and they had few new ideas for the 1970s and the Vietnam War. Billy Hargis had been discredited by a sexual scandal. Still, the Old Christian Right had gotten out its message and laid the foundation for the rise of the New Christian Right in the late 1970s. Some scholars see the Old Christian Right merging into the New Christian Right and that the latter is really an updated version of the former.[25]

Bedrock Theology

The bedrock beliefs of the New Christian Right closely resemble those of the Old Christian Right, but some new twists have arisen. Some of the issues are different and unlike its predecessor, the New Christian Right is at the very center of American politics—not at the margins of American society as was the Old Christian Right. Both the Old and New Christian Right have explicit and implicit theological positions. There are some very clearly stated beliefs and some unstated ideas that covertly shape the activities of the New Christian Right (from now on the Christian Right).

The Christian Right's explicit source of authority is an inerrant Bible interpreted literally. Its meaning is clear so there is no need for an interpretation by the educated elite. Because Scripture is accessible to all, this leads to a populist approach to politics. Political philosophies come from fallen human beings and are thus fallible. The evangelical Christian armed with Scripture, however, has direct access to God's will and needs no human authorities for his or her political insights. And evangelicals widely apply their interpretation of Scripture. Not only is the Bible the rule for personal morality and worship, but it is also the authority for politics and social organization. The attempt by many evangelicals to apply the commands of Scripture to the public arena is certainly a major factor in the culture wars.[26]

The implicit authorities are varied but important. The old Manichaean worldview, which pervades the evangelical subculture, encourages them to interpret the Bible and much else in black and white terms. Consequently, world events are viewed as part of the conflict between good and evil and one is either on God's side or the Devil's. This view obviously discourages compromise, which is essential to political discourse. Prevailing theologies such as dispensationalism are accepted by millions of evangelicals as synonymous with the Word of God and not as just another human approach to Scripture. Growing out of this theology is a sense of an impending end to history, a situation that also impacts one's political views. Christianity in the United States has been so Americanized that at times it is difficult to tell God's Word from American culture. The Christian Right indeed interprets the Bible through a "glass darkly," that is, the prism of American culture. This situation has dramatically influenced the Christian Right's stance on both domestic and international politics.

The evangelical distinctive centers on the conversion experience and informs its view of politics. As D. G. Hart notes, conversion is a "great leveler of privilege and rank because it results in a sanctified person who is capable of intuiting what is just or right in social and international affairs." Thus, evangelicals often find it difficult to understand how a truly converted person can oppose the political agenda of the Religious Right or embrace "liberal" views. Conversion is to produce a sanctified and pietistic person. This personal piety is broadened beyond the self to the wider society. It orientates evangelicals toward public issues that have more moral significance on a pietistic level but frequently blinds them to social problems. For example, evangelicals are often preoccupied with sexual sins while they ignore social evils such as poverty and racism. Conservative Protestants, indeed, believe that if religion is truly spiritual it will shape "the behavior of citizens" and order "the affairs of nations."[27]

Creationism is a big issue with the Christian Right. Believing in the literal interpretation of an inerrant Bible, in various degrees they are faithful to the Genesis account. God directly created the world—some say in six days, while others stretch his work over a vast period of time. Still, most reject evolution and this fuels a major issue for the Christian Right. They insist that creation science or intelligent design be taught as an alternative to evolution in the public schools. Related to the creation story is the preeminence of men over women and the Christian Right's rejection of feminism—a subject that will come later. The Genesis account in their view established woman as man's helpmate. Feminism and the struggle for equal rights thus upsets the divinely ordained role and the order of creation.[28]

The Christian Right accepts literally the Genesis account regarding the fall of humanity and the consequences of this original sin. Their dim view of the human condition has political implications. Because of their negative view of human nature, they regard individual conversion—not social programs—as the answer to societal problems. This view also inclines the Christian Right to take a law and order approach and advocate more social controls than would liberals. But conversion can reverse the effects of the original sin. That is why the Religious Right and evangelicals in general support the election of "Christian politicians." The new birth enables these "righteous ones" to rise above the usual corrupt situations that politicians face. This emphasis on conversion also reinforces the evangelical tendency to "Christianize" celebrity figures— whether in politics, business, athletics, or entertainment. That person "is a Christian" they say, so he or she is more trustworthy.[29]

While the covenant receives little attention from the evangelical pulpits, it has major political implications for the Christian Right. What are they? God had a covenant with Israel, which entailed moral injunctions. Would God bless or punish Israel? This depended on Israel's obedience to the covenant. The Puritans transferred the covenant to America. Since then American civil religion has viewed the United States as a "chosen nation" with a unique role to play in God's plan for the world. But America must be faithful to the divine commands. And since the 1960s, it has not been. This will bring God's judgment, such as the nation experienced on September 11.

As discussed in chapter 2, this chosen-nation concept has been applied to many aspects of American life—prayer in the schools, foreign policy, resistance to moral decadence, and support for military action. Gabriel Fackre writes that "the greatest departure from Christian doctrine" is the Religious Right's transfer of the divine covenant with Israel to America. What we have is a "functional elevation of America to the place of a chosen nation..." This breeds intense nationalism and military adventurism in foreign affairs while dampening internal criticism of such policies. Americas' "covenant status makes loyalty" to the nation an aspect of "loyalty to God."[30]

The end is coming say many evangelicals. This preoccupation plays an important but paradoxical role in the Christian Right's political views. While the Christian Right embraces several eschatological views, most hold to the premillennial, pretribulational position. Such a position says that the world will get worse until Christ returns to rapture out believing Christians. Current events are watched closely and interpreted in light of an impending end. The premillennialists believe that the world must get worse and worse. But they still have a moral reform agenda for America.

While many evangelicals believe the end is very near, they have moved up the social ladder and are planning to continue the good life for the foreseeable future. The Christian Right's view of the end closely relates to its dualistic worldview. What is going right before their eyes is a cosmic battle between the forces of light and darkness—and they are on God's side. Of great importance and as a result of its eschatology, the Christian Right has a great interest in Israel. The return of the Jews to Palestine set the divine clock ticking. Nothing else needs to be fulfilled before the end. Thus, the Christian Right staunchly supports Israel's interests in American foreign policy.[31]

One Nation Under God

Many contemporary evangelicals desire to remake and reform America. What fuels this passion? A central motivation is their vision of a Christian America. They believe that America was established on Christian principles and that it is a Christian nation with a special mission. They also insist that in recent years, the vision of a Christian American has been hijacked by the secularists and feminists.

The subject of a Christian nation has already been encountered in this study and will only be updated at this point. The Puritans believed that they had a covenant with God and that America was a "city on a hill," the "New Israel." This idea was continued and enlarged upon in the nineteenth century. America now became a redeemer nation with a millennial mission to civilize and Christianize the world. Wars and depressions tarnished this vision during the first half of the twentieth century. But the fundamentalists still clung to the notion that America had been a Christian nation. During the patriotic 1950s, under the guidance of a benevolent president and the threat of communism, the vision received new life.

In the late twentieth century, the idea of a Christian America has become an article of faith with many evangelicals. Throughout the 1960s and 1970s, the Vietnam War created much cynicism regarding America's divine mission. Some evangelicals countered this trend. Businessman George Otis wrote that "God's hand was in the founding of this country and the fiber of Christ is in the very fabric of America."[32] Dale Evans Rogers insisted that America "was in the mind of God before it became [an] earthly reality" and that it still occupied "a part of His purpose for mankind."[33]

Such beliefs took on new life in the 1980s and became part of the political rhetoric. In arguing for Christians to become involved in politics, Francis Schaffer contends that our founding fathers were deeply influenced by Judeo-Christian values. The ills that the nation has since encountered have come because America has forsaken its original value system. Instead, we are now embracing a materialistic and humanistic worldview.[34] Actually, the notion that America was founded on biblical principles is not as strident as the nine-teenth-century belief in America as a redeemer nation and chosen people. Some individuals involved with the Religious Right still insist on such a position, however.

During the 1980s, President Reagan frequently pushed the American civil religion theme. His rhetoric often drew on biblical imagery. In the star-spangled atmosphere of the 1984 Olympic games, President Reagan's speech referred to "a future of unlimited promise, an endless horizon lit by the star of freedom guiding America to supremacy." [35] At these games, the victory chant—"U.S.A.! U.S.A.!"—reinforced Reagan's optimism. In his 1988 presidential bid, Pat Robertson made several statements linking America to God. The Ten Com-mandments are the "bedrock of America," God "inspired our Founding Fathers to say that all men are created equal," and "we must never forget…that we are ONE NATION UNDER GOD."[36]

From the termination of the Moral Majority to the founding of the Faith and Values Coalition (about 1989 to 2004), Jerry Falwell gave evangelism and education a higher priority than political activities. He even asserts that "America is not the kingdom of God."[37] Still, he repeatedly speaks of America being founded on Christian principles. "I believe that God promoted America to greatness no other nation has ever enjoyed because her heritage is one of a republic governed by laws predicated on the Bible."[38]

Tim LaHaye also has high praises for America. If it were not for America, "our contemporary world would have completely lost the battle for the mind and would doubtless live in a totalitarian, one-world, humanistic state." Bill Bright, the founder of Campus Crusade, argued that because America has been so blessed by God it has enormous responsibilities. "God has given this coun-try unlimited resources…[and] has called America to help bring the blessing of His love and forgiveness to the rest of the world."[39]

Throughout the 1990s, evangelicals continued to proclaim the theme of "One Nation Under God." But the Clinton White House did not push this idea. Civil religion indeed came roaring back with the election of George W. Bush in 2000 and the terrorism of September 11. As people sought answers for this tragedy, religious explanations came to the forefront. Yes, God came back! Prayer and church attendance increased. The old theme of divine judgment befalling a sinful nation came to the forefront. Two days after the 9/11 terrorism, on Pat Robertson's *700 Club*, Jerry Falwell gave the answer believed by many evangelicals: God judged America because this nation tolerated "the pagans and the abortionists and the feminists and the gays and the lesbians." Pat Robertson agreed. They are responsible for "God lift-ing his protection over this nation." These men were resurrecting the old Puritan explanation for misfortune and calamity—God blesses the righteous but punishes evil-doers.[40] Such an answer often lurks behind the thinking of many evangelicals.

George W. Bush has pushed the old "civil-religious vision of America with the greatest energy of any president since Woodrow Wilson." Arguably, Bush may be the most overtly evangelical president in American history.[41] While his theology may be very simplistic and pietistic, he frequently verbalizes the Christian nation theme. Nearly every speech concludes with "God bless America." More than most past presidents, he has moved beyond vague statements of faith to overt Christian references. He believes that America has been called to bring God's gift of liberty "to every human being in the world." Without a doubt, this presidency "is the most resolutely faith-based in modern times."[42] His domestic policy largely conforms to the moral values of the evangelical community. In foreign policy, Bush believes that America has a special responsibility to the world—"to help the afflicted, and defend the peace, and confound the designs of evil men."[43] In all of this, we can hear an echo of the "redeemer nation" so prevalent in the nineteenth century.

Why is a Christian America so important for God's plans? America has four major tasks and if it fails, God's work will be set back. First, America must facilitate world evangelism. According to Falwell, "North America is the last logical base for world evangelization."[44] Who is to do the evangelism is unclear, but America must provide the resources. The next great task is to protect the nation of Israel. In dispensational theology, at the end of time God has great plans for Israel. Third, America must protect the free world from the onslaught of godless communism. When communism collapsed in 1991, the Christian Right turned to domestic issues. But after 9/11, terrorism replaced communism as the great external threat. Finally, America must be the guardian of liberty—religious, political, and economic. America must first preserve liberty at home from creeping liberalism and collectivism and export it to the rest of the world. Falwell regards liberty as "the basic moral issue of all moral issues" and is closely tied with biblical morality.[45] That his university is called *Liberty University* and sets on Liberty Mountain should come as no surprise.

Grant Wacker contends that the Christian Right can be "functionally defined by its commitment to the rebirth of Christian Civilization." As described by the Christian Right and other conservative Christians, a Christian civilization rests on three pillars. Most basic is the belief that there are "numerous moral absolutes human beings do not create but discover." As a result, there is only one correct answer for every moral question. Two, in a Christian civilization these moral absolutes ought to form "the laws that govern society." They should regulate both private and public conduct. Lastly, the moral absolutes undergirding society are revealed in nature but most explicitly in the Bible. Given these views, the Christian Right is "fired by an interventionist rather than libertarian vision of society."[46]

All evangelicals do not buy into the notion of civil religion as developed throughout American history and promoted by the Christian Right. Senator Mark Hatfield warned that an idolatrous civil religion that "enshrines" the political order "fails to speak of repentance, salvation, and God's standard of justice."[47] In evaluating civil religion, Robert Linder and Richard Pierard say that the promotion of political religion "not only shocks the sensibilities of many believers, but also casts doubt on the infallibility and immutability of divine truth itself."[48]

More recently, Christian Smith casts some doubt as to how widespread the concept of a Christian nation is upheld in the evangelical community. He acknowledges that many spokespersons for the Christian Right reinforce the belief that America was a Christian nation. For example, in his television program, the "Coral Ridge Hour," James Kennedy pushes this idea to an extreme. But Smith's surveys indicate that about "40 percent of the evangelicals" either question or doubt "the idea that America was once a Christian nation…" He further argues that the notion of a Christian America is not a single concept but has diverse meanings for different evangelicals. Moreover, Smith contends that only a minority of evangelicals desire to use political power to legislate Christian values on the rest of the population. If Smith is correct, the rhetoric of many evangelical leaders may not mirror the beliefs of the rank and file.[49]

In embracing the notion of the Christian nation, the Christian Right reflects the time tried evangelical political characteristics: "activistic, intuitive, populist, and biblicistic." While the movement has a body of theory, above all it is activistic. As a means to change America, it has motivated millions of evangelicals to be politically active. Consequently, the Christian Right is a powerful political block. Conservative evangelicals are deeply populist. They represent a grassroots movement desiring to reclaim America from the educated elite, the secularists, and feminists. Their model was Ronald Reagan, who rose from modest means and attended a small midwestern college. His lack of intellectual depth was no problem. They loved his one-liners, anecdotes, and ability to communicate in plain language. These same evangelicals instinctively knew right from wrong and that America was going the wrong way. And a simple, literal reading of the Bible told them the corrective was for the nation to return to its biblical moorings.

One Market Under God

Conservative politics and conservative economics are often fellow travelers. Evangelicalism's embrace of capitalism in the nineteenth century has been previously described. The same characteristics, however, that forged an early marriage between capitalism and evangelicalism are alive and well in the late twentieth and early twenty-first centuries. The marriage is thus stable. Ever since Max Weber, scholars have debated the linkage between Protestantism and capitalism. To see a cause and effect would be an exaggeration. They nevertheless share many characteristics that make for a compatible relationship. Many of these same features can be found in contemporary evangelism and make for its cozy relationship with capitalism.

Being an evangelical does not demand that one automatically embrace the free enterprise system. But there is certainly a close connection. Evangelicalism centers on the conversion experience, which is an individual's free decision. Conservative Protestants usually uphold the ideals of hard work, discipline, efficiency, and personal responsibility. All of these characteristics point the evangelical toward the free enterprise system and unregulated markets. Such evangelical features are also the requirements for running a small business. Evangelicals prize liberty of all forms and this intense devotion spills over into the market economic system. They hate all forms of collectivism and government control (unless it is to their benefit, of course). Individuals in their opinion should be free to use their talents and resources as they see fit. Many people will argue that free enterprise is the best economic system. But many conservative Protestants baptize this system, elevating it to the eleventh commandment.[50]

Even Carl Henry (1913-2003)—a leading evangelical moderate and an editor of *Christianity Today*—upheld the idea and practice of limited government. His influential book, *The Uneasy Conscience of Modern Fundamentalism*, criticized fundamentalism for ignoring the nation's social ills. He argued that all Christians should work to solve society's problems. Churches and other Christian institutions must show more concern for poverty and social injustice. Just how should this be done? In addressing this question, he remained a conservative. Henry would not advocate anything resembling a government program for redistributing wealth. His positions on social and economic matters were right at home in the late 1940s and early 1950s. They reflected the values of middle-class evangelicalism—the work ethic and private solutions to social ills. What made Henry different from most evangelicals of his time was his insistence that Christians must become involved with social problems.[51]

George Gilder, an economist who claims to be an evangelical Christian, staunchly supports the market economy. "Give and you'll be given unto is the fundamental practical principle of the Christian life, and when there's no private property you can't give it because you don't own it.... Socialism is inherently hostile to Christianity and capitalism is simply the essential mode of human life that corresponds to religious truth."[52] Elsewhere, he uses biblical references in support of the market economy. "Capitalism is not impugned but affirmed in the biblical parables: the parable of the talents, in which Jesus praises the man who invests and multiplies his money, or even the parable of the rich man, who is told to give away rather than hoard his wealth." Referring to Paul's writings, Gilder says, "the deepest truths of capitalism are faith, hope, and love."[53]

Jerry Falwell supports the free enterprise system—not just as his personal preference—but as a biblical principle. "I believe in capitalism and the free enterprise system and private property ownership...." He insists that "God is in favor of freedom, property ownership, competition, diligence, work, and acquisition. All of this is taught in the Word of God in both the Old and New Testaments." And to give legs to this belief, the free enterprise system is vigorously taught at Falwell's Liberty University.[54]

Other evangelicals make similar assertions. According to Pat Robertson, "free enterprise is the economic system most nearly meeting humanity's God-given need for freedom."[55] Ronald H. Nash—a professor of philosophy and theology—is alarmed about the growing trend toward socialism, which he sees in liberation theology. He contends that Christians should prefer capitalism because it is impossible to have "spiritual freedom" without "economic freedom."[56]

With some other evangelicals, the defense of capitalism is more toned down than with Falwell. Rather than endow the free enterprise system with divine sanction, they say that the market economy is relatively the best system. They compare capitalism with communism or fascism and contend for the relative merits of the free enterprise system as practiced in America. For example, evangelical Senator Bill Armstrong wrote: "Our form of government is vastly preferable to Marxism. But that doesn't prove that Christ would be a capitalist…[However] he would approve of those institutions of government or economy that foster human liberty. So I take it for granted that Christ would not approve of the arrangements in Nazi Germany or in the Soviet Union."[57]

Evangelicalism's embrace of the market economy has been fueled by more than theory and the fact that they share certain common characteristics. Post-World War II America, especially since 1980, has witnessed the triumph of consumerism. The nation has been riding a crest of prosperity, not withstanding the mounting personal and national debt. Conservative Protestants have not been left out of these developments. They have prospered and moved into the middle class and beyond. Evangelicals may be protesting the nation's moral breakdown, but they are not complaining about its materialism. They build large homes, shop until they drop, and use the plastic card like most Americans. In this sense, conservative Protestants have bought heavily into the American way of life.

Financial Answer Man

Evangelicalism has also put a populist face on the free enterprise system. This is best seen in the life and career of its economic guru, Larry Burkett (1939-2003). Through his organization, the Christian Financial Concepts (CFC), his books, and radio programs he became evangelicalism's financial answer man. His life and times can be seen as a microcosm of evangelical economics. He rose from modest circumstances to become a radio fixture, a best selling author, and an evangelical celebrity. His march to success and that of the CFC was closely connected with the economic developments of the 1980s and 1990s. That financial matters became a major concern for evangelicals, assumes an increase in their wealth and social status. Conservative Protestants shared in both the prosperity and the debt of the post-World War II era and had need for financial counseling. Burkett filled this void by offering evangelicals advice on financial matters. His guidance rested on two sources—principles derived from Scripture and common sense.[58]

Burkett epitomizes the evangelical characteristics—activism, populism, intuitive, and biblicism. In Burkett we have a former unbelieving electrical engineer who became for millions of evangelicals the last word in respect to financial matters. Yes, "when Burkett speaks, evangelicals listen." Working full time and going to college, he eventually earned two bachelor's degrees from Rollins College. One might think that the evangelical financial answer man would have an MBA or Ph.D. in economics. But not so with Burkett. He made the Bible his source of economic wisdom, amassing over 700 references. He organized these verses into a "financial concordance" that served as the foundation of his advice. These biblical principles were, of course, applied through the prism of common sense. [59]

Burkett emerged from a modest background. For even his first book—*Your Finances in Changing Times*—he had to raise $25,000 to cover the publishing costs. From this humble beginning he published a number of other books, began his own organization, and operated two daily radio shows. He offered his daily financial counsel on "How to Manage Your Money," which was heard on 600 stations from Guam to South Africa. "Your Money Matters" was a thirty-minute call-in show heard over 400 stations. Several of his books experienced phenomenal sales. By the late 1990s, *Your Finances in Changing Times* had sold over 1,300,000 copies. Other best sellers include *The Coming Economic Earthquake, Debt-Free Living, Using Your Money Wisely, The Financial Planning Workbook, and How to Manage Your Money.*[60]

What advice did this financial answer man give to evangelicals? Burkett's engineering background can be seen in his approach to economics. His information came largely in the form of economic nuts and bolts—budgets, handling taxes, investments, and debt-retirement. The very heart of his financial advice was that "God's people should be debt-free." No single subject gets more of his attention than the problem of debt, which he regarded as a form of bondage. Christians were to borrow only for a house and perhaps for a car. Another centerpiece of his philosophy is that all of a believer's possessions belong to God. Still, Christians were not to live a life of poverty, but to enjoy a comfortable life. Poverty in his view did not equal spirituality. Yet, he viewed the prosperity gospel with great scorn. In living such a life, however, the Christian had to give a minimum of 10 percent to the church. Additional giving to parachurches was to be above this minimum gift.[61]

Macroeconomics and economic theory were not Burkett's forte. His economic philosophy, nevertheless, squared with that of the Christian Right. He adhered firmly to the free enterprise system, believing that it reflected both biblical principles and America's Christian heritage. A market economy free of government controls faithfully embodied the Bible's guidelines on finances, so he believed. Such beliefs had deep roots in American society. But the events of two world wars, the Great Depression, and the New Deal placed America in debt and encouraged the rise of a big intrusive government. All of this undermined God's economic plan for America. Burkett linked America's abandonment of biblical principles in finances with the nation's overall moral decline. In his mind, godly economic principles and Judeo-Christian values go together.[62]

Burkett was a staunch Republican, supporting Reagan's attempt to place government on a diet. In fact, in admiring the Austrian libertarian economist Ludwig von Mises, Burkett became a major voice for the Christian Right. For Reagan's failure to reduce government, he blamed Congress for not enacting spending cuts. That George H. W. Bush did not follow Reagan's political and economic policies made Burkett unhappy. Believing that America was headed for an economic disaster by the mid-1990s, he penned *The Coming Economic Earthquake*. One would think that he would have approved of the economic boom of the 1990s and Clinton balancing the budget. No, in part Clinton did this by raising taxes—a sin to Burkett nearly as bad as the president's sexual scandals. And his later book, *Crisis Control in the New Millennium*, echoes his usual warnings and predicted that the economic bubble would burst by 2000. While Burkett did not push the Y2K theme, his thinking on economics in the 1990s was conditioned in part by the apocalyptic mood of that era.[63]

Limited Role of Government

If the free enterprise system has divine approval, what then is the role of government? Quite limited say many evangelicals. They viewed Franklin Roosevelt's New Deal with great suspicion and as intrusion into their God given liberties. In fact, evangelicals inclined toward dispensationalism regarded such developments as preparation for the "man of sin," and the "one world government." For the most part, a negative attitude toward big government has continued down to the present. In economic matters, the Christian Right agrees with Thomas Jefferson's statement that the government that governs least governs the best. The federal government in their opinion is the greatest threat to personal and economic freedoms. It has encroached upon the prerogatives of the family, church, school, and the business community. In the process, government has far exceeded its constitutional boundaries, which have been enlarged by activist judges.[64]

When it comes to the role of government, Falwell makes himself quite clear: "When America was founded, the legitimate purpose of government was to protect the lives, the liberties, and the property of the citizens. It was not the purpose of government to redistribute resources or to enforce any particular results in the relationships and dealings of the citizenry among themselves."[65]

In this view, the government protects rather than promotes rights. Scripture, in Falwell's opinion, mandates only two functions for the federal government: to protect citizens from foreign invasion and from criminals at home. The federal government has no biblical or constitutional authority to equalize wealth, provide food for the able-bodied, intrude upon the schools, regulate businesses, or establish race relations. Such tasks should be performed by the family, church, local schools, business community, and local or state governments.[66]

Given this philosophy, it is easy to see why the Christian Right enthusiastically supported Ronald Reagan in the 1980 election against a fellow evangelical, Jimmy Carter. They responded well to his promise to shrink government by reducing the bureaucracies. Evangelicals loved his belief that government should serve the people, not feed off of them. But in reality, Reagan failed to shrink the government and succeeded in running up record deficits. They also rejoiced in his social conservativism and rhetoric regarding traditional morals and patriotism. National pride became a high priority during the Reagan administrations, but social issues so dear to the Christian Right were largely put on the back burner. However, many in the evangelical community never noticed.

The logic of the Christian Right in respect to limited government contains an apparent paradox. They plead for less government in economic matters and on some social issues. But in respect to moral concerns—especially abortion, same sex marriages, homosexuality, and prayer in the schools—they desire government legislation to rectify the current situation. In the words of conservative columnist William Safire: "the Rightists wanted to remove the government from the private sector, yet have it govern such intimate matters as abortion, sexual lifestyles, and prayer."[67] In respect to abortion, conservative Protestants see their position as consistent with their philosophy that a government's primary role is to protect people—this time the unborn. They also justify legislation on other moral issues with this argument: once America returns to its Christian principles there will be no need to legislate morals.

In the last three sections—the Christian nation, the free enterprise system, and limited government—evangelicals have "baptized" America's political and economic systems, as they have sanctified many aspects of American culture. Limited government and the market economy may be outstanding systems—ones that have worked well in America. They may even be the key to America's freedom and prosperity. And, in part, they may reflect biblical principles. But they are also derived from secular sources, namely the classical economists and Enlightenment political thinkers. Assuming that liberty is a Christian virtue, it has sources other than the Bible. Much of this Christianizing of the political and economic systems can be attributed to evangelicalism's tendency to sanctify many aspects of the secular culture.[68]

Some Trigger Events

Driving the rise of the Christian Right are a number of beliefs—an inerrant Bible, the necessity of a conversion, America's Christian heritage, and the divinely sanctioned political and economic systems. But it took a series of events to trigger the conservative political resurgence of the late 1970s. Evangelicals were a political and intellectual minority since the 1930s. They were, however, still part of the conservative cultural majority. Most Americans shared a similar vision on how a well ordered society should be run. Evangelicals felt at home in the general religious tenor of the Eisenhower era. In their mind, America was "One Nation Under God." The traditional family values of the time suited them. Women understood their child-rearing role and abortion on demand was not yet legal. The new medium of television did not yet offend the evangelical community. They watched "Ozzie and Harriet" and "Leave It to Beaver" and could identify with this life style. In the public schools, the day still opened with Bible reading and the Lord's Prayer. After 1970, conservative Protestants longingly looked back to the America of the 1950s. They were not politically active from 1930 to 1970 in part because they did not have to be.[69]

But the social and political turmoil of the 1960s drastically changed America. Life altering events included the following: the civil rights movement, the counterculture, the women's movement, increased immigration, opposition to the war in Vietnam, a series of Supreme Court decisions, the sexual revolution, and an increased use of drugs.[70] Such developments made evangelicals increasingly uncomfortable with the America of the late twentieth century. The traditional values to which they adhered no longer held sway and often became the object of ridicule. It still took a series of events to push conservative Protestants into the political arena. And when they did get politically active, it came as a reaction to these developments.

Several Supreme Court decisions in the 1960s removed religion from the public schools. In particular, state laws permitting prayer and the reading of Scripture were declared unconstitutional. The First Amendment prohibited any laws from either establishing or prohibiting religion. In religious matters, the government must be neutral. As interpreted by the courts, this meant that for legislation to be legal, it could not give religion any special advantages or prevent anyone from freely exercising their faith. From the beginning of public education, the schools have included reading the King James Bible and prayer. To the dismay of Catholics, these activities had a Protestant flavor and reflected the Protestant dominance over public education. Even by the mid-twentieth century, about 35 to 50 percent of the public schools still opened school with religious exercises. Critics of these Supreme Court decisions, including evangelicals, saw these acts as removing God from the classroom and as a kind of forced secularization. Several proposed constitutional amendments attempted to reverse these decisions. They failed to gain the required two-thirds majority in Congress that would have sent them on to the states for ratification.[71]

The legalization of abortion ignited one of the bitterest conflicts in American religion, politics, and society. For many on both sides of the cultural divide, the abortion issue is a litmus test. Neither the pro-life nor pro-choice camps will compromise. Pro-lifers insist that abortion is murder. Pro-choice advocates say that women have the right to control their own reproductive systems. Among other issues, abortion has divided Americans into two camps— the more religious and the more secular. The old Protestant-Catholic or conservative-liberal divisions have been redrawn. Conservative Protestants, Catholics, Jews, and Mormons are on one side. Confronting them are the secularists and the more liberal Protestants, Catholics, and Jews. These cultural divisions have indeed prompted a realignment of America's political parties and voting patterns.[72]

What prompted this controversy? The Supreme Court decision *Roe v. Wade* (1973) set the stage for this moral and political confrontation. It legalized abortion during the first trimester of pregnancy. During the first three months of pregnancy, the state may impose no restrictions on a woman's right to acquire an abortion. In the second three weeks, some restrictions can be imposed. By the last three weeks, a child may be aborted only to preserve the life or health of the mother.

What are the real issues behind this decision and the controversy it has prompted? First, when does life begin? Conservative Protestants and Catholics say that life begins with conception. The Supreme Court and the more liberal religionists say no. Conception does not mean person-hood or that a human life has begun. Because conservatives believe life begins at conception, they regard abortion as murder. Such thinking helps to explain the intensity of their feelings. Second, the legal basis for the court's decision rested on the right to privacy. The majority interpreted this right broadly enough to encompass a woman's decision to continue or terminate her pregnancy. A more narrow interpretation of the right of privacy rejects this claim.[73]

This court decision prompted the battle lines to be drawn, but not as quickly as one might suppose. Liberal Protestants and Reform Jews applauded *Roe v. Wade*. At first, even the conservative Southern Baptist Convention was open to the decision, largely on their cherished stance regarding the separation of church and state. Even Jerry Falwell did not immediately protest the decision. The first outcry came from the Catholic community—at first from the clergy and then from Catholic housewives. By the late1970s, resistance to abortion became more confrontational. Leadership for this phase again came from the Catholic priests and women.[74]

As the decade proceeded, abortion—along with other issues such as homosexuality and pornography—mobilized many evangelicals into political action. Some such as Billy Graham and other moderate evangelicals stayed out of the fray. But spurred on by Francis Schaeffer's writings, others entered politics with a vengeance. Most prominent were Jerry Falwell, Tim LaHaye, James Dobson, and Pat Robertson.[75] Overturning *Roe v. Wade* heads the evangelical wish list and some conservative Protestants run the risk of making this objective a test of faith. The abortion issue has also blurred the lines between the pro-life movement and the Christian Right. The two movements are different. Ending abortion is the central issue with the pro-lifers and this movement contains many non-evangelicals. The Christian Right has a broader agenda and defines itself as pro-family. Moreover, not all evangelicals—despite their opposition to abortion—are identified with the Christian Right.[76]

Three other events—homosexual rights, the tax-exempt status of private schools, and the Equal Rights Amendment (ERA)—helped trigger the rise of the Christian Right. The ERA was closely related to feminism and will be noted in that context. The gay movement rose during the 1970s. Following the example of blacks and women, homosexuals sought to improve their rights. Evangelicals opposed gay rights as incompatible with the injunctions of Scripture and family values. Battles occurred on the local level, but one gained national attention. Christian singer Anita Bryant began a crusade to block legislation supporting gay rights. After local success she took her campaign nationally with mixed results. More local struggles against gay rights continued, however, and they helped lay the foundation for the Christian Right. By the late 1970s, two Christian Right organizations—Christian Voice and the Moral Majority—joined the fight against gay rights. Not all evangelicals took a strident position in this regard, however. Ralph Reed and the Christian Coalition were more moderate, referring the issue to the states.[77]

The tax-exempt status of private schools aroused evangelicals. The 1954 *Brown v. Board of Education, Topeka, Kansas* desegregated the public schools in America. In the wake of this decision, private schools sprang up. It became obvious that many of these schools were intended to get around the desegregation mandated by the Supreme Court. Such schools appeared to be "segregated academies." The government countered by having the IRS establish a standard for tax-exempt status. To retain its tax-exempt status, a private school had to take one of two courses of action. Of the proportion of minorities living in their local area, they had to enroll 5 percent. If they failed in this, they could retain their tax-exempt status by demonstrating that they had attempted in good faith to hire minority faculty.[78]

This plan of action aroused many fundamentalists who supported private schools. So they initiated a mass letter writing campaign. The IRS backed off and Congress removed the IRS's funds for implementing its proposal. For the rise of the Christian Right, the private school problem entailed two issues. It demonstrated that if conservative Protestants exerted political pressure, the government would listen. Two, the tax-exempt status of schools came in a larger context. Evangelical Christians were concerned about a number of developing trends in the public schools—the banning of religious exercises, the teaching of evolution, the use of text-books questioning America's Christian heritage and traditional values, and sex education.[79]

Those Women Won't Stay at Home!

For the Christian Right, the abortion issue does not stand by itself. It is closely related to feminism. "No issue has caused evangelicals more consternation in the second half of the twentieth century than feminism," says Randall Balmer. Such a situation contains several paradoxes. First is the difference between the nineteenth and twentieth centuries. While exceptions can be noted, in the nineteenth century evangelicals were at the forefront in the quest for equal rights for women. In the late twentieth, however, they went to great lengths to oppose it. Second, the resistance to feminism runs counter to the strength of women in the conservative movement. Women are an important element of the Christian Right, the pro-life movement, and the Republican Party. They are perhaps the staunchest opponents of abortion and the Equal Rights Amendment. Moreover, women do much of the work in evangelical churches and organizations. Finally, there exists a massive paradox between the ideal evangelical position regarding gender roles and economic realities. Many evangelical families cannot afford to have the wife stay at home and live on one income.[80]

Through much of Christian history, women have been viewed with great suspicion—as seductive, tempters, sensual, and evil. Only by being subordinate to men could such behavior be controlled. This line of thinking goes back to Adam and Eve in the Garden of Eden and made its way down to the Puritans. The Puritan husband was not only regarded as the head of the home but also responsible for the spiritual nurture of his household. Around the early eighteenth century, however, this attitude began to change. More women attended church than men. They embodied the tender and loving values in a coarse masculine world. Thus, women were now viewed as spiritually superior to men.[81]

The nineteenth century saw this line of thinking continue. The Arminian theology of the Second Great Awakening taught that everyone is equal before God. This prompted evangelical women to assert themselves and some became prominent in the church. Still, they rarely rose to positions of authority in the church or society. Economic changes such as the rise of the market economy prompted men to distance themselves from domestic duties. The wife now filled this void. She educated the children and also gave them spiritual, moral, and social guidance. As the Victorian era progressed, the home increasingly became the women's domain. And in this arena, spiritual nurture became her responsibility. As evangelicals entered the twentieth century, the belief in female domesticity and spiritual superiority held sway.[82]

In the early twentieth century, evangelicals attempted to counter the Victorian notion of a woman's spirituality. Billy Sunday pushed the masculine aspect of Christianity by declaring that in Jesus we find "the definition of manhood."[83] The fundamentalist John R. Rice echoed a similar theme: "God is a masculine God." He blesses women, "but He never intended any preacher to be run by a bunch of women."[84] The intensity of their remarks tells us two things: some reality lurked behind the myth of female spiritual superiority and men did not like it. The Promise Keepers of the late twentieth century—a subject that will be noted later—built on these attitudes.

In the late twentieth century, many evangelicals clung to this notion of feminine domesticity. To a considerable degree, this perspective has shaped the social and political attitudes of millions of conservative Protestants. The paradox, however, is quite evident. Evangelical men implicitly recognize female spiritual superiority while expecting them to be submissive. The popularity of Marabel Morgan's book *The Total Woman* (1973) indicates how deeply ingrained such an attitude was. She declared that a woman should submit in a servile way to her husband and enjoy her domestic role. " A Total Woman caters to her man's special quirks, whether it be in salads, sex, or sports."[85] In doing so, she will be fulfilled and make her husband happy.

The events of the late twentieth century dramatically challenged the traditional evangelical view of female domesticity. Society now rejected and even ridiculed a belief so dear to the hearts of conservative Protestants. The 1963 publication of Betty Friedan's *The Feminine Mystique* gave voice to the stirring feminist movement. The woman's movement called for changes in the workplace, politics, churches, home, and in society as a whole. It denounced sexism and discrimination against women in many areas of American life. Feminists founded their own magazines, centers to assist victims of rape and abuse and, after 1973, abortion clinics. Women organized to promote their demands. The National Organization of Women (NOW) became the most influential of their organizations. High on their wish list was passage of the Equal Rights Amendment (ERA), which eventually failed to get ratified. In a more quiet but effective way, women entered the work force in droves and became a major factor in the economy.

How did all of this effect the evangelical community? They did not like it. The women's movement challenged the worldview of conservative Protestants much like Darwinism and higher criticism did in the nineteenth century. As these earlier developments pushed evangelicals from the mainstream of American society, so did feminism. By the standards of contemporary society, their nineteenth-century view of a woman's role in society seemed anachronistic.

The situation for evangelicals was very confusing. On one hand, economic necessities encouraged women to work outside of the home. This development often settled the issue. In large numbers women moved out of the home and into the work place. On the other hand, conservative Protestant preachers blasted them for doing so. In particular, the Southern Baptists passed resolutions relegating women to a secondary position. There could be no female clergy and women were to submit to men in the home. Many evangelical women thus experienced a guilt trip for stepping out of the home and asserting themselves.[86] Such a paradoxical situation allowed evangelicals to preserve their claim to an inerrant Bible while largely ignoring the reality of the role of women in modern society.

Opposition to feminism predated the rise of the Christian Right in the late 1970s. The Senate passed the ERA in 1972. Phyllis Schlafly, a conservative Catholic, led a movement to derail the ERA. This movement consisted of numerous local and state units plus a national organization called STOP ERA. Because of this movement's efforts, ERA fell three states short of the three-quarters necessary for ratification. The victory over the ERA has been seen as a turning point in the battle between the feminists and the pro-family advocates [87]

The Christian Right now openly jumped into the fray and family values became central in their struggle against evil. The leader in this campaign was James Dobson's organization Focus on the Family. With a large structure in Colorado Springs and on over 2,500 radio stations in ninety-five countries, Dobson mustered the evangelical forces in this great crusade to save the American family. The Christian family faced a sinister conspiracy led by the radical feminists and the media. Their agenda included the ERA, the availability of abortion, and gay rights. Opposition to this perceived conspiracy thus shaped Dobson's mission and much of the Christian Right's political program. Dobson saw no gray in this great battle. "Nothing short of a great Civil War of Values rages throughout North America" he wrote. "Two sides with vastly differing and incompatible worldviews are locked in a bitter conflict that permeates every level of society."[88]

While Dobson is an educated man with a legitimate Ph.D., at heart he is a populist resisting the moral trends of the late twentieth century. As a populist and moralist, he offers simple answers to complex questions and demands immediate progress. "If you look at the culture war" most of it leads to death— "abortion, euthanasia, promiscuity in heterosexuality, promiscuity in homosexuality, [and the] legalization of drugs. There are only two choices.... It's either God's way, or it is the way of social disintegration." While he is a major player in the Christian Right, he could be critical of its leaders who compromised what he regards as traditional family values. Rather, Dobson was something of an Old Testament prophet denouncing the immorality of contemporary society.[89]

Evangelicals sought to refute the claim that women were repressed in the traditional marriage. Beverly LaHaye created another important Christian Right organization—Concerned Women for America. This organization countered feminism, homosexuality, abortion, the rising divorce rate, sex issues and others. But the source of this evil was feminism. By repudiating the divinely ordained patriarchal role, feminists were undermining the traditional values embraced by both the family and society.

LaHaye, however, did not want to paint a picture of repressed women. Within the framework of traditional values, she sought to liberate women. She affirmed that men were to lead in the home and church but not in society in general. Here women do not have to submit to men. She teamed up with her husband Tim LaHaye to write *The Act of Marriage* (1976). Reflecting the sexual revolution but still a counterattack against feminism, this book argues for a pleasurable sex life within marriage. In fact, the last decades of the twentieth century witnessed an explosion of evangelical sex manuals that became best sellers. These manuals were devoted to Christian heterosexual intercourse within marriage. While they often contained explicit information regarding the mechanics of sex, their general message was that evangelical Christians have the best sex. Why? They understand that God created man and woman to enjoy sex within the bonds of marriage.[90]

Not all evangelicals agreed with the patriarchal view of the family articulated by many of their leaders. Many came down somewhere between the two extremes of an equal or patriarchal relationship. According to Christian Smith, "Most [evangelicals] embraced more complex views that fell somewhere along the spectrum between the two extremes." They tended to base their ideas on pragmatic rather than ideological issues. Economics has played a big role. With women being important breadwinners in the family structure, men find it more difficult to be patriarchal.[91]

Some Facilitators

While beliefs and grievances propelled the Christian Right into action, several developments prepared the way. They include the Democratic Party's leftward drift, secular alliances, the Carter presidency, and the television evangelists. In the early twenty-first century, evangelical Christians are overwhelmingly housed in the Republican Party. (The exceptions would be black evangelicals and the evangelical left). But this current political alignment was not always the case. Prior to the 1970s, a majority of evangelicals were Democrats.

What caused this realignment? In the 1960s, the Democratic Party moved to the left. They elected to the presidency John Kennedy, a liberal and a Catholic president. During the same decade, Lyndon Johnson implemented the "Great Society," thus increasing the scope of big government. The demonstrations protesting the Vietnam War turned off many patriotic evangelicals. Both of these presidents supported civil rights and the Civil Rights Acts of 1964 and 1965 were passed during the Johnson presidency.

These developments prompted the once solid Democratic South to begin a move toward the Republican Party. Richard Nixon carried several southern states in the elections of 1960 and 1968. In 1964, Barry Goldwater carried only his home state of Arizona plus five states of the onetime Confederacy. By the time of the 1972 election, the liberal elites, women, minorities, and antiwar advocates dominated the Democratic Party. They proceeded to nominate the stridently liberal George McGovern, who carried only Massachusetts and the District of Columbia. These trends alienated southern whites, especially those with a lower socioeconomic status. The election of 1976 temporarily arrested the drift of evangelicals to the Republican Party. They supported Jimmy Carter, an evangelical from Georgia. The Carter presidency, however, disappointed evangelicals nationwide, and in the election of 1980 they turned in droves to Ronald Reagan.[92]

Since that time, the Republican Party has largely had a lock on the evangelical vote. But evangelicals have turned to the Republican Party for more than racial reasons. Moral and religious issues—increased secularization, abortion, homosexuality, pornography, indecency on television, liberal Supreme Court decisions, and the removal of religion from the public schools—have pushed evangelicals into the Republican ranks. A conservative alliance, indeed, has been formed. It embraces people with conservative religious, economic, social, and political beliefs. Political lines are now drawn between the more religious and the more secular people. Currently, the very bedrock of the Republican Party are conservative religious people—largely evangelicals but also Catholics.[93]

The Christian Right and the new secular right rose about the same time. The Old Christian Right had a cozy relationship with the secular right of the 1940s, 1950s, and early 1960s. Along with Joseph McCarthy and the John Birch Society, the ultra-fundamentalists joined in the anti-communist crusades. In doing so, they compromised their separatist values. The new Christian Right has traveled down a similar path. During the early 1960s, the number of conservative organizations grew because of dissatisfaction with the direction of society. The "Red Menance" and the big government in Washington with its liberal policies drove this discontent. During its formative stages, the Christian Right shared similar grievances. Its agenda had not yet shifted to family issues. Thus, the Christian Right and the New Right forged a working relationship.

Leaders of the New Right included Richard Viguerie, Paul Weyrich, Terry Dolan, and Howard Phillips. These men persuaded Jerry Falwell to become politically active and to form a political organization. They gave to the emerging Christian Right the skills necessary to become a successful political organization. The New Right brought to the Christian Right mass-mailing expertise, fund-raising skills, and ways to evaluate politicians based on specific issues. As time went on, the lines between the Christian Right and the New Right became increasingly blurred. While the emphasis may have been different, both groups upheld traditional morals, small government, a strong national defense, and resisted communism.[94]

The person and presidency of Jimmy Carter sparked a surge of evangelical political involvement. It represents a watershed for evangelicals. His successful bid for the presidency in 1976 proved that evangelicals could be mobilized for political action. After the corruption of Watergate, Americans looked for moral leadership in Washington and they turned to an evangelical. Carter, indeed, helped to make it respectable to be "born again." He did for evangelicals what John Kennedy did for Catholics—make them first-class citizens. *Newsweek* thus proclaimed 1976 "the year of the evangelical."[95]

As a person and a president, Carter embodied many evangelical characteristics. Most obviously, he displayed a deep-seated populism. While he was well educated with a master's degree in engineering, he conveyed a different image—that of a peanut farmer with limited political experience. Carter brought this Washington outsider anti-establishment attitude into the presidency. He wore a sweater in the White House, mended his own clothes while talking to reporters on a plane, carried his own luggage, stayed in the homes of ordinary people when he traveled, and listened to gospel music. Millions of common people who saw themselves shut out of politics now saw the most powerful nation in the world being governed by "a humble, everyday man—a man much like themselves."[96]

The evangelical community, however, turned against Carter. His *Playboy* magazine interview offended leading evangelicals. In America, two Christian traditions speak to political involvement. The Puritans believed Christian morality should be enforced legally. The free-church tradition contends that one's personal morals should be kept separate from public policy. Carter related more to the second tradition. For example, while he personally opposed abortion he did not support a constitutional amendment banning this practice. Moreover, Carter failed to support amendments restoring religion to the classroom. In the mind of the Christian Right, Carter was doing little to arrest the moral decline of America or to promote its agenda. So the Christian Right turned to Reagan in 1980.[97]

Another major development prompting the rise of the Christian Right was the television evangelists. The electronic church did not create the Christian Right, but without the televangelists it would not have had much success. For seven days a week, television sets beamed the image of charismatic preachers denouncing America's moral decline. While they may not have openly endorsed a particular candidate, their message regarding traditional morals left little doubt as to where they stood. They railed against the usual sins and evil organizations—homosexuality, abortion, the ERA., feminism, the American Civil Liberties Union (ACLU.), and removal of religion from the schools. Their worldview determined their foreign policy interests: pro-Israel and anti-communist. The advent of cable television has been a boon to the Christian Right. Distinctively Christian networks have broadcast the messages of preacher-politicians twenty-four hours a day seven days a week. [98]

Evangelicals have utilized the electronic media with great success. In the use of this medium, they have far surpassed liberal Protestants or Catholics. As noted in chapter 4, their radio ministries flourished. When television came along, conservative Protestants wasted no time in developing powerful ministries. Television was a perfect match for American culture, especially the evangelical subculture. Evangelicalism's populist impulse and need for instant expression found a home in television. As Erling Jorstad notes, "Television helped eliminate differences among educated and uneducated, offering knowledge to anyone who could see, without access to formal centers of learning." Events happened before the eyes of the viewer. Thus, television conveyed "a sense of immediacy and urgency..."[99]

Early celebrity-preachers included the Catholic Bishop Fulton J. Sheen and evangelicals Rex Humbard, Oral Roberts, and Billy Graham. While these men did not have an extensive political agenda, their success paved the way for others who did. By the mid-1970s, the electronic church as we think of it gained national prominence. Leading television preachers included Pat Robertson, Jim Bakker, Jerry Falwell, and James Robison. These men had their similarities and differences. Robertson and Bakker were charismatics while Falwell and Robison were not. Robertson and Bakker had daily television programs and could address current events more readily than those who preached only on Sunday. All four, however, were premillennialists who denounced America's moral decline and saw it as a sign of the last days. Since the mid-1970s, more televangelists have enunciated the message of the Christian Right. For example, James Kennedy has launched a crusade to restore America's Christian heritage.[100]

In other ways—especially in their populism and southern roots—the televangelists mirror the evangelical subculture. Few of them were well educated. Robertson and Kennedy are exceptions. None except Graham are associated with the old evangelical elite as represented by Wheaton College, Fuller Seminary, and *Christianity Today*. Most have come out of humble backgrounds and articulate sermons that connect with the common people. The vast majority are headquartered in the South and come from the fast growing Baptist and Pentecostal denominations. The populist and southern backgrounds of the televangelists have served them well, enabling them to bond with millions of viewers in a folksy way.[101]

The impact of the televangelists, however, should not be exaggerated. The sex scandals of the late 1980s—though limited to Bakker and Jimmy Swaggart—discredited televangelism in general. The lavish life style of others has not helped their image. The cost of television and this life style has prompted the televangelists to employ some distasteful fundraising methods. Moreover, some of the major figures (e.g., Roberts, Robert Schuller, Humbard, and Swaggart) have incorporated little or no politics into their ministries. Their messages cover a variety of subjects. Cultural fundamentalism has a clear connection with the Christian Right. But other evangelists focus on evangelism, the prosperity gospel, and self- improvement.[102]

How Shall We Then Live?

Prompting the birth of the Christian Right has been a number of developments and beliefs but few more important than the writings of Francis Schaeffer (1912-1984). Without impressive academic credentials and somewhat of a populist apologist, he unexpectedly emerged as an intellectual guru for millions of evangelicals. If people are to live right, they must think correctly, he argued. And this right thinking involved returning to a Christian worldview. In this, we see Schaeffer's great contribution. He made the issue of a worldview important to evangelicals.[103]

From the perspective of a Christian worldview, he interacted with the great thinkers and artists of Western culture. More specifically, this view came from a Reformed perspective, which emphasized the sovereignty of God over all areas of life. Schaeffer's greatest impact came in his book, *How Shall We Then Live?* (1976). This sweeping narrative of Western culture, also made into a film, argued that the defects of modern civilization can be traced to its rejection of God's sovereignty over all areas of life. Rather than accept God's rule, humans have asserted their own reasoning and this has led to the secularization of life. Schaeffer called this "secular humanism," which became the Christian Right's catchphrase for a wide range of social ills and ideological adversaries.[104]

What does this have to do with the Christian Right? Schaeffer's ideas have implications for society and politics. He regarded America as being founded on Christian principles. Currently, the nation was in moral decay because it rejected God's sovereignty over its public life. Appalled by abortion and other ills, Schaeffer urged Christians to become active in politics with the goal of returning America to its Reformation moorings. Speaking on college campuses and writing more books, his influence has been immense. More specifically, he inspired Falwell to get into the world of ideas and politics. Building on Schaeffer's suggestions, he founded Liberty College and the Moral Majority. Schaeffer's writings also prompted other evangelicals to attack secular humanism and the defects of American culture.[105]

Two examples of evangelical leaders following in the wake of Schaeffer's ideas are Tim LaHaye and Chuck Colson. LaHaye dedicated his book, *The Battle for the Mind* (1980), to Schaeffer. Building on Schaeffer's analysis of Western culture, LaHaye insisted that secular humanism was responsible for the ills of modern society—evolution, Freudianism, atheism, socialism, communism, rationalism, and existentialism. Colson also articulated Schaeffer's notion that America's moral decay could be directly attributed to its spiritual degeneration. In several books, Colson attempts to draw a connection between the question of worldview and cultural problems. Examples are *King-*

doms in Conflict (1987), *Against the Night* (1989), and *How Shall We Now Live* (1999).[106]

Phase One

The life of the Christian Right comes in two phases. While the Christian Right has deep historical roots, which have been described, it has had a short life. Phase one is seen as running from the late 1970s to 1988. The Christian Right formally began sometime between the elections of 1976 and 1980. This phase ended with the disappointments associated with the 1988 election and has been called the "age of discovery and disappointment." The second phase began after the election of 1988 and is seen as the "age of realism."[107]

The high points of phase one include the formulation of several Christian Right organizations, success in the 1980 elections, and the disappointments of the 1980s. Conservative Protestants had largely backed Carter in 1976 and were now out of the closet, so to speak. They had tasted victory in politics and wanted more. Thanks to the urgings of Schaeffer and the secular right, evangelicals now began to formulate political action groups. To combat a range of issues—relating to abortion, removal of prayer from the schools, the Equal Rights Amendment, homosexuality, pornography, social welfare, and increased government involvement in the schools—they formed a series of organizations. At first these structures were on the state and local levels and often led by pastors. These leaders focused on voter registration and the above issues that could be confronted at their level. The agenda of this early phase continued to be anti-communism but family issues driven by the war against secular humanism eclipsed this problem.[108]

National organizations began to spring up, the most prominent being the Moral Majority. In 1979, Jerry Falwell founded this organization in reaction to government decisions regarding abortion, homosexuality, feminism, and prayer in the schools. The goal of the movement was to counter the influence of secular humanism in politics and society by restoring traditional Christian morals and lifestyles. And it hoped to do this by means of education, political lobbying, and electing moral candidates to office. In 1989, Falwell disbanded this organization claiming victory and that the Christian Right has been integrated into society. The Moral Majority's end must also be seen in the context of the disappointments of the late 1980s. If viewed this way, Falwell's claims can be interpreted as dressing up defeat in the language of victory. Other Christian Right groups in these early years included Concerned Women for America, Christian Voice, the Freedom Council, the Religious Roundtable, and the American Coalition for Traditional Values.[109]

The early successes of the Christian Right centered on the 1980 election at two levels—the presidency and Congress. On the national level, Ronald Reagan defeated Jimmy Carter by a comfortable margin. For this the Christian Right deserves some of the credit, but scholars place more emphasis on the conservative tide that was swelling and the widespread dissatisfaction with the Carter presidency. What about the congressional races? The issue here is a little more difficult. Conservative candidates had considerable success and the Republicans gained control of the Senate for the first time in twenty-eight years. Again, scholars argue that these candidates would have won anyway. While the activity of the Christian Right helped, the 1980 election should be regarded as more of a Republican victory and the growth of conservatism. [110]

What about the disappointments? The Reagan presidency disappointed the Christian Right. He named only a few conservative Protestants to high offices. Beyond appointing conservative judges and giving lip service to the agenda of the Christian Right, Reagan did not push their issues. Particularly upsetting to the conservative Protestants was his appointment of pro-choice Sandra Day O'Connor to the Supreme Court. He had more secular concerns— reducing the size of government, cutting taxes, and building up the military. The election of 1988 also disappointed the Christian Right. To start, they were divided over which Republican to support—George Bush or Pat Robertson. On one hand, Bush's evangelical and conservative credentials were suspect. On the other, many conservative Protestants would not accept Robertson's Pentecostalism. Some of his controversial statements—such as claiming to turn away hurricanes by prayer—compounded this problem. Yet despite Robertson's defeat, this election prompted more Pentecostals to become politically active. In the end, evangelicals supported Bush but without much enthusiasm [111]

The disappointments did not end here. Jim Bakker and Jimmy Swaggart were involved in immoral sex acts. The sexual and financial scandals of the late 1980s had widespread repercussions. They discredited the televangelists in general. The public linked the televangelists with Christian Right and many of its leaders were guilty by association. Donations declined and the Christian Right's attack on America's moral decline was seen by many as hypocritical if not laughable. Referring to Bakker's Praise the Lord program, one journalist asked, "What do the letters PTL stand for? Pass the Loot." Oral Roberts brought ridicule upon himself by declaring that God would "call him home" if his followers did not come up with 8 million dollars. The end of the Moral Majority must be seen in the context of the total disappointments and scandals of the late 1980s.[112]

Phase Two

The events of the late 1980s brought some changes to the Christian Right. The Moral Majority was gone, some new organizations arose, some existing groups became more active, and different personalities rose to prominence. The agenda also took a decisive turn. With communism dead and the Soviet Union dissolved, foreign policy took a back seat. Pro-family issues, which had been on the rise, now became predominant. Or as Randall Balmer put it: "the collapse of the Soviet Union transformed the Cold War into a culture war." The events of September 11, however, did create more interest in foreign policy and caused evangelicals to emphasize American nationalism and the nation's Christian heritage. Still, the focus remained on national morality.[113]

In the 1990s, the Christian Right recovered from its mid-1980s slump. To a considerable degree, this resurgence can be credited to the activity of several Christian Right organizations. Very important was the Christian Coalition. Pat Robertson founded this organization in 1989 from the ashes of the Moral Majority. His defeat in the 1988 election convinced him of the need for a Christian organization to build on what the Moral Majority had begun. The objective of the Christian Coalition is "to promote Christian values in public life and give Christians a voice in American politics" notes D. G. Hart. While Robertson created the organization, he turned day-to-day control of operations over to Ralph Reed, a young Ph.D. in American history.[114]

Reed was determined not to repeat the mistake of the Moral Majority, namely its failure to establish a grassroots organization. As well as entering national politics, Reed focused the Christian Coalition on local issues. Evangelicals and conservative Catholics became active on school boards, city councils, and state legislatures. By this means, the Christian Coalition has come to dominate the Republican Party in a number of states. One might think that Bush's defeat in 1992 would have been a serious blow to the Coalition. But not so. Conservative Protestants were lukewarm to Bush and President Clinton provided a catalyst for the Christian Right and the Coalition. Both detested his liberal policies, his outspoken feminist wife, his opposition to pro-family values, and his personal moral failures.[115]

The Christian Coalition thus worked to defeat Clinton. In the mid- term elections of 1994, conservatives dealt a body blow to Clinton and his policies. The Republicans captured both houses of Congress for the first time since 1952. America had been turning right since the late 1980s, but this transformation now became quite obvious. Social and economic conservatives were burying their differences for a common cause—the defeat of liberalism. The Christian Coalition by now had built up a powerful grassroots organization and through its support behind the Republicans and their Contract with America.[116]

The Contract with America, however, said nothing about the pro-family issues so dear to the Coalition. Unlike conservative Protestants in the Reagan era, evangelicals were no longer satisfied for photo-ops or lip service. They had supported the Republicans and demanded action. Reed thus unveiled the Contract with the American Family. This program touched on most areas of the pro-family agenda. Included were the following proposals: restoring religious equality in the schools, returning control of education to the local level, promoting school choice, protecting parental rights, family-friendly tax relief, restoring respect for human life, support for private charities, restricting pornography, and privatizing the arts. While it was certainly conservative, it was not radical. It only restricted late-term abortions and made no mention of homosexuals.[117]

Reed demonstrated a pragmatic streak. By no means could he be considered an extreme conservative. He showed a willingness to work with diverse groups and compromise over certain issues—even allowing abortion in some circumstances. He realized that America was now a pluralistic society in respect to ideas and culture. He desired not the eradication of pluralism but a principled pluralism—one that upheld certain values but still permitted diversity. Such a situation would reject both a naked secularism and imposed religious values. The separation of church and state could be upheld while people debated competing claims to truth. Other members of the Christian Right were not this tolerant or flexible.[118]

James Dobson jumped into the fray. He rejected Reed's more pragmatic approach to Christian political involvement. Dobson would not compromise over abortion and threatened to bolt the Republican Party if it did so. The Republican leaders realized that millions of evangelicals listened to Dobson's "Focus on the Family," and they feared his influence. So in the party platform, they clearly condemned abortion. Robert Dole, who personally opposed abortion, argued that the Republican Party should welcome people with diverse views on this subject. In advocating this, he alienated many conservative Protestants. Thus, in the election of 1996, they regarded Dole as another "lukewarm" candidate for president and they longed for a "real conservative." The evangelicals got what they wanted in the 2000 election and in the administration of George W. Bush. A self-acknowledged evangelical, Bush has not governed from the middle but instead has promoted the interests of the Christian Right. As a result, evangelicals overwhelmingly supported Bush in the 2004 election.[119]

Promise Keepers (PK) began in 1990 and has attracted considerable attention since then. Founded by the successful University of Colorado football coach, Bill McCartney, PK can be viewed from several perspectives—a movement for transforming men, a right-wing political movement, a recent reincarnation of the "muscular Christianity movement," or an attempt to counter feminism. In various degrees PK incorporates all of these interpretations. It focuses on getting men to proclaim Christ and be more responsible family men. PK advocates values common to the Christian Right's political platform. It also stresses the interaction between sports, warfare, manliness, and Christianity. In doing so, PK attempts to restore men to their preeminent place in society and the home. PK boomed until mid-1997 when the movement began to sputter. But it continues to exist, even though McCartney no longer heads the organization.[120]

While PK lends itself to several interpretations, the current chapter deals primarily with politics. In this context, PK embodies the evangelical political characteristics, especially its populism and activism. Promise Keepers disavows any political inclinations. Still, its supporters and speakers are well-known Christian Right leaders—James Dobson, Chuck Colson, Pat Robertson, Bill Bright, Jerry Falwell, and D. James Kennedy. The primary message of Promise Keepers is that men must reassert themselves and reclaim their divinely ordained roles as head of the home and its spiritual leaders. This task is to be done in a loving manner, but critics regard it as a veiled call to patriarchy. The political message and the influence of James Dobson lurk beneath the surface. Abortion and homosexuality are severely condemned and the cause of America's moral decline has been a feminization of the nation's values. Feminism has indeed produced a nation of "sissified" men who have allowed this to happen. Promise Keepers also tracks the activities of politicians and urges men to pray for "godly politicians."[121]

Promise Keepers populist impulse can be seen in its leadership and masculine emphasis. Bill McCartney—or coach as he is affectionately called—embodies evangelical populism. He connects with men. Converted from a troubled background, he walked away from a successful football career at the top of his game. He had won a national championship at Colorado. He is definitely not an intellectual; his speeches are not polished and they resemble locker room pep talks. McCartney and other speakers frequently evoke athletic and military metaphors, as does Scripture.[122]

In doing so, PK taps into a long tradition. Throughout Christian history, church leaders—Paul, monks, crusaders, Jesuits, and evangelicals—have evoked athletic and military language to describe spirituality. In the late nineteenth and early twentieth centuries, such metaphors were commonly used to describe Christian piety and as an attempt to counter the notion of female spiritual superiority. As noted in chapter 4, many preachers and writers of this time portrayed Jesus as the epitome of masculinity—a successful businessman, an outdoorsman, and a real fighter. Much emphasis was placed on his driving the money-changers out of the temple. [123]

After World War II, muscular Christianity first focused on military metaphors but gradually athletics overshadowed the military as the primary metaphor for Christian spirituality. A number of organizations also combined athletics and Christianity. They would include Athletes in Action, Fellowship of Christian Athletes, and Power Team for Christ (a weight-lifting group). A number of organizations have also adopted military names—Salvation Army, the Knights of Columbus, and Campus Crusade for Christ. Military connotations can also be found in many Protestant hymns. Included are "Rise Up, O Men of God," "Onward Christian Soldiers," "We're Marching to Zion," and "the Battle Hymn of the Republic."[124]

Promise Keepers embodies an atmosphere of athleticism and even militarism. The meetings are in stadiums and speakers make liberal use of sport metaphors. Athletics, especially football, is a male domain and McCartney was highly successful in this realm, but he chose to step down for the cause of Christ and his family. To a lesser extent, PK conveys the image of an "army of God." In a 1993 meeting, McCartney even declared that "We're calling you to war." Promise Keepers can be seen as a fusion of elements from religion, sports, and male bonding: "the pep rally, the camp meeting, and the men's retreat."[125]

Whether intended or not, McCartney connected with some deep cultural trends. In drawing heavily on athletic and military metaphors, he brought to the surface the old evangelical tendency toward a dualistic worldview. On both the battlefield and athletic field there are winners and losers. And in the late twentieth century, white males feared that they might be the losers. Like a good coach, McCartney employed such metaphors to encourage men to be good husbands and implicitly to combat feminism—the arch-enemy.[126]

Critics on the Right

It would be misleading to think that all evangelicals went along with the program of the Christian Right. In respect to politics, Christian Smith has noted that evangelicals are considerably diverse. As noted earlier, they disagree over key issues: Was America ever a Christian nation? If so, what is meant by a Christian nation? Should biblical principles be enforced legally? Besides these general differences, there are evangelical groups both to the right and left of the Christian Right. Some believe that its ideas are too repressive while others object to its tolerance and want something resembling a theocracy. It also must be understood that not all conservative Protestants identify with the Christian Right. They are conservatives because they share with many Americans a commitment to democracy, limited government, and the market economy. The social agenda of the Christian Right is not high on their list.

On the Christian right wing there exists a group that goes by several names: Christian Reconstructionism, theonomy, dominion theology, and kingdom theology. It is a Christian splinter group that desires to take America and the world back to an Old Testament ethic. The leaders of this movement include Rousas John Rushdoony (1916-2001), Gary North, Gary DeMar, David Chilton, and Greg Bahnsen. While they quarrel among themselves over details, they come together over the big picture. Many see the Reconstructionist movement beginning in 1960 under the thinking of Cornelius Van Til (1895-1987). It did not gain an intellectual following, however, until 1973 when Rushdooney published his massive *Institutes of Biblical Law*.[127]

The Reconstructionists want nothing less than a complete transformation of the world, beginning first in America. Their program centers on six points. They are postmillennialists and see the Second Coming of Christ way in the distant future. Thus, they allow for a long gradual transformation of human society that will come largely by peaceful means. Two, every institution of every nation must be reclaimed for Christ from the Satanists and humanists. In this they will not compromise, as they believe the Christian Right has done. Next, they regard the Bible, especially the Mosaic Law, as the blueprint for this transformation. Four, Reconstructionism is a grassroots movement and is not something imposed from above by some religious or political hierarchy. Five, Christians should be involved in politics for this is one avenue for transforming society. Last, God established a covenant with America and he will be faithful to this nation so long as there exists a remnant obedient to him. (They, of course, see themselves as this remnant).[128]

Transformation will dramatically alter every aspect of American life. Society will not be reformed. It will be razed to the ground and rebuilt. All government props will be gone: social security, welfare, minimum wages, government regulation of business, public education, and all taxes except a 10 percent income tax. What will replace this government assistance? The elderly would be cared for by their children and a private retirement plan. After the harvest has been completed, the poor would be allowed to glean from the fields. America would return to the gold standard and loans will be valid for only seven years. The Reconstructionists desire to take America back to the world of radical libertarian economics.[129]

In respect to morals and religion, the transformation will be just as radical. The family will be run by strict patriarchal principles. Indentured servitude will solve many problems: unemployment, prison overcrowding, and idle teenagers. Old Testament laws will be strictly enforced. Homosexuals, adulterers, blasphemers, Sabbath breakers, habitual criminals, and disobedient children will be harshly punished—perhaps by stoning. Religious pluralism and toleration will be a thing of the past. There will be no place in America for Jews, Muslims, Hindus, Buddhists, atheists, humanists, and even non-Reconstructionist Christians. The First Amendment guaranteeing such freedoms will be gone and the government will not be neutral toward religion. Rather, it will enforce a biblical faith based on the Old Testament.[130]

The Religious Right has had a mixed reaction toward Reconstructionism. Pat Robertson has flirted with some of its ideas and made use of dominion language. In fact, Gary North has described him as a "halfway" house between the two movements. But because of Reconstructionism's postmillennism, Robertson has disassociated himself from the movement. Jerry Falwell and D. James Kennedy have endorsed Reconstructionist books. A number of Christian Right leaders also want to rebuild America, but they do not go as far as the theonomists. Their premillennialism presents a barrier. They see culminating events close at hand and not in the distant future. Christian Right leaders such as Reed and Dobson actually repudiate Reconstructionism. Reed can compromise and he wants Christians to have a place at the political table, not total domination. Dobson regards himself as pro-family and does not even relish the label of Christian Right, let alone Reconstructionism.[131]

Critics on the Left

Not all Christians, including many evangelicals, agree with the political and social agenda of the Christian Right. In their political views, they can be classified as moderates or liberals. These moderate evangelicals believe that the Christian Right has taken a secular political ideology and dressed it up in Christian clothes. They reject the notion that conservative religious beliefs and conservative politics must go hand in hand. Conversely, moderate evangelicals also reject the notion that politics is a strictly secular process. Unlike oil and water, religion and politics can mix. The public square should not be devoid of religious values. "The question is not *whether* religious faith should make a political contribution, but *how*," says Jim Wallis. Contrary to the Christian Right, however, these moderates normally do not attempt to force their values on other people.[132]

Moderate evangelicals believe that Christians should be involved in politics, but they have a different agenda than either the Christian Right or the secularists. Their program is more than a list of what many evangelicals oppose—abortion, homosexuality, secular humanism, liberalism, feminism, an intrusive government, and more. Rather, moderate or left-leaning evangelicals also advocate a politics of compassion, concern for the poor, civility, and community. This program often involves a more active central government, one that cares for the poor and provides health care for all its citizens. Herein lies a major point of disagreement with the Christian Right, which staunchly believes in a limited government. Liberty and individual rights are divinely ordained rights, they argue. Evangelical moderates and the Christian Right are at odds over their view of America. Unlike the Christian Right, evangelical moderates often criticize the nation's political and economic policies.[133]

Moderate or left-leaning evangelicals have been around for a while. Their roots can be found in the neo-evangelical movement, which separated itself from fundamentalism in the 1940s. While Carl F. H. Henry functioned within a conservative political framework, his book *The Uneasy Conscience of Modern Fundamentalism* (1947) hit like a bombshell. He challenged evangelicals to develop different social attitudes. As editor of *Christianity Today,* he continued to prod evangelicals to develop a social concern. By the 1960s, one could detect a revival of an evangelical social conscience. The climax to this developing evangelical social conscience was the Thanksgiving Workshop on Evangelical Social concern held in Chicago in 1973. About 100 evangelicals from several theological traditions produced *The Declaration of Evangelical Social Concern.* This document represented a turning point in evangelical social attitudes and was expressive of themes valued by the evangelical left.[134]

Since 1974, evangelical social concern has grown significantly. And it has cut across denominational traditions, including Calvinists, Wesleyans, and Mennonites. Prominent spokespersons enunciating evangelical political al-

ternatives to the Christian Right have been Jim Wallis, Ron Sider, and Tony
Campolo. Sider wrote *Rich Christians in an Age of Hunger* (1977), which
stayed on the best-seller list for years. In this book and others, he points out
that Americans represent only a small percent of the global population but
consume about a third of the earth's resources. He advocates a public policy
that is more just to the poor. He believes that such change can come if governments, non-government organizations, and churches cooperate. Still, Sider's
primary appeal is to Christians. They must be radical nonconformists and
share their wealth with the less fortunate. He takes a similar approach to violence. In obedience to Christ, Christians must practice peace—first in their
personal lives and then promote it on a societal level.[135]

In *The Scandal of the Evangelical Conscience* (2004), Sider echoes similar
ideas but also focuses on a different dimension—personal morality. He points
to polls that say evangelicals are not much holier or moral than the general
population. They divorce "their spouses just as often as their secular neigh-
bors. They were almost as materialistic and even more racist than their pagan
friends." Sexual promiscuity is only slightly less prevalent among evangelicals
than it is among their non-evangelical peers. And evangelicals give to chari-
table causes only marginally more than do members of the mainline churches.
In sum, Sider compares the evangelical church to the church at Laodicea,
which "was rich, self confident—and lukewarm." While the Christian Right is
attempting to improve the nation's public morals, it has not been doing so well
in respect to its own private morality. The solution, in his opinion, is "uncon-
ditional submission to Jesus as Lord as well as Savior." [136]

Sojourners magazine, edited by Jim Wallis, came into existence in the
1960s protesting the Vietnam War and has continued as a voice for the evangelical left. The title of Wallis' 1996 book—*Who Speaks for God? An Alternative to the Religious Right*—tells a story in itself. It is a counterpoint to Ralph
Reed's book, *Active Faith* (1996). In *God's Politics* (2005), Wallis presents an
alternative to both the political Right and Left and to Republican and Democratic policies. He criticizes both, contending that God is not partisan. He is
neither a Republican nor a Democrat. People of faith, according to Wallis,
must free themselves of both the Right and Left. The alternative is "'traditional' or 'conservative' on issues of family values, sexual integrity and personal responsibility, while being very 'progressive,' 'populist,' or even 'radical'
on issues like poverty and racial justice." Wallis' ideal political candidate
would be "decidedly pro-family, pro-life (meaning they really want to lower
the abortion rate)" and strong on moral values without being "right-wing,
reactionary, mean spirited, or scapegoating against any group of people, including gays and lesbians." In respect to more global issues, Wallis' alternative would promote good stewardship of the earth's resources and advocate a
more internationalist foreign policy, not a narrow nationalism. It would look
first to peaceful solutions for international problems.[137]

Both the Christian Right and the evangelical moderates have something in common—they reject the notion of a privatized Christian faith. They both believe that Christians should be active in the public square. They just disagree as to what the agenda should be and how it should be implemented. The Christian Right would focus more on issues related to sexual values, the family, evolution, and prayer in the schools while remaining uncritical of poverty, racism, and America's economic system and foreign policy. The evangelical moderates generally agree with the Christian Right in respect to sexual and family values. But they broaden the agenda to include poverty and racism and can be more critical of America's foreign policy, environmental practices, and economic inequities. In respect to implementing such policies, the evangelical moderates would focus more on education and persuasion than would the Christian Right who would rely largely on legislation.[138]

An Evangelicalism Microcosm

In many ways, evangelical political developments amount to a snapshot of the entire movement. Politics and religion are deeply intertwined, in part because these two areas mirror the most prominent evangelical cultural characteristics—populism, activism, moralism, biblicism, and individualism. Conservative Protestants believe that the wisdom of the common person is as good if not better than that of the educated elite. In science and medicine, they may defer to the experts, but not in religion and politics. This evangelical activism and moralism—based on their interpretation of Scripture—can be seen in their political orientation. At times, they have to choose between two candidates they do not prefer. But normally, they gravitate toward candidates who reflect their populism, moralism, and individualism.

For these reasons, evangelicals support political positions enhancing democracy, liberty, the market economy, and individual choice. Government should thus be limited, except when it is enforcing what they regard as biblical morals. These cultural characteristics have tended in recent years to push conservative Protestants toward the Republican Party and individuals and groups embracing their values. To use big words or enunciate complicated theories is poison in politics, even more so with the evangelical community. This is why evangelicals have supported individuals such as Carter, Reagan, and Bush the younger. Outside of politics, Burkett, McCartney, Dobson, and the televangelists have exerted considerable political influence because they appeal to the common instincts of many evangelicals.

In the political arena, the evangelical paradox runs deep. On one hand, the very birth pangs of the Christian Right can be seen in its resistance to modern cultural trends—secular humanism, feminism, abortion on demand, gay rights, homosexuality, liberalism, and an expanded government. In this sense, the Christian Right is truly a counter-cultural movement. On the other hand, few religious bodies have Americanized the Christian faith as have conservative

Protestants. You name it, they have Christianized it—America's heritage, democracy, market economy, foreign policy, military involvement, and great wealth. In baptizing America's political and economic systems, evangelicals tend to blur the distinctions between conservative religion and politics. They are seen as one and the same. Conservative political celebrities are at times regarded as evangelical Christians, despite a life style that might call such a conclusion into question. For example, take Rush Limbaugh, Oliver North, Gordon Liddy, Tom DeLay, and Pat Buchanan.

A paradox can also be seen in the differences between the evangelical left and right. While both the Christian Right and the evangelical left worship the same Lord, they have arrived at radically different visions for America. The role of women in the church and home has also presented conservative Protestants with a paradoxical situation. Many evangelicals desire to return to an earlier day when women were under control. But this is difficult when they do much of the work in the church and contribute significantly to the family income.

The rise of the Christian Right must be seen in a context—the rising tide of conservativism and southernization of evangelicalism. The Christian Right came to prominence at the same time secular conservativism was gaining strength. Many aspects of American conservatism—the business right, the patriot movement, the gun rights movement, and some hate groups—have little to do with the Christian Right. They are distinct movements. Still, as the political, social, and economic climate for secular conservatism rose, conservative religious groups also benefited. The conservative tide—whether it be political or religious—must be regarded as a reaction to the excesses of the political and cultural left. The counterculture and political developments of the 1960s and early 1970s prompted a reaction. Many conservative and moderate Democrats became Republicans and support the Religious Right. Without the radical left, the reactionary right would have less strength.

The Christian Right has also been southernized—that is, its leaders and values have a southern orientation. The southern Protestants never swallowed theological liberalism as did its northern cousins. By the 1870s, Protestants in the South had developed a southern civil religion. In order to ignore the slavery issue, before the Civil War, Protestants focused on a spiritual religion—one that avoided social, economic, and political issues. Instead, they emphasized the spiritual and pietistic dimension of religion. After the Civil War, this trend continued and to it Protestants added the notions of the South as chosen by God and "The Religion of the Lost Cause." Both of these ideas made close connections between the South and Israel. The South, these views contended, was more virtuous than the North and thus resembled Israel. After Vietnam, the counterculture, and Watergate scandal, these views were revived. Southern fundamentalists believed that it was their job to arrest America's moral decline. Thus, the leadership for the Christian Right and for much of evangelicalism came from the South or is based in the South.[139]

Notes

1. Dan Gilgoff, "The Morals and Values Crowd," *U.S. News and World Report* (15 November 2004): 42; Tom Carnes, "Wooing the Faithful," *Christianity Today* (October 2004): 32-35; Sheryl Henderson Blunt, "A Man and a Woman," *Christianity Today* (December 2003): 21, 22; "Religious Groups and Voting Behavior 2004 and 2000," *Religion and Ethics* http://www.pbs.org/wnet/religionandethics/week8/10data.html (11/12/04).

2. Clyde Wilcox, *Onward Christian Soldiers? The Religious Right in American Politics* (Boulder, CO: Westview Press, 1996), 5 (quote); Erling Jorstad, *The Politics of Moralism: The New Christian Right in American Life* (Minneapolis: Augsburg, 1981), 108; Michael Lienesch, "Right-Wing Religion: Christian Conservatism as a Political Movement," *Political Science Quarterly* 97, 3 (fall 1982): 407-09.

3. George Marsden, *Understanding Fundamentalism and Evangelicalism* (Grand Rapids: Eerdmans, 1991), 96, 97; Robert Wuthnow, "Divided We Fall: America's Two Civil Religions," *Christian Century* 20 (April 1988): 398; Robert Wuthnow, *The Restructuring of American Religion* (Princeton, NJ: Princeton University Press, 1988), 191-203; Sidney Blumenthal, "The Righteous Empire," *The New Republic* 22 (October 1984): 20; Wesley G. Pippert (intro), "Jimmy Carter: My Personal Faith in God," *Christianity Today* (4 March, 1983): 14-20.

4. Gilgoff, "Morals and Values Crowd," 42 (quote); Debra Rosenberg and Karen Breslau, "Winning the 'Values' Vote," *Newsweek* (15 November 2004): 23; Blunt, "A Man and a Woman," 21, 22; "Five Decisive Factors," *U.S. News and World Report* (15 November 2004): 24; Karen Tumulty and Mathew Cooper, "What Does Bush Owe the Religious Right?" *Time* (7 February 2005): 28-32; Tony Carnes, "Opportunity of a Generation," *Christianity Today* (February 2005): 66-68.

5. Debra Rosenberg and Rebecca Sinderbrand, "Of Prayer and Payback," *Newsweek* (22 November 2004): 46; "Bob Jones 111: Letter to President Bush," *Star Tribune* http://www.startribune.com/dynamic/story.php?template=print_a&story=5083301 (11/15/04) (quote); "The Faith and Values Coalition," http://faithandvalues.us/ (11/19/2004).

6. Marsden, *Understanding Fundamentalism and Evangelicalism*, 112 (quote); George Marsden, *Religion and American Culture* (New York: Harcourt Brace), 268; Harvey Cox, "The Warring Visions of the Religious Right," *Atlantic Monthly* (November 1995): 64-66; Randall Balmer and Lauren F. Winner, *Protestantism in America* (New York: Columbia University Press, 2002), 67.

7. Mark Noll, *The Scandal of the Evangelical Mind* (Grand Rapids: Eerdmans, 1994), 159-61.

8. Randall Balmer, *Blessed Assurance: A History of Evangelicalism in America* (Boston: Beacon Press, 1999), 56-58, 69, 70; Noll, *Scandal of the Evangelical Mind*, 156, 157.

9. Doug Koopman, "Religion and American Political Parties," in *In God We Trust? Religion and American Political Life*, ed. Corwin E. Smidt (Grand Rapids: Baker Books, 2001), 146, 147; Daniel Howe, *The Political Culture of American Whigs* (Chicago: University of Chicago Press, 1979), 176.

10. George M. Marsden, "Afterword: Religion, Politics, and the Search for an American Consensus," in *Religion and American Politics: From the Colonial Period to the 1980s*, ed. Mark Noll (New York: Oxford University Press, 1990), 383, 384; Koopman, "Religion and American Political Parties," 146, 147; Michael Corbett and Julia Mitchell Corbett, *Politics and Religion in the United States* (New York: Garland, 1999), 95, 96; Donald C. Swift, *Religion and the American Experience* (Amonk, NY: M.E. Sharpe, 1998), 224, 225.

11. Marsden, *Understanding Fundamentalism and Evangelicalism*, 90,91; Noll, *Scandal of the Evangelical Mind*, 162-64; Koopman, "Religion and American Political Parties," 149, 150; Robert Booth Fowler, Allen D. Hertzke, and Laura R. Olson, *Religion and Politics in America: Faith, Culture, and Strategic Choices*, 2nd ed. (Boulder, CO: Westview Press, 1999), 25, 26; Corbett, *Politics and Religion*, 97-100.

12. Marsden, *Understanding Fundamentalism and Evangelicalism*, 92, 93; Koopman, "Religion and American Political Parties," 150; Marsden, "Afterword," 386.

13. Koopman, "Religion and American Political Parties," 150; Marsden, *Understanding Fundamentalism and Evangelicalism*, 94.

14. D. G. Hart, *That Old-Time Religion in Modern America: Evangelical Protestantism in the Twentieth Century* (Chicago: Ivan R. Dee, 2002), 159, 160; Noll, *Scandal of the Evangelical Mind*, 151, 152.

15. Richard V. Pierard, "The New Religious Right: A Formidable Force in American Politics," *Choice* 19, 7 (1982): 864; Swift, *Religion and the American Experience*, 239-41; Robert S. Ellwood, *1950: Crossroads of American Religious Life* (Louisville: Westminister/John Knox Press, 2000), 185,186; Martin E. Marty, *Modern American Religion: Under God, Indivisible 1941-1960* (Chicago: University of Chicago Press, 1996), 371, 372.

16. Erling Jorstad, *The Politics of Doomsday: Fundamentalists of the Far Right* (Nashville: Abingdon Press, 1970), 21-24, 50 (quotes on 21); Ellwood, *1950: Crossroads of Life*, 85; William Martin, *With God on Our Side: The Rise of the Religious Right in America* (New York: Broadway Books, 1996), 36.

17. Jorstad, *Politics of Doomsday*, 24, 47, 60; John H. Redekop, *The American Far Right: A Case Study of Billy Hargis and Christian Crusade* (Grand Rapids: Eerdmans, 1968), 28-36.

18. Jorstad, *Politics of Doomsday*, 44-47; Swift, *Religion and the American Experience*, 241, 242; Blumenthal, "Righteous Empire," 20. For more on the tendency to buy into conspiracy theories in the late twentieth century, see Paul T. Coughlin, *Secrets, Plots and Hidden Agenda* (Downers Grove, IL: InterVarsity Press, 1999).

19. Jorstad, *Politics of Doomsday*, 49 (quote), 52, 60, 63); *Christian Beacon* 6 (September 1945): 1, 8.

20. Jorstad, *Politics of Doomsday,* 52, 65-67, 84-86, 118, 119; Ellwood, *1950: Crossroads of Life*, 90, 91.

21. Jorstad, *Politics of Doomsday*, 93-96 (quotes on 94); Billy Hargis, "The Truth About Segregation," A Christian Crusade pamphlet, pp.1, 2; Redekop, *The American Far Right*, 93; *Christian Beacon* 8 (May 1958): 5; *Christian Beacon* 2 (July 1964): 3; Martin, *With God on Our Side*, 78, 79.

22. Jorstad, *Politics of Doomsday*, 139, 140 (quotes); Richard V. Pierard, *The Unequal Yoke: Evangelical Christianity and Political Conservatism* (Philadelphia: Lippincott, 1970), 22, 23.

23. Jorstad, *Politics of Doomsday,* 141, 142; Robert Kingdon, "Social Welfare in Calvin's Geneva," *American Historical Review* 76, 1 (1971): 50-69; Pierard, *Unequal Yoke,* 24, 25, 37-39: Redekop, *The American Far Right*, 33-37; Hart, *That Old-Time Religion,* 159.

24. Jorstad, *Politics of Doomsday*, 104-111; Pierard, *Unequal Yoke*, 42-48; Martin Durham, *The Christian Right, the Far Right and the Boundaries of American Conservatism* (Manchester, UK: Manchester University Press, 2000), 1-9; Pierard, "The New Religious Right," 867.

25. Richard V. Pierard, "The New Religious Right in American Politics," in *Evangelicalism and Modern America*, ed. George Marsden (Grand Rapids: Eerdmans, 1984), 168, 169; Durham, *The Christian Right*, 9,10; Blumenthal, "Righteous Empire," 19.

26. Gabriel Fackre, *The Religious Right and the Christian Faith* (Grand Rapids: Eerdmans, 1982), 31-33; Hart, *That Old-Time Religion*, 145; Mark Noll, *American Evangelical Christianity: An Introduction* (Oxford: Blackwell, 2001), 190.

27. Hart, *That Old-Time Religion*, 86, 146 (quotes); Fackre, *The Religious Right*, 81,82; Pierard, *Unequal Yoke*, 38,39; Ellwood, *1950: Crossroads of Life*, 191.

28. Fackre, *The Religious Right*, 36-38.

29. Fackre, *The Religious Right*, 45,46 (quote); Pierard, *Unequal Yoke*, 38. See John Shelton Lawrence and Robert Jewett, *The Myth of the American Superhero* (Grand Rapids: Eerdmans, 2002).

30. Fackre, *The Christian Right*, 59, 62 (quotes). See Robert Jewett and John Shelton Lawrence, *Captain America and the Crusade against Evil: The Dilemma of Zealous Nationalism* (Grand Rapids: Eerdmans, 2003); Tony Carnes, "The Bush Doctrine," *Christianity Today* (May 2003): 38-40; Howard Fineman, "Bush and God," *Newsweek* (10 March 2003): 23-30; George Wills "Paradoxes of Public Piety," *Newsweek* (15 March 2004): 80.

31. For an overview of such materials, see Richard Kyle, *The Last Days Are Here Again: A History of the End Times* (Grand Rapids: Baker Books, 1998), 115-37; Timothy P. Weber, *On the Road to Armageddon: How Evangelicals Became Israel's Best Friend* (Grand Rapids: Baker Books, 2004).

32. George Otis, *The Solution to Crisis-America* (Old Tappan, NJ: Revell, 1972), 53.

33. Dale Evans Rogers, *Let Freedom Ring* (Old Tappan, NJ: Revell, 1975), 19, 20.

34. Francis A. Schaeffer, *A Christian Manifesto* (Weschester, IL: Crossway Books, 1981), 33; Wuthnow, *Restructuring of American Religion*, 245; G. Aiken Taylor, "Francis Schaeffer: America's Historical Underpinnings," *The Presbyterian Journal* 2 (March 1983): 7, 8.

35. President Reagan as quoted in Larry Rasmussem, "Patriotism Lived: Lessons from Bonhoeffer," *Christianity and Crisis* 24 (June 1985): 249; Erling Jorstad, *Being Religious in America: The Deepening Crises over Public Faith* (Minneapolis: Augsburg, 1986), 40.

36. Wuthnow, "Divided We Fall," 398 (quote).

37. Jerry Falwell, *The Fundamentalist Phenomenon: The Resurgence of Conservative Christianity* (Garden City, NY: Doubleday, 1981), 212.

38. Jerry Falwell, *Listen, America!* (Garden City, NY: Doubleday, 1980), 16.

39. Tim LaHaye, *The Battle for the Mind* (Old Tappan, NJ: Revell, 1980), 35 (quote); Bill Bright, *Come Help Change the World* (Old Tappan, NJ: Revell, 1970), 172 (quote).

40. James A. Morone, *Hellfire Nation: The Politics of Sin in American History* (New Haven, CT: Yale University Press, 2003), 494 (quote). See Michael E. Naparstek, "Falwell and Robertson Stumble," *Religion in the News* 4, 3 (fall 2001): 5, 27.

41. Will, "Paradoxes of Public Piety," 80.

42. Howard Fineman, "Bush and God," *Newsweek* (10 March 2003): 24, 25 (quote); Stephen Mansfield, *The Faith of George W. Bush* (New York: Tarcher/Penguin, 2003); Bruce Lincoln, "Analyzing the President's Theology: Bush's God Talk," *Christian Century* 5 (October 2004): 22-29.

43. Tony Carnes, "The Bush Doctrine: The Moral Vision that Launched the Iraq War," *Christianity Today* (May 2003): 38-40 (quote); Tony Carnes, "Bush's Defining Moment," *Christianity Today* 12 (November 2004): 38-42. See Mansfield, *The Faith of George Bush*. For a different view of national unity, see David Brooks, "One Nation, Slightly Divisible," *Atlantic Monthly* (December 2001): 53-65.

44. Falwell, *Listen America*, 244.

45. Robert Zwier, *Born-Again Politics: The New Christian Right in America* (Downers Grove, IL: InterVarsity, 1982), 42, 43 (quote).
46. Grant Wacker, "Searching for Norman Rockwell: Popular Evangelicalism in Contemporary America," in *The Evangelical Tradition in America*, ed. Leonard I. Sweet (Macon, GA: Mercer University Press, 1984), 297-99, 301.
47. Mark Hatfield, *Between a Rock and a Hard Place* (Waco, TX: Word, 1976), 92.
48. Robert D. Linder and Richard V. Pierard, *Twilight of the Saints: Biblical Christianity and Civil Religion in America* (Downers Grove, IL: InterVarsity, 1978), 156.
49. Christian Smith, *Christian America? What Evangelicals Really Want* (Berkeley: University of California Press, 2000), 21, 22, 24, 30, 36 (quote).
50. Hart, *That Old-Time Religion*, 106,107; Zwier, *Born-Again Politics*, 43; Gary Cross, *An All-Consuming Century: Why Commercialism Won in Modern America* (New York: Columbia University Press, 2000), 197, 198. See Robert Wuthnow, *God and Mammon in America* (New York: Free Press, 1994); Vincent J. Miller, *Consuming Religion: Christian Faith and Practice in a Consumer Culture* (New York: Continuum, 2003).
51. Carl F. H. Henry, *The Uneasy Conscience of Modern Fundamentalism* (Grand Rapids: Eerdmans, 1947); Hart, *That Old-Time Religion*, 108, 109, 153.
52. Interview by Rodney Clapp, "Where Capitalism and Christianity Meet," *Christianity Today* 4 (February 1983): 27 (quote). See also John R. Schneider, "On New Things," in *The Consuming Passion: Christianity and the Consumer Culture*, ed. Rodney Clapp (Downers Grove, IL: InterVarsity, 1998), 135-39.
53. George Gilder, "Moral Sources of Capitalism," *Society* (Sept/October 1981): 27 (quote). See also George Gilder, *Wealth and Poverty* (New York: Basic Books, 1981); George Gilder, *Recapturing the Spirit of Enterprise* (San Francisco: ICS Press, 1992).
54. Jerry Falwell, *Wisdom for Living* (Wheaton, IL: Victor Books, 1984), 102, 131 (quote). See also Falwell, *Listen America*, 13; Wuthnow, *Restructuring of American Religion*, 248, 249, 349.
55. Pat Robertson, *The Secret Kingdom: A Promise of Hope and Freedom in a World of Turmoil* (Nashville: Thomas Nelson, 1982), 151.
56. Ronald H. Nash, "The Christian Choice Between Capitalism and Socialism," in *Liberation Theology*, ed. Ronald H. Nash (Milford, MI: Mott Media, 1984), 60 (quote). See also Ronald H. Nash, *Why the Left is Not Right* (Grand Rapids: Zondervan, 1996).
57. "Bill Armstrong: Senator and Christian," *Christianity Today* 11 (November 1983): 23.
58. Larry Eskridge, " Money Matters: The Phenomenon of Financial Counselor Larry Burkett and Christian Financial Concepts," in *More Money, More Ministry: Money and Evangelicals in Recent North American History*, ed. Larry Eskridge and Mark A. Noll (Grand Rapids: Eerdmans, 2000), 311-25; Michael S. Hamilton, "We're in the Money," *Christianity Today* 12 (June 2000): 41,42. See Nicolaus Mills, ed., *Culture in an Age of Money: The Legacy of the 1980s in America* (Chicago: Ivan R. Dee, 1990).
59. Larry Eskridge, "When Burkett Speaks, Evangelicals Listen," *Christianity Today* 12 (June 2000) 45-47 (quote); Larry Burkett, *How to Manage Your Money* (Chicago: Moody Press, 2000), 7, 8; Eskridge, "Money Matters," 314-28.
60. Larry Burkett, *Your Finances in Changing Times* (Chicago: Moody Press, 1993); Burkett, *How to Manage Your Money;* Larry Burkett, *The Coming Economic Earthquake* (Chicago: Moody Press, 1991); Eskridge, "Money Matters," 320-24; Eskridge, "When Burkett Speaks," 45, 46.

61. Eskridge, "When Burkett Speaks," 46-48 (quote); Burkett, *Your Finances in Changing Times*, 49-61, 85-109; Burkett, *How to Manage Your Money*, 43-50, 89-96; Eskridge, "Money Matters," 327-32.

62. Burkett, *Coming Economic Earthquake*, 19-126; Eskridge, "Money Matters," 340-42; Eskridge, "When Burkett Speaks," 48, 49.

63. Eskridge, "Money Matters," 342-44; Eskridge, "When Burkett Speaks," 48, 49; Kyle, *The Last Days Are Here Again*, 190-94.

64. Zwier, *Born-Again Politics*, 44; Noll, *American Evangelical Christianity*, 190; Hart, *That Old-Time Religion*, 102, 160.

65. Falwell, *Listen America*, 69.

66. Falwell, *Listen America*, 69, 70; Zwier, *Born-Again Politics*, 44, 45.

67. Jorstad, *Politics of Moralism*, 107 (quote).

68. Jorstad, *Politics of Moralism*, 108; Smith, *Christian America?* 30. For a description of evangelicals baptizing the secular culture, see Carol Flake, *Redemptorama: Culture, Politics, and the New Evangelicalism* (Garden City, NY: Anchor Books, 1984).

69. Geoffrey Layman, *The Great Divide: Religious and Cultural Conflict in American Party Politics* (New York: Columbia University Press, 2001), 7, 8; Hart, *That Old-Time Religion*, 149, 150; Martin, *With God on Our Side*, 47, 48.

70. For a description of religion during the counterculture, see Mark Oppenheimer, *Knocking on Heaven's Door: American Religion in the Age of Counterculture* (New Haven, CT: Yale University Press, 2003).

71. Patrick Allitt, *Religion in America Since 1945: A History* (New York: Columbia University Press, 2003), 68-70; Hart, *That Old-Time Religion*, 96, 97; Robert S. Alley, *The Supreme Court on Church and State* (Oxford University Press, 1988), 186, 195, 203, 213. See Terry Eastland, ed., *Religious Liberty in the Supreme Court: The Cases that Define Debate Over Church and State* (Grand Rapids: Eerdmans, 1993); Marvin Frankel, *Faith and Freedom: Religious Liberty in America* (New York: Hill and Wang, 1994).

72. Layman, *Great Divide*, 12, 13; Koopman, "Religion and American Political Parties," 152, 153; James Davidson Hunter, *Culture Wars: The Struggle to Define America* (New York: Basic Books, 1991), 97-106.

73. Allitt, *Religion in America*, 159, 160; Zwier, *Born-Again Politics*, 24, 25; Bob Smietana, "When Does Personhood Begin?" *Christianity Today* (July 2004): 24-28.

74. Balmer, *Blessed Assurance*, 82, 83; Allitt, *Religion in America*, 162, 163; Martin, *With God on Our Side*, 234, 235.

75. Noll, *American Evangelical Christianity*, 22, 23.

76. Durham, *The Christian Right*, 85, 86.

77. Durham, *The Christian Right*, 43-52; Zwier, *Born-Again Politics*, 25; Martin, *With God on Our Side*, 197, 198; Balmer and Winner, *Protestantism in America*, 147-78.

78. Martin, *With God on Our Side*, 168, 169; Zwier, *Born-Again Politics*, 25, 26.

79. Zwier, *Born-Again Politics*, 25-27; Martin, *With God on Our Side*, 168, 169.

80. Balmer, *Blessed Assurance*, 71 (quote); Durham, *The Christian Right*, 38; Balmer and Winner, *Protestantism in America*, 121-48. For a different perspective on evangelicalism and feminism, see Virginia Ramey Mollenkott, "Evangelicalism: A Feminist Perspective," *Union Seminary Quarterly Review* 23, 2 (winter, 1977): 95-103.

81. Rosemary Radford Ruether and Rosmary Skinner Keller, eds, *Woman and American Religion*, 3 vols. (San Francisco: Harper and Row, 1981-86), 2:161; Balmer, *Blessed Assurance*, 74.

82. Balmer, *Blessed Assurance*, 75; Jan Lewis, "The Republican Wife: Virtue and Seduction in the Early Republic," *William and Mary Quarterly* 44 (1987): 689-721; Ruether and Keller, *Woman and Religion*, 1:36; 2: 402.

83. Quoted from Douglas Frank, *Less Than Conquerors: How Evangelicals Entered the Twentieth Century* (Grand Rapids: Eerdmans, 1986), 192. Americans have thoroughly Americanized their view of Jesus. See Stephen Prothero, *American Jesus: How the Son of God Became a National Icon* (New York: Farrar, Straus and Giroux, 2003); Richard Wightman Fox, *Jesus in America: Personal Savior, Cultural Hero, National Obsession* (San Francisco: HarperSanFrancisco, 2004); Richard Wightman Fox, "America's National Obsession," *Chronicle of Higher Education* 20 (February 2004): B7-B10.

84. Ruether and Keller, *Women and Religion*, 3: 260, 261 (quote); Balmer, *Blessed Assurance*, 79, 80.

85. Marabel Morgan, *The Total Woman,* (Old Tappan, NJ: Revell, 1973), 55 (quote).

86. Balmer, *Blessed Assurance*, 80, 81; Kenneth J. Collins, *The Evangelical Moment: The Promise of an American Religion* (Grand Rapids: Baker Books, 2005); 136-43.

87. Durham, *The Christian Right*, 35-36; Martin, *With God on Our Side*, 162-64.

88. Quoted in Wendy Murray Zoba, "Daring to Discipline America," *Christianity Today* 1 (March 1999): 31, 32; Mark Cooper, "God and Man in Colorado Springs," *The Nation* 2(January 1995): 9, 10; Michael J. Gerson, " A Righteous Indignation," *U.S. News and World Report* (4 May 1998): 24.

89. Quoted in Gerson, "Righteous Indignation," 24; Zoba, "Daring to Discipline America," 35, 36. For example, Dobson has criticized Ralph Reed's more moderate approach to moral engagement. Conversely, even conservative evangelicals question not so much Dobson's positions regarding the issues but the way he uses the political process. See Cal Thomas and Ed Dobson, *Blinded by Might* (Grand Rapids: Zondervan, 1999).

90. Allitt, *Religion in America*, 166, 167; Durham, *The Christian Right*, 37, 38; Amy DeRogatis, "What Would Jesus Do? Sexuality and Salvation in Protestant Evangelical Sex Manuals, 1950s to the Present," *Church History* 74, 1 (March 2005): 97-137.

91. Smith, *Christian America?* 177, 173.

92. Kenneth J. Heineman, *God is a Conservative: Religion, Politics, and Morality in Contemporary America* (New York: New York University Press, 1998), 54-56. See Earl and Merle Black, *The Rise of Southern Republicans* (Cambridge, MA: Harvard University Press, 2002). While Frank focuses on the Mid-West, his argument that social grievances have turned many Democrats to the Republican Party can be applied elsewhere. See Thomas Frank, *What's The Matter With Kansas?* (New York: Metropolitan Books, 2004).

93. Koopman, "Religion and American Political Parties," 152, 153; Geoffrey Layman, *The Great Divide: Religious and Cultural Conflict in American Party Politics* (New York: Columbia University Press, 2001), 9, 10.

94. Zwier, *Born-Again Politics*, 27,28; Jorstad, *Politics of Moralism*, 20, 21; Martin, *With God on Our Side*, 80, 88, 89.

95. Marsden, *Religion and American Culture*, 262, 263; Zwier, *Born-Again Politics*, 29,30; Allitt, *Religion in America*, 148, 149; Jorstad, *Politics of Moralism*, 70; Heineman, *God is a Conservative*, 5, 81.

96. Martin, *With God on Our Side*, 159 (quote); Heineman, *God is a Conservative*, 81.

97. Allitt, *Religion in America*, 148-52; Martin, *With God on Our Side*, 158; Heineman, *God is a Conservative,* 121, 123.

98. Razelle Frankl, *Televangelism: The Popular Marketing of Religion* (Carbondale: Southern Illinois University Press, 1987), 114; Zwier, *Born Again Politics*, 30, 31; Jeffrey K. Hadden and Anson Shupe, *Televangelism: Power and Politics on God 's Frontier* (New York: Henry Holt, 1988), 38-54; Jim Montgomery, "The Electric

Church," *Wall Street Journal* (19 May 1978): 1-15; William Hendricks, "The Theology of the Electronic Church," *Review and Exposition* 81 (winter 1984): 62.

99. Jorstad, *Politics of Moralism*, 25.

100. Hadden and Shupe, *Televangelism*, 161-80; Jorstad, *Politics of Moralism*, 31-37.

101. Wuthnow, *Restructuring of American Religion*, 191. See Mark A. Shibley, *Resurgent Evangelicalism in the United States* (Columbia: University of South Carolina Press, 1996).

102. Martin, *With God on Our Side*, 212, 213; Frankl, *Televangelism*, 113-115; Kenneth L. Woodward, " A Disneyland for the Devout," *Newsweek* (11 August 1986): 46, 47; Stephen Winnenburg, "Televangelist Report Card," *Christianity Today* 22 (October 2001): 88-91.

103. Hart, *That Old-Time Religion*, 134-39. For more on Schaeffer's influence, see Lane Dennis, ed., *Francis A. Schaeffer: Portraits of the Man and His Work* (Westchester, IL: Crossway, 1986); Ronald Ruegsegger, ed., *Reflections on Francis Schaeffer* (Grand Rapids: Zondervan, 1986).

104. Francis A. Schaeffer, *How Should We Then Live? The Rise and Decline of Western Thought and Culture* (Old Tappan, NJ: Revell, 1976); Hart, *That Old-Time Religion*, 138, 139; Allitt, *Religion in America*, 157. See Paul Kurtz, "Secular Humanism," 19 April 2003. http://www.secularhumanism.org/intro/declaration.html. (12/19/03).

105. Hart, *That Old-Time Religion*, 140,141, 162, 164, 165; Allitt, *Religion in America*, 157; Martin, *With God On Our Side*, 196, 197.

106. Hart, *That Old- Time Religion*, 140, 141, 162. See Charles Colson, *Kingdoms in Conflict* (New York: William Morrow, 1987); Charles Colson, *Against the Night* (Ann Arbor, MI: Vine Books, 1989); LaHaye, *Battle for the Mind*; Charles W. Colson, "Kingdoms in Conflict," *First Things* 1 (November 1996): 34-38.

107. Fowler, Hertzke, Olson, *Religion and Politics in America*, 141.

108. Allitt, *Religion in America,* 152-54; Fowler, Hertzke, Olson, *Religion and Politics in America,* 142; Martin, *With God on Our Side*, 159-74; Hart, *That Old-Time Religion*, 161-64.

109. Robert Zwier, "New Christian Right," in *Dictionary of Christianity in America*, ed. Daniel G. Reid et al. (Downers Grove, IL: InterVarsity Press, 1990), 818; Robert Zwier, "Moral Majority," in *Dictionary of Christianity in America*, 771; Martin, *With God on Our Side*, 258-79; Fowler, Hertzke, Olson, *Religion and Politics in America*, 142.

110. William C. Berman, *America's Right Turn: From Nixon to Clinton* (Baltimore, MD: Johns Hopkins University Press, 1998), 80-82; Zwier, *Born-Again Politics*, 73-81; Heineman, *God is a Conservative*, 120-23; Martin, *With God on Our Side*, 220; Lauren F. Winner, "Why America Turned Right," *Books and Culture* (March/April 2002): 30.

111. Heineman, *God is a Conservative*, 125-33, 161-79; Martin, *With God on Our Side*, 227, 228, 261-72; Hadden and Shupe, *Televangelisim*, 181-98; A. James Reichley, *Faith in Politics* (Washington, DC: Brookings Institution, 2002), 329, 330; Wilcox, *Onward Christian Soldiers,* 85; John B. Judis, "The Charge of the Light Brigade: Fundamentalists and Republicans in the Post-Reagan Era," *The New Republic* 29 (September 1986): 16-19; William Martin, "How Ronald Reagan Wowed Evangelicals," *Christianity Today* (August 2004): 48, 49.

112. Heineman, *God is a Conservative*, 167 (quote); Martin, *With God on Our Side*, 166-68, 275; Fowler, Hertzke, Olson, *Religion and Politics in America*, 142-45; Jeffrey Hadden, Anson Shupe, James Hawdon, and Kenneth Martin, "Why Jerry Falwell Killed the Moral Majority," in *The God Pumpers: Religion in the Electronic Age*, ed.

Marshall Fishwick and Ray B. Browne (Bowling Green OH: Bowling Green State University Press, 1987), 101-115.

113. Balmer, *Blessed Assurance*, 98 (quote); Dennis R. Hoover, "Is Evangelicalism Itching for a Civilization Fight?: A Media Study," *The Brandywine Review of Faith and International Affairs* 2, 1 (spring 2004): 11-16. See also Jewitt and Lawrence, *Captain America,* 26-43.

114. Hart, *That Old- Time Religion*, 167 (quote); Martin, *With God On Our Side*, 299-301.

115. Jeffrey H. Birnbaum, "The Gospel According to Ralph," *Time* (15 May 1995): 30, 31; Heineman, *God is a Conservative*, 198-200, 220; Martin, *With God on Our Side*, 309-16; Melissa Deckman, "Religion Makes the Difference: Why Christian Right Candidates Run for School Board," *Review of Religious Research* 42, 4 (2000): 349-71; James L. Guth et al., "God's Own Party: Evangelicals and Republicans in the 92 Election," *Christian Century* 17 (February 1993): 172-76; Karen Lange, "An Energized Religious Right? Strategies for the Clinton era," *Christianity Century* 17 (February 1993): 177-79. For a description of the activities of the Christian Right in various states, see John C. Green, Mark J. Rozell, and Clyde Wilcox, eds., *The Christian Right in American Politics: Marching to the Millennium* (Washington, D.C.: Georgetown University Press, 2003).

116. Berman, *America's Right Turn*, 175-77; Martin, *With God on Our Side*, 339-40; Birnbaum, "The Gospel According to Ralph," 30, 31; Heineman, *God is a Conservative*, 221-23; John C. Green et al., "Evangelical Realignment: The Political Power of the Christian Right," *Christian Century* (5-12 July 1995): 676, 677; Ronald Brownstein, "Evangelicals Found to Hold Largest Share of GOP Base," *Los Angeles Times* (25 June 1996): A8; Laurie Goodstein, "White Evangelicals a Powerful Block," *Washington Post* (25 June 1996): A6. See David Frum, *What's Right: The New Conservative Majority and the Remaking of America* (New York: Basic Books, 1996).

117. James W. Skillen, "The Political Confusion of the Christian Coalition," *Christian Century* (30 August-6 September 1995): 816-22; Heineman, *God is a Conservative*, 220-22; Martin, *With God on Our Side*, 340.

118. Durham, *The Christian Right*, 107; Heineman, *God is a Conservative*, 239; Wilcox, *Onward Christian Soldiers*, 114, 115; Martin, *With God on Our Side*, 358, 359.

119. Reichley, *Faith in Politics*, 332-36; Heineman, *God is a Conservative*, 237-39; Gerson, "A Righteous Indignation," 29; Zoba, "Daring to Discipline," 31, 32, 35.

120. James A. Mathisen, "The Strange Decade of the Promise Keepers," *Books and Culture* (September/October 2001): 36; Sean F. Evferton, "The Promise Keepers: Religious Revival or Third Wave of the Religious Right," *Review of Religious Research* 43, 1 (September 2001): 51, 52; Art Moore, "More PK Downsizing," *Christianity Today* 5 (October 1998): 20, 21; "Promise Keepers to lay off paid staff," *Christianity Today* 11 (March 1998): 254, 255; "Life After Coach," *Christianity Today* (December 2003): 25. For more on the muscular Christian movement, see Tony Ladd and James A. Mathisen, *Muscular Christianity: Evangelical Protestants and the Development of Sports in America* (Grand Rapids: Baker Books, 1999); Clifford Putney, *Muscular Christianity: Manhood and Sports in Protestant America, 1880-1920* (Cambridge, MA: Harvard University Press, 2001); Robert J. Higgs, "Muscular Christianity, Holy Play and Spiritual Exercises: Confusion about Christ in Sports and Religion," *Aretae* 1, 1 (fall 1983): 59-85.

121. Joe Conason, Alfred Ross, and Lee Cokorimos, "The Promise Keepers Are Coming: The Third Wave of the Religious Right," *The Nation* 7 (October 1996): 12, 13;

Martin, *With God on Our Side*, 350, 351; Nancy Novosad, "God Squad," *The Progressive* 16 (August 1996): 26; Everton, "Promise Keepers," 51, 52.

122. Edward Gilbreath, "Manhood's Great Awakening," *Christianity Today* 6 (February 1995):21-28; Mathisen, "Strange Decade of Promise Keepers," 36, 37.

123. Balmer, *Blessed Assurance*, 85, 86; Ladd and Mathisen, *Muscular Christianity*, 48-68; Putney, *Muscular Christianity*, 11-44; Brian W. Aitken, "The Emergence of Born-Again Sport," *Studies in Religion* 18, 4 (1989): 391-405; Guy Lewis, "The Muscular Christianity Movement," *Johper* (May 1966): 27,28.

124. Balmer, *Blessed Assurance,* 85, 86.See Richard J. Mouw, "Some Poor Sailor, Tempest Tossed: Nautical Rescue Themes in Evangelical Hymnody," in *Wonderful Words of Life: Hymns in American Protestant History and Theology*, ed. Richard J. Mouw and Mark A. Noll (Grand Rapids: Eerdmans, 2004), 238-40; Linda Kintz, *Between Jesus and the Market: Emotions that Matter in Right-Wing America* (Durham, NC: Duke University Press, 1997), 122, 123.

125. Mathiesen, "Strange Decade of Promise Keepers," 36, 37 (quote); Gilbreath, "Manhood's Great Awakening," 26; Novosad, "God Squad," 26; Concason, Ross, and Cokorinos, "Promise Keepers Are Coming," 18.

126. Balmer, *Blessed Assurance*, 92.

127. Bruce Barron, *Heaven On Earth? The Social and Political Agendas of Dominion Theology* (Grand Rapids: Zondervan, 1992), 13-16; Anson Shupe, "The Reconstructionist Movement on the New Christian Right," *Christian Century* 4 (October 1989): 880, 881; Anson Shupe, "Prophets of a Biblical America," *Wall Street Journal* (12 April 1989): sec. 1, p. 14, col. 3; Martin, *With God on Our Side*, 353.

128. Durham, *The Christian Right*, 109; Shupe, "Reconstructionist Movement," 880, 881; Barron, *Heaven on Earth?* 23-38. See Gary DeMar, *Last Days Madness: Obsession of the Modern Church* (Atlanta: American Vision, 1997).

129. Shupe, "Reconstructionist Movement," 881; Martin, *With God on Our Side*, 352; Barron, *Heaven on Earth?* 135-49; Shupe, "Prophets of a Biblical America," sec. 1, p. 14.

130. Shupe, "Reconstructionist Movement," 881; Martin, *With God on Our Side*, 352; Shupe, "Prophets of a Biblical America," sec. 1, p. 14.

131. Durham, *The Christian Right*, 110; Shupe, "Reconstructionist Movement," 882; Martin, *With God on Our Side*, 354; Barron, *Heaven On Earth?* 53-66; Shupe, "Prophets of Biblical America," sec. 1, p. 14.

132. Jim Wallis, *Who Speaks for God? An Alternative to the Religious Right—A New Politics of Compassion, Community, and Civility* (New York: Delta, 1996), 23 (quote); "Moderate Evangelicals Challenge Religious Right Ties to Republicans," *Church and State* (July/August 1995): 14; Jim Wallis, "A Wolf in Sheep's Clothing: The Political Right Invades the Evangelical Fold," in *Salt and Light: Evangelical Political Thought in Modern America,* ed. Augustus Cerillo, Jr. and Murry W. Dempster (Grand Rapids: Baker Books, 1989), 132-39; Timothy L. Smith, "Protestants Falwell Does Not Represent," *New York Times* (22 April 1980): op. ed. page.

133. See Randall L. Frame and Alan Tharpe, *How Right Is the Right?* (Grand Rapids: Zondervan, 1996), 17-22; Wallis, *Who Speaks for God?* 30-40.

134. Robert D. Linder, "The Resurgence of Evangelical Social Concern (1925-75)" in *The Evangelicals,* ed. David F. Wells and John D. Woodbridge (Nashville: Abingdon Press, 1975), 189-210; Robert E. Webber, *The Younger Evangelicals* (Grand Rapids: Baker Books, 2002), 38, 39; Richard Quebedeaux, *The Worldly Evangelicals* (San Francisco: Harper and Row, 1978), 83-94; Lewis B. Smedes, "The Evangelicals and the Social Question," *Reformed Journal* 16 (February 1966): 9-13; Leslie R.

Keylock, "Evangelical Protestants Take Over Center Field," *Publishers Weekly* (9 March 1984): 32-34.

135. See Ronald J.Sider, *Rich Christians in an Age of Hunger* (New York: Paulist Press, 1977); Ronald J. Sider, *Just Generosity: A New Vision for Overcoming Poverty in America* (Grand Rapids: Baker Books, 1999); Ronald J. Sider, *Christ and Violence* (Scottdale, PA: Herald Press, 1979); Ronald J Sider, ed., *Living More Simply* (Downers Grove, IL: InterVarsity Press, 1980); Ronald J. Sider and Diane Knippers, eds., *Toward An Evangelical Public Policy* (Grand Rapids: Baker Books, 2004).

136. Ronald J. Sider, "The Scandal of the Evangelical Conscience," *Books and Culture* (January/February 2005), 8, 9, 39-42 (quotes). See Ronald J. Sider, *The Scandal of the Evangelical Conscience* (Grand Rapids: Baker Books, 2004); Stan Guthrie, interviewer, "The Evangelical Scandal," *Christianity Today* (April 2005): 70-73.

137. Jim Wallis, "God's Politics: A Better Option," *Sojourners* 34, 2 (February 2005): 14-20 (quotes); Jim Wallis, *God's Politics: Why the Right Gets It Wrong and the Left Doesn't Get It* (San Franciso: HarperSanFranciso, 2005).

138. For more on the evangelical left or moderates, see Webber, *Younger Evangelicals,* 38, 39; Ted Olsen, "The Positive Prophet," *Christianity Today* (January 2003): 32-42; Ronald J. Sider, "Cautions Against Ecclesiastical Elegance," *Christianity Today* 17 (August 1979): 15-19; Joel A. Carpenter, "Compassionate Evangelicalism," *Christianity Today* (December 2003): 40-42; Amy Waldman, "Why We Need a Religious Left," *Washington Monthly* (December 1995): 37-43.

139. Philip Melling, *Fundamentalism in America: Millennialism, Identity, and Militant Religion* (Edinburgh: Edinburgh University Press, 1999), 104, 105. See Barry Hankins, *Uneasy in Babylon: Southern Baptist Conservatives and American Culture* (Tuscaloosa: University of Alabama Press, 2002.

7

Selling Jesus:
Megachurches and Televangelism

The acculturation of American evangelicalism has risen to new heights in two types of churches—megachurches and electronic churches. Both churches connect closely with contemporary culture. They are market driven and reflect the consumer approach to religion. Both arrange their services to suit the tastes and needs of their respective audiences. In doing so, they reinforce the existing religious and cultural inclinations of their constituencies. Both churches embody the American and evangelical approach to religion—populist, pragmatic, and individualistic. Like American society, the mega and electronic churches focus on quantity not quality. They are numbers driven. Bigger is better.

The services in these churches are not traditional and boring. Rather, they feature dramatic and exciting performances. A first-time visitor might think they were at the Jay Leno show rather than at church. Driving this style of doing church is the charismatic leadership that characterizes both types of churches. Both the mega and electronic churches also reflect the old evangelical paradox. On one hand, they have swallowed American culture hook, line, and sinker. These churches have indeed blurred the line between American culture and the Christian faith, often presenting them as one and the same. On the other, they generally embrace conservative religious and social beliefs. (The lifestyle, however, of these churches' leaders and followers often fails to match their rhetoric.)

The Next Church

"No spires. No crosses. No clerical collars. No hard pews. No kneelers. No biblical gobbledygook. No prayerly rote. No fire, no brimstone. No pipe organs. No dreary eighteenth-century hymns. No forced solemnity. No Sunday finery. No collection plates.... Centuries of European tradition and Christian habit are deliberately being abandoned, clearing the way for new contemporary forms of worship and belonging."[1] This new form goes by many names: megachurches, the Next Church, seeker-sensitive churches, the new paradigm, the shopping mall church, full-service churches, or the postmodern church.

The major characteristic of these churches is their sheer size. Over a weekend, many have more than 10,000 in attendance. They are indeed the fastest growing churches in the nation. Most observers list an average weekend attendance of 2,000 as the magic number for one to qualify as a megachurch. In the early twenty-first century, there are about 850 to 900 such churches in the United States. (Some sources claim that one megachurch develops every two weeks.) By the late twentieth century, about half of the churchgoing Americans attend 12 percent of the nations' 400,000 churches. As American consumers gravitate toward the shopping malls and supermarkets, they also embrace the super churches. The attraction is often the same—one-stop shopping to satisfy your "felt needs."[2]

Yes, "welcome to McChurch." No more boring, irrelevant sermons. They relate to certain themes and are coordinated with musical and dramatic productions. Our sermons touch you where you are. They are concrete, not abstract. They are practical, not theological. They connect with your feelings, not your mind. They are immediate, not distant. How do you like these Willow Creek sermon titles? "Authenticity," "Discovering the Way God Wired You Up," "The Power of Money," "The Art of Decision Making," "Maintaining a Healthy Attitude," "Fanning the Flames of Marriage," "Energy Management," and much more.[3] At America's megachurches, millions are being served, but critics question whether they are being fed.

Do you want a one-stop church, one that meets all of your needs? Second Baptist of Houston, or the "Exciting Second" as it is called, can do that. This megachurch, which claims a membership of over 17,000, can do it all. If sports are your thing, it fields about sixty-five softball teams, fifty basketball teams, and eighty-five teams in volleyball, soccer, and flag football. To boot, it has six bowling alleys, two basketball courts, and rooms for weight lifting, aerobics, and crafts. If your tastes are more musical, it has a music wing for the orchestra and a 500-member choir. According to one member, "It meets all of my needs, both spiritual and physical." I can take my family there for worship. My wife can teach or listen to music while I play or coach basketball.[4]

Perhaps you want to be entertained. Many megachurches can arrange for this. Some model their approach after Disney World. Second Baptist sends its pastoral staff to Disney for training and crafts its services as a Disney production. Phoenix's Community Church of Joy also credits Disney for inspiring its "Entertainment Evangelism." The pastoral staff attempts to provide exciting, dramatic services—ones that can compete with the theater and popular concerts. To do this, Church of Joy offers five different services each weekend: a spirited traditional, new contemporary, contemporary blend, contemporary country, and modern contemporary. The very heart of the seeker-sensitive church movement is its entertaining, lively, and contemporary services. In nearly every way, such services are non-traditional and non-liturgical. Ritual, contemplation, and abstract doctrine are out. Spontaneity, enthusiasm, and the dramatic are in.[5]

Or, maybe you are the practical type and want how-to-do-it seminars. The megachurches have this, too. They offer a number of twelve-step recovery meetings (e.g., drugs and alcohol). Do you want to be a better parent? Megachurches offer seminars for single parents or parents of teenagers. The standard classes for premarital couples are also available. If you are divorced, you can go to support meetings. There are seminars designed for men's and women's issues. If a loved one has passed away, grief support ministries are available. Do you have financial problems? You can attend a seminar for personal finances.[6]

Big Changes and Their Implications

Whether you love or hate these changes, American religion— especially its evangelical variety—is undergoing a revolution. Some call these developments a second reformation. This is probably an overstatement. The sixteenth-century Reformation challenged the very essence of the prevailing Catholic faith while the new paradigm has altered the form in which the evangelical faith is transmitted and practiced. The changes brought by the new paradigm churches do not run nearly as deep as those wrought by Luther, Calvin, and others. The contemporary reform of evangelicalism focuses on priorities and methods of delivery, not doctrine. The seeker churches still uphold the basics of generic evangelical theology—the authority of Scripture, divinity of Christ, and salvation by faith. While they ignore denominational distinctives and social issues, seeker theology must be regarded as conservative. Still, the changes are significant. While the Reformation emphasized faith over works and placed the Bible ahead of tradition, the new seeker churches have stressed experience over doctrine, emotion over serious Bible study, and spirituality over religious tradition.[7]

Herein lies a paradox that has run the course of evangelical history. At most points, especially the way the faith is propagated, evangelicals have caved in to the prevailing culture. They have adopted the most progressive methods for marketing the faith. Still, evangelicals have upheld the historic Christian faith and essential morals. At perhaps no point has this paradox been more obvious than in the late twentieth and early twentieth-first centuries. Since the 1960s, American culture has changed dramatically and the new paradigm churches must be seen as a response to this new situation.

While not obvious, however, a subtle change in theology may be in the offing. In the Next Church, evangelism has replaced worship as the major priority. Traditionally, evangelical churches have been believer's churches— they insist on a commitment to Christ as a standard for membership. Church

membership also centered on certain shared theological beliefs. Now they
are seeker churches. Such churches still require a similar response to Christ
and move believers to small groups but their priorities have changed. In
fact, attendance at these seeker services is usually greater than the church's
membership.

Church growth through evangelism and accommodating the seekers is on
the front burner—not worship or discipleship. Moreover, theology has taken a
terrible body blow. In a church that focuses on the practical or "felt needs," as
they would say, beliefs count for little. Doctrine is almost nonexistent. Seeker
churches only require an assent to a generic evangelical theology. The question is this: As user-friendly churches attempt to draw large crowds, are they in
danger of compromising the Christian faith? [8] Or as church growth expert
George Barna puts it: "There is a fine line between clever marketing and
compromised spirituality."[9]

Why Now?

In adopting new methods for presenting the gospel, evangelicals have created a stir. Why the concern? Evangelicals have used innovative methods to
promote the gospel throughout American religious history. In doing so, they
have met with considerable opposition, largely from other evangelicals.
Whitefield, Finney, Moody, Sunday, Graham and others have utilized progressive and culturally relevant methods to present Christ to the masses.

In removing state support from religion, the First Amendment has guaranteed such a situation. The churches have been forced to market their faith. And
to compete with other religious bodies and cultural attractions, they have had
to do it in the most effective manner. Such a situation has not hampered the
growth of religion in America. In fact, the opposite has happened. As Wade
Clark Roof notes: "Religion flourishes in an open, deregulated market where
it can respond in innovative ways to changing social realities and to people's
own recognized, but changing, needs and preferences." Adaptability to changing cultural situations has indeed been a key to evangelicalism's numerical
success.[10]

What is different about the contemporary changes? American religion, including the evangelical community, has experienced seismic changes in the
late twentieth century. Religion has had to adjust to many developments—the
conservative revival, increased pluralism, and the electronic church are examples. Still, three stand out as producing the rise of the megachurch and the
seeker movement. These are the themes of the counterculture and consumerism plus the impact of televangelism. The electronic church will be noted
separately later in this chapter.

The 1960s launched a cultural revolution that has altered the face of American religion. Thanks to the counterculture, in respect to religion Americans are
more therapeutic, individualistic, and anti-establishment. The therapeutic theme

is evident in the quest for openness, authenticity, and self-fulfillment. Individualism can be seen in the desire to interpret Scripture for oneself and to interact with God through prayer and other experiences. The anti-establishment theme comes out in the hostility toward bureaucracies, institutions, and organizational life in general.[11]

The new paradigm church must be seen as an evangelical response to these cultural developments. The baby boomers and generation X—who are the target audience for the seeker movement— have been reared on these counterculture themes. (Baby boomers were born from about 1945 to 1964 and the birth dates for generation Xers range from about 1965 to 1981.) In part, the numerical success of these churches can be attributed to their addressing the therapeutic, individualistic, and anti-establishment desires of these generations. These counterculture themes, of course, have been reinforced by the standard evangelical characteristics of populism and pragmatism.

Consumerism has also been a powerful force shaping the evangelical community. It has fostered a culture of choice and increased the already strong voluntary tendency within American religion. As religious pluralism has increased in modern America, so have the choices available to the seekers of religion. They have at their disposal a vast array of religious alternatives— traditional Catholicism, mainline Protestantism, fundamentalism, evangelical Protestantism, charismatic bodies, new age groups, Eastern religions, and more. Modern American culture, indeed, contains a religious smorgasbord. The religious choices in many parts of the country are almost limitless. In such a cafeteria setting, the religious seeker is sovereign. Of all religious groups, the quest culture has penetrated evangelical Christianity—especially it's the megachurches and parachurches.[12]

Several other factors have furthered the religious choices available to Americans. As noted in chapter 5, the 1965 laws restricting immigration to the United States were rescinded. Immigrants now poured into America primarily from Asia and Latin America. This development furthered cultural pluralism and the religious options available to Americans. Two, changes made by the Federal Communications Commission democratized the airwaves. They were open to anyone who could pay for access. Evangelical and charismatic Christians, especially the televangelists, raised enough money to dominate the religious dimension of television.[13] Next, denominationalism seriously declined. People did not attend the church of their family background but sought the church that best met their needs. Denominational loyalty became a thing of the past.[14] These three developments widened an already deregulated religious market.

The Market Mentality

Nearly everything in America is subject to market pressures. What to buy is an individual choice. So businesses must market their products. Marketing can be defined as "the process of planning and executing the conception, pricing, promotion, and distribution of ideas, goods and services" in a way that will satisfy both individual and organizational needs.[15] As the economies of North America and Europe evolved, marketing has gone through several stages of development. The production era dominated until the 1920s. This stage focused on producing quality products, assuming that if people needed a particular commodity they would purchase the best one available. In general, demand exceeded the supply so the customer did not reign supreme. From 1925 to 1950, a transition set in. Production increased and supply began to outstrip demand. The consumer thus became more important.

The big change, however, came after World War II. The situation now changed from a sellers' market (a shortage of goods and services) to a buyers' market (an abundance of goods and services). When a surplus exists, the consumer is "king." Consumers now have unprecedented power.[16] The producer must do two things. He/she must convince the consumer that his/her product is best for the given price. More than that, the producer must create a "felt need." Advertisements must convince the consumer that he/she needs a particular product.

As consumerism exploded in the late twentieth century, few areas of American life have been exempt from market pressures. Even the news media, education, and religion are dominated by the logic of the marketplace. And this situation presents a dilemma. Do you give the customer what is best for him/her or what he/she wants? The news media struggles over the issue of what is "news worthy" and what will attract the largest number of viewers or readers. Colleges and universities are torn between what they should teach and what the student (the customer) wants. Granting grades presents even a greater dilemma. Do you flunk your customer? Such problems exist because there is an abundance of colleges and universities. Unless you are an elite institution, the customer is sovereign.[17]

A similar problem confronts American religion. While it should not be subject to the logic of the market, it is. This is because Americans have a "supply-side spirituality." In religion they have an abundance of choices, not a scarcity. It is definitely a buyers' market and Americans have high expectations. They want more than a barebones spirituality. Rather, they expect a church to meet all of their spiritual and interpersonal needs. A notion of entitlement has shaped many areas of American life and religion is not immune to these expectations.[18] They demand much from the church and the traditional church has not risen to the occasion.

Church leaders did not set out to make religion a commodity in a market economy. They did not desire to make religion subject to the whims of the market. But it happened. As the consumer culture came to dominate American society, the churches felt pressure to tap the popular tastes and enthusiasms. They had to market their faith. Denominations that successfully did so grew; those who failed to do so declined.[19]

This market pressure and intense democratization of American religion has raised a significant issue, however. How should the Christian church operate in a society driven by democracy and the market economy? Or as Bruce and Marshall Shelley put it, "how can the Christian mission appeal to popular tastes without endangering the Christian message and the believing community? What if popular opinion conflicts with God's truth?" In a democratic society how do church leaders distinguish "the voice of the people from the voice of God?"[20]

The CEO Pastor

This consumer impulse inevitably led to another religious development— a managerial revolution. Running a megachurch requires considerable managerial expertise. In visiting Louisville's 9,000-member Southeast Christian Church, John Wilson noted that among the paid staff and especially the elders and other volunteers are "individuals who have had years of experience with the military, Federal Express, and similar organizations. A church like Southeast could not have existed 100 years ago, because the managerial science it embodies was then just being born."[21]

What is the role of the pastor in the new paradigm churches? The New Testament indicates that he should be the pastor-teacher. Such a person preaches and teaches the Word of God and shepherds a flock of believers. The role of the senior pastor in a megachurch, however, is quite different from that of the New Testament pattern. The new paradigm pastor is more like a CEO of a large corporation. While he may still be the primary preacher on Sunday morning, his tasks center on directing the operations of the church, which can be quite extensive. Some megachurches have hundreds of paid staff plus an army of volunteers. These individuals are in a chain of command, responsible to an area director, who, in turn, must report to the senior pastor. Many of these huge churches, indeed, function like large business corporations.[22]

Some Fortune 500 Pastors have lost their prophetic voices. Sermons cannot proclaim God's judgment or be critical and negative. In some churches, the word *sin* has become an expletive. Expository sermons, which proclaim God's Word are on a decline. Solid biblical teaching is too heavy for most congregations. Rather, preaching must be pleasing and entertaining. Preachers must proclaim God lite, a God who is your buddy and soul mate. Negative ideas must be so camouflaged that they are barely recognizable. Pastors face congregations who have been reared on hours of television and expect to be entertained. So the pastor must become a cross between an executive and an entertainer. Sermons must be short, relevant, and reinforced by visual images, including dramatization.

This model of the CEO pastor raises several questions. Are pastors being trained adequately for their new roles? To whom are these CEO's responsible? In recent years, seminaries have included more management training for their students. The Doctor of the Ministry degree focuses on practical training. On the whole, however, a seminary degree does not adequately prepare one for a ministry in the large seeker churches. As George Barna complains, at seminaries students conjugate Greek verbs, study theology and church history. Instead, they should be learning how to serve a target audience in their communities "as cost effectively and as meaningfully as might be done by McDonald's, Proctor and Gamble, or United Airlines..." Seminary training, in his opinion, should not be abstract or theoretical but be practical and oriented toward marketing.[23] In another place, Barna lists the functional competencies of a Christian leader. Preaching, teaching, and biblical knowledge do not make the list. The qualities he notes are those befitting a corporate CEO.[24]

For these reasons, seeker churches often do not hire seminary graduates to their staffs. Rather, they prefer to train their own staff members. The training offered by these large churches focuses on practical management skills—not the traditional seminary curricula. In fact, the growing trend suggests that "the large church will not be inclined to turn to the seminaries to staff itself, or for help in how to grow or how to serve its constituency."[25] Church consultant Lyle Schaller confirms this trend: "More than one-third of the senior ministers of megachurches do not hold a seminary degree." He wonders who will perpetuate the historic Christian faith if large churches do not turn to seminaries for leadership.[26] Seminaries, it would seem, are in the business of preparing students for a ministry in small churches.

The CEO pastor does not need seminary training. This can be seen in job descriptions for senior pastors at some megachurches. Personal and managerial qualities come to the forefront. These large churches seek winsome personalities with leadership characteristics. Note the qualifications listed by one large church for a senior pastor: "Knock-em dead platform skills, a transparent persona, aggressive leadership style and grueling background investigation required. Marketplace success respected over ministry credentials." Most desirable of these qualities is marketplace success. And since megachurches often center their ministry around a charismatic leader, his departure can create serious problems[27].

Our second question concerns accountability. To whom is the CEO pastor of a megachurch responsible? Most new paradigm churches are independent and have no denominational oversight. If they are part of a denomination, their affiliation is usually nominal. Besides, their success makes them nearly immune to denominational control. Most large churches do have boards who have legal control of the church. But the senior pastor is normally given a great deal of free rein. Assuming he does not engage in any scandalous behavior, he is primarily accountable to the market. The pastor will not be judged by his faithfulness to the gospel but whether, as Schaller puts it, "the people keep coming and giving." As in the world of corporate business, the enterprise must succeed or the CEO pastor will go.[28]

Super Churches Fit Right In

Many reasons can be given for the growth of the super churches in modern America. Most factors center on the rise of our consumer and therapeutic society. Within these large trends, however, there are a number of specific developments noted by Lyle Schaller. Our shopping and working styles lend themselves to the growth of megachurches. Suburban people are used to commuting distances to work. So driving five to twenty miles to church is not an inconvenience, especially when it can be done quickly on a freeway. For convenience, we desire one-stop shopping, so we go to the shopping malls or the Wal-Marts of the world. In doing so, we bypass the small store. So it is perfectly natural to ignore the small church and patronize a super church.

People born after 1945 are used to large convenient facilities and specialized services. Large high schools, supermarkets, shopping malls, and medical clinics are examples. Seekers get a religious version of this in the megachurches. They offer high-quality physical facilities, preaching, teaching, nurseries, and youth ministries. Many of the staff members are not even pastors but have a secular training that specializes in an area of church work. They may focus on sound effects, music, child-care, or financial matters. People seek intimacy within an impersonal society. Despite its size, the super church attempts to meet this need in its small groups.

Modern society minimizes commitment. The megachurches mirror this yearning. Like the shopping mall, there are different levels of interest. Some people go to the shopping mall to window shop while others make major purchases. At the super church, you can be a casual seeker or a committed believer. In fact, attendance at a megachurch worship service can double or triple the total membership. Conversely, at a small church, membership may double attendance.

The break down of denominational lines has prompted the growth of large churches. People born before 1945 have exhibited a high degree of denominational loyalty. Not so with the baby boomer generation. They gravitate toward the church that best meets their felt needs and will switch churches if these expectations go unmeet. Many of the seekers attending the super churches have migrated from churches previously on the edge of evangelical Christianity. Mainline Protestants including Episcopalians, Disciples of Christ, Lutherans, and Presbyterians have joined seeker churches. Large numbers of people have left Catholicism since 1945 and some have migrated to the megachurches. Conservative Protestants have been slow to welcome charismatic Christians into their ranks. Not only have the super churches opened their doors to charismatics, but many have a charismatic orientation.

The greatest attraction of the super churches might be their style of worship. Many people who came out of the Jesus movement of the 1960s are now the backbone of the megachurches. True to their Woodstock heritage, they prefer a lively style of worship, not a traditional service. The super church can offer a number of worship options, including a service with guitars and bands that play Christian rock. Indeed, the guitar has replaced the organ. [29] For the most part, this generation rejects liturgical services as found in Catholic and mainline Protestant churches. As Alan Wolfe says, "American society is a nonliturgical society, its pace of life too fast, its commitments to individualism too powerful, its treatment of authority too irreverent, and its craving for innovation too intense to tolerate religious practices that call on believers to repeat the same word or songs with little room for creative expression." [30]

As indicated earlier, the sermons at megachurches reflect a culture addicted to television. Our television culture has conditioned people to have a short attention span; something resembling the time between commercial breaks. People gain much of their inspiration from sound-bite cliques. Television has also replaced the spoken word with visual images. So sermons at many super churches are short with a liberal sprinkling of anecdotes, and they are practical, not theoretical. Visual images abound. They come in the form of large screens, film clips, and dramatizations. The modern church is moving in the direction of the medieval cathedrals where stained glass windows conveyed a message. [31]

Contemporary sermons and American culture connect in another way. Americans are always looking for quick answers and easy solutions. They hope to lose weight without dieting or exercise. They believe they can engage in analytical thinking with little knowledge about a particular subject. Somewhat related, contemporary sermons focus on application rather than any knowledge of Scripture. Parishioners want the end result without hearing any substantial biblical teaching. Modern sermons are long on practical application and short on substance.

Churches mirror our fast food culture. Americans want fast service with little inconvenience. After all, we are a people on the go. Some churches accommodate this desire by offering express services. These services guarantee to get you out in forty-five minutes. The sermons are a condensed twenty-minute version of the one given at the regular ninety-minute service. Do you want an abbreviated version of the Bible? In the 1990s, you could have "Kwik-scan," an edition which requires no more than thirty half-hour readings to go from Genesis to Revelation. [32] Better yet, there are drive up church services. You do not even have to get out of your car. And you can even stay in your pajamas and bring your pet. Americans like low calorie beverages—Diet Coke, Bud Lite, or Miller Lite. Evangelicals also have the option of church-lite.

In yet several other ways, the megachurch portrays American culture. The atmosphere is very casual. Most people—sometimes even the pastor—dress very casually. This removes the obstacle of formal dress and helps the unchurched to feel at home. It also reflects the populism so common in evangelical circles. Like the rest of America, the super churches are numerically driven.

Quantity counts, not quality. Success is often measured by church growth. With some justification, the super churches have been described as McChurch. Individuals in the seeker movement do counter this by contending that the small groups offer believers considerable substance in respect to worship and Bible study.[33]

The Spiritual Quest

A future chapter will address the therapeutic and self-fulfillment mentality so prevalent in evangelical circles. At this point, however, some mention should be made of these characteristics as they relate to the super churches. What are the megachurches marketing? The gospel, to be sure. But they are also promoting a spirituality so common in American culture.

Spirituality rather than religion is in vogue in America. What is spirituality? It is a very difficult concept to grasp. It may or may not include traditional religion. For some spirituality connects with a faith tradition. For many, however, it is not bound by any doctrinal or creedal categories. Wade Clark Roof contends that any definition would include "reference to a relationship with something beyond myself (known as 'Creator,' 'God,' 'transcendent power,' etc.) that is intangible but also real. It would recognize that spirituality is the source of one's values and meaning, a way of understanding the world, [and] an awareness of my 'inner self'..."[34]

Other observations add to this definition. Nearly one-third of those surveyed in a Gallup poll "defined spirituality with no reference to God or a higher authority." About three-quarters of the people thought of spirituality more in a personal and individual sense than in terms of the church or doctrine. Spirituality, indeed, has "swung away from what is beyond us [God or the church] to what is within us." Such individualism is one of the reasons contemporary Americans are reluctant to make a commitment to participate in congregational life.[35]

The late twentieth century has witnessed a major shift in religion toward the inward, subjective, and experiential. The baby boomers and generation Xers have been raised in a therapeutic self-help environment. Out of this has come a tremendous quest for self-fulfillment. The boomers and Xers became seekers for a spirituality that went beyond the mechanics of some self-improvement program. They have given a spiritual, inward and experiential twist to the notion of self-improvement. This new dimension to self-improvement might be better described as a desire for self-transformation.[36]

In their pursuit of spiritual self-improvement and inner meaning, boomers and Xers have turned to many sources. New Age beliefs, Eastern religions, occult activities, mysticism, evangelical Christianity, and the charismatic movement make the list. Very important, the monistic worldview related to New Age, occult, and Eastern activities has been dressed in Western clothes and has penetrated evangelical Christianity. And with the decline of doctrine and serious thinking within the evangelical community, many boomers and Xers are oblivious to this trend toward an eclectic spirituality. They have little knowledge of worldviews and fail to see how they connect with their lives.[37]

While it may not have taken on heretical proportions, the gospel of self-improvement has acquired a spiritual dimension and has become common in the evangelical community. It is an important aspect of the consumer mentality that drives the large seeker churches. With many spiritual choices, "the seeker and chooser has come increasingly to be in control," notes Martin Marty. When one enters a large chain bookstore, this trend becomes obvious. The seeker can chose books from a bewildering range of subjects relevant to evangelical Christians: the Bible, evangelicalism, angels, prophecy, mysticism, meditation, spiritual journeys, church growth, prayer, spiritual gifts, and much more.[38] In fact, some books are best sellers because they speak to the needs of evangelical Christians.

Surveys indicate that over half of the church-goers in America attend because "it's good for you," and that about 25 percent go for "peace of mind and spiritual well-being." Most appear to be "looking for that inner and more subjective kind of payoff" from religion. They desire "support, not salvation, help rather than holiness, [and] a circle of spiritual equals rather than an authoritative church or guide." [39] In fact, it is difficult to "tell where the immensely popular language of self-help therapy begins and the language of salvation through Jesus ends." [40]Self-fulfillment became a dominant theme of the 1960s and 1970s and it linked up with the materialism of the 1980s and 1990s. As a result, the quest for spiritual fulfillment has acquired a powerful consumer dimension. "Spirituality, like hamburgers, was increasingly something one could get quickly and in a variety of places," notes Robert Wuthnow.[41]

"We live in an experience saturated culture," says George Gallup. Advertisements do more than try to sell you a quality product; they promise you an ecstatic moment. As a result, in religion experience has taken precedence over belief. People seek authenticity by means of an experience, not through ideas. This trend has accelerated as the vitality of conservative Protestantism has shifted from fundamentalism to evangelicalism and on to Pentecostalism.[42] In an age when people seek personal fulfillment through an experience, the large seeker churches open the door to many options. You can experience self-fulfillment through contemporary music, sermons, drama, small groups, how-to-do-it sessions or even athletic activities. Take your choice.

Forerunners of the Megachurches

The megachurches did not hatch from an egg in the late twentieth century. They had precursors and prototypes that reach way back into American history. Before moving to this subject, however, some terms need clarification. The terms *megachurch* or *super church* are not synonymous with the seeker movement. Not all megachurches are seeker churches. Some like Jerry Falwell's

Thomas Road Baptist Church and the First Baptist Church of Hammond, Indiana, are large fundamentalist churches. Also, many seeker churches are not large enough to qualify as megachurches. Furthermore, some churches only incorporate aspects of the seeker-sensitive methods for reaching the unchurched. My subject in this context is the large super churches. Some may be seeker churches, others may not.

As noted several times in this study, evangelicals have frequently employed innovative methods to reach the unsaved. These techniques, moreover, have been successful because they have connected with the popular culture. Whitefield organized and advertised his services and dramatized his sermons. Finney was pragmatic to the core. His "new methods" featured lively songs, a dramatic style of preaching, and the "anxious bench" for those repenting of their sins. Of significance, he reversed the relationship of worship to evangelism. Previously, pastors believed that evangelism came as a product of worship. Finney made soul winning the priority.

As a businessman, Moody organized and advertised his services much like a large corporation. While his sermons were not dramatic, he appealed to the urban middle-class population of his day. Sunday also had a well-oiled organization. His simple messages squared with the moods of the day—patriotism, temperance, anti-communism, and masculinity. By entertaining the masses and connecting the gospel with their cultural context, these evangelists provided an example for the modern super churches.

More directly, the large churches of the late nineteenth and early twentieth centuries can be seen as prototypes of the modern megachurches. The late nineteenth century witnessed the rise of the large institutional churches. Rather than move out of the inner city, these churches provided many services for the urban area. In addition to preaching the gospel, prayer meetings, and Sunday school these churches addressed other needs. These services touched upon the social, intellectual, and physical aspects of life and included reading rooms, day nurseries, gymnasiums, sewing rooms, drama clubs, lecture series, concerts, and other entertaining activities. By 1900, about 175 churches could be categorized as institutional churches. Like the modern super churches, these institutional churches were full service institutions intended to meet the needs of the community. They declined for several reasons, especially their very high cost and cozy relationship with theological liberalism.[43]

Several churches in the early twentieth century foreshadowed the modern megachurces. Built in 1922, Paul Rader's Chicago Gospel Tabernacle drew large crowds for over a decade. Why? The services included popular music, dramatized sermons, and a charismatic preacher who was somewhat of an entertainer. A former boxer and rugged individualist, Rader (1879-1938) told funny and compelling stories and dressed in a casual manner. During the week, a paid staff ran many more services—food programs for the needy, prayer services, men and women's groups, clubs for children and summer camps.[44]

Even more of a prototype was the sensational ministry of Aimee Semple McPherson (1890-1944). She engaged in many activities: Pentecostal evangelist, founder of the Foursquare Gospel Church, a pioneer radio evangelist, and the founder of the Angelus Temple in Los Angeles. This church contained the ingredients of the modern super churches. At its peak, more than 10,000 people attended the Sunday services. The church was a structural marvel and one of the largest buildings of its time. Designed more like a theater than a church, it had tremendous visual and acoustic features, one of the first sound systems in use, and an orchestra pit. The Temple featured a variety of quality musical performances—an outstanding choir for traditional hymns, gospel songs, and the "best jazz in Los Angeles."[45]

The Temple contained no pulpit but a stage for McPherson's dramatic presentations. Her messages were rather ordinary, but her presentations were anything but that. She presented a simple, unsophisticated gospel message in an extremely dramatic and unpredictable fashion. McPherson brought "to life the glories of heaven, the torments of hell, and allure of the fleshpots of Egypt." Showmanship was her middle name. She used drama, costumes, makeup, scenery, live animals, ships filled with musicians, screaming sirens, motorcycles, and a variety of props. For example, McPherson would preach on Jesus as the Good Shepherd dressed as Little Bo Peep or on the wages of sin astride a motorcycle and dressed as a policeman. Outside, search-lights lit up the Temple as if it were a casino in Las Vegas.[46]

Church Growth Movement

Closely related to the rise of the super churches is the church growth movement. This movement can be defined as "a missiological movement founded by Donald McGavran (1897-1990) and characterized by a pragmatic approach to planting and nurturing the growth of churches, based on a systematic analysis of growing churches."[47] Os Guinness views the church growth movement as having three phases. McGavran's work in the 1950s gave rise to the church growth movement. When the movement spread beyond the missionary stage to the United States, the second phase began. Guinness regards the rise of the megachurches as a highly popularized third phase of the church growth movement.[48]

The homogeneous unit formed the cornerstone of McGavran's mission theory. Crossing racial, linguistic or class lines presents a barrier to becoming a Christian. So he contended that people in self-contained cultural groups are more receptive to the gospel. The movement also employed social science methods to develop an elaborate methodology for surveying and analyzing groups of people as to their readiness to receive the gospel. McGavran also argued for a pragmatic approach in mission work. Outdated and unproductive methods must be abandoned.[49]

McGavran's student, C. Peter Wagner, discovered that these methods worked in the United States. He popularized a similar approach to church growth by his publications and classes at Fuller Theological Seminary. Wagner even mentored some of the leading pastors of the seeker movement—for example, Rick Warren, John Wimber, and Walt Kallestad. The church growth movement's practical emphasis attracted many pastors and church leaders to classes and conferences on building the church. From the church growth movement, the megachurches have learned much. The church service focuses on a target group, the unchurched. The service is to be visitor-friendly, that is, welcoming and hospitable. Environmental factors are important. The church complex and ministries—the parking lot, sanctuary, nursery, worship aids, music, and youth ministries—must be attractive.[50]

While not connected with Fuller Seminary, George Barna has promoted many of the ideas practiced by the megachurches. He is an expert market researcher and pollster who practices his skills in both the church and business community. He founded the Barna Research Group and has published many books related to church growth. Most significant have been *Marketing the Church* (1988), *The Frog in the Kettle* (1990), *User Friendly Churches* (1991), and *The Second Coming of the Church* (1998).[51]

Essentially, he is urging churches to communicate and market the gospel effectively to target audiences. While this general principle is not controversial, his specific marketing principles did arouse criticism. He has been accused of watering down the gospel and pandering to the felt needs of the people. Barna does not regard the megachurch as the answer to all of the church's problems. Still, he is a staunch supporter of the Willow Creek seeker approach and hopes that "one day [there] would be 100,000 Willow Creek churches in this country."[52]

A Few Megachurches

Many super churches dot the American religious landscape. While they are in most parts of the country more can be found in the suburbs and in certain geographical locations—especially California, Texas, and the South. But two churches stand out: Willow Creek in Illinois and Saddleback in California. In part, this is because they have extended themselves by creating associations that promote their vision of the ministry. Before focusing on these two churches, however, some mention should be made of a few other megachurches.

In fact, the largest concentration of super ministries and perhaps the capital of evangelicalism might be Dallas, Texas. Yes, "don't mess with Texas." Things are really big down there. Dallas "has more megachurches, megaseminaries, and mega-Christian activity than any other American city." I will only mention a few. Some observers believe that First Baptist of Dallas was the first modern super church. Under the leadership of W. A. Criswell from 1944 to 1991, the church implemented many innovative ministries. As a result, the church grew to 28,000—believed to be the largest in the nation for the time. The church's roll now stands at 10,000 with about 5,000 active members.

Dallas can count at least eight other super churches from a variety of religious traditions; the largest being T. D. Jakes's Potter's House, which attracts 23,000 each weekend. There is also the 3,600-member Cathedral of Hope—which claims to be evangelical and the world's largest gay church.[53]

More will be said about the ministry of Robert Schuller in a chapter focusing on the power of possibility thinking. At this point, however, a few words should be said about The Crystal Cathedral and its role in the megachurch movement. The Crystal Cathedral was the first church in America to place marketing and church growth techniques at the heart of its ministry. While Schuller did not use the term *seeker*, he surveyed his locality to determine their spiritual needs. He thus built his ministry around the executives and entrepreneurs of affluent Orange County, who preferred a practical Christianity to meet their everyday needs. In the context of Orange County suburbanites, this entailed a positive message, a mixture of traditional and contemporary music professionally performed, and one of the most distinctive church buildings ever built. In fact, Schuller counts Bill Hybels of the Willow Creek Church and Rick Warren of the Saddelback Church as his disciples.[54]

Bellevue Baptist Church in Cordova, Tennessee (a suburb of Memphis), is one of the largest megachurches in the nation. In the 1990s, this Southern Baptist church had 22,000 members, a 7,000-seat sanctuary, and a 376-acre facility. In this church, the evangelical paradox is evident. Adrian Rogers, the senior pastor, led the conservative wing of the Southern Baptist Convention while his church utilized innovative methods for church growth. Aided by twenty-two assistant ministers, Rogers and staff put on a spectacular show Sunday after Sunday. The services were also broadcast on 1,600 television stations. In good megachurch fashion, however, Rogers understood the value of small groups. Here assistant pastors and lay people led Bible studies and other groups.[55]

Willow Creek

Willow Creek Church in South Barrington, Illinois, is the prototype of the megachurch and has been called one of the most influential churches in the United States. Founded in 1975, Bill Hybels and its other leaders dreamed of building "a church that would speak the language of our modern culture and encourage nonbelievers to investigate Christianity at their own pace, free from the traditional trappings of religion that tend to chase [non-believers] away."[56] To achieve this objective, the church implemented entertaining and unchurch-like services for its baby boomer constituency.

By any standard, the Willow Creek Church was remarkably successful in achieving this goal. Approximately 100 people gathered at the first service in 1975. Twenty years later, weekend services at the church averaged from 15,000 to 20,000 and it had 260 employees with an annual budget of $12, 500,000. By 2000, the church staff had grown to 500 plus 6,000 volunteers and 17,000 people were participating in 2,600 small groups.[57]

During the main weekend services, visitors "sat in plush theater seats rather than pews, listened to an electric band and vocalists, and watched interpretative dancers accompanying Christian songs in the vast auditorium, and could join in the songs by following the words flashed on massive overhead screens."[58] The sermons are lively, entertaining, culturally appealing, professional and focus on timely subjects. For visitors speaking Spanish and Mandarin-Chinese, the sermon was immediately translated.[59]

The small groups also contained considerable variety and contemporary relevance. One could attend sessions on divorce counseling, auto repair, women in the workplace, hairdressing, vacuum-cleaner repair, career transition, marital restoration, and many more. Despite this variety, the groups included some combination of Bible study, prayer, sharing, and accountability. In fact, Hybels regards the small groups as the center of Willow Creek's ministry.[60]

Willow Creek took a very businesslike approach to church growth. In senior pastor Hybel's office, a sign reads, "What is our business? Who is our customer? What does the customer value?"[61] Consequently, the church did market research to determine the needs and desires of its potential customers— that is, the middle-class professionals of upscale suburban Chicago. The first step in reaching "unchurched Harry or Mary" was to understand how they think and feel. Such individuals personify the baby boomers whom Willow Creek is determined to reach.[62]

Step two entails designing the weekend services for unchurched Harry or Mary. These services became a time for seekers, not worship services for believers. Weekends are more convenient for the unchurched. The committed believers can come at a less convenient time during the week. In these seeker services, the unchurched are not asked to participate or respond. Rather, they are spectators who want and receive a polished performance.[63]

Third, for the Sunday services, Willow Creek puts on an impressive multimedia show. Spending up to $100,000 for stage and sound equipment, the church's use of sophisticated lighting, sound, and visual imagery was right in sync with the media age. Drama is certainly not new to religious services. But Willow Creek closely coordinated a five-minute drama with the theme of the sermon. The themes and topics for such services have been determined months in advance.[64]

Willow Creek's innovative approach to doing church is not confined to South Barrington. Willow Creek has many offspring. Its popularity in part rests on the fact that many churches have adopted its seeker sensitive methods. In 1992, Willow Creek Church established the Willow Creek Association (WCA) for the purpose of providing training for those pastors fascinated by Willow Creek's methods and success. The WCA claims to be a "network of like-minded churches."[65]

Is it at the early stages of becoming a denomination? Probably not. The churches in the WCA have very different ministries and they value their independence. Perhaps more important, denominationalism is on a decline. Old denominational loyalties are difficult to maintain. So why create a new one? Actually, the WCA fits well into the current trend toward religious decentralization. If anything, the WCA might represent the postmodern denomination— a loose alliance of churches based more on the methods of conducting church than on theology or tradition.[66]

Or, the WCA might be as Michael Hamilton suggests: "It's probably more accurate to think of the Willow Creek Association as a parachurch organization providing a proprietary product line." Churches affiliated with the WCA stand at about 3,300 in the United States, 200 in Canada, and 2,500 outside of North America. Absent from this list are most of the other super churches. They are already large and do not need the WCA's help. Rather, the WCA largely consists of small churches that want to grow.[67]

Saddleback

Next to Willow Creek, Saddleback Valley Community Church in Orange County, California, is the nation's most famous megachurch. Weekend services average 15,000 and the atmosphere is extremely casual. The church has a staff of 175 and its thirteen pastors all have seminary degrees. Saddleback's relationship with the Southern Baptist Convention is paradoxical. On one hand, it keeps its affiliation nearly invisible to the public. On the other, Saddleback supports the denomination financially, especially its mission programs.[68]

Saddleback is a seeker-sensitive church with services remarkably similar to those at Willow Creek. Its target audience, known as "Saddleback Sam," resembles that of Willow Creek: "well educated, likes his job, likes where he lives, likes contemporary music, is skeptical of organized religion, is self-satisfied...prefers the casual and informal over the formal, and is overextended in both time and money."[69] The music is lively and contemporary. The church staff surveyed its members as to their favorite radio station and proceeded to fashion the church's music accordingly. In the words of senior Pastor Rick Warren: "Match your music to the kind of people God wants your church to reach."[70]

Pastor Warren also changed his style of preaching, moving from verse by verse expository sermons to topical messages. For believers, he still used the verse by verse approach, but for the unchurched he preached topical sermons. The starting point was no longer the biblical text but the interests, needs, and hurts of the target audience. Warren describes it this way: "The Bible determines our message, but our target determines when, where, and how we communicate it." These topical sermons focus on the practical aspects of the Christian life and must be presented in a way that captures the attention of the audience. "When God's Word is taught in an uninteresting way, people don't just think the pastor is boring, they think God is boring," says Warren. To improve their attention, listeners are given fill-in-the-blank outlines to help them follow the sermon.[71]

Saddleback regards itself as a Purpose-Driven church. The theological or methodical foundation for its ministry rests on Purpose-Driven principles. What are they? Warren uses two diagrams to describe them. Using a baseball diamond, going to first base is church membership, which entails a commitment to Christ and the church and signing a covenant. Second base moves toward maturity and features a commitment to a daily quiet time, tithing, and a small group. Going to third base means actively serving the church. Home base is mission and entails evangelicalism. At the center of the diamond is magnification, which stands for worship.[72]

Concentric circles representing target audiences make up the second diagram. The widest circle is the Community, which is the target of evangelism. The next circle is called the Crowd: the seekers who come to the seeker-sensitive services. The third circle represents the Congregation, individuals who have committed themselves to the church. Circle four contains the Committed—the mature in faith. Last is the Inmost Core, which contains individuals committed to the ministry of the church.[73]

What Warren strives for in the Purpose Driven church is a balanced ministry. While evangelism and church growth are important, they are only one component of a healthy church. Most churches, in Warren's view, focus on one aspect of the Christian ministry—evangelism, worship, discipleship, etc. The Purpose Driven church endorses no specific theology. Rather, its theology is its methodology of a balanced ministry. This ministry strives to integrate evangelism, discipleship, fellowship, service, and worship.[74]

Saddleback has gained fame for more than its size and innovative ministry. Its ministry has been extended in two ways—Warren's best-selling books and conferences for pastors. *The Purpose Driven Church* has sold over 1,000,000 copies in twenty languages. This book sets down the principles for a healthy church. Selling over 6 million copies is *The Purpose Driven Life*. This book focuses more on individuals, directing them on a forty-day spiritual journey that addresses life's most important question: "What on earth am I here for?" [75]

While Saddleback has not formed an association as has Willow Creek, it has conferences for pastors. They flock to Saddleback's pastoral conferences by the thousands, and it is they who have made the *Purpose Driven Church* a best seller. At these conferences, pastors are taught Warren's concept of a balanced ministry. Like other seeker pastors, Warren claims that methods determine church growth: "the primary factor affecting the growth or decline of a church is the methods the church uses…. Change the method, change the results."[76]

The Electronic Church: An Introduction

The impact of television on evangelicalism has already been mentioned several times in this study and will again be encountered in chapter 8. So I will confine my comments to aspects of the electronic church not directly related to politics, the health and wealth gospel, or possibility thinking. What is the electronic church? Broadly speaking, it refers to a variety of religious broadcasting methods and organizations, including both radio and television. By the 1980s, the term *electronic church* came to refer to the television programs produced by evangelicals, fundamentalists, and Pentecostals.[77] While mainline Protestants and even Catholics were active in the early years of television, in the last thirty years or so it has been the domain of evangelicals—especially the Pentecostals.

Quentin Schultze lists six characteristics that distinguish the electronic church and televangelism from religious broadcasting in general. One, they are "audience supported," meaning that the television viewers must donate to the ministry to keep it on the air. Two, the electronic churches are "personality-led." The program centers around a charismatic personality who can attract large numbers of viewers. Three, the broadcasts are "experientially validated," that is, viewing the program provides people with a religious experience. Four, the electronic churches are "technologically sophisticated." They employ the most current broadcasting technology, rivaling in professional quality even popular secular programs. Five, televangelism is "entertainment-oriented." In an entertainment age, religious programs cannot be boring. They must capture the interest of the viewer or they will turn the dial. Six, the electronic church is "expansionary-minded." The audience, ratings, and donations must grow. If not, the ministry may go off the air.[78]

Given, these six criteria, Schultze would not regard an evangelist such as Billy Graham as a televangelist. But he does contend that three-quarters of the highest rated religious programs met these standards and must be regarded as part of the electronic church. Examples of those he would list as televangelists are Oral Roberts, Rex Humbard, Jerry Falwell, Pat Robertson, Kenneth Copeland, Jimmy Swaggert, and Jim Bakker. With the rise of cable television, the televangelists have another outlet for their programs. The Trinity Broadcasting Network (TBN), operated by Paul Crouch, carries primarily religious programs. A majority of these broadcasts feature televangelists, especially those of a health and wealth gospel (or Word-Faith movement) persuasion.[79]

Why did the mainline Protestants and Catholics largely abandon television? Why have the evangelicals been so successful in this regard? In part, the mainline Protestants and Catholics have not accommodated American popular culture to the degree that evangelicals have. And as we shall see, adaptation to American culture is a huge factor in the numerical success of the televangelists. Second, liturgical and sacramental services as found in mainline Protestant and Catholic churches do not entertain television audiences.[80]

For that matter, the more traditional sermons from the mainline pulpits are often sophisticated and boring. Television is not suited for complex religious ideas. It best conveys simple concepts that connect with a person's feelings. Entertainment, indeed, is a necessary ingredient for holding the attention of a television audience. Conversely, evangelicals—especially those from the South—preach with a popular gusto that captivates television audiences. Exciting and emotional revivals, which are a staple of evangelicalism, lend themselves to television.

Lastly, as noted in chapter 4, liberals were given free broadcasting time on radio and early television and did not develop strategies for financing such broadcasts. Conservative Protestants had to raise money for their programs and thus honed these skills. When in 1960 the FCC mandated that networks did not have to give free broadcasts in order to meet their public service obligations, paid religious broadcasting became the norm. The evangelicals were well positioned for the new age of self-financed religious television programs. Their years of successful radio broadcasting had prepared them well for the television era. They knew how to use the technology, finance programs, and reach target audiences.[81]

Televangelism: The Pioneers

The roots of televangelism go back to America's great revivalists—Whitefield, Finney, Moody, and Sunday. As mentioned previously, they employed well-organized strategies and entertaining ways to promote the gospel. As Razelle Frankl notes, the televangelists are a hybrid of earlier revivalism and modern secular television programming. To this could be added the parachurches. Some television ministries have no formal church affiliation and perform specialized religious tasks. Modern televangelists such as Rex Humbard, Oral Roberts, Billy Graham, and Jimmy Swaggart are "direct descendents" of the urban revivalists. Others such as Pat Robertson and Jim Bakker are more directly related to commercial television. The roots of televangelism must also include the nineteenth-century Bible and tract societies that pioneered in the publishing and distribution of religious literature. In particular, the successful radio broadcasts, financed by many small donations, paved the way for televangelism.[82]

ABC televised the first religious program in 1949. This broadcast featured prominent theologians discussing the relevance of religion for daily life. The 1950s saw an increase in religious programs. While Bishop Fulton Sheen excited many with his weekly programs, most broadcasts featured Protestants. During 1950s, conservative Protestants also took to the airwaves. Several Pentecostals led the charge: Rex Humbard was first, followed by Oral Roberts and Kathryn Kuhlman. They appeared on local television stations, from which they purchased time. Billy Graham appeared on national television. While an evangelical, he was becoming a prominent figure and acceptable to the national networks.[83]

Despite rising costs, during the 1960s and 1970s paid television programs—dominated by evangelicals, fundamentalists, and Pentecostals—increased significantly. Such broadcasts jumped from about 50 to 90 percent of all religious programs. Free public programs, featuring mainline Protestants, had become a thing of the past. The networks realized that religious broadcasting could be profitable and conservative Protestants became eager customers, purchasing the great bulk of the air time. Many of their programs appeared on local stations and at off-peak times. In fact, Sunday morning, when there are fewer viewers and the costs are reduced, became known as "The Sunday Morning (Religious) Ghetto."[84]

The rising costs of air time also prompted the televangelists to explore ways to attract larger audiences. One method was to adopt different formats for their television programs. To stereotype the television evangelists in respect to their programs would be a mistake. While they had much in common, considerable diversity existed in respect to their broadcasts. Beginning in the 1960s, a number of different program and evangelistic styles emerged. In the 1950s before auditoriums were designed for television programs, Rex Humbard had his church built specifically for high-tech TV. While he televised traditional services, he also imitated the musical and variety shows so popular in secular television. Billy Graham had his weekly radio program, "Hour of Decision," but he never undertook the expense of a weekly television program. Rather, he televised his revival services over national networks. His programs, however, had their trademark: the altar-call. Every telecast ended with the call to leave your seats, come forward, and give yourself to Jesus.[85]

Another pioneer was Oral Roberts, who must be regarded as a descendent of revivalism. First a Pentecostal, later a Methodist and a university president, Roberts employed several types of broadcast formats. Typical of his Pentecostal ministry, his early programs featured spiritual and physical healing. Millions of people observed his vigorous prayers, the laying on of hands, and the testimonies of individuals claiming to be healed. The faithful supported him with their prayers and donations. Roberts' critics regarded his ministry as showmanship, his claims to healing as scientifically unverifiable, and his pleas for money as a turn-off. As a Methodist and a university president, Roberts changed his broadcast format. In 1969, he launched his remarkable primetime specials. Shorn of their Pentecostal distinctives, these programs were attractive, professional, entertaining, and attracted a range of viewers.[86]

More Televangelists

The success of these pioneers encouraged other preachers to start television ministries. A number of televangelists began as local pastors and then took their churches into television. They were pastors first and television evangelists second. Examples include Robert Schuller, D. James Kennedy, Charles Stanley, and Lloyd Ogilvie. Their churches are part of traditional denominations and except for Schuller, these pastors have effectively submitted them-selves to a local congregation.[87]

Robert Schuller (1926-) began broadcasting his Sunday services as early as 1970 and employed a variety of highly professional and celebrity-oriented formats to convey his possibility thinking theology. Avoiding a pulpit thump-ing fundamentalist message with political implications, Schuller televised his "Hour of Power" nationally from the spectacular Crystal Cathedral. Every facet of this Sunday broadcast is minutely planned. Market research has indi-cated what the audience wants. With this in mind, the themes and messages are determined one year in advance. Songs and testimonies are then tailored to the message and everything is edited for an upbeat tone and appropriate length. The professionalism of the "Hour of Power" stands in stark contrast to the telecasts of the Pentecostal-orientated services. But both approaches have their respective audiences.[88]

A gifted expository preacher, D. James Kennedy built a large church in the 1970s and early 1980s. His early services were simple broadcasts of his church services. Compared to most televangelists, his services were quite tame. By the mid-1980s, Kennedy increasingly began to address issues concerning public morality: abortion, prayer in the schools, evolution, and sex and violence in the motion pictures. The answer to these problems, according to Kennedy, was to return America to its perceived Christian past. Increasingly, this has become the theme for his services.[89]

Charles Stanley, a Southern Baptist, is one of the few televangelists who broadcasts a simple church service with traditional preaching and music. His success on television can be attributed to preaching that has balanced content with emotions and doctrine with practical application. During the 1980s, his humility and sincerity also stood in contrast with the scandalous behavior of several televangelists. It also seems that his recent divorce has not severely harmed his ministry. Even in this regard, he submitted to the authority of the local congregation.[90]

Jerry Falwell also began his ministry as the pastor of an independent Bap-tist church. Since then he has become the pastor of a megachurch, a televangelist, the founder of the Moral Majority, the Faith and Values Coalition, and a university, and a national celebrity. For a number of years, he pulled back from political involvement and televangelism and focused on preaching the gospel and Liberty University. The centerpiece of Falwell's television ministry was the national weekly broadcasts of his Sunday morning services from Thomas Road Baptist Church.

"The Old-Time Gospel Hour," as it was called, lived up to its name—lots of prayers and singing, Scripture reading, and preaching from a fundamentalist perspective. Unlike many televangelists, Falwell was no charismatic or advo-cate of the health and wealth gospel. In addition to the gospel, he also de-nounced America's national sins—abortion, homosexuality, feminism, sex, and the removal of prayer from the schools. For a period of several years, Falwell's messages had a distinctively political flavor. His services are still highly nationalistic and millennarian. He regards America as the greatest nation on the earth. In these last days before the return of Christ, however, America must be rescued from the "godless secular humanists." Christians must stand with the nation's founders and bring America back to its traditional morals and values.[91]

Falwell's successful television ministry prompted others to use television as a vehicle to bring America back to God. James Robison of Fort Worth echoed many of Falwell's themes, especially those representative of cultural fundamentalism. He lacked, however, Falwell's resources and is best known in the Southwest, where most of his programs have been broadcast. Robison did reach a national audience in a television special, which presented the Christian Right's indictment of America's moral decay. In this program and elsewhere, he launched a standard attack on the nation's sins—abortion, gay rights, the ERA, banning religion in the public schools, and America's military decline. In addition to his crusades and television ministry, Robison actively pushed the agenda of the Christian Right in other formats. In particular, he believed that it was a sin for Christians to be indifferent toward the political issues of the day.[92]

The wildest pulpit thumper of them all was Jimmy Swaggert. Unlike Falwell and Robison, Swaggert was an old-fashioned Pentecostal rather than a fundamentalist and he did not push a political agenda. Swaggert's television programs are edited versions of prerecorded church services or revival meetings. These programs borrow little from commercial television and represent an unadulterated Pentecostal worship service, "complete with speaking in tongues, dancing in the Spirit, shouting, gospel singing, and hell-fire-and-damnation preaching."[93]

In total contrast to Schuller and Kennedy who preached in academic garbs, Swaggert pranced back and forth across the stage waving his arms frantically and perspiring profusely. His animated messages mirrored his physical actions. Using confrontational rhetoric, he condemned the secular world in no uncertain terms. His fiery attacks called down God's judgment on many areas of society—the news media, the entertainment industry, the federal government, the judicial system, educational institutions, and more. In Swaggert, anti-intellectualism reached extreme heights. He condemned nearly anyone who did not speak plainly and directly and accused them of being secular humanists.[94]

Before his sexual scandals, Swaggert had a devoted television audience and he raked in more money than any other televangelist—a half a million dollars a day. His offices had their own zip code and his organization received more mail than any other address in Louisiana. Swaggert's empire consisted of a college, a Christian school, and a broadcasting network that according to his claims reached more than 100 countries and 500,000,000 people. Insisting that the end of the world was at hand, he launched his D-Day or Delay campaign for evangelizing the world before Christ's Second Coming.[95]

Christian Talk Shows

Broadcasting revival crusades and church services were not the only options for the televangelists. As cable television gained strength, some of them turned to the format of talk-shows. Three examples are Pat Robertson, Jim Bakker, and Paul Crouch. Televangelists such as Roberts, Swaggert, and Falwell are descendents of the revivalists. Not so with Robertson, Bakker, and Crouch. They have taken their format from television, not from the church or revival meetings. As Robertson told an interviewer, "The biggest mistake that pastors make is to superimpose their 'thing' on the media. They should discover what the media are doing and then adapt to the media format." [96]

This talk-show approach combined the revivalist sentiment with the folksy variety and talk show formats. Drawing from Arthur Godfrey's radio programs and Johnny Carson's "Tonight Show," Robertson fashioned his television ministry and others followed in his wake. His talk show, the "700 Club," began in 1963 from scratch. In order to finance his monthly budget, he asked 700 people to pledge $10.00 a month. The "700 club" was born. Within two years came the Christian Broadcasting Network (CBN)—a strong cable network and production studio. By the late 1970s, Robertson had established a full graduate university focusing on communications.[97] In describing how all of this began, he stated, "We simply took a format that had worked on commercial networks and applied it to CBN. It was a proven format that had reached millions of Americans."[98]

If a viewer did not know what the "700 Club" was about, they would think that they had turned to a news and entertainment program on secular television. Following the magazine-show format, the program begins with the host (Pat Robertson) giving a news preview. Subjects include current social issues, domestic politics, and international events. The program then moves to human-interest stories, guest interviews, and discussions by the host and guests regarding current or practical subjects. Subjects include advice on financial matters, marital relations, child rearing, and more. The background music is often light rock and resembles what is heard on commercial or public television. The entire program is professionally done, appealing, and resembles secular television.[99]

The "700 Club" may be an attractive and captivating program, but what is Christian about it? What are its evangelical distinctives? The "700 Club" does not resemble a televised traditional church service or revival meeting. "There is no gospel singing or congregational singing. There is no sermon. (There is no pulpit.) There is no shouting. There is no altar call."[100] In particular, Robertson's Pentecostal background does not come through in his program as it does with other Pentecostal televangelists. A Pentecostal flavor does become more apparent in the prayers for healing and in the phone-in spiritual counseling centers.

Conservative Protestant religion, however, is present in the content of the program. The issues discussed are of particular interest to evangelical Christians—abortion, separation of church and state, evolution, judicial decisions impacting religion, sex and violence on television, Israel, the Middle East, and much more. Conservative Christianity is also obvious in the perspective given to these issues. While guests with opposing opinions are invited to the program, the backdrop to all issues is a conservative Protestant worldview. In such a format, evangelical Christianity comes across as tasteful, informed, intelligent, practical, up-beat, and respectful of other opinions.[101] Worlds separate this program from the pulpit thumping and world-rejecting approach adopted by Jimmy Swaggert.

Jim and Tammy Bakker also departed from the standard church and revivalist format for religious broadcasts. Bakker began his television ministry on Robertson's "700 Club." From there the Bakkers went to California and helped start the Trinity Broadcasting Network (TBN). They eventually moved to Charlotte, North Carolina, and in 1974 developed their own television ministry, the PTL (Praise the Lord) Club. When financial and sexual scandals brought the PTL Club to an end in 1987, the Bakkers began another short-lived ministry, "The Jim and Tammy Show." Out of the PTL Club, the Bakkers built an impressive empire including a television ministry and Heritage USA, a 2,300-acre evangelical theme park. This Christian Disneyland provided a sanctified vacation area for the devout. It had hotels, time-share condominiums, shops, pools, rides for children, a water park, an amphitheater, and a conference center.[102]

As far as a television format, the PTL Club must be regarded as a cross between a talk show and a soap opera. The program was broadcast from a large TV studio and opened with popular music played by a live stage band, which included snappy drums and trumpets. The Bakkers were smartly dressed and spoke in a friendly informal manner. The broadcast captivated people with its blend of preaching, storytelling, and folksy Christian talk show.[103] What made the PTL such a success were the Bakkers themselves. They could put on an incredible show—complete with human drama and heart-wrenching emotions all poured out within a spiritual framework. "The truth was that the Bakkers were enormously gifted television performers who turned the program into a real-life soap opera about their own lives and the life of the ministry itself," notes Quentin Schultze.[104]

The theme of the PTL Club's broadcasts pitted the Bakkers and their followers in a cosmic struggle against conspiratorial forces. Sinister powers led by the secular media were determined to destroy the PTL Club. The show frequently mentioned the tribulations faced by the Bakkers and their followers—illnesses, financial burdens, domestic problems, the loss of jobs, and mistreatment by the secular community. In the face of such trials, the Bakkers urged their followers to stand up for themselves, band together, pray, and love one another. The Bakkers prayed for emotional, physical, and spiritual healing for their followers. These prayers often took place over the phone and Bakker, indeed, became "Pastor Jim" to millions of his followers. Tammy was not to be left out of the show. While Jim prayed, she provided the tears. She had a remarkable talent for crying at will and over nearly any subject. Because of her heavy mascara, her tears created dark streams as they flowed down her cheeks. Jim and Tammy's emotional closeness with their viewers provided perhaps the major drawing card for the PTL Club.[105]

The 1987 Scandals

The scandals of 1987 severely tarnished the public image of the televangelists. They became the butt of jokes and sensational news coverage. Money, sex, and religion have always provided a volatile mixture for the news media and fiction writers. Sinclair Lewis's *Elmer Gantry* (1927) told the story of a lecherous minister and a seductive prophetess and has since provided the stereotype for clerical misconduct. John Updike's *A Month of Sundays* (1975) introduces us to a sexually promiscuous minister who pursues his female parishioners. Truth, however, can be stranger than fiction. Enter Jim Bakker and Jimmy Swaggert. Even fiction writers would have a hard time topping their stories.[106]

Scandals are not new or representative of evangelists and religious broadcasting, however. For example Aimee Semple McPherson, who had been previous divorced, disappeared in 1926 for several weeks—allegedly with a male friend. Also, evangelists like Billy Graham have been above the fray. He and others have neither engaged in sexual affairs nor lavish living. The financial issue, nevertheless, continues to dog those in the electronic church. While constantly begging for donations, a number of them have lived extravagantly. To combat this problem, the National Religious Broadcasting association (NRB) devised new ethical guidelines for the electronic church. Still, compliance is voluntary and cannot be enforced by either the NRB or the government. And it has not curtailed financial irregularities. As late as 2004, for example, *Christianity Today* noted the lavish lifestyles of televangelist Joyce Meyer, Trinity Broadcasting Network president Paul Crouch, and Hank Hanegraaff, host of the "Bible Answer Man"—a nationally syndicated daily radio program.[107]

The evangelical scandals of 1987 have been hashed over by the media and have become a part of the saga of modern televangelism. So only a brief survey will be given here. While his improprieties are pale in comparison with those of Bakker and Swaggert, Oral Roberts's behavior is an aspect of the evangelical scandals of 1987. In building Oral Roberts University, he added graduate programs, including a medical school, and a controversial hospital. (Tulsa did not need another hospital, but Jesus had told Roberts in a dream to build it.) This growing empire—especially the medical school and hospital—cost huge sums of money, and in desperation Roberts pulled out all of the stops. On his television show of January 1987, he declared that if he did not receive $8 million by March, God was going to "call him home"—that is, take his life. (In sarcasm, some believed that "home" meant one of his luxurious homes.)[108]

Roberts went into isolation in the universities' prayer tower. Here he prayed and fasted while awaiting the financial outcome. The crisis tactics worked and $9.1 million came in. Roberts' earthly life was spared. But that was not enough— he thanked his donors and then declared that this amount of money would have to be raised each year until the return of Christ. (The medical school was sold off before Christ returned, thus diminishing the problem.) The media criticized Roberts, regarding his actions as a deplorable gimmick for raising money. Yet, as one writer acknowledged, they worked. Roberts had "given new meaning to the word *deadline*." His contribution to financial ploys was to turn "the threat against himself." But this strategy could only work once.[109]

The PTL scandal captivated the nation in 1987. The major news shows including "Good Morning America," "Nightline," and the evening news all featured this real-life soap opera. This sex, money, and religious scandal caused their ratings to soar. The most imaginative scriptwriter would have had a hard time duplicating this drama. Even in the best of times, Jim and Tammy Bakker invited ridicule. He is small in stature, uneducated, insecure, but folksy and charismatic. Tammy is one of a kind—so emotional that she could cry at the drop of a hat and she wore so much makeup that it could be pealed off.

Building the PTL ministry and Heritage USA cost great sums of money. Donations poured into the PTL Club, but so did the bills. The Bakkers' lavish lifestyle added to the financial burden. They were paid $1.6 million in salaries the year before the PTL Club filed for bankruptcy. They owned six luxury dwellings with gold-plated bathroom fixtures, houseboats, a Rolls Royce, and a Mercedes-Benz. And Tammy had gargantuan spending habits, including a wardrobe worthy of Imelda Marcos and a famous air-conditioned doghouse. Convinced that the Bakkers were defrauding their donors and investors to pay for their extravagance, two journalists began to investigate the finances of the PTL Club. News stories—interpreted by the Bakkers as demonic conspiracies—began to circulate throughout the nation. If these financial irregularities were not enough, two other embarrassing disclosures emerged. It became known that Tammy had been admitted to the Betty Ford clinic for drug addiction. Worse than that, several years earlier Jim had had a sexual affair with Jessica Hahn, a nineteen-year-old secretary, and had paid hush money to keep it quite.[110]

Adding to an already sordid situation, two other evangelists entered the drama. Bakker asked Falwell to intervene and save the PTL Club. Despite disagreeing with Bakker's Pentecostalism and health and wealth gospel, Falwell believed that the PTL Club merited saving. Bakker later accused Falwell of stealing his ministry. Heightening the drama, a war of words then proceeded between Falwell and the Bakkers. This spectacle enthralled the nation.[111]

And more was to come. Jimmy Swaggert jumped into the fray, insisting that Bakker's sexual affair had not been an isolated event. Other PTL clergy also had sex with Hahn, he claimed. Allegations surfaced that Bakker had also visited prostitutes and had homosexual encounters. In fact, in a sworn statement, one former aid at PTL claimed that "the Reverend Bakker, in the nude, at PTL, seduced him." While this purported seduction was never consummated, Tammy defended her man by insisting that "He's not homosexual, or is he bisexual."[112]

Loyal PTL viewers continued to donate to Bakker's ministry. But their efforts were not enough. Three months after Falwell's intervention, the PTL Club went into bankruptcy. Ever resilient, the Bakkers rebounded and began a new program, called "The Jim and Tammy Show."[113] Legal troubles cut these efforts short. The federal government tried Jim for conspiracy and fraud. At his conviction, dramatic events again captured the media's attention. Facing prison time, Bakker emotionally came apart: "Sobbing, bent and broken, Bakker was led by federal officers from the courtroom to a car, where he again curled in a fetal position in the backseat..."[114] He was sentenced to forty-five years in prison but only served six.

If the average person had squandered vast sums of money in luxurious living and had immoral sexual encounters, conservative Pentecostals would disown him. Right to the bitter end, however, the Bakkers had their loyal supporters. Why? In part, people were vicariously living their lives through the Bakkers. Pentecostals had been rising socially and they desired more of the world's pleasures. The Bakkers' version of the health and wealth gospel affirmed this desire: "God wants you to be rich and enjoy the pleasures you thought were forbidden." As the Bakkers described the ups and downs of their lives with great emotion, people could empathize with their struggles. "Supporters identify with the televangelists as much for their personalities as their evangelism," says Schultze. "And Bakker, more than any other of the televangelists—way, way, more—created a program in which the viewers are vicarious participants in his family, its trials and triumphs."[115]

Jesus set some guidelines for judging others: "Why do you look at the speck of sawdust in your brother's eye and pay no attention to the plank in your own eye?... You hypocrite, first take the plank out of your own eye, and then you will see clearly to remove the speck from your brothers eye" (Luke 6:41, 42). One of the televangelists—Jimmy Swaggert—apparently did not heed this advice. Rather than follow Christ's admonition, Swaggert gave life to the Elmer Gantry stereotype.

Swaggert's dynamic preaching and confrontational style attracted millions of viewers who regarded him as the voice of God. He attacked sinful living and the secular culture in a no-holds-barred-fashion, occasionally interrupting his tirades with a burst of speaking in tongues. (The language of the Holy Spirit.) He used the most strident language to attack what he regarded as immoral. Speaking of the entertainment business, he said "(We are) sick of long-haired, smelly, stinky, beer-guzzling, coke-snorting, marijuana-smoking freaks." He called homosexuality "the worst sin in the world" and said that a gay person should be described as a pervert, queer, or faggot. Such harsh language would disturb many people, but his audience often burst into a round of applause.[116]

But Swaggert's hands were not clean. He was photographed with a prostitute going into a motel and his empire came crashing down. As a member of The Assemblies of God, he fell under their authority. Their normal course of action was to suspend erring clergy for a year. The collapse of Swaggert's ministry, however, would cost people their jobs and have financial implications. So they reduced his punishment to three months. Swaggert still would not go away without a fight. In a televised event, he went before his congregation—weeping, confessing his sin, and begging for their forgiveness.[117] Quentin Schultze calls Swaggert's confession "one of the most masterful TV programs of all time, perhaps even the single most effective televisual performance of any American evangelist."[118]

Swaggert succeeded in regaining his pulpit but since then his ministry and influence has been greatly diminished. His personal wealth, nevertheless, is still very great and he is grooming his son to be his successor. His anger toward homosexuality has also not abated. In a 2004 television sermon, he stated, "I've never seen a man in my life I wanted to marry. And I'm gonna be blunt and plain; if one ever looks at me like that, I'm gonna kill him and tell God he died." (Swaggart later apologized for this comment.)[119]

Electronic Church Theology

Does the electronic church have a theology? In any pure sense, the answer is no. Some people, indeed, would regard the terms *electronic church* and *theology* as an oxymoron. Not having a theology, however, is a key to the success of the electronic church. Or as Ben Armstrong approvingly says, "Relying on the everyday language of the work-day world rather than the language of theologians and Bible commentaries, Schuller (and most others as well) captures the interest of the viewer."[120]

In a disapproving way, William F. Fore contends that the televangelists have an "inherent bias toward gross, simplified linear messages which fit commercial needs."[121] Some individuals even contend that theology is an elitist discipline. If this is so, it runs counter to the ethos of the televangelists, who are populists and practical to the core. Simplicity is the key characteristic of the electronic church's belief system.[122]

While the electronic church may not have a formal theology, the televangelists repeatedly target certain religious themes. From their messages, Jeffrey Hadden and Charles Swann have distilled twelve elements. The Bible is the "central authority " for all areas of life and it is interpreted literally. Or as one bumper sticker declared, "God spoke it. The Bible declares it. I believe it." Two, they staunchly oppose evolution. Three, the televangelists adopt "a mechanical view of providence," viewing the hand of God in most activities. Four, they clearly distinguish between God's love and wrath, believing that God blesses the righteous and punishes the wrong doers.

Five, missions are given a high priority. The gospel must be proclaimed throughout the world before the return of Christ. Closely related is their "conversionist theology," which makes the new birth the criterion for being a Christian. Seven, many televangelists have a Pentecostal orientation and speak of being "Spirit-filled." Eight, an active satanology reinforces their Manichaean worldview. Satan is at work in the world and is the source of all evil and disagreements. Nine, nearly all televangelists embrace a premillennial eschatology, insisting that the Second Coming of Christ looms on the horizon.

Ten, their theological-political views were staunchly anti-communist (before communism collapsed) and are still pro-Israel—a position that coincides with their eschatology. Eleven, the televangelists embrace American nationalism, insisting that the nation has been chosen by God to perform his work in the world and fight the Antichrist. Finally, they proclaim moral absolutes that uphold their social views: family values, the male-dominated family, prayer in the schools and opposition to abortion, homosexual rights, and the ACLU.[123]

At Home in the Culture

American culture has powerfully influenced the electronic church as it has nearly all aspects of religion. Television, in turn, has had a tremendous impact on the nation's economic, social, cultural, and political trends. As a result, the electronic church more accurately reflects American culture than it does the Christian faith. One should regard it as more of an American phenomenon than a Christian development. As in many aspects of evangelicalism, it is difficult to tell just where the culture lets off and the faith begins. The electronic church can be legitimately criticized at many points. But an attack on televangelism is an assault on American culture itself.[124]

In what general ways does the electronic church mirror American culture? Americans love entertainment and dramatic presentations, which the televangelists provide. They also proclaim messages of affluence, individualism, and answers to felt needs. Like the rest of American society, the electronic church is market driven—it must give its viewers what they want to hear. Reflecting the impulses of the evangelical subculture, the televangelists are populists and pragmatists. Their message is simple and avoids complex ideas and is proclaimed in emotional tones. Television provides its viewers with an experience and evangelicals insist on a personal experience as central to the Christian faith.

America is an entertainment-driven culture, and in the late twentieth-century television became the primary vehicle for amusement. Thanks to television, Americans expect to be entertained in many areas of life, including the church. There is only a fine line between entertainment and worship. Instead of being an expression of adoration to God, contemporary worship has often become a form of entertainment and the electronic church has excelled in this. Televangelists are first and foremost entertainers. They package a church service in a dramatic way that captivates their audiences. They have figured out "how to dress the old-fashioned gospel in novel, entertaining clothing."[125]

A sense of the dramatic can captivate a congregation. Evangelicals have been employing drama as a means to present the gospel since the days of George Whitefield. Television, however, magnifies the drama inherent in Christianity and often sensationalizes the Christian life by hyperbole and excesses. The televangelists present the Christian faith in the most dramatic terms. A great cosmic battle is raging. In this conflict, Christians are aligned with the forces of God against Satan. The struggles of life do not have natural causes: they are caused by Satan. The liberals, secular humanists, Hollywood entertainers, media (except Fox News) and feminists are doing the work of Satan.[126]

Television has caused major problems for the local pastor. Entertainment programs present life in simple black and white terms. In doing so, television has enhanced its viewers' taste for entertainment, drama, and has reduced their ability to think about complex issues. To accommodate this trend, successful televangelists entertain and present their message in simple dramatic terms. The traditional seminary-trained pastor, who preaches a content-based sermon with notes, cannot compete with the televangelist. Such sermons are not as entertaining or dramatic, and they often raise complex issues. Television also elevates a sense of the dramatic by portraying evil as outside of us: the criminal, the gun-slinger, the drug dealer, the Indian, or the terrorist. The hero has no taint of evil. Thus, evangelicals often do not to see the "speck in their own eye." Rather, they tend to neglect spiritual discernment and embrace a "knee-jerk" morality. Moral or social wrongs are always in the enemies' camp, not in their own backyard.[127]

A closely related issue is the cult of the personality. Lacking strong religious traditions, Americans, especially evangelicals, have always been obsessed with celebrities. They are not primarily interested in issues and ideas, but in people and personalities. Radio and television have only accelerated this trend. The electronic church rests on this foundation. Without the celebrity status of the pastor or host, such churches would collapse. Conservative Protestants long for their own popes or gurus and the televangelists meet this need. They are the last word in nearly everything. They are the interpreter of God's Word, whether it be Scripture or God speaking directly to them. Or, as Quentin Schultze puts its, "The televangelist is presumed to be like God, communicating through space directly to millions of individuals and personalities. He is not only a person, but the special person that represents God to his people."[128]

Evangelical Christianity has been a primary recruiting ground for aberrant or fringe religious groups, often labeled as cults. Several factors account for this development, but one reason is that evangelicals are caught up with the "cult of the personality" and defer to authoritarian leaders who have a "new word of truth." This tendency is not limited to some groups on the fringes of evangelicalism. Rather, it can be detected close to the center of evangelicalism—in the mega and electronic churches, especially those that embrace the health and wealth gospel. These churches are often dominated by charismatic personalities, who have created personal kingdoms in which the king is beyond discipline.[129]

This obsession with personalities has led to another problem for the electronic church—succession of leadership. The electronic church's existence rests on the shoulders of one charismatic leader. It does not have strong denominational or institutional roots. What happens when the leader is gone or discredited? Sometimes the ministry dissolves. A number of contemporary televangelists have attempted to deal with this problem by grooming their sons as their successors. Roberts, Schuller, Robertson, Falwell, Swaggert, and Graham have made it a family affair. Their sons and even grandsons have either replaced them or are waiting in the wings.[130]

In yet other ways, celebrity status is important. Throughout history, Christians have been enthralled by testimonies of successful people. Television has increased this fascination. Evangelicals love to hear testimonies. The electronic church meets this need by focusing on the testimonies of unique or famous people. Quite often, such testimonies tend to dwell on the material or physical blessings that God has bestowed or even their own accomplishments. The televangelists and megachurch leaders gain celebrity status in another way—quantity. The televangelist points to the stack of letters, donations, or TV ratings. The super church pastor looks to the size of his church. In doing this, both churches are more American than they are Christian.[131]

The cult of the personality rests on another evangelical characteristic—biblical illiteracy. Such ignorance can be traced back to the colonial days, but the electronic church has given it a new boast. In the old democratic market-driven spirit, the nineteenth-century revivalists gave their listeners what they wanted to hear—the simple gospel in a very popular style. This type of preaching has reduced what evangelicals know about the Bible. Despite people parading into churches with Bibles, twenty-first-century evangelicals have only a shallow understanding of Scripture. And the electronic church has furthered this ignorance. From the televangelists, one usually hears the simple gospel, a shallow pop faith, or sermons that rant and rave about secular society. This biblical ignorance is one of the reasons evangelicals tend to donate millions of dollars to questionable religious enterprises—especially programs advocating the health and wealth gospel.[132]

Related to biblical illiteracy is the educational background of the televangelists. The vast majority of them have a limited education—Bible school or less. Some even regard a seminary education as a disadvantage: it dulls the voice of the Holy Spirit and introduces one to complex and unnecessary ideas. This lack of respect for higher education, of course, squares with evangelicalism's populist and pragmatic character. Early in the nineteenth century, the educated elite ceased to direct the thinking of popular evangelicalism. And they still do not. On a popular level, the modern evangelical mind is largely being shaped by uneducated preachers or writers.

Also connected with personality types is the southern character of the televangelists. Most of the popular televangelists either come from the South or have a southern orientation: Roberts, Robertson, Falwell, Stanley, Swaggert, Robison, Copeland, Humbard, and Graham. But Schuller and Bakker do not come from the South. Northern churches tend to be more middle-class, professional, and rational. Their sermons often resemble academic lectures. Not so with the southern evangelicals who were reared on revivalism. Reflecting the oral tradition of the South, their sermons tended to be simple, spontaneous, emotional and resembled story telling. Such sermons engage a television audience and have become the norm with televangelists. In turn, the electronic church has influenced preaching styles in all areas of the country, including the local church.[133]

Closely related to this southern style of preaching is the Pentecostal orientation of the televangelists. Even more than southern preachers, Pentecostals can whip up an audience into an emotional frenzy. Such fervent expressions of feeling connect well with television's emphasis on the experiential, not the rational. With the rise of cable television, the dominance of Pentecostals in the electronic church has become even more pronounced.

Perhaps the closest relationship between the electronic church and American culture rests in their market orientation. In America's free market, religion must compete with many cultural attractions or it will not survive. Of any religious group, evangelicals have evidenced a competitive and entrepreneurial spirit. Throughout history, they have constantly adapted their methods of presenting the gospel to the surrounding culture and changing circumstances. The old-fashioned gospel has been shaped to the tastes of its audience. Consequently, this Americanized gospel reflects the values of the popular culture and not just the historic faith.[134]

The electronic church has carried these entrepreneurial trends even further. Television air time is very expensive. So the televangelists must not just preach the gospel, they must convince viewers that their ministry deserves financial support. Such a situation has many implications. The televangelists are under pressure to increase their audience, ratings, and contributions. This prompts them to embrace an old American marketing concept, that is, to adjust their message to suit their audience. They cannot preach "what people ought to hear, but must preach what people desire to hear."[135]

In American society, only a fine line separates the preacher from a salesman (or a politician for that matter). And in fund raising the televangelists often step over this line and become hucksters. In persuading their viewers to finance their ministry, they issue threats and claims. They say that their ministry will go off the air if money does not come in. Or, it is God's will that you give and he will bless you if you do. The televangelists may exaggerate the influence of their ministry and insist that any opposition comes from Satan.[136]

The electronic church's marketing strategies can also be seen in its embrace of technology. Throughout their history Americans, including evangelicals, have been fascinated with technology. Evangelicals have always used the most advanced technology to promote the gospel and the televangelists are no exception to this trend. In its television productions and presentations, the electronic church is very sophisticated, often on the cutting edge of technological innovations. The old stereotype of a backward people does not hold up in most respects, especially in the use of technology. In fundraising and promoting its product, the electric church is also quite advanced. On the air, televangelists offer "specials" as do businesses. If you make a donation of a certain amount, you will receive some object—a cup, a memento, a book, a tape, jewelry, and more. With the advent of computer-driven direct-mail solicitations, the televangelists jumped on board. Like a business, they mass mail to millions of viewers, soliciting money or publicizing their ministry.[137]

What's the Impact?

What impact is the electronic church having on the local church? Is it drawing people and money away from local congregations? The answer to both of these questions is generally no. The faithful still attend and support the local church. Are large numbers of people being converted to Christianity through the programs of the electronic church? No! Studies show that few people are converted because of the ministry of the electronic church. The major impact of the electronic church is subtle but profound. It is changing the way evangelicals are doing church. [138]

Most important, because the electronic church is market driven it caters to popular expectations. It is entertainment and experience driven. In moving in this direction, it forces the local church to compete or decline. Compared to the electronic church or megachurch, traditional services are boring and not "spirit-filled." Denominational leaders and pastors thus change the way church life is practiced. They also strive to accommodate popular tastes in music, sermons, and church activities. Worship becomes a form of entertainment and popular music replaces traditional songs. Sermons are watered down; charismatic preaching replaces biblical exposition. Experience and feelings become more important than serious thinking.[139]

The electronic church is a private religion. You do not have to meet people; you turn the dial to the right station. On the contrary, the New Testament knows of only one kind of Christianity—a congregational faith. The electronic church will not become a denomination, largely because it is so independent. Still, as described by Robert Wuthnow, the electronic church is furthering the restructuring of American religion. Religion is moving away from the denominational structure to more decentralized forms—the parachurch, nondenominational churches, loose federations, and private forms of the faith. And the electronic church should be seen as a factor in this transition.[140]

The Emergent Church

The confluence of democracy, capitalism, individualism, and religious freedom has produced a dynamic faith in America. But it is a faith that is at one with the culture. Few religious bodies—Christian or otherwise—have been able to resist the powerful tug of American popular culture. In America, the evangelical church has not clashed with the modern world, except for its resistance to certain moral issues. Rather, Christianity has become so enmeshed with society that it is difficult to distinguish between the faith and culture.

Alan Wolfe comments on this situation. "To people of faith, I say this: You have shaped American culture far too much to insist that you remain countercultural. You do not want to admit the extent to which your religion has accommodated itself to modern life in the United States for fear that this would somehow detract from your piety." Christians have indeed yielded to the individualism and occasionally to the narcissism of American life.[141] As a result, Christians—especially evangelicals—have baptized secular culture. This enables them to retain their piety while still enjoying the fruits of modern society. And no religious type has been more mainstream than the mega and electronic churches.

To be truly countercultural, a church cannot condemn certain moral practices while accommodating the culture in most other respects. The notion of the church running against cultural trends nearly vanished in the late twentieth century. The megachurches, in fact, built their entire strategy for growth around the principle of being culturally sensitive. In the twenty-first century, however, one type of church is attempting to be more countercultural. This church goes by several names, but most often is called the emergent church.

While acknowledging that conservative Protestants have resisted some current moral trends, most have largely yielded to the surrounding culture. This generalization especially fits the pragmatic megachurches. In the way they do church, evangelical congregations throughout the nation have been greatly influenced by the mega and electronic churches. Such churches are pragmatic and gear their services to cultural trends and market forces. The emergent church can be seen as an alternative to this pragmatic way of doing church.[142]

The emergent church is difficult to describe. Being rather recent and having no major institutional centers or rigid boundaries, it is currently taking shape. In nearly every aspect of ministry—preaching, worship, leadership, and prayer—the emergent church is improvisational and eclectic. Rob Bell, the pastor of a large emergent church, sees it as culturally relevant but resisting trends within both liberalism and evangelicalism. Rather, it reflects shades of postmodernism. "The Bible is still in the center for us," he says, "But it's a different kind of center. We want to embrace mystery, rather than conquer it." The emergent church is "rediscovering Christianity as an Eastern religion, as a way of life." While the evangelicals tend to view Christianity in black and white terms, liberals see shades of gray. The emergent church seeks a faith colorful enough to embrace mystery and doubt and they are willing to abandon some of the issues that evangelicals have often defended.[143]

Brian McLaren is often regarded as the de facto spiritual leader for the emerging church. In his influential book, *A New Kind of Christian* (2001), he contends that we are entering an ill-defined postmodern world where objectivity, control, and analysis are less important. Rather, postmodern values such as mystery and wonder—which are embraced by the emergent church—carry more weight. McLaren criticizes the old evangelical model of ministry. It is about getting saved and improving yourself. If these needs are met, you serve the church and if anything is left over, the church can serve the world. McLaren contends that the church is not about meeting personal needs. Rather, church is about joining God's people who have a mission to serve the world. McLaren even challenges the evangelical notion of getting saved. To most it means accepting Jesus as your personal savior or walking down an aisle. McLaren asserts that the emergent church must concentrate on making disciples— "on training disciples who practice, rather than just believe, the faith."[144]

Robert Webber speaks very favorably of the emergent church. In *The Younger Evangelicals* (2002), he describes it by comparing it to the super or pragmatic churches. In fact, the emergent church developed as a reaction against the Wal-Mart type churches. Megachurches minimize theology and regard Christianity as a form of therapy intended to meet felt needs. The emergent church sees Christianity as a community of faith and emphasizes the beliefs of the Reformation and early church.[145]

Contrary to the megachurch, which is ahistorical and focuses on the present, the emergent church has great respect for the ancient or pre-Constantinian church. The pragmatic approach to Christianity views faith as largely experiential and that the church should be growth driven and culturally sensitive. Conversely, the emergent church places more emphasis on communal relationships and is somewhat countercultural. The megachurch is usually found in the suburbs and is driven by market principles designed to attract people of a similar background. Size is not the goal of the emergent church. It is often located in the inner city and has a culturally diverse congregation.[146]

Between the two types of churches, leadership styles differ significantly. The pastor of a super church is a CEO with charismatic qualities. In the emergent church, there is an emphasis on team leadership and the priesthood of the believer. Megachurch services are geared for the unchurched, not believers. Thus, evangelism, not worship, is the major focus. On the contrary, the emergent church is primarily for believers and activities center on worship, spiritual growth, and discipleship. While the megachurches are more in tune with the felt needs of the baby boomers, generation Xers are more at home in the emergent church.[147]

The type of worship is a controversial subject in many evangelical churches. In the pragmatic church, the approach is contemporary and designed to entertain. The emergent church uses both traditional and contemporary forms of music, but emphasizes majesty and awe in worship. Rather than have a loving, intimate relationship with God as do people in the pragmatic church, the emergent church prefers to worship a transcendent, unknowable God. The modern super church does not want to appear as a church, so it removes traditional Christian symbols from the meeting place. It prefers the church to look like a theater or gym. Conversely, the emergent church emphasizes God's grandeur in worship and visibly displays signs of the faith.[148]

The emergent church serves as an alternative to the traditional and megachurches. It is doubtful, however, whether it will ever have the same impact as have the super or electronic churches. Why? The emergent church does not connect with American culture as do these two churches. And being at one with the culture is a key to numerical success. Unlike the super and electronic churches, the emergent church places less emphasis on key American characteristics: individualism, populism, pragmatism, affluence, size, market orientation, and self-fulfillment. A smaller number of people, nevertheless, will be attracted to this emerging movement because it is swimming against the stream of American culture.

Notes

1. Quoted from Charles Truehart, "The Next Church," *Atlantic Monthly* (August 1996): 37.
2. Trueheart, "The Next Church," Richard N. Ostling, "Superchurches and How They Grew," *Time* (5 August 1991): 62, 63. Some sources say the megachurches represent less than one percent of the church going population. See "Close-knit Megachurches," *Christian Century* (12-19 September 2001): 11; "Good Morning America," ABC (13 December 2004).
3. Kimon Howland Sargeant, *Seeker Churches: Promoting Traditional Religion in a Nontraditional Way* (New Brunswick, NJ: Rutgers University Press, 2000), 18; Charles Colson, "Welcome to McChurch," *Christianity Today* 23 (November 1992): 28-32.
4. Kenneth L. Woodward, " A Time to Seek," *Newsweek* (17 December 1990): 53 (quote).

5. Os Guiness, *Dining with the Devil: The Megachurch Movement Flirts with Modernity* (Grand Rapids: Baker Books, 1993), 27, 28; Sargeant, *Seeker Churches*, 4, 54, 55; Patrick Allitt, *Religion in America since 1945: A History* (New York: Columbia University Press, 2003), 227-30; Thomas Spence, "A Rock 'N' Roll Worship Service," *Regeneration Quarterly* http://www.theimarketplace.com/spence/index.cfm?fusiation=section 18. (12/12/02).

6. Trueheart, "The Next Church," 39; Rebecca Prewett, "Seeker-Sensitive Churches," http://www.fix.net/rprewelt/seeker.html. (12/12/02).

7. Donald E. Miller, *Reinventing American Protestantism: Christianity in the New Millennium* (Berkeley: University of California Press, 1997), 11; Sargeant, *Seeker Churches*, 33; Stephen Prothero, *American Jesus: How the Son of God Became a National Icon* (New York: Farrar, Straus, and Groux, 2003), 92-101; Richard N. Ostling, "The Church Search," *Time* (5 April 1993): 44-48; Mark Wingfield, "Pastor Defends 'Seeker' Churches," *Biblical Recorder* http://www.biblicalrecorder.org/news/7-98/pastor.html 30 July 1998. (7/30/98).

8. See David Wells, *No Place for Truth. Or Whatever Happened to Evangelical Theology* (Grand Rapids: Eerdmans, 1993); Os Guiness, *Fit Bodies Fat Minds: Why Evangelicals Don't Think and What To Do About It* (Grand Rapids: Baker Books, 1994); Mark A. Noll, *The Scandal of the Evangelical Mind* (Grand Rapids: Eerdmans, 1994); Mark Noll, Cornelius Plantinga, Jr., and David Wells, "Evangelical Theology Today," *Theology Today* 51, 4 (January 1995): 503; Franklin B. Krohn, "The Sixty-Minute Commercial: Marketing Salvation," *The Humanist* (November-December 1980): 26-30; Peter Jennings, "In the Name of God," ABC News Special (16 March 1995).

9. Quoted in Douglas D. Webster, *Selling Jesus: What's Wrong with Marketing the Church* (Downers Grove, IL: InterVarsity Press, 1992), 9.

10. Wade Clark Roof, *Spiritual Marketplace: Baby Boomers and the Remaking of American Religion* (Princeton, NJ: Princeton University Press, 1999), 87 (quote). See also Roger Finke, "Religious Deregulation: Origins and Consequences," *Journal of Church and State* 32, 3 (summer 1990): 609-26; Roger Finke and Laurence R. Iannaccone, "Supply-Side Explanations for Religious Change," *Annals of the American Academy of Political And Social Science* 527 (May 1993): 27-39.

11. Miller, *Reinventing American Protestantism*, 20-22.

12. Roof, *Spiritual Marketplace*, 94, 110; Sargeant, *Seeker Churches*, 11. For a general description of the consumer culture, see Gary Cross, *An All-Consuming Century: Why Commercialism Won in Modern America* (New York: Columbia University Press, 2000); Vincent J. Miller, *Consuming Religion: Christian Faith and Practice in a Consumer Culture* (New York: Continuum, 2003).

13. Razell Frankl, *Televangelism: The Marketing of Popular Religion* (Carbondale: Southern Illinois University Press, 1987), 66, 67; Roof, *Spiritual Marketplace*, 89, 90.

14. See Robert Wuthnow, *The Restructuring of American Religion* (Princeton, NJ: Princeton University Press, 1988), 71-99.

15. Louis E. Boone and David L. Kurtz, *Contemporary Marketing,* 7th ed. (Fort Worth: Dryden Press, 1992), 6 (quote). For a similar statement, see John M. Rigby, "Church Marketing and other Oxymorons," *John Cooper Online* http://www.jardoncopper.com/resources/churchmarketing.html. (12/12/02).

16. Philip D. Kenneson and James L. Street, *Selling Out the Church: The Dangers of Church Marketing* (Nashville: Abingdon Press, 1997), 38, 39; Robert Wuthnow, *After Heaven: Spirituality in America Since the 1950s* (Berkeley: University of California Press, 1998), 66; Ben Primer, *Protestants and American Business Methods* (N.P. Umi Research Press, 1979), 93-119.

17. Kenneson and Street, *Selling Out the Church*, 38-40; Webster, *Selling Jesus*, 116; Lynne Drury Lerych, "Meeting the Bottom Line in the College Biz," *Newsweek* (9 April 2001): 12.

18. Wade Clark Roof, *A Generation of Seekers* (San Francisco: HarperSanFrancisco, 1993), 68; Franklin B. Krohn, "The Sixty-Minute Commercial: Marketing Salvation," *The Humanist* (November/December 1980): 26-30.

19. R. Laurence Moore, *Selling God: American Religion in the Marketplace of Culture* (New York: Oxford University Press, 1994), 119; Christian Smith, *American Evangelicalism: Embattled and Thriving* (Chicago: University of Chicago Press, 1998), 73. See Roger Finke and Rodney Stark, *The Churching of America 1776-1990: Winners and Losers in Our Religious Economy* (New Brunswick, NJ: Rutgers University Press, 1992).

20. Bruce Shelley and Marshall Shelley, *Consumer Church: Can Evangelicals Win the World Without Losing Their Souls?* (Downers Grove, IL: InterVarsity Press, 1992), 98 (quote). See also Richard Mouw, "Ending the Cold War Between Theologians and Laypeople," *Christianity Today* 18 (July 1994): 27.

21. John Wilson, "Not Just Another Megachurch," *Christianity Today* 4 (December 2000): 64.

22. See Guinness, *Dining with the Devil*, 52, 53; Os Guinness, "Sounding Out the Idols of Church Growth," in *No God But God*, ed. Os Guiness and John Seel (Chicago: Moody Press, 1992), 164, 165.

23. George Barna, *Marketing the Church: What They Never Taught You About Church Growth* (Colorado Springs, CO: NavPress, 1988), 37 (quote); Guinness, *Dining with the Devil*, 53; David F. Wells, "The D-Min-ization of the Ministry," in *No God But God*, 175-202.

24. George Barna, *The Second Coming of the Church* (Nashville: Word Publishing, 1998), 113.

25. Sargeant, *Seeker Churches*, 149 (quotes); "Teaching Churches," (Tyler, TX: Leadership Network, 1990), 8, 22.

26. Lyle Shaller, "Megachurch!" *Christianity Today* 5 (March 1990): 23; "Close-knit Megachurches," 51.

27. *The Exchange,* Willow Creek Association (September 1993) (quote); Sargeant, *Seeker Churches*, 149; Shaller, "Megachurch," 23.

28. Shaller, "Megachurch," 22 (quote); Woodward, "A Time to Seek," 52, 53; Guinness, *Dining with the Devil*, 53.

29. Much of the above material comes from Schaller, "Megachurch!" 20, 21. See also "Megachurch Methods," *Christian Century* 14 (May 1997): 482, 483; David Goetz, "Suburban Spirituality, " *Christianity Today* (July 2003): 31-37.

30. Alan Wolfe, *The Transformation of American Religion* (New York: Free Press, 2003), 17.

31. See Edward Gilbreath, "Farther in and Deeper Down," *Christianity Today* 1 (April 2002): 52-56; Arthur W. Hunt, "Back to the Dark Ages: How Electronic Media Are Pulling Us Back to Barbarism," *Christian Research Journal* 24, 1 (2001): 26-31, 48, 49; John G. Stackhouse, Jr. *Evangelical Landscapes* (Grand Rapids: Baker Books, 2002), 92-101.

32. "Church Guarantees Express Service for Busy Believers," *Christianity Today* 10 (July 2000): 21; Woodward, "A Time to Seek," 54.

33. Wolfe, *Transformation of American Religion*, 204; Wilson, "Not Just Another Megachurch," 62-65; Verla Gillmor, "Community is Their Middle Name," *Christianity Today* 13 (November 2000): 48-55; Michael Maudlin and Edward Gilbreath, "Selling Out the House of God," *Christianity Today* 18 (July 1994): 20-25.

34. Clark, *Spiritual Marketplace*, 34,35.
35. George Gallup, Jr. and Timothy Jones, *The Next American Spirituality* (Colorado Springs: Victor, 2000), 48-54 (quotes on 49, 50); Roof, *A Generation of Seekers*, 27. For more on these trends, see Robert N. Bellah et al., *Habits of the Heart* (New York: Harper and Row, 1986).
36. Roof, *Spiritual Marketplace*, 9.
37. See James A. Herrick, *The Making of the New Spirituality: The Eclipse of the Western Religious Tradition* (Downers Grove, IL: InterVarsity Press, 2003); Catherine Albanese, "Religion and the American Experience: A Century After," *Church History* 57, 3 (1988): 337-51; Richard Kyle, *The New Age Movement in American Culture* (Lanham, MD: University Press of America, 1995); LaTonya Taylor, "The Church of O," *Christianity Today* 1 (April 2002): 38-45.
38. Martin E. Marty, "Where the Energies Go," *Annals of the American Academy of Political and Social Science* 527 (May 1993): 15 (quote); Roof, *Spiritual Marketplace*, 7.
39. Quotes from Colson, "Welcome to McChurch," 29,30.
40. Wolfe, *Transformation of American Religion*, 83.
41. Wuthnow, *After Heaven*, 67 (quote). See also Michael Scott Horton, *Made in America: The Shaping of Modern American Evangelicalism* (Grand Rapids: Baker Books, 1991), 73-89.
42. Gallup, *The Next American Spirituality*, 53 (quote); Wolfe, *Transformation of American Religion*, 80, 81.
43. Winthrop S. Hudson and John Corrigan, *Religion in America*, 6th ed. (Upper Saddle River, NJ: Prentice Hall, 1992), 295, 296; Michael S. Hamilton, "Willow Creek's Place in History," *Christianity Today* 13 (November 2000): 64; Peter W. Williams, *America's Religions: From Their Origins to the Twenty-First Century* (Urbana: University of Illinois Press, 2002), 261.
44. Hamilton, "Willow Creek's Place in History," 62, 63; Harold P. Shelly, "Paul Rader," in *Dictionary of Christianity in America*, ed. Daniel G. Reid et al. (Downers Grove, IL: InterVarsity, 1990), 970.
45. Hamilton, "Willow Creek's Place in History," 64 (quote). See Lately Thomas, *Storming Heaven* (New York: William Morrow, 1970); Edith Blumhofer, "Aimee Semple McPherson," in *Dictionary of Christianity in America*, 696, 697.
46. Hamilton, "Willow Creek's Place in History," 65 (quote); Blumhofer, "Aimee Semple McPherson," 696; "The Seeker Service," www.wileyeurope.com/cda/cover. (7/25/02).
47. Wilbert R. Shenk, "Church Growth Movement," in *Dictionary of Christianity in America*, 271.
48. Os Guinness, "Sounding Out the Idols of Church Growth," 152; Woodward, "A Time to Seek," 52, 53.
49. James D. Berkley, "Church Growth Comes of Age," *Leadership* (fall 1991): 108, 109; Donald A. McGavran, *How Churches Grow* (New York: Friendship Press, 1959); Donald A. McGavran, *Understanding Church Growth* (Grand Rapids: Eerdmans, 1980); John Sweetman, "Homogeneous Church versus Heterogeneous Church," http.//www.kawanabaptist.org.ou/Pastor-resoruces/John-Sweetman/homogenerous-vs-heter...; (12/12/02); John H. Armstrong, "The Mad Rush to Seeker Sensitive Worship," *Modern Reformation* http.://www.modernreformation.org/mr95/janfeb/mr950/madrush.html. (12/12/02).
50. Berkley, "Church Growth Comes of Age," 108-10; Guinness, "No God But God," 152; John H. Armstrong, "The Contemporary Church," *The Highway* http://www.thehighway.com/articlesept97.html. (12/12/02).

51. See Barna, *Marketing the Church;* George Barna, *The Frog in the Kettle* (Ventura, CA: Regal Books, 1990); Barna, *The Second Coming of the Church;* George Barna, *What Americans Believe* (Ventura, CA: Regal Books, 1991); George Barna, *The Barna Report* (Ventura, CA: Regal Books, 1992); George Barna, *Invisible Generation: Baby Busters* (Glendale, CA: Barna Research Group, 1992); George Barna and William Paul McKay, *Vital Signs* (Weschester, IL: Crossway Books, 1984).
52. Quote from Barna, *Marketing the Church*, 7, 8; Tim Stafford, "The Third Coming of George Barna," *Christianity Today* 5 (August 2002): 33-38.
53. Edward Gilbreath, "The New Capital of Evangelicalism," *Christianity Today* 21 (May 2002): 38-40 (quotes). See Richard Wightman Fox, *Jesus in America: A History* (San Francisco: HarperSanFrancisco, 2004), 389-94.
54. *Seeker Churches*, 31, 95, 101, 102, 194; Bob De Waay, "Robert Schuller and the Seeker Sensitive Church," *Twin City Fellows* http://www.twincityfellowship.com/iu/articles/issue56.htm. (12/12/02).
55. Allitt, *Religion in America*, 229; Robert Kerr, "Rev. Rodgers Rolls On," *Memphis Commercial Appeal* (29 September 1991): E1.
56. Sargeant, *Seeker Churches*, 190 (quotes); "Church History," *Welcome to Willow Creek*, Willow Creek Community Church, 14; "Worship," *Impact Fellowship* http://www.impactfellowship.org/worship.php. (12/12/02); "Rev. Bill Hybels Biography," *Christian Stewardship Association* http://www.stewardship.org/index.cfm/method/context.6ffa5184-4efc-407c-96e2f5059. (12/12/02).
57. Allitt, *Religion in America*, 228; Barbara Dolan, "Full House at Willow Creek," *Time* (6 March 1989): 60; "Bill Hybels," *Making a Difference* http://www.straightistheway.com/warning/hybels/general.httml. (12/12/02).
58. Allitt, *Religion in America*, 228 (quotes); Dolan, "Full House at Willow Creek," 60.
59. Sargeant, *Seeker Churches*, 19, 36, 64, 78, 80-83; Allitt, *Religion in America*, 228.
60. Gillmore, "Community is Their Middle Name," 49-55; Lauren F. Winner, "The Man Behind the Megachurch," *Christianity Today* 13 (November 2000): 58-60; Sargeant, *Seeker Churches*, 118-22; Dolan, "Full House at Willow Creek," 60; "Answers to Common Misunderstandings About Seeker-Targeted Churches Like Discovery Church," http://discoverychurchj.com/seeker.htm. (12/12/02).
61. Truehart, "The Next Church," 40 (quote).
62. Stewart M. Hoover, "The Cross at Willow Creek," in *Religion and Popular Culture in America*, ed. Bruce David Forbes and Jeffrey H. Mahan (Berkeley: University of California Press, 2000), 153; David S. Luecke, "Is Willow Creek the Way of the Future?" *Christian Century* 14 (May 1997): 479; James Emery White, "Why Seekers Come to Church," *Leadership Journal* http://www.christianitytoday.com/le/813/813.49. (12/12/02).
63. Luecke, "Is Willow Creek the Way of the Future?" 480; Sargeant, *Seeker Churches*, 193. See Gregory A. Pritchard, *Willow Creek Seeker Services: Evaluating a New Way of Doing Church* (Grand Rapids: Baker Books, 1995); George G. Hunter III, *Church for the Unchurched* (Nashville: Abingdon, 1966); James Sunguist, Willow Creek Church and Bill Hybel's Theology," http://www.deceptioninthechurch.com/willowcreek.html.(12/12/02). Faith in Focus "Proclaiming the Good News at Willowcreek," http://www.reformed-churches.org.nz/resources/fnf/a47.htm. (12/12/02).
64. Luecke, "Is Willow Creek the Way of the Future?" 481; Sargeant, *Seeker Churches*, 2, 64, 69, 182.
65. Hamilton, "Willow Creek's Place in History," 67 (quote); Sargeant, *Seeker Churches*, 191; Mark Mitteberg, "Seeker-Sensitive for the Sake of the Gospel," *CRI* http://www.quip.org/free/dc249.htm. (12/12/02).

66. Sargeant, *Seeker Churches*, 134; Miller, *Reinventing American Protestantism*, 1; Wuthnow, *Restructuring of American Religion*, 71-99; Trueheart, "The Next Church," 56, 57.

67. Hamilton, "Willow Creek's Place in History," 67 (quote); Sargeant, *Seeker Churches*, 13, 134-62; David S. Leucke, "Is Willow Creek the Way of the Future?" http://www.religion-online.org/cgi-bin/relsearch.dl/showarticle?stem-d=288. (12/12/02).

68. Tim Stafford, "A Regular Purpose Driven Guy," *Christianity Today* 18 (November 2002): 44; Miller, *Reinventing American Protestantism*, 174.

69. Rick Warren, *The Purpose Driven Church* (Grand Rapids: Zondervan, 1995), 170.

70. Warren, *Purpose Driven Church*, 279-81 (quote); Sargeant, *Seeker Churches*, 65,66.

71. Warren, *Purpose Driven Church*, 157, 231 (quotes) 295-300; Sargeant, *Seeker Churches*, 78.

72. Warren, *Purpose Driven Church*, 130, 144, 145; Stafford, "Regular Purpose Driven Guy," 46.

73. Warren, *Purpose Driven Church*, 130, 153-58; Stafford, "Regular Purpose Driven Guy," 46.

74. Warren, *Purpose Driven Church*, 127-36; Stafford, "Regular Purpose Driven Guy," 46, 47.

75. Rick Warren, *The Purpose Driven Life* (Grand Rapids: Zondervan, 2002), 16.

76. Sargeant, *Seeker Churches*, 108 (quote).

77. Quentin J. Schultze, "Electronic Church," in *Dictionary of Christianity in America*, 385.

78. Quentin J. Schultze, *Televangelism and American Culture* (Grand Rapids: Baker Books, 1991), 28.

79. Schultze, *Televangelism and American Culture*, 29; Robert M. Bowman Jr., *The Word-Faith Controversy: Understanding the Health and Wealth Gospel* (Grand Rapids: Baker Books, 2001), 8, 9.

80. See Gregor T. Goethals, *The TV Ritual: Worship at the Altar* (Boston: Beacon Press, 1981), 125-44.

81. R. Laurence Moore, *Selling God: American Religion in the Marketplace* (New York: Oxford University Press, 1994), 245; Quentin J. Schultze, "Evangelical Radio and the Rise of the Electronic Church, 1921-1948," *Journal of Broadcasting and Electronic Media* 3, 32 (1988): 292-94; Tona J. Hangen, *Redeeming the Dial: Radio, Religion, and Popular Culture in America* (Chapel Hill: University of North Carolina Press, 2002), 48-53; Douglas Carl Abrams, *Selling the Old-Time Religion: American Fundamentalism and Mass Culture, 1920-1940* (Athens: University of Georgia Press, 2001), 58, 59; Dave Berkman, "Long Before Falwell: Early Radio and Religion—As Reported by the Nation's Periodical Press," *Journal of Popular Culture* 21 (spring 1988): 1-11; Spencer Miller, Jr. "Radio and Religion," *The Annals of the American Academy of Political and Social Science* 177 (January 1935): 135-40.

82. Frankl, *Televangelism*, 5, 6; Quentin J. Schultze, "TV Revivalism: Show Biz and Big Biz," *Christianity Today* 7 (August 1987): 51, 52; Jeffrey K. Haden and Anson Shupe, *Televangelism: Power and Politics on God's Frontier* (New York: Henry Holt, 1988), 44.

83. Bobby C. Alexander, *Televangelism Reconsidered: Ritual in the Search for Human Community* (Atlanta: Scholars Press, 1994), 59, 60; Frankl, *Televangelism*, 65-73.

84. Alexander, *Televangelism*, 59, 60 (quote); Peter G. Horsfield, *Religious Television: The American Experience* (New York: Longman, 1984), 9, 10; Thomas C. Durfey and James A. Ferrier, *Religious Broadcast Management Handbook* (Grand Rapids: Academic Books, 1986), 34.

85. Schultze, *Televangelism and American Culture*, 38, 55; Schultze, "Electronic Church," 385; Erling Jorstad, *The Politics of Moralism* (Minneapolis: Augsburg, 1981), 26, 27; Frankl, *Televangelism*, 106-15; Hadden and Shupe, *Televangelism*, 119.

86. David Edwin Harrell, Jr. *Oral Roberts: An American Life* (San Francisco: Harper and Row, 1985), 268-70; Jorstad, *Politics of Moralism*, 26; Schultze, *Televangelism and American Culture*, 55; John Mariani, "Milking the Flock: Television Evangelism," *Saturday Review* 3 (February 1979): 79; David Edwin Harrell, Jr., *All Things Are Possible: The Healing and Charismatic Revivals in Modern America* (Bloomington: Indiana University Press, 1975), 155, 156.

87. Schultze, *Televangelism and American Culture*, 29, 205, 228.

88. Frankl, *Televangelism*, 76, 84, 123; Mariani, "Milking the Flock," 25.

89. Schultze, *Televangelism and American Culture*, 111,112.

90. Ibid., 84, 85, 108.

91. Alexander, *Televangelism Reconsidered*, 97-100 (quote on 99); Frankl, *Televangelism*, 113; Hadden and Shupe, *Televangelism*, 163, 164, 179.

92. Jorstad, *Politics of Moralism*, 55-57; Frankl, *Televangelism*, 114, 120; Hadden and Shupe, *Televangelism*, 125.

93. Alexander, *Televangelism Reconsidered*, 125 (quote); Frankl, *Televangelism*, 115.

94. Alexander, *Televangelism Reconsidered*, 125, 126; Schultze, *Televangelism and American Culture*, 30, 31; Frankl, *Televangelism*, 98, 99; Hadden and Shupe, *Televangelism*, 124.

95. Allitt, *Religion in America*, 194; Schultze, *Television and American Culture*, 60; Frankl, *Televangelism*, 73, 108, 123, 129; Hadden and Shupe, *Televangelism*, 123, 124.

96. Schultze, *Televangelism and American Culture*, 66 (quote).

97. Frankl, *Televangelism*, 108,109; Schultze, *Televangelism and American Culture*, 102; Mark G. Toulouse, "Marion Gordon 'Pat' Robertson," in *Dictionary of Christianity in America,* 1021, 1022; Moore, *Selling God*, 249, 250; Carol Flake, *Redemptorama: Culture, Politics, and New Evangelicalism* (New York: Penguin Books, 1984), 135.

98. "The Gospel Boom," *Saturday Evening Post* (April 1979): 36 (quote). See also Richard A. Blake, "Catholic, Protestant, Electric," *America* 15 (March 1980): 213.

99. Alexander, *Televangelism Reconsidered*, 113, 114; Hadden and Shupe, *Televangelism*, 195; Richard Ostling, "Evangelical Publishing and Broadcasting," in *Evangelicalism and Modern America*, ed. George Marsden (Grand Rapids: Eerdmans, 1984), 52, 53.

100. Alexander, *Television Reconsidered*, 115 (quote).

101. Alexander, *Television Reconsidered*, 115-17. Flake's view is not as positive. See Flake, *Redemptorama*, 135.

102. Allitt, *Religion in America*, 194, 195; Conrad E. Ostwalt, Jr. "James (Jim) Orson Bakker," in *Dictionary of Christianity in America*, 102; Kenneth L. Woodward, "A Disneyland for the Devout," *Newsweek* (11 August 1986): 46, 47; Frankl, *Televangelism*, 129; Joe E. Barnhart, *Jim and Tammy* (Buffalo: Prometheus Books, 1988).

103. Alexander, *Televangelism Reconsidered*, 143,144; Allitt, *Religion in America*, 192; Mariani, "Milking the Flock," 24.

104. Schultze, *Televangelism and American Culture*, 114 (quote); Hadden and Shupe, *Televangelism*, 18; John Corry, "Preachers: Mastery of Medium," *New York Times Television* (2 April 1987): C26.

105. Alexander, *Televangelism Reconsidered*, 142, 143; Allitt, *Religion in America*, 192; Jean Seligmann, "The Inimitable Tammy Faye," *Time* (8 June 1987): 69.

106. Allitt, *Religion in America*, 191; Richard N. Ostling, "Enterprising Evangelicalism," *Time* (3 August 1987): 50-53.

107. Schultze, *Televangelism and American Culture*, 27; Schultze, "Electronic Church," 386. Marshall Allen, "Naïve Bookkeeping," *Christianity Today* (August 2003): 19, 20; Corrie Cuter, "Joyce Meyer Ministry Flap," *Christianity Today* (March 2004): 22; Thomas C. Oden, "Truth or Consequences: A Biblical Guide to Accountability," *Christianity Today* 18 (March 1988): 33-39; "TBN Under the Microscope," *Christianity Today* (November 2004) 19.

108. Allitt, *Religion in America*, 195; Ostling. "Enterprising Evangelism," 53; Randy Frame, "Did Oral Roberts Go Too Far?" *Christianity Today* 20 (February 1987): 43, 44.

109. Victoria Sackett, "Oral Roberts Bucks Eternity," *New York Times* (30 March 1987): A19 (quote); Allitt, *Religion in America*, 195.

110. Allitt, *Religion in America*, 193; Russell Watson, "Fresh Out of Miracles," *Newsweek* (11 May 1987): 70-72; Ostling, "Enterprising Evangelism," 51.

111. Russell Watson, "Heaven Can Wait," *Newsweek* (8 June 1987): 58-60; John D. Hull "The Rise and Fall of Holy Joe," *Time* (3 August 1987): 54, 55; David Brand, "God and Money," *Time* (3 August 1987): 48,49; Ostling, "Enterprising Evangelicalism," 52,53.

112. Watson, "Heaven Can Wait" (quotes), 58, 61; Allitt, *Religion in America*, 193.

113. Randy Frame, "PTL: A Year After the Fall," *Christianity Today* 18 (March 1988): 44, 45; Alexander, *Television Reconsidered*, 141, 142.

114. Quoted from Walter Capps, *The New Religious Right: Piety, Patriotism, and Politics* (Columbia: University of South Carolina Press, 1994), 137; Allitt, *Religion in America*, 194.

115. Quotes from Watson, "Heaven Can Wait," 65; Alexander, *Televangelism Reconsidered*, 141-43.

116. Alexander, *Televangelism Reconsidered*, 137 (quote).

117. Lawrence Wright, *Saints and Sinners* (New York: Alfred A.Knopf, 1993), 52 (quote); Allitt, *Religion in America*, 194.

118. Schultze, *Televangelism and American Culture*, 104.

119. "Perspectives," *Newsweek* (4 October 2004): 23.

120. Ben Armstrong, *The Electric Church* (New York: Thomas Nelson, 1979), 112.

121. William F. Fore, "The Church and the Electronic Media," *Ministry* (January 1979): 5.

122. William Hendricks, "The Theology of the Electronic Church," *Review and Expositor* 81 (winter): 59.

123. Jeffrey K. Hadden and Charles E. Swann, *Prime Time Preachers: The Rising Power of Televangelism* (Reading, MA: Addison-Wesley, 1981), 85-102 (quotes). See also Hendricks, "Theology of the Electronic Church," 59-75.

124. Schultze, "Electronic Church," 386.

125. Bruce David Forbes, "Introduction," in *Religion and Popular Culture in America*, ed. Bruce David Forbes and Jeffrey H. Mahan (Berkeley: University of California Press, 2000), 13; Schultze, *Televangelism and American Culture*, 39, 40 (quote). Most of the rest of the section entitled "At Home in the Culture" has been drawn from Schultze's *Televangelism and American Culture*. General citations will be given at the end of most paragraphs. Supporting sources will also be noted.

126. Schultze, *Televangelism and American Culture*, 98, 117. See Harry S. Stout, *The Divine Dramatist: George Whitefield and the Rise of Modern Evangelicalism* (Grand Rapids: Eerdmans, 1991); Frank Lambert, "Peddlar in Divinity: George Whitefield and the Great Awakening, 1737-1747," *Journal of American History* 77, 3 (1990): 812-29.

127. Schultze, *Televangelism and American Culture*, 19, 117, 118. See John Shelton Lawrence and Robert Jewett, *The Myth of the American Superhero* (Grand Rapids: Eerdmans, 2002).

128. Schultze, *Televangelism and American Culture*, 32, 33, 70, 74, 79 (quote); Richard Quebedeaux, *By What Authority: The Rise of Personality Cults in American Christianity* (New York: Harper and Row, 1982), 53-69. See Douglas F. Barnes, "Charisma and Religious Leadership: An Historical Analysis," *Journal for the Scientific Study of Religion* 17, 1 (1978): 1-18.

129. Richard Kyle, *The Religious Fringe: A History of Alternative Religions in America* (Downers Grove, IL: InterVarsity Press, 1993), 328, 329.

130. Schultze, *Televangelism and American Culture*, 87, 90; Ostling, "Enterprising Evangelicalism," 53.

131. Schultze, *Televangelism and American Culture*, 36,72; Martin Marty, "I Think," *The Lutheran Standard* (2 January 1979): 13.

132. Schultze, *Televangelism and American Culture*, 19, 129; Quebedeaux, *By What Authority*, 76, 77.

133. Schultze, *Televangelism and American Culture*, 19, 83, 84; Mark A. Shibley, *Resurgent Evangelicalism in the United States: Mapping Cultural Change since 1970* (Columbia: University of South Carolina Press, 1996), 1-23.

134. Schultze, *Televangelism and American Culture*, 31, 159.

135. Ibid., 16, 17, 131 (quote).

136. Ibid., 162, 163.

137. Schultze, *Televangelism and American Culture*, 37, 38; Randall Balmer, *Blessed Assurance: A History of Evangelicalism* (Boston: Beacon Press, 1999), 10.

138. J. Thomas Bisset, "Religious Broadcasting: Assessing the State of the Art," *Christianity Today* 12 (December 1980): 28-31; Schultz, *Televangelism and American Culture*, 203, 204; Marty, "I Think," 12; William D. Romanowski, *EyesWideOpen: Looking for God in Popular Culture* (Grand Rapids: Brazos Press, 2001), 71.

139. William F. Fore, "Beyond the Electronic Church," *The Christian Century* (7-14 January 1981): 29,30.

140. Marty, "I Think," 11,12; Wuthnow, *Restructuring of American Religion*, 71-99. See Thomas Luckmann, *The Invisible Religion* (New York: Macmillian, 1967); Alan Jamieson, *A Churchless Faith* (London: SPCK, 2002).

141. Wolfe, *Transformation of American Religion*, 4 (quote). See also Christopher Lasch, *The Culture of Narcissism: American Life in An Age of Diminishing Expectations* (New York: Norton, 1978).

142. See Dan Kimball, *The Emerging Church: Vintage Christianity for New Generations* (Grand Rapids: Zondervan, 2003).

143. Andy Crouch, "The Emergent Mystique," *Christianity Today* (November 2004): 37-41 (quotes).

144. Crouch, "Emergent Mystic," 37-41 (quotes); "Emergent Evangelism," *Christianity Today* (November 2004): 42, 43. See Brian McLaren, *A New Kind of Christian* (San Francisco: Jossey-Bass, 2001); Brian D. McLaren, *The Church on the Other Side: Doing Ministry in a Post-Modern Matrix* (Grand Rapids: Zondervan, 2000).

145. Robert E. Webber, *The Younger Evangelicals: Facing the Challenges of the New World* (Grand Rapids: Baker Books, 2002), 18, 112; James Davison Hunter, "The New Class of the Young Evangelicals," *Review of Religious Research* (December 1980): 155-69; Norman Jameson, "Emerging Church Makes Contemporary Obsolete," *Biblical Recorder,* www.biblicalrecorder.com/content/news/2002/12_13_2002/text/tne131202emerging.shtml, 1-3. (12/12/02); Mark Wingfield, "A Generation Beyond Willow Creek: Reaching Austin Al and Alice," *Pastor.com* http://

www.pastors.com/articles/BeyondWillowCreek.asp. (12/12/02). Weber is writing about a group of evangelicals in a way that Quebedeaux did. See Richard Quebedeaux, *The Young Evangelicals* (New York: Harper and Row, 1974).

146. Weber, *Younger Evangelicals*, 18, 107-23; Jameson, "Emerging Church," 1.

147. Weber, *Younger Evangelicals*, 18, 147-59; Rob Moll, "Has the Emergent Church Emerged?" *LeadershipJournal.net* www.chrsitianitytoday.com/leaders/newletter/2003/cln31230.html, 4. (8/10/04).

148. Weber, *Younger Evangelicals*, 18, 201-10; Jameson, "Emerging Church," 2; "Worship Wars," http://www.nefi.net/aboutus/epistle/worship-wars.html. (12/12/02).

8

If You Can't Beat 'em Join 'em

By the late twentieth century, there existed little appreciable difference between the evangelical subculture and mainstream American culture. Gone were the days when evangelicals opposed much of the popular culture. For all of their denunciation of sex and violence in society and in the media, evangelicals flourish at the most superficial levels of America's affluent and celebrity-driven popular culture. This is particularly evident with the subjects of this chapter—evangelicals and the popular culture, the health and wealth gospel, and the positive thinking movement.

Throughout their history, evangelicals have had a hate–love relationship with American culture. By the late twentieth century, they loved it more than they hated it. Evangelicals have wavered between three of H. Richard Niebuhr's categories: "Christ Against Culture," "Christ Above Culture," or "The Christ of Culture." For much of the nineteenth century, they experienced considerable success in their attempt to Christianize culture. The alliance between Victorian morals and the evangelical ethos worked well for much of the century. Evangelicals constantly warred against "worldly entertainment." In addition to condemning the usual vices such as drinking alcohol and gambling, they regarded dancing, the reading of novels, and theater attendance as worldly.

This evangelical influence in the nineteenth century, however, never entailed dominance. Large segments of society ignored the attempt by conservative Protestants to sanctify the nation's popular culture. In fact, even at this time evangelicals began to offer alternatives to worldly amusements. Included were sports, the YMCA, museums, and camp meetings (especially the Chautauqua Association).[1] By the early twentieth century, even this tenuous evangelical sway over culture had declined and the fundamentalist defeat in the 1920s prompted them to separate from culture. William Romanowski indicates that the relationship between religion and entertainment has been "something like a pendulum swinging back and forth between vicious attack and uneasy cooperation."[2] From about the mid-1920s to the 1970s, the swing of the pendulum generally prompted conservative Protestants to attack and reject many aspects of the popular culture.

By the late twentieth century, many fundamentalists had now become evangelicals and they came out of their self-imposed religious ghetto. Rather than retreat from culture, they have attempted to impose their ethos upon American society. In doing so, evangelicals evidenced their usual paradoxical behavior. They have endeavored to restore public morals to their pre-1960s condition. This entailed resisting aspects of the secular society and using their newly found political clout to influence the political agenda. But in coming out of their religious cocoon, evangelicals have also harmonized Christ with American culture, especially its popular aspects. They saw little tension between Christ and culture and had in effect adopted Niebuhr's model—"The Christ of Culture." For the most part, evangelicals no longer rejected the world—they sanctified it. They gave it a Christian veneer.

At this point some definitions would be useful. What is popular culture? This can best be defined by comparing it with the traditional or high culture. An easy definition would say that it is what most people are currently doing, wearing, eating, feeling, viewing, or listening to.[3] The popular culture focuses on the new, the instant, the trivia, the quantitative, the spectacular, and is very subjective. Moreover, the popular culture derives its content and form from the market. Conversely, the high or traditional culture has standards and convictions about objective reality. It focuses on the timeless; requires training; emphasizes knowledge and wisdom; and suggests the transcendent. And because culture is market driven, two things happen to the high culture—it is patronized by a narrow section of society or adapts to the popular culture.[4]

Buying into the Pop Culture

Caving in to American culture is not a new experience for evangelicals, but by the early twenty-first century it has reached new proportions. What has brought this about? Such a development has many parents. The evangelical tendency to accommodate itself to society and create "Christian" alternatives has deep roots. The evangelical ethos with its populist, pragmatic, and individualistic tendencies has encouraged conservative Protestants to move in this direction. The popular culture, indeed, is rooted in the common people, not elite society. Being evangelistic and market driven, evangelicals have used popular culture as a means to witness to the world. This is especially true with the megachurches and televangelists who, as we have seen, have adopted a "bring-em-at-any-cost" approach to evangelism.[5]

Americans are an impatient people. They want things to be done now, immediately. They do not like to wait. Both the popular culture and the evangelical subculture connect closely with this American characteristic. The popular culture specializes in instant gratification. It caters to our desire for instant food, drink, love, entertainment, and solutions to problems. And thanks to television, computers, fax machines, credit cards, microwaves, drive-through food service, and fast food restaurants all are available. All of this has a spiritual parallel in the evangelical subculture. Evangelicals, of course, stress the conversion experience—usually at one moment in time. They minimize discipleship, which is a lengthy growth process, and have tailored many worship services around popular music and preaching.[6]

For evangelicals to move rapidly in the direction of embracing popular culture, they had to overcome a long history of opposition to it. For many, participating in the popular culture was to open the door to the Devil and all kinds of evil influences. Finney could not understand how anyone "who has ever known the love of God can relish a secular novel..." On the contemporary scene, Bob Jones University and Donald Wildmon of the American Family Association are examples of fundamentalists who view popular culture as the servant of the Antichrist.[7]

Throughout the nineteenth century, evangelicals gradually embraced forms of the popular culture—circuses, theatrical performances, vaudeville acts, novels and more. In the late nineteenth and early twentieth centuries, the adjustment to popular culture became more obvious. Conservative Protestants adopted many forms of the mainstream culture while rejecting its explicit content. Included were Christian magazines, books, publishing houses, and radio programs. Even such modest steps were inadequate because in reality, evangelicals were creating a subculture within mainstream society. If evangelical moralists wanted to successfully resist the secular popular culture, they had to create a popular culture of their own. This they did and such a tendency reached explosive proportions by the middle years of the twentieth century.[8]

In the late twentieth century, Romanowski points to three approaches that conservative Protestants have taken toward popular culture—condemnation, appropriation, and consumption. The condemnation approach can be seen in their boycotts of products and places. Without a great deal of success, fundamentalists have boycotted Disney, ABC, Proctor and Gamble, Harry Potter and more. More representative of the condemnation approach is the attitude that links Hollywood and the media with the Devil. If aspects of popular culture are of Satan, the only Christian recourse is abstinence. Such a mindset regards avoidance of the secular popular culture as a mark of being a true believer.[9]

Most conservative churches realized that resisting the popular culture was not working, so they decided to Christianize it. They adopted Romanowski's appropriation approach. In his words: to be "in the world but not of it," entailed creating a "Christianzed version of the secular culture by appropriation of mainstream practices and trends, infusing them with a spiritual justification. In this model, the hallmark of popular art is overt Christian content—an explicit statement of Christian belief." Without giving it much thought, many evangelicals have also opted out for the consumption approach. They may object to some aspects of popular culture such as R-rated movies, but on the whole, they participate in most aspects of the popular culture. This approach gives little thought as to how viewing and listening habits can impact one's faith. Both the appropriation and consumption models are driven by the consumer ethos of modern American society. The former, however, attempts to infuse the popular culture with at least a Christian veneer or message.[10]

Along came several factors that accelerated this evangelical tendency to create a Christian popular culture—the omnipresence of the media, the seductive nature of American popular culture, affluence, mass consumerism, and a celebrity-driven culture. The media, especially television, has massively shaped modern American society, including the evangelical subculture. About 90 percent of the evangelical households have cable or satellite television and a VCR. On this score and the time watching television, little difference exists between conservative Protestants and the rest of society. Even though some fundamentalist preachers denounce television, their church members seem to patronize it at the same rate as do most other people.[11]

Television has changed America from a print to a visual society and has replaced a cerebral emphasis with one on experience. More than this, television has brought the popular culture into the living rooms of most Americans. It has made it an immediate experience. And the American pop culture has been easy to digest. It is attractive and alluring. For centuries, American popular culture has enticed millions of people both in the United States and abroad. The tug of the popular culture has been enhanced by its celebrity appeal. People in our impersonal society have a desire for the personal. The popular culture provides for this need in the form of celebrities. Prominent athletes, movie stars, rock musicians, and television personalities endorse the products of the pop culture. So it became difficult for even conservative Protestants to resist an attraction that confronts them at every turn in life—television, radio, billboards, magazines, and websites.[12]

Evangelicals have shared in the prosperity of modern America. Like the rest of American society, evangelicals are affluent and consumer driven and can thus afford to patronize the popular culture. According to one source, evangelicals spend about double on entertainment as they donate to the church. Today evangelicals are nearly as comfortable with American popular culture as are other Americans. Many areas of life, once strongly discouraged by evangelicals—sports and shopping on Sunday, rock music, television, movies, extensive use of cosmetics, and dancing—have now become the norm in the evangelical community.[13]

A Christian Pop Culture

A form of Christian capitalism drives this evangelical fascination with the popular culture. Of all the major religious groups in America, evangelicals have been infused with the entrepreneurial spirit. Conservative Protestants did not like what they saw in secular culture. So they set out to change it by sanctifying it. This they would do by competing with the mainstream culture and defeating it. As noted in chapter 6, they jumped into politics in order to change America. They also competed in the marketplace of culture, and in the process created a Christian popular culture. Since the 1970s, conservative Protestants ceased being countercultural (except in certain respects) and have instead created a counterfeit culture.[14] More than that, the traffic runs in both directions. Not only have evangelicals created their own sanctified subculture, but they have also influenced the secular culture. Or, as Alan Wolfe says, "we are all evangelicals now." By this he means "evangelicals are agents as well as victims of cultural accommodation."[15]

In creating this counterfeit culture, many evangelicals have trivialized the Christian faith and turned it into a superficial commodity. While such a tendency has always been present in the evangelical subculture, it has perhaps reached a new low in the modern era. The evangelical subculture represents a powerful economic bloc, something that has not gone unnoticed by either secular or evangelical enterprises. Thus, people of all religious stripes have hawked commodities with the evangelical subculture in mind.

What would Jesus do? Many contemporary evangelicals believe that he would embrace their lifestyle. Many marketing ventures begin by contending that Jesus would eat, wear, or drive their commodity. In making this pitch, these entrepreneurs are baptizing the products they desire to market. Evangelicals have been prone to give secular institutions and commodities a Christian makeover. To many people, this evangelical tendency to sanctify every aspect of the larger American culture is shallow at best and perhaps even irreverent or dishonest.

What aspects of the mainstream culture have evangelicals baptized? The list is lengthy and only a few examples will be given. Many of the products connect with the desire for self-improvement. In the desire to please God and to improve oneself, many evangelicals believe that the sacred and the secular connect. Conservative Protestant women want to lose weight to please God and become more attractive. The have lots of help in this endeavor. Some recent books include: *More of Him and Less of Me* (Jan Christiansen); *What Would Jesus Eat?* (Don Colbert); *Daily Word for Weight Loss* (Colleen Zuck and Elaine Meyer); *The Prayer Diet* (Matthew Anderson), and *The Makers's Diet* (Jordan S. Rubin). These books and the programs associated with them have become very popular in many evangelical congregations. While the authors recognize that there are physical aspects to losing weight, they also spiritualize the quest by equating it with giving oneself up to God and urging daily prayers.[16]

Are you having financial or business problems? In addition to Larry Burkett's organization, there are other services. ChristianDebthelpers.com offers you a Christian themed approach to debt elimination. Another group, Christian Debt Advisors claims Matthew 6:12 as their motto: "And forgive us our debts, as we forgive our debtors." (Most scholars translate the word *debts* as sins or wrongs, not financial indebtedness.)

Do you want to buy a home? Christianrealestate.net is a network of Christian real estate listings—both domestic and commercial. Perhaps you want a job. ChristianEmployment.com is an online job search engine that brings together Christian employers and employees. Maybe you need an attorney. Christianattorneysonline.com will make an online connection for you. If you want to sell something, there is Christianclassfiedonline.com.

Perhaps you want something face to face. In most urban localities, there exist Christian yellow pages listing many businesses that claim a Christian connection. For example, the Christian business guide in central Kansas (where I live) lists nearly every type of business from A to W (except taverns) and lists its e-mail number as www.galatians610.com and its phone as (316) 838 NOAH.

Are you single and lonely and desire love, romance, and sex? Perhaps ChristianSingles.com can help you. This is a Christian dating service that links people up for marriage, not sexual immorality. It has a generic evangelical statement of faith and a statement of purpose. If you are over fifty-five, ChristianSingleSeniors.com might be for you. This connects seniors for marriage or companionship. If things work out and a wedding is on the horizon, try ChristianWeddings.net. It lists Christian wedding services for most areas of the country.

There is a crasser side to this evangelical entrepreneurial activity. In addition to an array of self-help books covering nearly every subject, Christian bookstores stock many other "Christian commodities"—frisbees, tablemats, coffee mugs, greeting cards, videos and DVDs. One can see T-shirts labeled as "Fast Break" and depicting Christians disappearing in the rapture. Bumper stickers read "Jesus is my rock and My Name is on the Roll." Sex sells well even in the evangelical market. There are Christian romances, sex manuals, and lovemaking guides.[17] Not to be left out of the evangelical market, Hooters Restaurants now offer their customers more than buffalo-wings and attractive women. They have begun Bible studies.[18]

In an attempt to provide a comfortable cultural setting for youth, churches have changed their outlook on several previously forbidden practices—"dirty dancing," hair length, jewelry, makeup, and tattooing. Except with strict fundamentalists, this list of once forbidden activities is no longer relevant. Jewelry and makeup are not even subjects for discussion. Dancing is now well accepted—there are Christian dances and evangelical churches commonly provide activities for their youth after the senior prom. Tattoos are now chic and many evangelical youth are getting Christian tattoos—crosses, sacred hearts, angels, and symbols of the Trinity. To be competitive with the secular world, evangelicals have begun Christian rock bands, soap operas, nightclubs, and talk shows. There is even a Christian Wrestling Federation, where the violence is less and the combatants go by biblical names—Michael the Arc Angel, Sampson, David, and Gideon.[19]

What would Jesus drive? This question has ignited considerable discussion on Christian websites. More environmentally conscious evangelicals contend that Jesus would be driving a fuel-efficient vehicle or travel on public transportation. They speak from the perspective of Christ's lordship over creation. Others say no! Jesus was a carpenter and he hung around with twelve guys. So for practical considerations, he would drive a Ford F-250 "six-pack" truck or a Chevy Suburban. Because Jesus was an unconventional type of guy with long hair, some say he may have driven a Harley Davidson. Others consider the entire matter a silly question. Nowhere does the Bible hint at Christ's philosophy regarding the vehicle he would drive.[20]

Selling the Printed Word

For centuries the printed word has been a major vehicle for spreading the Christian message. Without thousands of monks copying manuscripts during the Middle Ages, the advance and even the preservation of Christianity would have been in serious jeopardy. Thanks to the printing press, the Reformation returned the Word of God to the people. Without this invention, the message of the Reformation would not have reached the laity and this movement would not have been successful. In the late twentieth century, television began to bring the gospel to millions of people, but books are still important.

In evangelical thinking, reading fiction has undergone a serious change—from being regarded as worldly to becoming a vehicle of popular entertainment. Well into the nineteenth century, people read for self-improvement, not entertainment. As the century progressed, advances in printing techniques reduced the price of books. This, in turn, made books more accessible and changed reading habits. Reading for entertainment shocked the clergy who saw fiction as debasing the mind. More progressive evangelicals, however, believed that people could be trusted to make responsible choices. So Protestant authors began to adapt religious literature to suit popular tastes. As time went on, people had more money for books and time to read. While some Protestants still resisted fiction, the novel was here to stay and the evangelical realists accepted this fact. They now attempted to publish fiction that was useful and instructional. A popular genre was fictional Bible stories or tales set in the biblical context. On the negative side, Protestants launched crusades to silence wicked or sensationalized fiction.[21]

From these beginnings in the nineteenth century, evangelical publishing became a huge business in the twentieth century. The Fleming H. Revell Publishing Company led the charge in religious publishing and many companies followed. By the early twenty-first century, Thomas Nelson had become the largest evangelical publisher with sales over $300 million. At this time, there were over 6,000 Christian bookstores plus large religious sections at the mass retailers—Barnes and Noble, Borders, Amazon.com, and Wal-Mart. In 1980, Christian publishers produced over $1 billion worth of sales. By 2002, this figure jumped to over $4 billion. This incredible surge, however, was built on the practice that had begun in the nineteenth century—namely, to make the Christian message interesting and relevant to the contemporary context.[22]

Evangelicals have published many serious and scholarly books and have demonstrated considerable intellectual vitality.[23] But the skyrocketing evangelical book market rests more on popular, publications—both fiction and nonfiction. So well have these books sold that secular publishers look at the lucrative evangelical market and have begun to publish books on subjects of interest to evangelicals. Mainstream bookstores now feature evangelical publications. The types of books that have driven this market relate to personalities, self-improvement, and especially prophecy. Books by evangelical celebrities have sold well. Examples would include Billy Graham, Jimmy Carter, Chuck Colson, Francis Schaeffer, James Dobson, Hal Lindsey, Max Lucado, and Tim LaHaye.[24]

Being a pragmatic people, how-to-do-it books have hit the best-seller lists. Some books in this genre relate to secular problems (e.g., losing weight) but give a spiritual twist to these issues. Others focus more directly on the spiritual dimension, but are still practical. Two examples are *The Prayer of Jabez* and *The Purpose Driven Life*. Both books are practical and focus on spiritual issues driving evangelicals. The former helps believers acquire the blessed (or affluent) life; the later enables them to discover the meaning of life.[25]

Of all the subjects launching the sky-rocketing evangelical book market, prophecy books rank first. On this subject, the late twentieth century witnessed an explosion of fiction and non-fiction publications. Leading the charge was Hal Lindsey's *The Late Great Planet Earth* (1970). This book was the best non-fiction seller of the 1970s and by 1990 it had sold 28 million copies. Many other non-fiction prophecy books sold well. A small sampling would include books by John Walvoord, John Hagee, Grant R. Jeffrey, Jack Van Impe, Pat Robertson, Tim LaHaye, and Dave Hunt. Nearly all of these authors are writing from a dispensational perspective, which lends itself to a dramatic, exciting end of the world scenario.[26]

Driving the strongest interest in prophecy, however, has been the fictional books on this subject. The dispensational interpretation of the Bible has all of the ingredients for entertaining science fiction and has been turned into such by a number of writers.[27] In the dispensational scheme of things, believers are on God's side in a great cosmic struggle but they will be raptured at the last minute, right before the horrible events of the great tribulation. Those who are left behind experience tremendous hardships in their struggle against the Antichrist. Everything needed for the grist of fiction is there—a dramatic battle, conspiracy theories, good versus evil, and heroes. Very important, this end-time scenario connects with the way many evangelicals view the Christian life—get saved and God will rescue you from trouble.

Leading this fictional approach to prophecy in the 1980s were Frank Peretti's novels. *The Present Darkness* (1986) and *Piercing the Darkness* (1989) made the Christian best-seller lists well into the 1990s. The plots of Peretti's novels center on the unfolding of biblical prophecy in small-town America. These stories depict average believers caught up in a cosmic struggle against evil and feature New Age cultists and secular humanists plotting against America. In doing so, they connect with evangelical interests regarding end-time and conspiracy themes. His spine-tingling novels paved the way for other evangelical fiction writers, and his later novels did not sell as well in part because other evangelical authors flooded the market with similar books.[28]

Leading this pack, of course, is *The Left Behind* series co-authored by Tim LaHaye and Jerry Jenkins. The first novel, *Left Behind: A Novel of the Earth's Last Days,* appeared in 1995 and the series has continued at a little more than one sequel per year. Volume 12, *The Glorious Appearing*, came out in 2004. By then sales had sky rocketed to 62 million copies. This is the final volume but a prequel has been published and a sequel is planned. These novels tell a story about what happens on earth after Jesus returns and takes Christians up to heaven. Volume 1 kicks off with millions of Christians being raptured and then through subsequent volumes follows airline pilot Rayford Steele and journalist Buck Williams—who have been left behind—as they tough it out and struggle with the forces of the Antichrist. Volume 12 has the return of Christ, the battle of Armageddon, and the judgment.[29]

Who are the people reading these books? Seventy percent are sold in the Red States, the Republican areas of the Midwest and South, and the average readers are born-again Christian women in their forties. Why are so many people buying these books? Take a look at the news! The culture and political climate of the late twentieth and early twenty-first centuries has produced an audience with an apocalyptic mindset. Throughout the twentieth century, the dominant mood in Western society has been one of pessimism. Successive military conflicts, the specter of nuclear annihilation, energy shortages, regional famines, threats to the environment, and financial crises have cast a foreboding shadow across the future of humanity. And then came September 11 and the trouble in the Middle East. In such a scary environment, the premillennial doomsday predictions appear quite credible.[30]

Other factors contribute to the appeal of *The Left Behind* series. In a time of terror and tumult, people are looking for certainty—something that can be gleaned from a dispensational reading of the Book of Revelation. Of great importance, LaHaye and Jenkins connect with evangelicalism's populist impulse. Their commonsense reading of Scripture and lay language speak to multitudes of average people. As Jenkins says, "I write to pedestrians. And I am a pedestrian...I don't claim to be C. S. Lewis...I wish I was smart enough to a write a book that's hard to read..." LaHaye and Jenkins are outsiders and populists and proud of it. They grew up this way. Both have blue-collar backgrounds and LaHaye has a particular disdain for the educated elite. He graduated from Bob Jones University and Jenkins has no college degree. LaHaye also has strong right-wing political views, which emerge at times in this series.[31]

Movies and Television

The issues and trends that evangelicals confronted in the movies and television are similar to those they encountered in publishing. They had to straddle between two worlds: the Christianized subculture they had created and the secular society they were attempting to avoid. As time went on, it became difficult to tell the difference between the two. By the last part of the twentieth century, a shift became noticeable. Previously, evangelicals wrote books and produced movies and television programs primarily to evangelize. The focus now shifted from evangelization to Christian entertainment. They desired to provide the evangelical subculture with sanitized alternatives to secular entertainment.[32]

For centuries Protestants condemned the theater as the "Devil's workshop." In their view, it ran counter to Christian values, especially those that related to hard work, frugality, sobriety, and sexual restraint. With evangelicalism dominant in America for much of the nineteenth century, the belief that any form of amusement was wrong remained strong. It is estimated that about 70 percent of the Protestants rejected the theater on theological and moral grounds. By 1900, the Protestants let up. Resistance to the theater was deemed unrealistic and out of touch with the modern world. Both the Protestant and Catholic clergy turned from resistance to accommodation. Rather than condemn theater outright, they left the decision to individual discernment.[33]

The movies, nevertheless, were a different matter. Their tremendous popularity made them a competitor with many aspects of culture, including the church. More than most forms of entertainment, Protestants viewed them as a threat to Christian society. As late as the mid-twentieth century, conservative Protestants condemned the cinema as "degrading, polluting, ruining souls and bodies and poisoning the minds of men, especially the young and inexperienced." They described the movies as "godless," a "moral bubonic plague," a "maelstrom of iniquity," and where "Satan has his throne." Even mainstream Protestants were upset about theaters being open on Sunday, which was the day working-class people had free.[34]

Such condemnation could not last long. As in the case of the theater, resistance to movies became unrealistic. Television and then VCRs and cable TV brought similar programs into the living room. Even the most legalistic fundamentalist could not monitor such a situation. At first, the movie industry was less threatening to conservative Protestants. They produced films such as *Ben Hur* and *The Ten Commandments*, which contained a Christian message. In fact, Hollywood continued to produce movies for the general public until the late 1960s. But competition from television forced the movie industry to make changes. They then began to make movies intended to attract the youth. Such productions were not as middle-class friendly as were earlier movies. Another turning point came when the Supreme Court extended free speech protection to the entertainment industry. This further reduced the influence of the church and left the entertainment industry to regulate itself. Under competition from television and people desiring more realistic movies, Hollywood allowed more sex, violence, and profanity in its productions.[35]

Gone were the days when the movie, recording, and publishing industries designed their products for the middle class, thus keeping sex and profanity out of their productions. How did conservative Protestants respond to this situation? They could not stop their followers from viewing unacceptable programs. They moved in two directions. They attempted to monitor the situation and create Christian alternatives. In both cases, they were attempting to sanctify the secular culture.

A number of evangelical watchdog groups monitor the television and movie industries. As noted earlier, Don Wildmon and his American Family Association have critiqued several aspects of culture and organized boycotts against various industries. More focused on film and television are Ted Baehr of the Christian Film and Television Commission, John Evans of the Movie Morality Ministries, and the Dove Foundation led by Brad Curl. Baehr and the Catholic Cardinal Mahony called for an updating of the old code of ethics Hollywood once followed. Such a code summons the movie industry to uphold the dignity and value of human life and to refrain from presenting violence, sex, obscene language, and racial hatred. Moreover, Hollywood was not to demean religion. These groups view hundreds of films and publish their recommendations. While the specifics of their suggestions differ, they share a common philosophy: "the Christian public speaks loudest with its pocketbook." Christians are urged to patronize certain films and to refrain from viewing others. If enough economic pressure is put on Hollywood, they will produce more family-friendly films, the watchdogs argue. In addition, evangelicals have even used high tech watchdogs to sanitize television. They have the options of hooking up to SkyAngel Christian satellite network or TV Guardian—a "cover your-ears technology" which uses closed captions to replace offensive words on television.[36]

Best known of the watchdog groups is James Dobson's Focus on the Family. This organization functions as more than a Christian political lobby. It performs two other tasks. Focus on the Family monitors the popular culture and offers guidance as to the content of films, television, and contemporary music. Second, it produces family-oriented entertainment alternatives and educational materials. In doing all of this, Focus on the Family has been thoroughly assimilated into the mainstream society. The issue is not whether evangelicals will patronize the popular culture, especially movies and television. Rather, the question is which movies and television programs will conservative Protestants view. The goal is to monitor secular culture and to make it more palpable to the evangelical subculture.[37]

Despite their criticisms of the movie industry, the watchdog groups were not rejecting film entertainment, they were attempting to sanitize it. In fact, other enterprises carried the baptizing process a step further—they produced films with a Christian flavor. The first movie to be a commercial success was *The Restless Ones* (1965). Portraying a boy tempted by sex and drugs but victorious over these sins, this film ran throughout the nation in first-run theaters. Another film intended both to evangelize and to entertain was *A Thief in the Night* (1973). This film did not run at major theaters but was very popular in evangelical circles.[38] Years later, *The Passion of Christ* (2003)—produced by a conservative Catholic, Mel Gibson—captivated evangelical audiences as well as mainstream viewers. While recommended by the evangelical film critics, it was also a booming financial success, in part because evangelicals flocked to it in droves. Youth groups and entire churches came in buses to view it.

As noted in chapter 7, evangelicals also imitated secular television programs. Using the variety show format, Oral Roberts' special programs began to blur the lines between the secular and the sacred. Pat Robertson continued the move in this direction. His "700 Club" is a Christian imitation of a talk show. With Robertson as the host, various personalities discuss the pressing issues of the day, usually ones that interest the Christian Right. The parent company of the "700 Club" was the Christian Broadcasting Network (CBN). Now called the Family Channel, this company not only broadcasted religious programs but also family friendly shows such as "Leave It to Beaver" and "Father Knows Best."[39]

Modern America is currently in a full-scale culture war and many of the skirmishes center around the movie and television industries. The battle lines in this war do not follow traditional denominational structures but pit social conservatives against more moderate to liberal elements of society. The primary combatants are often not churches but parachurch organizations. While the social conservatives also include other groups such as Mormons and conservative Catholics, evangelicals and fundamentalists make up the lion's share of this movement. Moreover, the driving convictions are not just religious but a confluence of religious beliefs and political ideology.

Conservative Protestants have launched an attack upon Hollywood and television. They have done so largely because these entertainment industries have promoted sex and violence. Many evangelicals have reduced sin to sexual immorality while ignoring structural and social injustices. As is so often the case with the evangelical subculture, a paradox arises. Despite offending the morals of many conservative Protestants, the movie and television industries reinforce other evangelical values—especially that of individualism. Hollywood films tend to reduce social and economic problems to individual weakness, not structural problems. The solution is for the individual to shape up or for some hero to come on the scene and rescue people. The film industry exaggerates the existing individualistic and celebrity culture so prevalent in mainstream America and the evangelical subculture.[40]

Good-bye Bach

Listen to the music at many megachurches. Turn on some Christian radio stations. Or listen to many contemporary Christian CD's. What do you hear—Christian or secular rock music? It may be difficult to tell. In music, the convergence of the evangelical subculture and mainstream American culture becomes quite obvious—perhaps more so than in any other area. The values of individualism, feelings, experience, subjectivity, self-fulfillment, and materialism come to the forefront in both contemporary Christian music (CCM) and popular secular music. But this has not always been the case. Prior to about the 1970s, one could tell the difference between secular and sacred music.

In their passion for communicating the gospel message, evangelicals have always identified with the common people. So it has been natural for them to popularize Christian music. The surge of evangelicalism in the eighteenth and nineteenth centuries registered a sea change for many areas of Western religion, including music. Previously, many songwriters composed hymns relating to the nature of God, Christ, the church, the sacraments of baptism and the Lord's Supper, events at the end of history, and particular denominational convictions. Such subjects did not always connect with the common people. Evangelicalism then came along and interjected a heart-felt experience into the faith. This significantly changed the nature of songwriting. Ordinary believers could now express themselves in song. Hymns now focused on the element of personal salvation—the love of God for sinners, the need of sinners for Christ, the joy of salvation by Christ, and hope of life eternal in Christ.[41]

Isaac Watts furthered the development of this new hymnody. Connecting with the surge of evangelicalism under Edwards, Whitefield, and the Wesleys these new hymns proclaimed that Christianity was more than dogma, church membership, or participation in the sacraments. They focused on the necessity for repentance, faith in Christ, and the new birth. Edwards promoted Watts' hymns in the Great Awakening and hymn singing became a key aspect of this awakening.[42]

Adapting to the needs of the common people and the trends of the time must be seen as a key to the success of Methodism. The Methodists did not limit their flexibility to doctrine or the circuit riders. They also adapted their hymns to the revivals in both America and England. Such choruses struck at the heart and electrified the common people. The frontier camp meetings of the Second Great Awakening may have been the first large-scale entertainment in United States history. The fiery preacher was the central attraction, but lively hymn singing also gripped the emotions of country folk.[43]

After the Civil War, music continued to be a favorite vehicle for expressing the evangelical faith. In the urban rivals of the last half of the nineteenth century, Dwight Moody teamed up with the song leader and composer Ira B. Sankey. They became an inseparable team and hymn singing must be regarded as a major drawing factor for the middle-class evangelicals who attended these rivals. Music was also an important psychological and emotional ingredient in Billy Sunday's revivals of the first part of the twentieth century. Like Moody's revivals, Billy Graham's crusades of the 1950s and 1960s were a team effort. The gospel singer George Beverly Shea performed regularly at these revivals. Before the advent of contemporary Christian music in the 1970s, popular music was thus used in conjunction with evangelicalism. The line between evangelism and entertainment, however, had not yet been blurred. And evangelism, not entertainment, was the primary motive for this popular music.[44]

A new Christian music tradition—embracing popular musical idioms, instrumentation, and performance styles—emerged in the late 1960s and early 1970s. Contemporary Christian music, as this new trend is called, has been defined by William Romanowski: It is "evangelical popular music that co-opted existing popular music styles with religious lyrics added for ecclesiastical purposes, specifically worship and evangelism." Like all forms of popular music, CCM is a product of cultural and musical fusion. Artists draw from various forms of gospel, folk, and contemporary music traditions. Of the music styles generically labeled as gospel music, CCM has been by far the most successful.[45]

This new tradition, nevertheless, had its roots in the 1940s and 1950s. Key actors in this change were the leaders of Youth for Christ. Since the 1920s, evangelicals had gone into a self-imposed cultural exile. They adopted a very narrow view of culture, focusing only on personal piety while ignoring large areas of public life. Thanks to the neo-evangelicals led by Carl Henry and Fuller Theological Seminary, evangelicals began to interact with the modern world. Youth for Christ (YFC) provided a similar service, helping evangelicals connect with mainstream culture.[46]

These teenagers and their sympathetic adult leaders paved the way for the revolution in musical tastes that took place among Protestants between 1940 and 1970. And the controversy that they began has still not abated. What has developed is a new sectarianism over worship. While differences over doctrine have died down and denominational loyalties have weakened, people are fighting and dividing over music and how one does church. For the baby boomers who regard self-fulfillment as important, music is a major factor in their choice of church. The innovators are accused of "turning worship into a rock concert." Conversely, the traditionalists are charged with "turning it into a music appreciation class." Music sparks controversy because "it mediates between sacred and secular, youth and old, emotion and restraint" notes Thomas Bergler.[47]

Even the transition sparked by YFC had its precedents. Other evangelicals bridged the gap between secular and sacred music. Radio evangelists such as Paul Rader and Percy Crawford in the 1920s and 1930s used modern music to attract the youth. These pioneers influenced early YFC leaders such as Jack Wyrtzen, Torrey Johnson, and Bob Cook. Wyrtzen, in fact, had played in a dance band before his conversion. In the transition of Protestant worship from traditional to contemporary styles, Ralph Carmichael played a particularly key role. He introduced syncopated rhythms bearing resemblance to a rock beat. His arrangements for YFC as well as those for movies, television, and musicals pointed to the revolution in music that was looming on the horizon. When compared to what would come in the 1960s, the innovations brought about by YFC and Carmichael seem tame. Still, they paved the way by lobbying for a new music that expressed the thrill and emotions of the Christian life. In doing so, they were also helping to break down the barriers between the evangelical subculture and secular society.[48]

Why the Guitars Won?

During the 1970s, the lines between contemporary Christian and secular music became indistinct. For popular music to travel between the secular and evangelical communities was not new. Southern gospel, country gospel, and black gospel had a cultural compatibility with other forms of music. Contemporary Christian music differed from these forms of gospel music in that it had a strong religious orientation and was marketed primarily to the evangelical subculture, especially the youth. In many ways, CCM did not retain its original focus on ministering to the evangelical youth.[49]

What brought this change about? At this point four factors must be noted. First, the evangelical subculture has become submerged in the larger American culture. At most points, there are few differences between the two—despite outcries to the contrary. Evangelicalism has been thoroughly fused into the mass democratic consumer American society.[50] Contemporary Christian music's adaptation to secular rock must be seen as just a small segment of the larger acculturation that evangelicalism has undergone. CCM can be regarded as an expression of the democratic and populist components within evangelical and American culture. As popular music, CCM does not represent the high cultural tradition. Flashing the words on a screen, rather than using a hymnal, is a democratic expression. Even those who cannot read music can fully participate in the songs.[51] The differences between sacred and secular music have largely been cultural, not artistic. The culture indeed changed in the 1960s and evangelicalism, including its musical expressions, changed with it.

Two, in a market-driven society, music or anything else must sell. The evangelical youth culture represented a small market, and it is not easy to be successful in such a specialized area. Why not win souls and make a profit also? In order to be profitable, CCM had to refocus its music to a mass market, especially to a secular youth audience. This merger was accomplished by marrying Christian lyrics (words) with a secular musical style.[52]

As time went on, the demands of consumerism made Christian lyrics the junior partner in this marriage. In the effort to satisfy the demands of the secular market, the Christian music industry reoriented its goals, efforts, and strategies. If the lyrics are taken out of Christian rock, one can barely tell Christian rock from secular rock. CCM now promoted music that was based on the rules of commercialization and consumer tastes, not the values of the church or Christian doctrine.[53] Like much of evangelism, CCM has a chameleon-like character. It will change to suit the market or circumstances.

Three, as noted several times in this study, the 1960s witnessed a cultural explosion called the counterculture. The Jesus Movement, which combined an unusual mixture of fundamentalism and the counterculture, became a religious expression of this broader social movement. These evangelical hippies created "Jesus Rock" by employing existing rock music for the purpose of evangelizing the alienated youth of the 1960s. "Jesus Rock" is a forerunner of contemporary Christian music.[54] While the baby boomers were born from 1946 to 1964, many of their cultural tastes—including their preferences for music—were fashioned during the 1960s and have continued to the present.

Four, the charismatic movement added a new twist to contemporary Christian music. Drawing from historic Pentecostalism and the youth culture, the charismatic movement elevated the immediate voice of the Holy Spirit as the source of authority, not Scripture or doctrine. This movement accentuated the existing emotional and pietistic strain within evangelicalism. It also influenced a new form of CCM that was emerging in the 1970s. Often called Praise and Worship, the Jesus People promoted a more lively form of worship as a way to counter cold, impersonal church services.[55]

Rock the Flock

Christian rock took a definite shape in the 1970s. Larry Norman is regarded as the first Jesus rock artist. His album *I Love You* became a big hit and a major record company signed him to a contract. Norman's participation in Christian rock, of course, encountered some criticism. His defense of Christian rock can be best summed up in the title of one of his songs: "Why Should the Devil Have All the Good Music?" One of the lines read, "I want people to know that he saved my soul/But I still like to listen to the radio." By 1978, the CCM industry had grown large enough to publish its own magazine, *CCM Magazine*. Bob Dylan, who had converted to Christianity through the Vineyard movement, also gave CCM a boast with his three Christian albums—the first being *Slow Train Coming* (1979).[56]

At this time, contemporary Christian music depended considerably on the baby boomer or Woodstock generation. While evangelical parents attempted to reverse the results of the counterculture, their children were straddled between two worlds. Being affluent and idealistic, they sympathized with the aspirations of their peers while still holding to their evangelical faith. As a result, they combined counterculture and evangelical values. Such young people formed the mainstay of the Jesus movement. They promoted a more socially relaxed version of evangelicalism as a way to heal the nation's divisions. One result of their approach was Jesus rock, which they regarded as both biblical and hip.[57]

Many sections of the evangelical community looked with great disfavor on Christian rock. Such disapproval came to a head when the rock band Stryper merged Christianity with heavy metal. The image of some Christian rock artists—with spiked hair, seductive makeup, and tight clothes—did not endear them to conservative Protestants. Their loud, heavy metal music with lyrics that testified to their faith appeared to be a contradiction. Pentecostal and fundamentalists especially condemned Christian rock as inherently evil. They labeled it as Satanic, spiritual fornication, vulgar, and orgiastic. Segments of the evangelical community, however, accepted this Christianized version of rock as better than the secular version. They also contended that musical style did not matter. Rather, the lyrics made music Christian or secular.[58]

By the 1980s many of the Jesus People had cut their hair, began careers, and started families. The 1980s placed more emphasis on affluence and a conservative reaction to the 1960s was well underway. In such a context, the genre of Jesus rock became assimilated into contemporary Christian music. Two previously mentioned factors prompted this development. One, the major recording companies realized that gospel music—a broad category including country, rock, and folk music with religious lyrics—could generate substantial sales. This propelled CCM into the mainstream market and once this happened, commercial interests began to overshadow religious values. CCM now became a major player in the entertainment industry.[59]

This budding relationship can best be illustrated in the career of Amy Grant. Her album, *Age to Age* (1982) sold more than one million copies. Grant's next album, *Straight Ahead* (1984), also garnered over a million sales and earned a platinum status for her. Sales for *Unguarded* reached 500,000 in only two months and the company awarded her a gold status. CCM had generated such sales that it occupied a significant place in the mainstream recording industry.[60]

Praise and Worship

Another factor assimilating Jesus rock into contemporary Christian music was the charismatic movement. By the 1970s this movement had produced a new form of worship, often called Praise and Worship. This style of worship began to influence the church services of many American Christian traditions. This new form of worship came out of the Jesus movement of southern California. Chuck Smith of Calvary Chapel, a church in the Pentecostal orbit, invited the hippies into church to play their music. Not only could they wear their casual clothes and sandals, they could play their music. He even went so far as to give these new converts a stage for their music. The audience liked their music and Smith invited them back.[61]

The music of the Jesus people began to take hold, so much so that Smith helped them to establish a record company, Maranatha Music. This company distributed the music of the young artists. Maranatha Music drew tens of thousands of young people not only to Calvary Chapel and its related churches but also to the Vineyard movement. The Vineyard Christian Fellowship began in the 1970s and also embraced a charismatic form of worship. Maranatha Music drew scores of young people because it signaled that religion was going to be done in a different way. "People were getting high—on life, love, and Jesus" and the music said that religion could be culturally relevant, notes Donald Miller. Cultural movements have their own sounds and the guitar drove the cultural rhythm of the Jesus People.[62]

Praise and Worship music had a staying power and has moved well beyond the Jesus movement. It became popular in many churches, appealing to the youth but alienating more traditional worshippers. Coming across as more than a Christianized version of rock music, Praise and Worship gave more respectability to CCM. Praise and Worship can be most readily identified by the presence of a praise band on the stage at the front of the church. Very similar to Jesus rock, the praise band consists of electric guitars, drums, bass, and singers with microphones. In more pragmatic churches, this praise band or worship team has replaced the symbol of the traditional church—the church choir. The Praise and Worship music comes early and often lasts for about thirty minutes. The service begins with a round of songs, punctuated with an opening prayer and more choruses, followed by a sermon.[63]

Praise and Worship has taken hold because it connects with many of the historic evangelical characteristics. It offers the churchgoer an experience—a sense of encountering God, a reminder of their conversion, and dramatizes the trials they face. Like most Americans, evangelicals desire to be entertained. Praise and Worship is lively and offers them music similar to what they will hear on the radio. It also reflects the populist impulse within evangelicalism. Evangelicals are often uncomfortable with traditional churches because they convey an atmosphere of formality, rationality, structure, and professionalism. Praise and Worship services are informal, subjective, emotional, and expressive. Such services also blend the sacred and secular as evangelicals do in many areas of life.[64]

Contemporary Christian music has certainly been a numerical success. It has appealed to the youth, contributed to the megachurch phenomenon, and generated huge sales in the record market. Still, some questions have been raised. Marva Dawn contends that it is a "misnomer to call (church) services worship if their purpose is to attract people rather than to adore God." And attracting people is what megachurches do, largely through their use of CCM. The primary purpose of CCM, that of winning the youth, has been challenged. Many youth who attend services featuring CCM are already Christians. It may be that the major function of CCM is entertainment. If this is so, the words of Stephen Prothero are appropriate. "Rather than making America more Christian" CCM and the megachurches "have tried to make Christianity more American. They have molded Jesus to the world instead of molding the world to Jesus."[65]

Word-Faith Movement

Another late twentieth-century development pointed to the marriage between segments of conservative Protestantism and American culture. Like the rest of American society, evangelicals passionately pursed the quest for health and wealth. This can be seen in the popularity of the Word-Faith movement, and a small book, *The Prayer of Jabez*, by Bruce Wilkinson. While not directly connected, this movement and book represent an attempt by evangelicals to reconcile their faith with the materialistic, consumption-driven American society.[66]

In the last half of the twentieth century, evangelicals have bought into a new religious fad—the Word-Faith movement. Critics have called it by several other names: the health and wealth gospel, name-it-claim-it gospel, positive confession, or simply Faith movement. This movement proclaims that physical health and material prosperity are the rights of every Christian if they will claim them by faith. The secret for acquiring these blessings is an unwavering faith. The Christian must make a positive confession, that is, "stating in faith what one desires or is requesting from God and believing that God will honor it."[67]

Well-known personalities of this movement include Kenneth Hagin, Kenneth Copeland, Paul Yonggi Cho, Benny Hinn, Marilyn Hickey, Frederick K. C. Price, John Avanzini, Charles Capps, Jerry Savelle, Morris Cerullo, Robert Tilton, and Paul and Jan Crouch. With the death of Hagin in 2003, Copeland must be regarded as the leading spokesman for the movement. His wife Gloria plays an important role in his ministry. Tilton was discredited by an ABC news special but is staging a comeback. Though not a Word-Faith teacher, Oral Roberts significantly influenced the movement. The Word-Faith proponents have become well known because of their international television coverage. Most of these programs are broadcast on the Trinity Broadcasting Network (TBN), which is operated by Word-Faith advocates, Paul and Jan Crouch. TBN is the largest Christian-based television station in the world.[68]

The roots of the Word-Faith movement are disputed. Bruce Barron states that its historical origins reside in the Pentecostal and charismatic movements. D. R. McConnell says no. Rather, its roots can be traced back to E. W. Kenyon

(1876-1948), who had connections with several metaphysical groups. McConnell says Kenyon, not Hagin, deserves the title of father of the Faith movement. Hagin plagiarized his writings and usurped the title. Robert Bowman, Jr. takes a mediating approach. While acknowledging the influence of Kenyon and that Hagen did plagiarize him, Bowman still regards Pentecostalism as the source of the Word-Faith movement and that Hagin is the real father of the movement.[69]

Divine Healing: Several Streams

The precise origins of the Faith movement are not central to this study. So the various streams of the movement should be mentioned. One current goes back to the divine healing teachings of several influential evangelicals—A. J. Gordon, A. B. Simpson, and John Alexander Dowie. From different perspectives, these men preached Christ's power to heal the body. A second avenue was the Pentecostal tradition. Early Pentecostal leaders such as Charles Parham and William Seymour said that the gifts of the Spirit—including speaking in tongues and divine healing—were operational in the twentieth century. Following these leaders, the early Pentecostals staunchly believed in divine healing. While they did not reject medical science, they believed healing to be preferable.[70]

The early Pentecostals recognized two types of healing. The first model involved the Christian community. The church prayed for healing while the elders laid hands on the sick or injured individual. The second type concerned the "gift of healing." God endowed certain individuals with the power to heal. For a successful outcome, they applied their gift to a recipient who was only required to exercise faith. Throughout Christian history, many groups have practiced the first model. The second version gained prominence in Pentecostal circles and led to a surge of healing revivalism in the 1950s. Nationally known Pentecostal leaders—Oral Roberts, Asa A. Allen, William Branham, T. L. Osborn, William Freeman, and Jack Coe—conducted healing revivals throughout the nation. In the process, they gained considerable publicity for healing practices and momentarily made them the center of the Pentecostal world.[71]

A third stream for early Pentecostalism remained largely unnoticed until the 1960s. The theological framework came from Kenyon who drew from such groups as Christian Science, Unity, and Divine Science. Such New Thought movements argued that true reality is spiritual. The human mind, by means of a positive mental attitude and positive confession, can create its own reality—especially health and wealth. Kenyon did not formally join any New Thought groups, though he acknowledged its influence. Moreover, he never became a Pentecostal, though he traveled in those circles and significantly influenced the Word-Faith movement.[72]

A fourth current centers on Kenneth Hagin (1917-2003), the widely ac-knowledged father of the Faith movement. While the precise origins of the movement are disputed, Hagin certainly popularized the Faith teachings and gave them an institutional structure. As a child, he experienced several life threatening health problems. By age 16, he was paralyzed and at times uncon-scious. In this condition, he began an intensive Bible study, focusing on Mark 11:24: "Therefore I tell you, whatever you ask for in prayer, believe that you have received it, and it will be yours." Hagin prayed for God to heal him and after months of lying in bed, he believed that God had healed him. He con-fessed that his paralysis was gone and got up from his bed. This miraculous recovery catapulted his ministry.[73]

In 1937, Hagin received the baptism of the Holy Spirit and became an Assemblies of God pastor. After pastoring Assemblies' churches for twelve years, he began an independent ministry and moved to the forefront of the developing Word-Faith movement. Furthering his rise to prominence was his acquisition of two offices: teacher and prophet. Despite having little formal education, by means of a mystical experience he was anointed with the gift of teaching. Several years later, he had another experience and felt called to be a prophet, which he defined as one who receives visions and revelations. In subsequent years, Hagin claimed to have had eight personal visitations by Christ and many more visions. Combining these two offices gave Hagin tre-mendous authority in the Faith movement. The teacher expounds Scripture and the prophet receives and communicates divine revelations. Thus, his min-istry appeared to be both biblical and supernatural.[74]

Moving his office to Tulsa in 1966, Hagin's ministry surged dramatically. He began to circulate his *Word of Faith Magazine,* which reached a circulation of over 200,000. In 1974, he founded the $20 million Rhema Bible Training Center, which has sent out thousands of disciples propagating Word-Faith teachings. In 1979, Hagin and several other evangelists established the Inter-national Convention of Faith Churches and Ministry in Tulsa—an organiza-tion that functions as a de facto denomination for the Word-Faith movement. The Hagin ministries have had a long-lasting impact on the Faith movement, producing many of the next generations' leading preachers, especially Ken-neth and Gloria Copeland and Fred Price.[75]

Blessed are the Rich

While the Word-Faith movement at first focused on health, the acquisition of wealth soon became an important component. Writing in 1975, David Harrell indicates that as early as the 1930s prosperity was an important message with some Pentecostals. "But in the 1960s the message almost supplanted the ear-lier emphasis on healing: every evangelist came to advertise his own master key to financial success."[76] The evolution of the belief that divine healing can be claimed by a positive confession of faith can be traced from Kenyon and several Pentecostal teachers. The development of the idea that prosperity can also come by the positive confession is more difficult to trace.

For centuries, Protestantism has been linked with the rising commercial classes and the acquisition of wealth. With the seventeenth-century Puritans, there emerged the notion that wealth and prosperity were a sign of divine blessing to the just and a sign of being God's elect. With the rise of industrialization and advertising, the practice of consumerism exploded. Religious people responded in two ways to this rising materialism. Some people reasserted the simple life. Others incorporated materialism into their religious framework. Instead of regarding materialism and godliness as in conflict, they saw the two existing in a sympathetic relationship.[77] Two examples of this thinking can be noted. In the nineteenth century, Horace Bushnell said that Christians had the duty to prosper. Around the turn of the twentieth century, Russell Conwell delivered his sermon "Acres of Diamonds" over 6,000 times. According to this message, it is one's Christian responsibility to become wealthy in order to aid the cause of Christ. No links, however, have connected such men and ideas with the Word-Faith movement.[78]

Many of the Word-Faith teachings can be traced to Kenyon. In respect to prosperity, however, the connections with Kenyon are tenuous and indirect. He defined prosperity in terms of freedom from poverty and meeting the believers' basic needs, not in the acquisition of wealth. And he personally died with little money. But he did believe that Christians should not be in bondage to poverty. A connection, nevertheless, can be made with the Unity School of Christianity and New Thought, which influenced Kenyon. It taught the existence of laws for acquiring prosperity. Also, Kenyon's formula for claiming healing by a positive confession can readily be applied to the acquisition of wealth. In insisting that God will meet the desires (not only needs) of believers, the modern Word-Faith teachers have gone well beyond Kenyon, however.[79]

Definite connections can be made between the prosperity doctrine and the Pentecostal evangelists. Hagin acknowledged that prosperity came late to his belief system. He began to push it in the 1960s and many have followed him since then. This prosperity doctrine came directly from God and not from human sources, he insisted. Hagin contended that God not only wants to free Christians from poverty, "He wants his children to eat the best, He wants them to wear the best clothing, He wants them to drive the best cars, and He wants them to have the best of everything." Fred Price echoed similar statements, insisting that God's children should drive luxury cars.[80]

Prosperity was important in Oral Roberts' early ministry. He began pushing it in the 1950s, and based his teaching on 3 John 2: "I pray that you may enjoy good health and that all may go well with you, even as your soul is getting along well." When seeking funds for his television ministry, Roberts pushed the prosperity doctrine even further. His "Blessing-Pact" promised to everyone giving $100 to his ministry that they would receive the gift back from a completely unanticipated source within a year. Such a plan, he believed, would bring prosperity to his followers. In 1955, Roberts published his first book on the subject, *God's Formula for Success and Prosperity.*[81]

While the prosperity doctrine preceded Hagin, it exploded in the 1960s when he aggressively promoted this belief. Foremost of his followers were Kenneth and Gloria Copeland. They published two books on the subject— *The Laws of Prosperity* and *God's Will is Prosperity.* In the Faith movement, one can detect two general teachings regarding prosperity. The egocentric approach promises success and prosperity from God to those who give to a particular evangelist's ministry. This is egocentric because it benefits the one pleading for money and centers on his or her personality. Taking a broader view is the cosmic approach. This teaching is cosmic because it promises prosperity from God to those who follow the divine laws of the universe that govern prosperity. Kenneth Copeland pushed the cosmic teaching. He contended that there are "certain laws governing prosperity in God's Word. Faith causes them to function.... The success formulas in the Word of God produce results when used as directed." God has worked out an arrangement. When individuals give to his cause, they have activated the law of reciprocity. God, in turn, is obligated by this law to increase the believer's wealth.[82]

In Mark 10:29 and 30, Jesus said, "No one who has left home or brothers or sisters or mother or father for me and the gospel will fail to receive a hundred times as much in this present age...and in the age to come, eternal life." Gloria Copeland put a dollar figure on that principle: "You give $1 for the Gospel's sake and $100 belongs to you; give $10 and receive $1000; give $1000 and receive $100,000. I know that you can multiply, but I want you to see it in black and white and see how tremendous the hundredfold return is.... In short, Mark 10:30 is a very good deal." Given this good deal, she declares, "Christians should be the wealthiest people on earth." This good deal can even apply to nonbelievers, notes Hagin. If they apply the divine laws of prosperity, they will work. They are the laws of universe and God will honor them.[83]

Core Teachings

Hagin and Copeland are the most prominent leaders of the Word-Faith movement. Other teachers may differ over specific points, but any teaching embraced by both of them can be regarded as a standard for the movement. While the Faith movement is best known for insisting that all Christians can gain health and wealth by a positive confession of faith, certain doctrines must precede this belief. These core beliefs center on the nature of God, Christ, and humanity and the relationship between faith, prayer, and confession.[84]

The Faith movement views human nature as spirit, soul, and body. Spirit is basic and more real than the physical. It is the real person and was made in God's image. This permits the Faith teachers to claim that humans are little gods and the exact duplicates of God. Moreover, rather than communicate with the mind, God communicates with this spirit made in his image. The problems encountered by humans arise because they have allowed their bodies—not their spirits—to control their lives. This line of reasoning is basic to the Faith teachers. If our senses tell us that we are sick or poor, we are to ignore this impulse. When our reason tells us that the Word-Faith teachings are false or illogical, we are to disbelieve this rational thinking.[85]

The Faith movement teaches that while God is in essence a spirit, he is more like a human being than people think. Like humans God is spirit, soul, and body. God is also a god of faith and accomplishes his will by exercising faith. Conversely, humans are more like God than usually believed. We are in a "god-class" or small gods. In fact, Christ came to restore humanity to godhood, that is, to create a new race that would become God incarnate like Jesus. This potential to become little gods, however, became destroyed by the fall of humanity. Sin gave Satan dominion over the world and sickness and poverty became the plight of humanity.[86]

To correct the problem of sin in the world, God became human. The Word-Faith teachers affirm that Jesus was God incarnate but they give a different twist to the meaning of incarnate. They are unclear as to whether the preexistent Son of God became incarnate in the person of Jesus. To further confuse the issue, they say Christians are also incarnations of God as was Jesus. How does this unusual view of Christ affect the doctrine of salvation? The Word-Faith teachers say Jesus died both physically and spirituality. In doing so, he took upon himself the nature of Satan and went to hell for three days. Here Jesus was born again and rose from the dead with God's nature, which they imply was lost when he died spiritually. In doing all of this, Jesus prepared the way for humankind to be born again and acquire God's nature.[87]

Such ideas regarding God, Christ, and humanity pave the way for the Faith movement's distinctive ideas regarding the acquisition of health and wealth by a positive confession. Faith is traditionally defined as believing what God says. Because God has said that he will grant our requests, faith also entails believing that we will receive what we ask from him. We are divine spirits and if we utter a positive confession, that is, state in faith what we want from God he will honor that faith. In fact, God must grant our request because his Word states that he will. The Word-Faith teachings turn the positive confession into a command obligating God to grant our requests. For example, if one prays to be healed one must claim it and believe he/she is well. To even repeat a prayer is to allow doubt to creep in.[88]

The Word-Faith teachings also rest on a particular view regarding Christ's atonement. Jesus died to free us from the curse of the law. "By his stripes we were healed." Traditionally, this has been interpreted to mean that Christ's death has freed believers from the punishment of their sin. The Word-Faith teachers go a step further and say that Christ's death frees us from the entire curse of the law, including sickness and poverty. Christians thus have the potential to be free from illness and impoverishment. In fact, when Christians live healthy and affluent lives they are testifying to the power of God.[89]

To further the idea that God wants Christians to be wealthy, some Word-Faith teachers contend that Jesus was affluent. For evidence, they cite several examples. Jesus did not have to be born in a manger. His father was a business-man and he could afford to rent a room at Bethlehem, but none were available. At his birth, the wise men brought costly gifts to Jesus and he and his family went to Egypt. As a carpenter, Jesus was a capitalist and a successful business-man. Kenneth Copeland tells us that "Jesus was not poor in His ministry. He had a treasurer!" Moreover, at his crucifixion, he wore a robe so expensive that the Roman soldiers cast lots for it. Was Jesus poor? Oral Roberts insisted that such a teaching was Satan's lie. In urging people to read his book, *How I Learned Jesus Was Not Poor*, Roberts said, "Read this book and you'll never be poor again."[90]

While it may not be systematic, the Word-Faith teachers have created both a rationale and a psychology for the acquisition of wealth. One, God is con-cerned with the material condition of his followers. It is God's will for Chris-tians to be prosperous. Next, the Faith teachers provide a set of actions necessary for acquiring personal wealth. If the believer takes a step, this activates the divine principle bringing prosperity. Three, the Word-Faith movement offers an explanation for misery and poverty in the world and insulates its followers from guilt feelings or the motivation to correct such problems. This thinking and mindset allows the followers to accept the lavish lifestyles of the prosper-ity evangelists. Their personal affluence is a reward for their godliness and a promise of what their followers can also acquire.[91]

Gain without Pain

"No gain without pain." In an attempt to inspire people to work out, locker rooms and gymnasiums often post this sign. *The Prayer of Jabez* by Bruce Wilkinson seems to reverse the order. It offers divine blessings and makes no mention of life's struggles. It connects with the American desire for shortcuts to success without paying the price. This slim, ninety-two-page book rides the tide of American materialism and narcissism. The author focuses on two sen-tences of the two verses in the Bible devoted to Jabez. "Jabez cried out to the God of Israel, Oh that you would bless me and enlarge my territory! Let your hand be with me, and keep me from harm so that I will be free from pain. And God granted his request" (1 Chronicles 4:10).

Wilkinson has turned this prayer into something resembling a mantra— insisting that if faithfully recited with the right motives, it will bring blessings. And millions of Americans have bought into its message. *The Prayer of Jabez* has appeared on best-seller lists, registering more than 9 million sales. Unlike the Word-Faith movement, which resides at the margins of evangelicalism and has been labeled as heretical, *The Prayer of Jabez* comes right out of the heart of evangelicalism. Wilkinson is an Atlanta evangelist who has a global ministry. Still, with the exception of James Dobson of Focus on the Family, most evangelical writers and organizations have been critical of *The Prayer of Jabez*.[92]

These critics argue that this book promotes something resembling the prosperity gospel advocated by the Faith teachers. The prayer focuses on the individual who is uttering it, and he/she is guaranteed success if he/she repeats the prescribed prayer. Moreover, Wilkinson gives the Jabez prayer a materialistic orientation. "If Jabez had worked on Wall Street, he might have prayed, 'Lord, increase the value of my investment portfolios.'" Christian executives ask Wilkinson: "Is it right for me to ask God for more business?" His response is, "Absolutely!"[93] As one critic said, "God will bless you with a bigger paycheck if you promise not to squander it on high living…" Also, one can search this small book and find nothing indicating that the Christian life may entail sacrifice.[94]

However, Wilkinson does insist that the prayer for blessing assumes that one is doing God's will. "If you're doing business God's way, it's not only right to ask for more, but he is waiting for you to ask." Jabez's prayer for blessing is for a reason—to help him to do God's work. Wilkinson indeed rejects the health and wealth gospel. He talks of no laws that require God to bless the one praying. Wilkinson notes that "it is entirely up to God to decide what the blessings would be and where, when, and how Jabez would receive them." He insists the Jabez prayer has no connection with "the popular gospel that you should ask God for a Cadillac, a six-figure income, or some other material sign…"[95]

The Word-Faith movement, indeed, tends to reduce God to a pawn in the hands of the one uttering the positive confession of faith. Despite Wilkinson's disclaimers, however, many evangelicals have linked this prayer with their personal and material success. Also, Wilkinson seems to imply that the Jabez prayer has somewhat of an automatic character. While God decides on the when, what, and how, a blessing will come to the one uttering the prayer.

Why the Explosion?

Modern America has witnessed an explosion of consumerism and materialism and evangelical Christians have participated in this development. The prosperity gospel and to some extent *The Prayer of Jabez* must be seen as an attempt to reconcile conservative Protestantism with the materialism of modern America. Both have promoted a narcissistic view of religion. The Word-Faith movement may be the most Americanized version of Protestantism. The prosperity gospel that it promotes "amounts to a baptism of American materialism and consumerism," notes Randall Balmer. "Jesus will save your soul and your marriage, make you happy, heal your body, and even make you rich. Who wouldn't look twice at that offer?"[96]

This teaching connects with the American desire for affluence and easy solutions. It appeals to middle-class aspirations and has made inroads into the evangelical subculture, especially with those who interpret Scripture literally with no concern for the context. Many evangelicals want gain with no pain. They seem to have forgotten the scandal of the gospel and Jesus' invitation to forsake all for his sake. Instead of resisting the values of American culture, advocates of the Word-Faith movement—along with many other evangelicals—have embraced them. The health and wealth teachings promise Christians "the best of both worlds: the blessing of God and the respect of society."[97]

More specifically, the rise of the prosperity gospel mirrors several economic and social trends. It connects with televangelism and the money needed for these national and international ministries. Expensive television and radio programs require tremendous sums of money and the televangelists promise financial blessings if one contributes to their ministry. Two, the health and wealth gospel is most readily found in the Pentecostal subculture. Along with much of American evangelicalism, the Pentecostals have either prospered financially or desire to do so. They have sought the American dream and have moved up the financial and social ladder.

Three, in particular the 1980s saw a surge of prosperity teachings. This decade also marked a time of self-aggrandizement and the quest for affluence. The Reagan administration promoted "trickle down" economics, that is, the wealth starts at the top and will flow down to the middle and lower classes. Everyone will thus be better off. The health and wealth gospel can be seen as an evangelical version of "trickle down" economics. "Prosperity in this case would trickle down from heaven, but it would reach the faithful, of course, only after it had cycled through the rain barrel of the televangelists," says Balmer.[98] Four, the health and wealth gospel connects with the American character. Americans are so "optimistic and pragmatic, they believe that such a God-winning system must exist," states Quentin Schultze. They think that by obeying simple laws they will be able to overcome the trials of life.[99]

Another component contributing to the acceptance of the Word-Faith movement is biblical illiteracy and a parallel emphasis on feelings. Catholics have the pope and mainline Protestants have denominational structures and the liturgy to give them direction. Lacking these supports, evangelicals have focused on doctrine, celebrities, experience, and emotions. But belief and doctrine have been on a serious decline in recent years. The dumbing down of beliefs has left evangelicals with not much else but an emphasis on feelings, experience, and celebrities.[100]

In part, this biblical ignorance stems from the way evangelicals approach Scripture. Believing that truth can be found in the literal words of the Bible, they take a cut-and-paste-approach to Scripture. They see no need for systematic thinking, the principles of biblical exegesis, or interpreting Scripture in its historical context—as have most Christian traditions. Rather, evangelicals engage in proof texting. They play "Bible roulette," that is, they use random texts to support the idea at hand.[101] In adopting this approach to Scripture they reflect the populism and pragmatism of the evangelical subculture. Understanding Scripture in its proper context requires some theological training. Conversely, a literal reading of certain proof texts with no knowledge of the context can be done by the untrained laity and has a populist appeal.

Moreover, evangelicals are not interested in doctrine or theology; they want an immediate application of Scripture. As Nancy Ammerman has observed in her study of fundamentalist churchgoers: "Although they often read the Bible from cover to cover, believers rarely refer to the themes of the whole Bible or even to the whole books or stories. Rather, they search the scripture to find the word or phrase that seems to answer the question at hand." In fact, "Any portion of scripture, no matter how small, can be used."[102]

How does this relate to the Word-Faith movement? At best many of its teachings must be regarded as aberrant. Some critics say *heretical* might be a better word. While the faith teachers do uphold most essentials of the Christian faith, they support their health and wealth teachings by tearing Scripture out of its context and by extra biblical sources. Their leaders have little or no theological training. They thus find verses and give them a literal interpretation not related to the total thrust of Scripture. Worse yet, they support many beliefs by dreams or visitations by God. This approach fits into the tendency of evangelicals to gravitate toward celebrity figures. Such charismatic figures carry much authority in the Pentecostal subculture. They are often seen as the voice of God.

You, Too, Can Be a Winner

An important American cure all—self-esteem—is purported to fix everything from juvenile delinquency to mental illness. We are told that there are no bad people, just people who feel badly about themselves. Negative thoughts can afflict even the most successful of people. But such individuals have overcome these feelings. Self-esteem can be empowerment. It can motivate people to great heights and be the building block upon which personal effectiveness is based. While self-esteem as a concept has no clear line of origins, theorists such as Carl Rogers and Abraham Maslow have given it the most prominence.[103]

Nearly every area of American society has embraced the concept of self-esteem. Television programs encourage children to feel good about themselves. Self-esteem can free people from addictive behaviors and substance abuse. Businesses use self-esteem to motivate employees. No area of society has accepted the notion of self-esteem as has education. Some school districts have abolished failing grades or pressured teachers into not giving such grades because they might damage a young person's self-esteem. Self-esteem is less a matter of scientific proof than faith. Many people believe that positive thoughts can bring out an individual's inherent goodness and enhance his or her performance. Americans have been very favorable to this brand of naïve optimism.[104]

Religion has been caught up big time in the allure of self-esteem. In the constant quest to attract new members, many churches—especially the growth-oriented churches—have shelved worship, doctrine, and denominational loyalties. To this list one must add sin. They want to avoid making people feel uncomfortable. These churches have not completely disregarded the concepts of sin and judgment; they just couch them in non-judgmental terms. They have found that low-esteem is less of an affront to congregations than sin. When the pastors of such churches speak of sin, they usually do so without using the word. And *hell* is even a more forbidden word. Most seeker churches have banished this word from their vocabulary.[105]

Seeker-sensitive church preachers often frame the discussion of human misbehavior "in terms of how sin harms the individual, rather than how it is offensive to a holy God. Sin, in short, prevents us from realizing our full potential." These pastors "believe that if they can successfully portray God as reasonable rather than mystical they will be able to attract more seekers."[106] In pursuit of this goal, they do not present Christianity as an authoritative religion but as a nurturing faith—one that uplifts people instead of condemning them for their shortcomings.

The carrier of this focus on self-esteem has been the therapeutic revolution of the modern era. This therapeutic revolution or the arrival of the "psychological man" came from Europe and has taken such deep roots in America that it has been hailed as the "triumph of the therapeutic." In America, it has flowered into an alternative faith, which can be traced back to the New Thought movement of the late nineteenth century.[107] Robert Ellwood says this development "is not so much a cult or a church in itself as a type of teaching which has influenced a number of groups."[108] New Thought was so diffuse that it lacked boundaries and could not be confined to a specific religious body. The basic assumption of New Thought is that mind is fundamental and causative. New Thought can be regarded as a Western adaptation of this concept—largely it emphasizes that every event is an internal, nonmaterial idea. New Thought's tenets are the basis of several churches, including Unity, the Church of Religious Science, and the Church of Divine Science.[109]

New Thought relates well to American culture, for it appealed to the practical and material side of American life. In very concrete ways, New Thought teachers have attempted to demonstrate how thoughts of health, wholeness, and success can create equivalent material realities. Assuming that mind is the basis of the physical world, altering one's thoughts should bring changes in the physical world. Even if an individual's thoughts focus on a specific objective, such as acquiring a new job, these thoughts will bring such a reality into existence. [110]

A line can be traced from New Thought to the Power of Positive Thinking and today's Possibility Thinking. Individuals in this stream of influence include Ralph Waldo Emerson, William James, Harry Emerson Fosdick and down to Norman Vincent Peale and Robert Schuller. New Thought's greatest impact has come through its publishing endeavors. Many of its books have become well known in the self-help market. Very importantly, New Thought has infiltrated liberal Protestantism to the extent that many in the religious mainstream have absorbed its ideas and values and spread them.[111]

Norman Vincent Peale (1898-2003) is an example. Millions of Americans learned of mental healing and the success ethic from his message of "positive thinking." As a minister of the Reformed Church of America, early in his career he recognized the need for integrating psychiatry with ministry. Drawing from his interpretation of Scripture, Peale combined psychological themes and therapeutic prescriptions into simple principles and presented them in everyday language. These therapeutic themes became evident in his publications: *The Art of Living* (1937), *You Can Win* (1939), *A Guide to Confident Living* (1948), *The Art of Real Happiness* (1950), and especially his best selling book *The Power of Positive Thinking* (1952).[112]

Appealing to traditional Protestants, who sought answers to their personal and spiritual needs, Peale reminded them that the answers to their problems lay within themselves. They only had to tap the divine energy stored up within their unconscious through affirmative prayers and positive thinking. His message resonated with a largely lower middle-class, female, Protestant audience and had a strong populist appeal. Expressed in the language of the masses and communicated through the most advanced technology, Peale's message was pragmatic, empirical, nonsystematic, and designed to reach large numbers of people. He regarded his message as practical Christianity, as the old time gospel applied to contemporary problems. The major adjustment came in the form of what he called "thought power" or positive thinking. Peale regarded this way of thinking as a link between the individual and divine energy. [113]

Through its metaphysical connections, Peale's message contained the theme of cosmic oneness so prevalent in the nineteenth century and must be seen as part of the American "harmonial" religion. Sydney Ahlstrom has described this tradition as "those forms of piety and belief in which spiritual composure, physical health, and even economic well-being are understood to flow from a person's rapport with the cosmos." Related to this approach, Peale presented Jesus from several alternating vantage points: a personal friend and companion and as a Christ synonymous with God or Divine Mind. Critics have viewed his positive thinking as religious pragmatism that has watered-down Christian theology and promoted the American values of self-reliance and material rewards.[114]

Possibility Thinking

Peale's blend of evangelical and New Thought ideas have reached the present through his protégé Robert Schuller (1926-). Schuller is a minister of the Reformed Church in America and a televangelist. But he is perhaps best known for his possibility thinking, an updated version of Peale's positive thinking with an evangelical twist. In fact, Schuller fully credits Peale with fine-turning his own positive faith and laying the foundation for his message of possibility thinking.[115]

In 1955, Schuller accepted a call to start a mission church in southern California. Beginning in a drive-in theater, his church grew rapidly. By 1961, Garden Grove Community Church had a building. With further growth came more buildings including the Tower of Hope (1968) and the spectacular Crystal Cathedral (1980)—an edifice with 10,000 windows, huge video screens, and an angel hovering from the roof by a rope of gold. In 1970, he began to televise the Sunday worship service known as the "Hour of Power." This program is directed to the unchurched and professionally designed to hold their attention. It is currently viewed by millions of people internationally. Schuller has also authored more than twenty-five books, several of which have been best sellers.[116]

Whether Schuller can be placed in the evangelical camp is a matter of debate. But one thing is for sure: he has been a genius at fusing Christ and culture, at adapting (or distorting as some would say) the gospel to conform to American society. In Orange County of southern California, the icons of culture are sunshine, affluence, and Disney Land. Schuller built a monument that would rival the great cathedrals of Europe, except that his church is not dark and gloomy. God could be worshipped under the glow of his great sun. As a member of a Reformed denomination he has taken this tradition from the austere Puritan churches of New England to a modern sun-belt Tower of Babel. Reflecting the wealth of one of the most affluent counties in America, the Crystal Cathedral cost over $20 million—a tidy sum for the 1970s. As Schuller declared, "We are trying to make a big, beautiful impression upon the affluent non-religious American who is riding by on this busy freeway."[117] Only a stone's throw from Disney Land, the Crystal Cathedral fits well into the surrounding area. The see-through church is so spectacular that it seems like a mirage, something akin to the nearby fantasyland.[118]

In respect to doctrine, Schuller has further adapted the Reformed faith and possibly orthodox theology to American culture. His Puritan forefathers would not recognize his possibility thinking. It is as far removed from their theology as the Crystal Cathedral is from the simple Puritan house of worship. He confidently claims that his new insights into Scripture and the gospel amount to a "new reformation" of the church. Schuller says, "classical theology has erred in its insistence that theology be God-centered, not man-centered." "It was appropriate for Luther and Calvin to think theocentrically." At that time most people were in the church and the issues were theological. Today many people are unchurched and the issues center more on human needs. So another approach is needed and "the scales must tip the other way."[119]

The heart of Schuller's new Reformation is the concept of self-esteem. While he claims to affirm the essentials of the historic Christian faith, he gives it a new twist.[120] Schuller says that the Reformation theology—which serves as the foundation for the Protestant and evangelical faith— is imperfect. It places too much emphasis on God and not enough on humankind. In doing so, Reformation theology has elevated "theocentric communication above the meeting of the deeper emotional and spiritual needs of humanity." The traditional doctrine of sin "is not incorrect as it is shallow and insulting to the human being." Instead of demeaning people, the church should be in the business of building up their self-esteem, which is necessary for both a proper concept of sin and salvation.[121]

Schuller builds his theology of self-esteem "on a solid core of religious truth—the dignity of man." This is shortchanged in Reformation theology, which "failed to make clear the core of sin is a lack of self-esteem."[122] Schuller rejects federal theology, which argues that because of Adam's original sin, humankind has since been enslaved to sin. He also spurns the Pelagian view that contends people are born sinless but do fall into sin by committing acts of sin. Rather, Schuller argues that individuals are born in sin but that sin is unbelief before it becomes rebellion. "The core of sin is lack of faith, a total inability to trust oneself, one's parents, or God."[123]

The answer is to be saved from sin. But what does Schuller mean by salvation? He affirms the Reformation doctrine of salvation by faith, but gives it a new twist. Salvation "means to be permanently lifted from sin (psychological self-abuse with all of its consequences…) and shame to self-esteem and its God-glorifying, human need-meeting, constructive and creative consequences. To be saved is to know that Christ forgives me…and that I am somebody…"[124] Sin is to be in a state of shame. Salvation, in turn, is a faith that brings glory to both God and human beings. Traditional evangelical theology argues that individuals must see themselves as helpless sinners before they can come to Christ. Schuller reverses this. Only the person who recognizes moral values and their self-worth can know he or she is a sinner and turn to Christ.[125]

In his new Reformational thinking, Schuller has translated traditional theological concepts into the vocabulary (and possibly the meaning) of popular psychology. While he affirms the major tenets of the Christian faith—even accepting "the Apostles, Nicene and Athanasian Creeds"—he has managed to subjectivize traditional theology. In places he has turned it on its head. The focus is not God but the human craving for self-worth. Sin is more of a psychological defect than rebellion against God. While he says there is a literal hell, he emphasizes that it is also being less than your full self.[126]

Kenneth Kantzer does not see Schuller as unorthodox but as overreacting against some doctrines and deficient in others. Many evangelicals have pushed the doctrine of total depravity to an extreme, regarding humans as totally worthless. They have lost sight of the dignity of humanity and that they were created in God's image. Schuller, in turn, has elevated his notion of self-worth and reduced sin to a negative self-concept. He is also overreacting against a method—"one that, in a 30-minute gospel message, allots 29 minutes to sin, and the need for repentance. Only at the last moment, almost as an after thought, does it allow for mention of God's overflowing love for the sinner...[and] his reaching out for the sinner in grace, and his call to faith."[127]

These new interpretations connect with several components of modern American culture—its optimism, quest for success, and therapeutic mentality. There is no limit to American optimism. We can do it all—an attitude evident in building the Crystal Cathedral from its beginnings in a drive-in movie. Failure is not an option in our success-driven society. You can be anything you want to be, proclaims Schuller and other apostles of the American success story. And to be successful, Schuller is willing to compete with the best of secular society—professional sports, soap operas, newscasts, etc. His Crystal Cathedral and "Hour of Power" are "Show-Biz" at its best. They are operated as professionally as any program in the secular culture.

Especially appealing to modern American society is the therapeutic mentality. "[The] self improved, is the ultimate concern of modern culture," notes Phillip Rieff.[128] Schuller's focus on the therapeutic is in step with the evangelical world. James Hunter tells us that evangelicals are preoccupied with the therapeutic understanding of self. As do many other elements of American society, they believe "the attention the self is receiving is legitimate and that the self, as the repository of human emotions and subjectivity, has intrinsic and ultimate worth and significance."[129] Because Schuller has focused on the therapeutic, David Wells has described him as a minister "riding the stream of modernity." By telling us "don't worry, be happy," Schuller "is offering in easily digestible bites the therapeutic model of life through which the healing of the bruised self is found."[130] And with a son and grandson waiting in the wings, the ministry of possibility thinking will continue after his retirement.

Notes

1. R. Laurence Moore, *Touchdown Jesus: The Mixing of Sacred and Secular in American History* (Louisville: Westminster John Knox Press, 2003), 51-53.
2. William D. Romanowski, *Pop Culture Wars: Religion and the Role of Entertainment in American Life* (Downers Grove, IL: InterVaristy Press, 1996), 34.
3. Catherine L. Albanese, "Religion and American Popular Culture: An Introductory Essay," *Journal of the American Academy of Religion* 64, 4 (1997): 733-42; James B. Gilbert, "Popular Culture," *American Quarterly* 35 (1983): 140-54; Mark Hulsether, "Interpreting the 'Popular' in Popular Religion," *American Studies* 36, 2 (1995): 127-37.

4. Kenneth A. Myers, *All God's Children and Blue Suede Shoes: Christians and Popular Culture* (Wheaton, IL: Crossway Books, 1989), 105, 106, 120.

5. Alan Wolfe, *The Transformation of American Religion* (New York: Free Press, 2003), 212 (quote); Wade Clark Roof, *Spiritual Marketplace: Baby Boomers and the Remaking of American Religion* (Princeton, NJ: Princeton University Press, 1999), 155, 156.

6. Myers, *All God's Children*, xiv, xv.

7. Quoted in Wolfe, *The Transformation of American Religion*, 206.

8. Moore, *Touchdown Jesus*, 50, 51; Romanowski, *Pop Culture Wars*, 44-49; Wolfe, *Transformation of American Religion*, 207; Marc Peyser, "God, Mammon, and 'Bibleman,'" *Newsweek* (16 July 2001): 46.

9. William D. Romanowski, *Eyes Wide Open: Looking for God in Popular Culture* (Grand Rapids: Brazos Press, 2001), 12.

10. Romanowski, *Eyes Wide Open*, 12, 13 (quote); Romanowski, *Pop Culture Wars*, 44, 45; Myers, *All God's Children*, 18; Roof, *Spiritual Marketplace*, 186, 187.

11. Romanowski, *Eyes Wide Open*, 12.

12. Bruce David Forbes, "Introduction," in *Religion and Popular Culture in America*, ed. Bruce David Forbes (Berkeley: University of California Press, 2000), 13; Myers, *All God's Children*, 84, 161; Gregor Goethals, "The Electronic Golden Calf," in *Religion and Popular Culture*, 139.

13. Romanowski, *Eyes Wide Open*, 28, 29.

14. Carol Flake, *Redemptorama: Culture, Politics, and the New Evangelicalism* (New York: Penguin Books, 1984), 21, 22; Peyser, "God, Mammon, and 'Bibleman,'" 46. See also Richard Wightman Fox, *Jesus in America: A History* (San Francisco: HarperSanFrancisco, 2004), 193-400.

15. Quoted in R. Stephen Warner, "They're Ok, We're Ok," *Books and Culture* (March/April 2004): 17; Martin E. Marty, "At the Cross Roads," *Christianity Today* (February 2004): 39.

16. Wolfe, *Transformation of American Religion*, 159, 160; Arian Campo Flores, "Now, Milk and Honey," *Newsweek* (19 April 2004): 14.

17. Moore, *Touchdown Jesus*, 50, 51 (quote); R. Laurence Moore, *Selling God: American Religion in the Marketplace of Culture* (New York: Oxford University Press, 1994), 254; 50, 51; Flake, *Redemptorama*, 22; Amy DeRogatis, "What Would Jesus Do? Sexuality and Salvation in Protestant Evangelical Sex Manuals, 1950s to the Present," *Church History* 74, 1 (March 2005): 97-137.

18. Reported on CNN Headline News (14 April 2004).

19. Jack Anderson, "Crusading Clergy Shape the Course of Dance," *New York Times* (27 September 1992): H6; "Tattoos as Evangelical Chic," *Christian Century* (23-30 December 1998), 1240; Myers, *All God's Children*, 18; Peyser, "God, Mammon, and 'Bibleman,'" 45; Arian Campo-Flores, "Get Your Praise On," *Newsweek* (19 April 2004): 56, 57.

20. Tom Walsh, "What Would Jesus Drive? Oh, Please," *Detroit Free Press* http://www.freep.com/money/business'walsh22_20021122.htm. (11/22/02); Michelle Cole, "What Would Jesus Drive? Faith Leaders Ask Detroit to Ponder," *The Oregonian* http://www.oregonlive.com/living/oregonian/index.ssf?/xml/story.ssf/html_standard.xsl?base/living/103779. (11/22/02); Jane Lampman, "Should Churches Convert Drivers of SUVs?" *Christian Science Monitor* (22 November 2002), http://www.csmonitor.com/2002/1122/p02s01-ussc.htm (11/22/02); "What Would Jesus Drive," http://www.whatwouldjesusdrive.org/resources/fs_jesus.php. (11/22/02).

21. Moore, *Touchdown Jesus*, 51-53.

22. Steve Rabey, "No Longer Left Behind," *Christianity Today* 22 (April 2002): 31-33; Moore, *Selling God,* 252, 253; Peg Tyre, "The Almighty Dollar: Christian Bookstores Go Bust after Chains Find Religion," *Newsweek* (24 January 2005): 68.

23. For discussions on this issue, see Alan Wolfe, "The Opening of the Evangelical Mind," *Atlantic Monthly* (October 2000): 55-76; George M. Marsden, *The Outrageous Idea of Christian Scholarship* (New York: Oxford University Press, 1997); Michael S. Hamilton and Johanna G. Yngvason, "Patrons of the Evangelical Mind," *Christianity Today* 8 (July 2002): 42-46; Michael S. Hamilton, "Reflection and Response: The Elusive Idea of Christian Scholarship," *Christian Scholars Review* 31, 1 (fall 2001): 13-21; James C. Turner, "Something to be Reckoned With: The Evangelical Mind Awakens," *Commweal* 15 (January 1999): 11-13.

24. Roof, *Spiritual Marketplace*, 99, 100; Flake, *Redemptorama*, 161-64; Rabey, "No Longer Left Behind," 26-30; Cindy Crosby, "America's Pastor," *Christianity Today* (March 2004): 58-63.

25. Kenneth L. Woodward, "Platitudes or Prophecy?" *Newsweek* (27 August 2001): 47; Rabey, "No Longer Left Behind," 26; Bruce Wilkinson, *The Prayer of Jabez* (Sisters, OR: Multnomah Publishers, 2000); Rick Warren, *The Purpose Driven Life* (Grand Rapids: Zondervan, 2002); Roof, *Spiritual Marketplace*, 101-103.

26. For examples, see Hal Lindsey, *The Late Great Planet Earth* (Grand Rapids: Zondervan, 1970); John Hagee, *The Battle for Jerusalem* (Nashville: Nelson, 2003); David Hunt, *Global Peace and the Rise of the Antichrist* (Eugene, OR: Harvest House, 1990); Tim LaHaye, *No Fear of the Storm* (Sisters, OR: Multnomah, 1992); Grant R. Jeffrey, *Prince of Darkness: Antichrist and the New World Order* (Toronto: Frontier Publications, 1994).

27. D. G. Hart, *That Old-Time Religion in Modern America* (Chicago: Ivan Dee, 2002), 188.

28. Hart, *That Old-Time Religion*, 186, 187; Rabey, "No Longer Left Behind," 26. See Frank Peretti, *The Present Darkness* (Wheaton, IL: Tyndale, 1986); Frank Peretti, *Piercing the Darkness* (Wheaton, IL: Tyndale, 1989).

29. David Gates, "The Pop Prophets," *Newsweek* (24 May 2004): 45-50; Hart, *That Old-Time Religion*, 187, 188. Other titles in *The Left Behind* series include: *Tribulation Force; Nicolae; Soul Harvest; Are We Living in the End Times?; Apollyon; Assassins; The Indwelling; The Mark; Desecration;* and *The Remnant.* The prequel is *The Rising* (2005). The first and last volumes, which are mentioned in the text, are not noted here. Also subtitles have not been given. The publisher for all of these volumes is Tyndale House.

30. Richard Kyle, *The Last Days Are Here Again: A History of the End Times* (Grand Rapids: Baker Books, 1998), 136; Stanley J. Grenz, *The Millennial Maze* (Downers Grove, IL: InterVarsity Press, 1992), 20-22; Gates, "The Pop Prophets," 47, 48. See also Amy Johnson Frykholm, *Rapture Culture: Left Behind in Evangelical America* (New York: Oxford University Press, 2004); Timothy P. Weber, *On the Road to Armageddon: How Evangelicals Became Israel's Best Friend* (Grand Rapids: Baker Books, 2004); Bruce David Forbes and Jeanne Halgren Kilde, eds., *Rapture, Revelation, and The End Times: Exploring the Left Behind Series* (New York: Palgrave, 2004); Glenn W. Shuck, *Marks of the Beast: The Left Behind Novels and the Struggle for Evangelical Identity* (New York: New York University Press, 2005).

31. Gates, "The Pop Prophets," 47-49 (quote).

32. Peyser, "God, Mammon, and 'Bibleman,'" 46; Hart, *That Old-Time Religion*, 186, 189-91; Roof, *Spiritual Marketplace*, 186, 187.

33. Romanowski, *Pop Culture Wars,* 42-44.

34. Ibid., 50, 51 (quote).

35. Marshall Allen, "Multi(per)plexed" *Christianity Today* (March 2004): 64; Romanowski, *Pop Culture Wars,* 29, 30; Romanowski, *Eyes Wide Open*, 84.
36. Joe Maxwell, "The New Hollywood Watchdogs," *Christianity Today* 27 (April 1992): 38-40 (quote); Allen, "Multi(per)plexed," 64-67; "A 'Message' for Hollywood," *Newsweek* (5 October 1992): 35; Christine A. Scheller, "See No Evil," *Christianity Today* (January 2005): 36-40 (second quote).
37. Michael J. Gerson, "A Righteous Indignation," *U.S. News and World Report* (4 May 1996): 20-29; Hart, *That Old-Time Religion*, 179-83; Wendy Murray Zoba, "Daring to Discipline America," *Christianity Today* 1 (March 1999): 35-38.
38. Hart, *That Old-TimeReligion*, 184, 185.
39. Bobby C. Alexander, *Television Reconsidered* (Atlanta: Scholars Press, 1994), 113-15; Hart, *That Old-Time Religion*, 185, 186; Richard Ostling, "Evangelical Publishing and Broadcasting," in *Evangelicalism and Modern America*, ed. George Marsden (Grand Rapids: Eerdmans, 1984), 52, 53; Goethals, "Electronic Golden Calf," 136, 137; Moore, *Selling God*, 248, 249.
40. Romanowski, *Eyes Wide Open*, 15, 16. See also John Shelton Lawrence and Robert Jewett, *The Myth of the American Superhero* (Grand Rapids: Eerdmans, 2002).
41. Mark Noll, "The Defining Role of Hymns in Early Evangelicalism" in *Wonderful Words of Life: Hymns in American Protestant History and Theology*, ed. Richard J. Mouw and Mark A. Noll (Grand Rapids: Eerdmans, 2004), 3-6. See also Stephen A. Marini, *Sacred Song in America* (Urbana,: University of Illinois Press, 2003); Steve Turner, *Amazing Grace: The Story of America's Most Beloved Song* (New York: ECCO, 2002).
42. Noll, " The Defining Role of Hymns," 4-6.
43. William D. Romanowski, "Evangelicals and Popular Music," in *Religion and Popular Culture,* 113; Noll, "The Defining Role of Hymns," 4-6; Moore, *Selling God*, 45, 46.
44. William D. Romanowski, "Roll Over Beethoven, Tell Martin Luther the News: American Evangelicals and Rock Music," *Journal of American Culture* 15, 3 (1992): 79.
45. Romanowski, "Roll Over Beethoven," 79 (quote). See Flake, *Redemptorama*, 183, 184.
46. Thomas E. Bergler, "I Found My Thrill: The Youth for Christ Movement and American Congregational Singing, 1940-1970," in *Wonderful Words of Life,* 123, 124. See Bruce L. Shelley, "The Rise of Evangelical Youth Movements," *Fides et Historia* 18, 1 (1986): 47- 63; Joel A. Carpenter, ed., *The Youth for Christ Movement and Its Pioneers* (New York: Garland, 1988).
47. Bergler, "I Found My Thrill," 123 (quotes); Don Cusic, *The Sound of Light: A History of Gospel Music* (Bowling Green, OH: Bowling Green State University Press, 1990), 129-39; Milburn Price, "The Impact of Popular Culture on Congregational Song," *The Hymn* 44, 1 (January 1993): 13; Michael S. Hamilton, "The Triumph of the Praise Songs," *Christianity Today* 12 (July 1999): 30.
48. Bergler, "I Found My Thrill," 124-27; Cusic, *Sound of Light*, 70-74; Clarence Woodbury, "Bobby Soxers Sing Hallelujah," *American Magazine* (March 1946): 26, 27, 121.
49. Romanowski, "Roll Over Beethoven," 79; Bob Millard, "Gospel Music Buoyed By Rising Sales: Execs See Bright Future in New, Upscale Market," *Variety* 20 (April 1983): 179, 180; Quentin J. Schultze and William D. Romanowski, "Praising God in Opryland," *The Reformed Journal* (November 1989): 10-14.
50. Romanowski, "Evangelicals and Popular Music," 107, 108.
51. Hamilton, "The Triumph of the Praise Songs," 34.

52. Romanowski, "Evangelicals and Popular Music," 108, 109; Romanowski, "Roll Over Beethoven," 81; Hart, *That Old-Time Gospel*, 193; Millard, "Gospel Music Buoyed By Rising Sales," 20.
53. Romanowski, "Evangelicals and Popular Music," 108, 109; Romanowski, "Roll Over Beethoven," 81; David Hazard, "Holy Hype," *Eternity* (December 1985): 32-40; "New Lyrics for the Devil's Music," *Time* (11 March 1985): 60; Lorraine Ali, "The Glorious Rise of Christian Pop," *Newsweek* (16 July 2001): 38-44.
54. Romanowski, "Roll Over Beethoven," 79; Hart, *That Old-Time Religion*, 192, 193; Balmer, "Hymns on MTV," 35; Todd Hertz, "Jesus' Woodstock," *Christianity Today* (July 2003): 46-53. See Ronald M. Enroth, Edward M. Erickson, Jr., and C. Breckinbridge Peters, *The Jesus People: Old-Time Religion in the Age of Aquarius* (Grand Rapids: Eerdmans, 1972); Edward E. Plowman, *The Jesus Movement* (Elgin, IL: Cook Publishing, 1971); Richard G. Kyle, *The Religious Fringe: A History of Alternative Religions in America* (Downers Grove, IL: InterVarsity Press, 1993).
55. Hart, *That Old-Time Religion*, 194, 195.
56. Hart, *That Old-Time Religion*, 191 (quote); Stephen Prothero, *American Jesus: How the Son of God Became a National Icon* (New York: Farrar, Straus, and Giroux), 152.
57. Hart, *That Old-Time Religion*, 191, 192; Hertz, "Jesus Woodstock," 46-53; Bill Young, "Contemporary Christian Music: Rock the Flock," in *The God Pumpers: Religion in the Electronic Age*, ed. Marshall Fishwick and Ray B. Browne (Bowling Green, OH: Bowling Green State University Press, 1987), 141-58.
58. Romanowski, "Roll Over Beethoven," 83, 84; Romanowski, "Evangelicals and Popular Music," 117-19; Romanowski, *Pop Culture Wars*, 210-12; Elmer J. Thiessen, "Contemporary Worship Culture," *Mennonite Brethren Herald* (3 May 2002): 3-6; Paul O'Donnell, "God and the Music Biz," *Newsweek* (30 May 1994): 62, 63; Ali, "Glorious Rise of Christian Pop," 43; "New Lyrics for the Devil's Music," 60; William Romanowski, "Where's the Gospel?" *Christianity Today* 8 (December 1997): 44,45; Prothero, *American Jesus,* 152.
59. Hart, *That Old-Time Religion*, 190-93; Romanowski, "Evangelicals and Popular Music," 112, 113; Steve Rabey, "Fast-growing Gospel Music Now Outsells Jazz and Classical," *Christianity Today* 16 (March 1984): 42,43; Hazard, "Holy Hype," 32-40; Ali, "Glorious Rise of Christian Rock," 40-44.
60. Hart, *That Old-Time Religion*, 192, 193; William D. Romanowski, "Move Over Madonna: The Crossover Career of Gospel Artist Amy Grant," *Popular Music and Society* 17, 2 (summer 1993): 47-67; John W. Styll, "Amy Grant: The CCM Interview," *Contemporary Christian Magazine* (July/August 1986): 30-34; Romanowski, "Where's the Gospel?" 44, 45.
61. David E. Miller, *Reinventing American Protestantism: Christianity in the New Millennium* (Berkeley: University of California Press, 1997), 82, 83.
62. Miller, *Reinventing American Protestantism*, 83 (quote). See Tim Stafford, "Testing the Wine from John Wimber's Vineyard," *Christianity Today* 8 (August 1986) 17-22.
63. Hart, *That Old-Time Religion*, 196.
64. Ibid., 196, 197.
65. Prothero, *American Jesus*, 154; (quote); Marva Dawn, *Reaching Out Without Dumbing Down* (Grand Rapids: Eerdmans, 1995), 81 (second quote); Wolfe, *Transformation of American Religion*, 28; Gary A. Parrett, "9.5 Theses on Worship: A Disputation on the Role of Worship," *Christianity Today* (February 2005): 38-42.
66. Wolfe, *Transformation of American Religion*, 32; Anita Sharpe, "More Spiritual Leaders Preach Virtue of Wealth," *Wall Street Journal* (5 April 1996): B10, B13; Robert Johnson, "Preaching a Gospel of Acquisitiveness, A Showy Sect Prospers," *Wall Street Journal* (11 December 1990): A4, A 9.

67. James R. Goff, Jr. "The Faith that Claims," *Christianity Today* 19 (February 1990): 18 (quote); Bruce Barron, "Faith Movement," in *Dictionary of Christianity in America*, ed. Daniel G. Reid et al. (Downers Grove, IL: InterVarsity, 1990), 426. See James R. Goff, "Questions of Health and Wealth," in *Pentecostals from the Inside Out*, ed. Harold B. Smith (Wheaton, IL: Victor Books, 1990), 65-80.

68. Robert M. Bowman, *The Word-Faith Controversy* (Grand Rapids: Baker Books, 2001), 8, 9; Gary E. Gilley, "The Word-Faith Movement," http://www.rapidnet.com/ -jbeard/bdm/Psychology/char/more/w-f.htm. (5/7/04). For an influence on the African-American community, see Milmon F. Harrison, *Righteous Riches: The Word of Faith Movement in Contemporary African American Religion* (New York: Oxford University Press, 2005).

69. Bruce Barron, *The Health and Wealth Gospel* (Downers Grove, IL: InterVarsity, 1987), 9-12; D. R. McConnell, *A Different Gospel* (Peabody, MA: Hendrickson, 1988), 3-14; Bowman, *Word-Faith Controversy,* 10, 11; Eryl Davies, "The Faith Movement: Its Origins and History," *Evangelical Magazine of Wales* (April 2002): 5.

70. Goff, "Faith That Claims," 19, 20; Charles E. Hummel, *The Prosperity Gospel* (Downers Grove, IL: InterVarsity, 1991), 6. See James R. Goff, Jr. and Grant Wacker, *Portraits of a Generation: Early Pentecostal Leaders* (Fayetteville: University of Arkansas Press, 2002); Barron, *Health and Wealth Gospel*, 38-46.

71. David Edwin Harrell, Jr., *All Things Are Possible: The Healing and Charismatic Revivals in Modern America* (Bloomington: Indiana University Press, 1975), 53-83; Goff, "Faith That Claims," 20. See Oral Roberts, *3 Most Important Steps to Better Faith and Miracle Living* (Tulsa: Oral Roberts Evangelistic Association, 1976).

72. McConnell, *Different Gospel*, 24-52; Hummel, *Prosperity Gospel*, 6,7; Barron, *Health and Wealth Gospel*, 61, 69; Bowman, *Word-Faith Controversy*, 36-41.

73. Goff, "Faith That Claims," 20; Barron, *Health and Wealth Gospel*, 47, 48; Hummel, *Prosperity Gospel*, 9.

74. Bowman, *Word-Faith Controversy*, 93, 94; Hummel, *Prosperity Gospel*, 9; Goff, "Faith That Claims," 20.

75. Bowman, *Word-Faith Controversy*, 93; Goff, "Faith That Claims," 20; Barron, *Health and Wealth Gospel*, 55-58.

76. Harrell, *All Things Are Possible*, 229.

77. Jill Dubisch and Raymond Michalowski, "Blessed Are the Rich: The New Gospel of Wealth in Contemporary Evangelism," in *The God Pumpers*, 33-36.

78. George Marsden, "The Gospel of Wealth, The Social Gospel, and the Salvation of Souls in Nineteenth-Century America," *Fides et Historia* 5, 1 (spring 1973): 10-21; George Charles C. Cole, *The Social Ideas of the Northern Evangelists 1826-1860* (New York: Octagon, 1966), 169, 170; Daniel Bjork, *The Victorian Flight and the Crisis of American Individualism* (Washington, D.C.: University Press of America, 1978).

79. E. W. Kenyon, *Advanced Bible Course: Studies in the Deeper Life* (Seattle: Kenyon's Gospel Publishing Society, 1970), 59; McConnell, *A Different Gospel*, 172-175.

80. Quote from Kenneth Hagin, *New Thresholds of Faith* (Tulsa: Faith Library, 1980), 54, 55; McConnell, *Different Gospel*, 175; Barron, *Health and Wealth Gospel*, 62, 63; Kenneth Hagin, *How God Taught Me Prosperity* (Tulsa: Kenneth Hagin Healing Ministries, 1985).

81. Oral Roberts, *God's Formula for Success and Prosperity* (Tulsa: Healing Waters, 1955); Barron, *Health and Wealth Gospel*, 61,62; David Edwin Harrell, Jr. *Oral Roberts: An American Life* (Bloomington: Indiana University Press, 1985), 65, 66, 129, 130.

82. Kenneth Copeland, *The Laws of Prosperity* (Fort Worth: Kenneth Copeland Publications, 1974), 18-20 (quote) 92; McConnell, *Different Gospel*, 171; Michael Scott Horton, *Made in America: The Shaping of Modern American Evangelicalism* (Grand Rapids: Baker Books, 1991), 86.

83. Gloria Copeland, *God's Will is Prosperity* (Tulsa: Harrison House, 1978), 13, 54 (quotes); Kenneth Hagin, "The Law of Faith," *Word of Faith* (November 1974): 2, 3.

84. Bowman, *Word-Faith Controversy*, 31.

85. Bowman, *Word-Faith Controversy*, 31, 32. See E. W. Kenyon, *The Father and His Family* (Lynwood, WA: Kenyon's Gospel Publishing Society, 1937), 56; Kenneth Copeland, *The Force of Faith* (Fort Worth: Kenneth Copeland Ministries, n.d.), 6-9; Kenneth Hagin, *New Thresholds of Faith* (Tulsa: Kenneth Hagin Ministries, 1972), 31, 32.

86. Bowman, *Word-Faith Controversy*, 31, 32, 115-21. See Hagin, *New Thresholds of Faith*, 53, 54, 74-76; Copeland, *Force of Faith*, 16, 17; Copeland, *Laws of Prosperity*, 18, 19; Frederick K. C. Price, *How Faith Works* (Tulsa: Harrison House, 1976), 93; Kenneth Copeland, *Our Covenant with God* (Fort Worth: Kenneth Copeland Publications, 1987), 7; Kenneth Copeland, *Walking in the Realm of the Miraculous* (Fort Worth: Kenneth Copeland Ministries, n.d., 15,16).

87. Bowman, *Word-Faith Controversy*, 32, 147-78. See Kenneth Copeland, "Take Time to Pray," *Believer's Voice of Victory* (February 1987): 9; Kenneth Copeland, "Question and Answer," *Believer's Voice* (August 1988): 8; Kenneth Hagin, "The Incarnation," *The Words of Faith* (December 1980): 14; Kenneth Copeland, "What Happened from the Cross to the Throne," tape 02-0017 (Forth Worth: Kenneth Copeland Ministries, 1990); Kenneth Hagin, *The Name of Jesus* (Tulsa: Kenneth Hagin Ministries, 1979), 28.

88. Bowman, *Word-Faith Controversy*, 33, 193-217.

89. Bowman, *Word-Faith Controversy*, 33, 193-228. See Kenneth Hagin, *You Can Write Your Own Ticket with God* (Tulsa: Kenneth Hagin Ministries, 1979), 18; Kenneth Hagin, *Having Faith in Your Faith* (Tulsa: Kenneth Hagin Ministries, 1980), 3-5; Copeland, *The Force of Faith*, 13,14; Hagin, *New Thresholds of Faith*, 9-12, 53,54.

90. Copeland, *Laws of Prosperity*, 57 (quote); Walter Unger, "Confronting the Get-Rich God," *The Christian Leader* (10 April 1990): 5; (Roberts quoted in) Horton, *Made in America,* 85, 86.

91. Dubisch and Michalowski, "Blessed are the Rich," 38, 39, 43, 44.

92. Kenneth L. Woodward, "Platitudes or Prophecy?" *Newsweek* (27 August 2001): 47; Wolfe *Transformation of American Religion*, 33, 34. See also Bruce Wilkinson, *Beyond Jabez* (Sisters, OR: Multnomah, 2005).

93. Wilkinson, *Prayer of Jabez*, 31.

94. Andrew Chase Baker, "Gain, No Pain," *Religion in the News* 4, 3 (2001), 3 (quote); Wolfe, *Transformation of American Religion*, 33,34.

95. Wilkinson, *Prayer of Jabez,* 24, (quote); Baker, "Gain, No Pain," 3, 4. See also Timothy C. Morgan, "Mr. Jabez Goes to Africa," *Christianity Today* (November 2003): 45-50.

96. Randall Balmer, *Mine Eyes Have Seen the Glory* (New York: Oxford University Press, 1989), 231 (quote). See Christopher Lasch, *The Culture of Narcissism* (New York: Norton, 1978).

97. Hummel, *Prosperity Gospel,* 29 (quote); Balmer, *Mine Eyes Have Seen the Glory*, 231.

98. Randall Balmer, *Blessed Assurance: A History of Evangelicalism in America* (Boston: Beacon Press, 1999), 60 (quote). See Nicolaus Mills, ed., *Culture in an Age of Money: The Legacy of the 1980s in America* (Chicago: Ivan R. Dee, 1990).

99. Quentin J. Schultze, *Televangelism and American Culture* (Grand Rapids: Baker Books, 1991), 135.

100. Wolfe, *Transformation of American Religion*, 71,74, 76, 81.

101. Mary Jo Neitz, *Charisma and Community: A Study of Religious Commitment within the Charismatic Renewal* (New Brunswick, NJ: Transaction Publishers, 1987), 28 (quote); Wolfe, *Transformation of American Religion*, 68, 69.

102. Nancy Ammerman, *Bible Believers: Fundamentalists in the Modern World* (New Brunswick, NJ: Rutgers University Press, 1987), 53.

103. Jerry Adler, "Hey, I'm Terrific," *Newsweek* (17 February 1992): 46-50; Paul C. Vitz, "Leaving Psychology Behind," in *No God But God*, ed. Os Guinness and John Seel (Chicago: Moody Press, 1992), 96.

104. Adler, "Hey, I'm Terrific," 50.

105. Wolfe, *Transformation of American Religion*, 166, 167; Adler, "Hey, I'm Terrific," 46, 47.

106. Kimon Howland Sargeant, *Seeker Churches: Promoting Traditional Religion in a Nontraditional Way* (New Brunswick, NJ: Rutgers University Press, 2000), 87, 89 (quote).

107. Os Guinness, "America's Last Men and Their Magnificent Talking Cure," in *No God But God*, 129 (quotes). See Paul Rieff, *The Triumph of the Therapeutic* (New York: Harper and Row, 1966).

108. Robert Ellwood, *Religious and Spiritual Groups in Modern America* (Englewood Cliffs, NJ: Prentice Hall, 1973), 79.

109. Kyle, *Religious Fringe*, 115, 116; Charles S. Braden, *Spirits in Rebellion: The Rise and Development of New Thought* (Dallas: Southern Methodist University Press, 1963), 14-19. See Horatio W. Dresser, *A History of the New Thought Movement* (New York: Thomas Y. Crowell, 1919).

110. Kyle, *Religious Fringe*, 116; Ellwood, *Religious and Spiritual Groups*, 79, 80; Braden, *Spirits in Rebellion*, 14-19.

111. Kyle, *Relgious Fringe*, 116; J. Stillson Judah, *The History and Philosophy of the Metaphysical Movements in America* (Philadelphia: Westminister Press, 1957), 192, 193; Catherine Albanese, *America: Religions and Religion* (Belmont, CA: Wadsworth, 1981), 182; Braden, *Spirits in Rebellion*, 323-405.

112. Donald Meyer, *Positive Thinkers,* 2nd ed. (New York: Pantheon Books, 1980), 45, 260-63, 284, 285; Donald G. Reid, "Norman Vincent Peale," in *Dictionary of Christianity in America*, 877. See Arthur Gordon, *Norman Vincent Peale: Minister to Millions* (Englewood Cliffs, NJ: Prentice Hall, 1958); Clarence Westphal, *Norman Vincent Peale: Christian Crusader* (Minneapolis: Denison, 1964).

113. Carol V. R. George, *God's Salesman: Norman Vincent Peale and the Power of Positive Thinking* (New York: Oxford University Press, 1993), viii, ix, 129-44; Meyer, *Positive Thinkers,* 259-80.

114. Sydney E. Ahlstrom, *A Religious History of the American People* (New Haven, CT: Yale University Press, 1972), 1019 (quote); George, *God's Salesman*, ix; Reid, "Norman Vincent Peale," 877.

115. George, *God's Salesman*, 214; Guinness, "America's Last Men and Their Magnificent Talking Cure," 129.

116. George Reid, "Robert Harold Schuller," in *Dictionary of Christianity in America*, 1054, 1055; Flake, *Redemptorama*, 56-58. See Dennis Voskuil, *Mountains into Goldmines: Robert Schuller and the Gospel of Success* (Grand Rapids: Eerdmans,

1983), Michael Nason and Donna Nason, *Robert Schuller: The Inside Story* (Waco, TX: Word Books,1983).

117. Robert Schuller, *Your Church Has Real Possibilities* (Glendale, CA: Regal Books, 1974), 117; (quote); Flake, *Redemptorama*, 57, 58; Richard Quebedeaux, *By What Authority: The Rise of Personality Cults in American Christianity* (New York: Harper and Row, 1982), 73.

118. Flake, *Redemptorama*, 58.

119. Robert Schuller, *Self-Esteem: The New Reformation* (New York: Jove, 1982). See especially the introduction and quote from page 64. See also Horton, *Made in America*, 80, 81.

120. See Kenneth S. Kantzer, "A Theologian Looks at Schuller," *Christianity Today* 10 (August 1984): 22-24; "Hard Questions for Robert Schuller About Sin and Self-Esteem," *Christianity Today* 10 (August 1984): 14-20. These articles are based on an interview conducted by Kenneth Kantzer, David Wells, and Gilbert Beers. In this interview, Schuller affirms the essentials of the historic Christian faith. Admittedly, his answers to these pointed questions seem at odds with some statements in his writings. See also Alfred Klassen, "Robert H. Schuller and the Ethics of Success," *Direction* 12, 4 (1983): 27-37.

121. Schuller, *Self-Esteem,* 12, 14, 15, 65, 98, 150 (quotes); Sargeant, *Seeker Churches*, 102.

122. Schuller, *Self-Esteem*, 146, 150 (quotes); Sargeant, *Seeker Churches*, 102.

123. Robert Schuller, "Schuller Clarifies His View of Sin," *Christianity Today* 10 (August 1984): 21.

124. Schuller, *Self-Esteem*, 99, 100.

125. Schuller, "Schuller Clarifies His View of Sin," 21; Kantzer, "A Theologian Looks at Schuller," 23.

126. "Hard Questions for Robert Schuller," 16, 19 (quote); Sargeant, *Seeker Churches*, 102.

127. Kantzer, "A Theologian Looks at Schuller," 23 (quote).

128. Phillip Rieff, *The Triumph of the Therapeutic* (Chicago; University of Chicago Press, 1966), 66.

129. James Davison Hunter, *Evangelicalism: The Coming Generation* (Chicago: University of Chicago Press, 1987), 71.

130. David Wells, *No Place for Truth* (Grand Rapids: Eerdmans,

Epilogue

The movie *Saved* (2004) irreverently satirizes the evangelical subculture. While this comedy crosses the line of decency at many points, it does point out the superficiality of much of evangelicalism. The scene is at American Eagle Christian High School. Nearly everything has a Christian veneer—the nation of America, sex outside of marriage, haunted houses, Halloween (giving tracts instead of candy to trick or treaters), skate board leagues, quiz shows with Bible questions, rock music, and the senior prom (called "The Light of the World Prom").

Saved notes the hypocrisy of these Christian teenagers. The school has a statue of a white Jesus, despite objections that Jesus came from the Middle East. Hilary Faye, the most overtly pious of the students, comes across as a mean-spirited hypocrite despite her efforts to convert other students. The school has a pious principal, who regards the Bible as black and white with no gray in respect to interpretation. But he is having an affair with a student's mother, which they regard as being led by the Lord. While this movie exaggerates some evangelical tendencies, it accurately makes two points: the extent that evangelicals have baptized secular culture and how non-evangelicals often view evangelicals. *Saved* is full of evangelical jargon, but, unfortunately, the characters do not walk the talk. In this movie, evangelicals offer only one answer for the problems of life—receive Jesus in your heart and get saved.

Martin Marty offers a more balanced view of evangelicalism: "Evangelicals have become major players in American culture, and that may be their biggest problem." For all of their "cultural bogeys," they "have chosen to adapt more to the mainlines of American life than most other groups."[1] From one-quarter to one-third of Americans generally identify themselves as evangelicals. Perhaps more important, they have access to political power, ample wealth, and considerable cultural influence. For much of the twentieth century, mainline Protestantism and Roman Catholicism dominated the American religious landscape. In the early twenty-first century, however, the story is different. Mainline Protestantism is in decline and can hardly be described as mainline anymore. Catholicism faces many staggering problems—an acute shortage of priests plus charges of sexual abuse by the clergy. Thus, evangelicalism, as diverse as what it is, can be regarded as a "third force."

In fact, evangelicalism may be going beyond being a "third force." In the twenty-first century, it may become the prevailing form of religion in America. As Kenneth Collins points out, "Who would have guessed back in the 1920s that conservative religion would bypass its liberal cousins in so many ways by the turn of the twenty-first century?"[2] And yet it has. Or as Alister McGrath projects, "There is every indication that it [evangelicalism] will soon become— if it is not already—the dominant form of Protestantism in North America." He points out that of the currently growing churches in the United States, "89 percent were found to be evangelical."[3] Perhaps more important is the strength of evangelical institutions. A higher percent of evangelicals attend church than do mainline Protestants or Catholics. Indeed, as Collins notes, "The outsiders have become insiders; the marginalized are now mainstream."[4]

In the nineteenth century, evangelicalism played an important role in shaping American society. During the first half of this century, it significantly influenced the nation. By the second half of the century, however, the cultural impact ran in the opposite direction. American culture had so shaped Protestantism—especially the evangelical variety—that American civilization and Christianity appeared to be one and the same. Or as Richard Hughes puts it, "Christianizing the culture…involved a trade-off: The world might absorb bits and pieces of the Christian faith, while the church would absorb bits and pieces of the values common to the larger society." The first half of the nineteenth century witnessed such a process when Christians attempted to create a *de facto* Christian establishment in America—one that lasted into the early twentieth century.[5]

Why the Comeback?

For much of the twentieth century, nevertheless, the evangelicals lost their place at the table of political and cultural influence. By the late twentieth century, they had regained a measure of that influence. How did they achieve this? First, they have developed something of an evangelical ecumenism. Denominational lines have broken down, theology has been diluted, religious traditions have gone by the way side, and the parachurches have become increasingly important. Consequently, a generic evangelicalism has come to the forefront. While this version of evangelicalism may be superficial, it has had a greater cultural impact than the old sectarian or separatist version of evangelicalism.

Second, evangelicals have moved beyond their private pietism. They have become involved in the political and social arenas. To be sure, for the most part they still have only a minimal social conscience. They generally do not concern themselves with social and economic injustices. Rather, they focus on a narrow range of issues concerned with pietistic and sexual matters. Evangelicals have, nevertheless, come out of their cocoons and have become involved in the political process and social issues related to what they regard as immoral and sinful. They are at the forefront in the drive to return America to its Christian roots, as they perceive them to be.

Three, evangelicals have to a large extent been assimilated into American culture. Despite their strident criticism of American society and how it has strayed from its Christian moorings, they have thoroughly adapted to American popular culture. Instead of creating a Christian America, evangelicals have Americanized Christianity. In theory they reject big government, but readily accept it when it enforces their moral views. They desire to reduce Washington's influence on their lives but largely support the Bush administration, which has significantly enlarged the scope of the federal government. Evangelicals are among the most patriotic of Americans, advocating a strong military and an often go-it-alone foreign policy. They are also staunch supporters of the market economy, viewing any kind of government involvement as akin to socialism. Many evangelicals even contend that America's political and economic systems are divinely inspired.

Evangelicals have even Americanized salvation. To be sure, salvation entails a personal commitment to follow Jesus Christ. The new birth is not gradual. While an individual may not know when it occurs, the new birth begins at a moment in time. But many evangelicals believe that this decision must come in a revivalistic format, that is, they must be able to identify when they invited Jesus into their heart or responded to an invitation. Moreover, they often only make a shallow commitment to Christ. They accept him as savior while largely ignoring his lordship over their lives. By focusing on the one time experience and cheap grace, many evangelicals have in effect "McDonaldized" salvation. They like their salvation like their fast food—quick and cheap.

When it comes to publishing, more than any other religious group evangelicals have produced and bought bestsellers. The beat of popular music, once regarded as demonic, has been thoroughly embraced by the evangelical community and now plays a major role in their worship services. When it comes to religious television, evangelicals practically own the airwaves. It is difficult to find a program without an evangelical perspective. If one can exclude the pope, only evangelicals have produced religious celebrities but this squares well with their celebrity-oriented culture.[6]

The "confluence between capitalism, democracy, and religious freedom" in early national America has benefited all religious groups, notes R. Laurence Moore. Such a situation has turned religion into a market commodity. When religion is viewed "as something to be sold rather than as something imposed—something advanced in the prospect of a mutually beneficial contract, which parties are free at all times to accept or reject—religious toleration advances."[7]

Of all religious bodies, evangelicals have capitalized on this market model and thrived in this free environment. They have done well in the face of competition. They have successfully competed with mainline Protestants,

Catholics, and many aspects of the general culture. Believing that people must be won to Christ, they have vigorously marketed the gospel. From the colonial period on, evangelicals have employed culturally relevant and technologically current methods in presenting the message of salvation. In particular, Americans are great talkers. They would rather pick up the telephone than write a letter; they are addicted to radio and television talk shows; and cell phones abound. In a nation that values talkers, from the eighteenth-century revivals to the twenty-first-century televangelists, evangelicals have mastered the art of persuasive rhetoric.

More than any other religious group, evangelicalism is typically American. From the 1920s to perhaps the 1960s, they gained a reputation for being out of sync with the mainstream of American thought and culture. But this must be seen as an aberration. Prior to and after these years, they connected well with the various expressions of American culture. Like good missionaries, they have tailored their services to their audience—whether it be middle-class suburbanites of Chicago or black Pentecostals of southern Mississippi.

Except for obvious sinful behavior, the surrounding culture poses no problem for evangelicals. In particular, they have tapped into the populist pulse beat of America. Americans prize informality and evangelicals have capitalized on this. Their casual preaching and worship comes across well; they call their pastors by their first names and have a fixation with celebrities. Materialism and consumerism have presented few problems for the evangelical subculture. For a long time, evangelicals have found ways to reconcile their version of the Christian faith with the consumer-driven American culture. This has been particularly true for the years following World War II when they have participated in the rise of American prosperity and indulged in its consumerism. For this reason, many evangelicals have accepted the extravagant lifestyles of the televangelists and their success-oriented and prosperity preaching.

In the other direction, evangelicalism's support of traditional values also has an appeal in an age that appears to have lost its moral compass. But even in this, evangelicalism can be regarded as typically American. Reflecting the old Puritan heritage and American individualism, evangelicals focus on abortion and sexual immorality while downplaying the issues of poverty, racism, and social injustice. And when they address such problems, they believe that they can be solved primarily through individual, church, or local efforts.

It would be inaccurate, however, to say that evangelicals are not concerned with social problems. Many evangelical parachurch organizations have a social dimension and a substantial ministry among the poor. And the evangelical left even contends for more social justice in respect to public policy. But, on the whole, evangelicals generally do not argue for a public policy designed to elevate social problems.

Paradoxically, the opposite is frequently true in respect to personal morality. In this area, evangelicals often focus on public policy—laws restricting abortion, homosexuality, pornography, and same sex marriages—while ignoring important aspects of Christian values. Evangelicals seldom engage in the previously mentioned sins. But as pointed out by Ronald Sider —in respect to divorce, spouse abuse, materialism, and racism—there exists little difference between evangelicals and the general population. They do not practice what they preach. Thus, hard-core skeptics smile "in cynical amusement at this blatant hypocrisy."[8]

Somewhat related to the issues of personal and public morality is the developing rapport between conservative Protestants and Catholics. Fundamentalists once regarded the papacy as the Antichrist. Evangelicals came to revere John Paul II. Why? Evangelicals and conservative Catholics both share many views in respect to the "culture of life." In fact, on the Religious Right's list for presidential candidates for 2008 are Catholics such as Senators Sam Brownback and Rick Santorum. However, evangelicals and Popes John Paul II and Benedict XVI would not see eye to eye on social issues. Both popes take a left of center stance in respect to social justice. But for the most part, their ideas have not trickled down to the Catholic grassroots in America. So evangelicals can conveniently ignore the papacy's views regarding social issues and war and still maintain a working relationship with Catholics.

Years ago, Dean Kelly argued that conservative churches were growing because of their commitment to Christian orthodoxy, strong doctrine, and a strict lifestyle. Such a theory calls for a reinterpretation. In their attempt to be relevant to the surrounding culture, evangelicals have stepped over the line. They have been absorbed by the culture. They have grown significantly because of their acceptance of American culture and do not look so strict.[9] The more liberal churches have declined, it is argued, because they have surrendered the historic faith. In part, this is true. But they have also decreased because they have not accommodated the popular culture to the extent that evangelicals have. Indeed, it can be said that mainline Protestantism has caved into the elite culture while evangelicals have been engulfed by the popular culture.

The Paradox and Problems

Herein lies the paradox. To call evangelicalism a form of conservative Protestantism, as I have done, is something of an oxymoron. Evangelicals have been anything but conservative. Being market oriented, they have adopted the most progressive methods of presenting the gospel and current forms of worship. They have been geniuses at fusing Christ and culture and adapting the gospel to any medium of expression and presentation. Rather than resist the surrounding culture, evangelicals have realized that they are better off attempting to influence this culture.

In part, this has developed because evangelicalism tends to blur the lines between the sacred and secular and between things religious and common.

They insist that the faith must influence all aspects of life and have become uncomfortable with the creeping secularization of American society. To an extent, evangelicalism has influenced America, but more often the impact has gone in the other direction. And, sadly, evangelicals are oblivious to this trend. They have superficially sanctified aspects of culture and have mistaken this for genuine Christianity. In this attempt to Christianize America, they have relied heavily on civil religion and baptized the American political and economic systems, which they often equate with biblical Christianity.

By the early twenty-first century, evangelicalism has much to brag about. Evangelicals now wield considerable political, economic, and cultural influence. Their numbers are strong and growing. Evangelical churches are the largest and most dynamic in the nation. They have established numerous parachurch organizations, some of them with budgets greater than many denominations. Hundreds of colleges with an evangelical orientation dot the American landscape. These churches and institutions have won people to Christ and shaped many lives. In general, they have succeeded in being culturally relevant and achieving considerable numerical success while maintaining the timeless essentials of the old time gospel. Furthermore, evangelicals have moved to the highest levels of American society, including the corridors of economic and political power. Moreover, they are no longer considered ill-educated but have their respected scholars.

Still, evangelicals have not rolled back the increased secularization and pluralization of American public life that has taken place since the 1960s. In the early twenty-first century, the nation remains sharply divided between those people who advocate secular values and those who advocate traditional values. While some battles have been won, the nation has not been restored to what evangelicals view as its "Christian past." Evangelicals have not yet won an anti-abortion amendment to the Constitution or restored prayer to the public schools. They have had some success in promoting family values but the media has not been purged of the sex and violence that offends them. Worse yet, because they could not defeat or separate from the mainstream culture, they have created a Christianized counterfeit culture.

Even this limited success has come at a price. Due to its democratic and populist urges, evangelicalism's popularity is due more to its determination to find out what people want and to give it to them than to any drive to promote doctrine. Thus, any danger posed to American society by the megachurches and other aspects of growth-oriented evangelism is not bigotry but triteness and superficiality. "Television, publishing, political campaigning, education, self-help advice—all increasingly tell Americans what they already want to hear," declares Alan Wolfe. "Religion, it would seem, should now be added to that list."[10] Bigotry may raise its head, but this will come in respect to the insistence that national morals confirm to those of the evangelical subculture, not to theology.

Evangelicalism has its elite culture and its scholars. But evangelicalism's cultural, political, and economic influence has not come from them. Rather, it has come from below, from the popular evangelical culture. Take, for example, the city of Orlando, Florida. The city has the Reformed Seminary with a number of respected scholars. Orlando was also the home of Benny Hinn (he has since moved to Texas) , an ill-educated but charismatic evangelist. Who has had the greatest impact? A scholarly and intellectual influence may bear great fruit over the years. But millions of people flock to Hinn's healing services and watch his television programs. They crave after his version of the health and wealth gospel. This is because evangelicals are populists, pragmatic, and experiential—not intellectuals. They want tangible results now, not down the road. They want an experience, not something to think about.

In commenting on some of our mediocre political leaders, the president of DePauw University often said, "The world is being run by 'C' students."[11] In politics (except for a Bachelor's degree), education counts for little. In fact, thinking in complex terms can be a liability, and being cerebral is the kiss of death. Our populist culture prefers politicians who give simple, black-and-white answers in terms that can be readily understood. The same can be said for religion. As noted in chapter 2, in the 1820s and 1830s, the populist culture overthrew the elite culture. In medicine, science, and law, the elite culture has recovered its dominance. This has not been so in religion and politics. Here the popular culture still calls the shots.

No religious group has been controlled by the popular culture as has American evangelicalism. For much of its history, evangelicalism has been propelled by populist revivals. The common people have always desired to hear their ministers preach fiery, simple, practical, and emotional sermons. Thanks to television and the megachurches, this populist tendency has increased. As denominational lines have been blurred, theology has been reduced to its lowest common denominator. As a practical people, evangelicals regard doctrine as boring and irrelevant. They want down-to-earth sermons to help them get past the week.

Along with the therapeutic nature of American culture, this lack of interest in dogma has encouraged evangelicals to flock to small groups. In these small groups, doctrine is seldom discussed for it can promote discord. Rather, small groups tend to be populist and pragmatic and the dialogue promotes harmony, good feelings, and offers help for life's immediate problems. Like other people living in urban and suburban situations, evangelicals crave intimacy and fellowship. They desire to be connected with people of similar interests and problems. Small groups thus provide evangelicals with fellowship, support, and are a practical form of therapy.

Closely related to this lack of interest in theology and drive to satisfy interpersonal needs are new forms of worship. As conservative Protestantism has moved from fundamentalism to evangelicalism it has received a substantial infusion of Pentecostalism. This influx has come by means of the charismatic movement and in the form of worship, not Pentecostal beliefs and practices. Pentecostal forms of worship have come to the forefront because, like many Americans, evangelicals are seeking "authenticity through experience rather than through ideas." As they have often chafed over arid doctrine, they are impatient with liturgy and traditional hymns. Rather, they want "joyful, emotional, personal, and emphatic" patterns of worship.[12] In worship as in other aspects of spirituality, the focus has moved away from what transcends individuals (God) to what is within them (personal feelings).[13]

If the United States is a nation being run by "C" students, the same can be said for the evangelical subculture. Despite having many respected scholars, on the whole, the thinking and behavior of the evangelical community is driven by uneducated popularizers. Millions of evangelicals accept as gospel truth the ideas found in the messages and books of the televangelists and evangelical gurus. Their books sell by the millions and they are regarded as the last word on many subjects. They claim to have some new insight into Scripture. Believers are told how they should live their lives, acquire prosperity, or interpret current events. The voices of the evangelical scholars have indeed been largely drowned out by a deluge of popular opinions.

These evangelical popularizers are believed to have a corner on the correct interpretation of Scripture. Unfortunately, they tear Bible verses out of their context and limit themselves to "proof texting." Behind this "proof texting" is a populist appeal. The evangelical popularizers frequently lack the theological training necessary to interpret Scripture in its context and their populist audience often wants a simple and direct interpretation. Their interpretations concerning the relationship of Christianity to the origins of America are also regarded by millions of evangelicals as akin to "holy writ." To question the sacred origins of America is tantamount to heresy. When professional evangelical historians do so, most evangelicals will accept the word of the untrained popularizer, not the historians.

The tremendous intellectual influence of the evangelical popularizers can be traced to several sources. First, they are in sync with the evangelical mindset. The ideas they present resonate with the populist, pragmatic, and experiential tendencies found in the evangelical subculture. They scratch where evangelicals itch; they speak to where evangelicals are in life. Second, the popularizers write and speak in a down-to-earth language that evangelicals understand. Third, the popularizers address subjects of interest to a broad audience. Thus, publishers readily publish their works in large quantities. Finally, the ideas of the popularizers are widely distributed. They skillfully use the mass media, be it television or inexpensive paperbacks. Their ideas are seen on television by a mass audience or read in popular books that sell by the millions. The local pastor who has not caved in to the popular trends or the serious Christian scholar cannot compete with such mass distribution. But, unfortunately, they often do not even try. They insist on preaching dry sermons or writing on esoteric subjects that have little relevance to life.

In *Evangelical Landscapes,* John Stackhouse notes two trends related to the acculturation of evangelicalism: perpetual adolescence among evangelicals and the Christian church in the new Dark Age. Evangelicals evidence many adolescent trends. They chase the latest fads in religion. In music, they limit themselves to popular choruses. Evangelicals often prefer problem-solving or therapeutic sermons to serious Bible study. Worse yet, they venerate heroes and uncritically accept what they say as the last word. Adolescents are loyal only as long as they like something. If they become bored with a particular church or denomination or feel that it is not meeting their needs, they find another. And in America there are thousands of religious options to choose from.[14]

Like other scholars, Stackhouse sees American culture, including the evangelical subculture, as sinking back into the Dark Age. During the early Middle Ages, learning and culture seriously declined. Ignorance and a thin veneer of Christianity characterized this Dark Age. In this time of illiteracy, religious learning came through visuals—stained glass windows and other sacred symbols. Stackhouse sees parallels with our day and age. Much of our knowledge also comes through visuals—television and computer screens, power points, and the theater. Even in the church we no longer have to open a Bible or a hymn-book. The information is on a screen at the front of the church. Like television, church sermons and music offer the believer only bits and pieces of information. Thus, many evangelicals are theologically and biblically illiterate. They do not have even a basic knowledge of the Christian faith.[15]

Taking a different approach, Mark Shibley argues for the southernization of American religion and the Californication of conservative Protestantism. Theological liberalism never dominated in the South as it did in the North. In the Bible belt of the South, the old time gospel remained intact despite the challenges of the twentieth century. It never had to be revived. So the South became "a kind of repository for American evangelicalism." Challenged by the social changes following the 1960s, Americans looked for religious answers and the South provided them. Thus, in the late twentieth century, many of the megachurches and national evangelicals leaders were located in the South.

By the Californication of evangelicalism, Shibley is referring to the fact that much of evangelicalism has adopted contemporary worship and social trends while remaining theologically conservative. Herein lies a paradox. California has led the way in the acculturation of evangelicalism. The latest fads in worship have come from there. Moreover, the sun and beaches of California often encourage a lively lifestyle, something frowned on by conservative Protestants. While obvious sin is rejected, modern cultural trends are accepted and operate parallel to the preaching of the old time gospel. Much of contemporary evangelicalism is indeed traveling down the same path.[16]

This survey of evangelicalism points to a problem that confronts all religions: how to be relevant to the surrounding culture without being absorbed by it. In a free religious market, most religious groups desire to grow. The key to growth is to connect with the surrounding culture and to offer people what they want. But as we have seen, evangelicals have often stepped over the line and have been assimilated into the mainstream culture. On the whole, they still proclaim the old-time faith but they often do so in a Christianized counterfeit culture they have created. In order to grow and spread the good news, evangelicals have indeed "become all things to all people." But can they do this without being absorbed by the culture?

This is a dilemma—one that evangelicalism has not handled well. So strong is its "desire to copy the culture of the hotel chains and popular culture that it loses what religious distinctiveness it once had," notes Alan Wolfe.[17] Eugene Petersen is a prominent writer on Christian spirituality. He also condemns evangelicalism's tendency to accommodate its message to current trends: "When you start tailoring the gospel to the culture, whether it's a youth culture, a generation culture or any other kind of culture, you have taken the guts out of the gospel. The gospel of Jesus Christ is not the kingdom of this world. It's a different kingdom."[18]

Notes

1.   Marty E. Marty, "At the Crossroads," *Christianity Today* (February 2004): 38, 40.
2.   Kenneth J. Collins, *The Evangelical Moment: The Promise of an American Religion* (Grand Rapids: Baker Books, 2005), 181.
3.   Alister McGrath, *Evangelicalism and the Future of Christianity* (Downers Grove, IL: InterVaristy, 1995), 10, 184.
4.   Collins, *The Evangelical Moment,* 182 (quote); Christian Smith, *American Evangelicalism: Embattled and Thriving* (Chicago: University of Chicago Press), 33.
5.   Richard T. Hughes, *Myths America Lives By* (Urbana: University of Illinois Press, 2004), 77.
6.   Except for the quote by Hughes, the general ideas for the last four paragraphs have come from Marty, "At the Crossroads," 38-40.
7.   R. Laurence Moore, *Selling God: American Religion in the Marketplace of Culture* (New York: Oxford University Press, 1994), 272.
8.   Ronald J. Sider, "The Scandal of the Evangelical Conscience," *Books and Culture* (January/February 2005): 8. See Ronald J. Sider, *The Scandal of the Evangelical Conscience* (Grand Rapids: Baker Books, 2005); Michael Horton, "Beyond Culture Wars," *Modern Reformation* (May-June 1993), 3.
9.   See Dean M. Kelley, *Why Conservative Churches are Growing* (New York: Harper and Row, 1972); Michael A. Hout, Andrew Greeley, and Melissa J. Wilde, "The Demographic Imperative in Religious Change in the United States, " *American Journal of Sociology* 107 (September 2001): 468-500; James A. Mathisen, "Tell Me Again: Why Do Churches Grow?" *Books and Culture* (May/June 2004): 38-41.
10.   Alan Wolfe, *The Transformation of American Religion* (New York: Free Press, 2003), 36.
11.   Quoted in Kenneth J. Heineman, *God is a Conservative: Religion, Politics, and Morality in Contemporary America* (New York: New York University Press, 1998), 155.

12. Wolfe, *Transformation of American Religion*, 80, 81.
13. George Gallup, Jr. and Timothy Jones, *The Next American Spirituality* (Colorado Springs, CO: Victor, 2000), 50.
14. John Stackhouse, Jr. "Perpetual Adolescence: The Emerging Culture of North American Evangelicalism," *Crux* 29, 3 (1993): 32-37; John G. Stackhouse, Jr. *Evangelical Landscapes: Facing Critical Issues of the Day* (Grand Rapids: Baker Books, 2002), 13-23.
15. Stackhouse, *Evangelical Landscapes*, 89-102.
16. Mark A. Shibley, *Resurgent Evangelicalism in the United States* (Columbia: University of South Carolina Press, 1996), 1-9, 108, 109.
17. Wolfe, *Transformation of American Religion*, 256, 257.
18. Quoted in Mark Galli, interviewer, "Spirituality for All the Wrong Reasons," *Christianity Today* (March 2005): 42-45.

Selected Bibliography

Ahlstrom, Sydney E. "The Radical Turn in Theology and Ethics: Why It Occurred in the 1960s." *The Annals of the American Academy of Political and
Social Science* 387 (January 1970): 1-13.

Albanese, Catherine. "Religion and American Popular Culture." *Journal of
the American Academy of Religion* 64, 4 (1997): 733-42.

Allitt, Patrick. *Religion in America Since 1945: A History.* New York: Columbia University Press, 2003.

Balmer, Randall. *Blessed Assurance: A History of Evangelicalism in America.*
Boston: Beacon Press, 1999.

_____. *Mine Eyes Have Seen the Glory.* New York: Oxford University Press,
1989.

Barron, Bruce. *The Health and Wealth Gospel.* Downers Grove, IL: InterVarsity,
1987.

Bebbington, David. *Evangelicalism in Modern Britain.* Grand Rapids: Baker
Books, 1992.

Bellah, Robert N. "Religion and the Legitimation in the American Republic."
Society 15, 4 (1978): 16-23.

Bowman, Robert M. *The Word-Faith Controversy: Understanding the Health
and Wealth Gospel.* Grand Rapids: Baker Books, 2001.

Bruce, Dickson D. *And They All Sang Hallelujah.* Knoxville: University of
Tennessee Press, 1974.

Carpenter, Joel A. *Revive Us Again.* New York: Oxford University Press, 1997.

Clapp, Rodney, "Why the Devil Takes Visa." *Christianity Today* (October
1996): 19-33.

_____, ed., *The Consuming Passion: Christianity and the Consumer Culture.*
Downers Grove, IL: InterVarsity Press, 1998.

Collins, Kenneth J. *The Evangelical Moment: The Promise of an Evangelical
Religion.* Grand Rapids: Baker Books, 2005.

Cooper, Marc. "God and Man in Colorado Springs." *Nation* 2 (January 1995):
9-12.

Cross, Whitney R. *The Burned-Over District.* New York: Harper Torchbooks,
1965.

Dark, David. *The Gospel According to America.* Louisville: Westminster John
Knox, 2005.

Dayton, Donald W. *Discovering an Evangelical Heritage.* New York: Harper
and Row, 1976.

Dayton, Donald W., and Robert K. Johnston, eds. *The Variety of American Evangelicalism.* Knoxville: University of Tennessee Press, 1991.

Durham, Martin. *The Christian Right, the Far Right and the Boundaries of American Conservatism.* Manchester, UK: Manchester University Press, 2000.

Ellwood, Robert S. *1950: Crossroads of American Religious Life.* Louisville: Westminister John Knox, 2000.

Eskridge, Larry. "When Burkett Speaks, Evangelicals Listen." *Christianity Today* 12 (June 2000): 44-52.

Eskridge, Larry, and Mark A. Noll, eds. *More Money, More Ministry.* Grand Rapids: Eerdmans, 2000.

Finke, Roger, and Rodney Stark. *The Churching of America, 1776-1990.* New Brunswick, NJ: Rutgers University Press, 1992.

Flake, Carol. *Redemptorama: Culture, Politics, and the New Evangelicalism.* New York: Penguin, 1984.

Fox, Richard Wightman. *Jesus in America.* San Francisco: HarperSanFranciso, 2004.

Frank, Douglas W. *Less Than Conquerors.* Grand Rapids: Eerdmans, 1986.

Frankl, Razelle. *Televangelism: The Marketing of Popular Religion.* Carbondale: Southern Illinois University Press, 1987.

George, Timothy. "If I'm an Evangelical, What Am I?" *Christianity Today* 9 (August 1999): 62.

Gilbreath, Edward. "The New Capital of Evangelicalism, *Christianity Today* 21 (May 2002): 38-48.

Goff, James R. "The Faith that Claims," *Christianity Today* 19 (February 1990): 18-21.

Guinness, Os. *Dining with the Devil.* Grand Rapids: Baker Books, 1993.

———. *Fit Bodies Fat Minds.* Grand Rapids: Baker Books, 1994.

Guinness, Os, and John Seel, eds., *No God But God.* Chicago: Moody Press, 1992.

Hadden, Jeffrey K., and Anson Shupe. *Televangelism: Power and Politics on God's Frontier.* New York: Henry Holt, 1988.

Hamilton, Michael S. "The Triumph of the Praise Songs." *Christianity Today* 12 (July 1999): 29-35.

Handy, Robert T. *A Christian America: Protestant Hopes and Historical Realities*, 2nd ed. New York: Oxford University Press, 1984.

Hangen, Tona J. *Redeeming the Dial: Radio, Religion and Popular Culture in America.* Chapel Hill: University of North Carolina Press, 2002.

Harris, Harriet. *Fundamentalism and Evangelicals.* Oxford: Clarendon Press, 1998.

Hart, D. G. *Deconstructing Evangelicalism.* Grand Rapids: Baker Books, 2004.

———. *That Old-Time Religion in Modern America.* Chicago: Ivan R. Dee, 2002.

Hatch, Nathan O. *The Democratization of American Chrisitianity.* New Haven, CT: Yale University Press, 1989.

Heineman, Kenneth J. *God is a Conservative.* New York: New York University Press, 1998.

Horton, Michael Scott. *Made in America: The Shaping of Modern American Evangelicalism*. Grand Rapids: Baker Books, 1991.

Hughes, Richard T. *Myths America Lives By*. Urbana: University of Illinois Press, 2004.

Hunter, James Davison. *American Evangelicalism: Conservative Religion and the Quandry of Modernity*. New Brunswick, NJ: Rutgers University Press, 1983.

_____. *Evangelicalism: The Coming Generation*. Chicago: University of Chicago Press, 1987.

_____. *Culture Wars: The Struggle to Define America*. New York: Basic Books, 1991.

Johnson, Curtis D. *Redeeming America: Evangelicals and the Road to the Civil War*. Chicago: Ivan R. Dee, 1993.

Jorstad, Erling. *The Politics of Doomsday: Fundamentalists of the Far Right*. Nashville: Abingdon, 1970.

Kenneson, Philip D., and James L. Street. *Selling Out the Church: The Dangers of Church Marketing*. Nashville: Abingdon, 1997.

Kyle, Richard. *The Religious Fringe: A History of Alternative Religions in America*. Downers Grove, IL: InterVarsity Press, 1993.

_____. *The Last Days Are Here Again: A History of the End Times*. Grand Rapids: Baker Books, 1998.

Ladd, Tony, and James A. Mathisen. *Muscular Christianity*. Grand Rapids: Baker Books, 1999.

Lambert, Frank. *Peddlar in Divinity: George Whitefield and the Transatlantic Revivals*. Princeton, NJ: Princeton University Press, 1994.

Lasch, Christopher. *The Culture of Narcissism*. New York: W.W. Norton & Co., 1979.

Linder, Robert D., and Richard V. Pierard. *Twilight of the Saints*. Downers Grove, IL: InterVarsity Press, 1978.

Long, Kathryn Teresa. *The Revival of 1857-58*. New York: Oxford University Press, 1998.

Marsden, George, ed. *Fundamentalism and American Culture*. New York: Oxford University Press, 1980.

_____. *Evangelicalism and Modern America*. Grand Rapids: Eerdmans, 1984.

_____. *Religion and American Culture*. New York: Harcourt Brace, 1990.

_____. *Understanding Fundamentalism and Evangelicalism*. Grand Rapids: Eerdmans, 1991.

Martin, William. *A Prophet with Honor: The Billy Graham Story*. New York: William Morrow, 1991.

_____. *With God on Our Side: The Rise of the Religious Right in America*. New York: Broadway Books, 1996.

Marty, Martin, E. *Righteous Empire*. New York: Dial Press, 1970.

_____. *Modern American Religion: The Noise of Conflict 1919-1941*. Chicago: University of Chicago Press, 1991.

_____. *Modern American Religion: Under God, Indivisible 1941-1960*. Chicago: University of Chicago Press, 1996.

_____. *A Nation of Behavers*. Chicago: University of Chicago Press, 1976.

Mathisen, James A. "The Strange Decade of the Promise Keepers." *Books and Culture* (September/October 2001): 36-39.

McConnell, D. R. *A Different Gospel*. Peabody, MA: Hendrickson, 1985.

McGrath, Alister. *Evangelicalism and the Future of Christianity*. Downers Grove, IL: InterVarsity Press, 1995.

McLoughlin, William G., Jr. *Modern Revivalism*. New York: Ronald Press, 1959.

_____. "Pietism and the American Character." *American Quarterly* 17, 2, pt. 2 (1965): 163-202.

_____. *Revivals, Awakenings and Reform*. Chicago: University of Chicago Press, 1978.

Mead, Sidney E. *The Nation with the Soul of a Church*. New York: Harper and Row, 1975.

Miller, Donald E. *Reinventing American Protestantism*. Berkeley: University of California Press, 1997.

Moore, R. Laurence. *Selling God: American Religion in the Marketplace of Culture*. New York: Oxford University Press, 1994.

_____. *Touchdown Jesus: The Mixing of Sacred and Secular in American History*. Louisville: Westminister John Knox Press, 2003.

Mouw, Richard, and Mark A. Noll, eds., *Wonderful Words of Life*. Grand Rapids: Eerdmans, 2004.

Noll, Mark A. "Common Sense Tradition and American Evangelical Thought." *American Quarterly* 37 (summer 1985): 216-38.

_____. *The Scandal of the Evangelical Mind*. Grand Rapids: Eerdmans, 1994.

_____. *American Evangelical Christianity*. Oxford: Blackwell, 2001.

_____. *America's God: From Jonathan Edwards to Abraham Lincoln*. New York: Oxford University Press, 2002.

_____. *The Rise of Evangelicalism*. Downers Grove, IL: InterVarsity Press, 2003.

Pierard, Richard V. *The Unequal Yoke: Evangelical Christianity and Political Conservatism*. Philadelphia: Lippincott, 1970.

Prothero, Stephen. *American Jesus*. New York: Farrar, Straus and Giroux, 2003.

Quebedeaux, Richard. *The Worldly Evangelicals*. New York: Harper and Row, 1978.

_____. *By What Authority*. New York: Harper and Row, 1982.

Romanowski, William D. "Roll Over Beethoven, Tell Martin Luther the News: American Evangelicals and Rock Music." *Journal of American Culture* 15, 3 (1992): 79-88.

_____. *Pop Culture Wars*. Downers Grove, IL: InterVarsity Press, 1996.

_____. *Eyes Wide Open: Looking for God in Popular Culture*. Grand Rapids: Brazos Press, 2001.

Roof, Wade Clark. *A Generation of Seekers*. San Franscisco: HarperSanFransciso, 1993.

_____. *Spiritual Marketplace*. Princeton, NJ: Princeton University Press, 1999.

Sargeant, Kimon Howland. *Seeker Churches: Promoting Traditional Religion in a Nontraditional Way*. New Brunswick, NJ: Rutgers University Press, 2000.

Schuller, Robert H. *Self Esteem: The New Reformation*. Waco, TX: Word Books, 1982.

Schultze, Quentin J. *Televangelism and American Culture*. Grand Rapids: Baker Books, 1991.

Shelley, Bruce. *Evangelicalism in America*. Grand Rapids: Eerdmans, 1967.

_____. "The Rise of Evangelical Youth Movements." *Fides et Historia* 18, 1 (January 1986): 47-63.

Shelley, Bruce, and Marshall Shelley. *Consumer Church*. Downers Grove, IL: InterVarsity Press, 1992.

Shibley, Mark A. *Resurgent Evangelicalism in the United States*. Columbia: University of South Carolina Press, 1996.

Sider, Ronald J. *The Scandal of the Evangelical Conscience*. Grand Rapids: Baker Books, 2005.

Smith, Christian. *American Evangelicalism: Embattled and Thriving*. Chicago: University of Chicago Press, 1998.

_____. *Christian America? What Evangelicals Really Want*. Berkeley: University of California Press, 2000.

Stackhouse, John G., Jr. *Evangelical Landscapes: Facing Critical Issues of the Day*. Grand Rapids: Baker Books, 2002.

Stout, Harry S. *The Divine Dramatist: George Whitefield and the Rise of Modern Evangelicalism*. Grand Rapids: Eerdmans, 1991.

Sweeney, Douglas A. *The American Evangelical Story: A History of the Movement*. Grand Rapids: Baker Books, 2005.

Sweet, Leonard I., ed., *The Evangelical Tradition in America*. Macon, GA: Mercer University Press, 1984.

Sweet, William Warren. *Revivalism in America*. Nashville: Scribner's, Tuscaloosa: 1944.

Szasz, Ferenc M. *The Divided Mind of Protestant America 1880-1930*. University of Alabama Press, 1982.

Truehart, Charles. "Welcome to the Next Church." *Atlantic Monthly* (August 1996): 37-58.

Tuveson, Ernest Lee. *Redeemer Nation*. Chicago: University of Chicago Press, 1968.

Wacker, Grant. *Heaven Below: Early Pentecostals and American Culture*. Cambridge, MA: Harvard University Press, 2001

Wallis, Jim. *God's Politics: Why the Right Gets It Wrong and the Left Doesn't Get It*. San Francisco: HarperSanFrancisco, 2005.

Warren, Rick. *The Purpose Driven Church*. Grand Rapids: Zondervan, 1995.

Webber, Robert E. *The Younger Evangelicals*. Grand Rapids: Baker Books, 2002.

Webster, Douglas D. *Selling Jesus*. Downers Grove, IL: InterVarsity Press, 1992.

Weisberger, Bernard A. *They Gathered at the River*. New York: Octagon Books, 1979.

Wells, David F. *No Place For Truth*. Grand Rapids: Eerdmans, 1993.

Wilcox, Clyde. *Onward Christian Soldiers: The Religious Right in American Politics*. Boulder, CO: Westview Press, 1996.

Wolfe, Alan. "The Opening of the Evangelical Mind." *Atlantic Monthly* (October 2000): 55-76.

_____. *The Transformation of American Religion.* New York: Free Press, 2003.

Wuthnow, Robert. *After Heaven: Spirituality in America Since the 1950s.* Berkeley: University of California Press, 1998.

_____. *The Restructuring of American Religion.* Princeton, NJ: Princeton University Press, 1988.

Zwier, Robert. *Born Again Politics.* Downers Grove, IL: InterVarsity Press, 1982.

Index